LEARNING
DISABILITIES

LEARNING DISABILITIES

Second Edition

Stanley W. Johnson
State University of New York at Plattsburgh

Robert L. Morasky
Montana State University

Allyn and Bacon, Inc.
Boston, London, Sydney, Toronto

Library of Congress Cataloging in Publication Data

Johnson, Stanley W.   1928–
            Learning disabilities.

    Bibliography: p. 405
    Includes indexes.
  1. Learning disabilities.   I. Morasky,
Robert L., 1940–   joint author.   II. Title.
LC4704.J64   1980   371.9   79-21030
        ISBN 0-205-06898-7

       Art Editor: *Armen Kojoyian*
   Preparation Buyer: *Linda Card*
 Production Editor: *Joanne Dauksewicz*
    Series Editor: *Miggy Hopkins*

To
Karen and Sandra

and

To
Alice Moyer,
who was singing the tune to her students
long before we learned the words

Contents

xiii Preface to the First Edition
xvii Preface to the Second Edition

Part I
An Introduction to Learning Disabilities

1
3 Learning Disabilities—A Historical Survey
9 Historical Development of the L.D. Field
14 A Brief Outlook

2
15 Learning Disability Behaviors
17 Orientation of this Book
17 Incidence of Learning Disabilities
19 General Problem Behaviors
21 Principle of Disparity
25 Types of Learning Disabilities
32 Summary

3
33 Issues, Trends, and Needs
Identifying the Major Issues

46   Trends
48   Needs
53   Summary

4
55   Roles of Different Professions in Diagnosis and Treatment
60   Educational Disciplines
65   Medical Disciplines
75   Clinical Disciplines
78   Summary

Part II
79   General Models and Strategies

5
81   Different Orientations, Approaches, and Strategies
82   Examining Approaches to Learning Disabilities
84   Developmental Approach
87   Basic Processes Approach
90   Deficit-Behavior or Task Approach
94   Assessment Approach
97   Management Approaches
100   Summary

6
102   Remedial Approaches Representing Different
      Theoretical Positions
104   A General Developmental Approach
107   A General Basic Process Model
111   A Deficit-Behavior Task Model
116   An Assessment-Correlated Model
119   Management Models
120   A Systems-Programming Approach
121   A Program Displaying Management-Arranged Materials
122   Summary

7
124   Remedial Approaches to Different Problem Areas
125   Language Problems
134   Reading Problems

137   Arithmetic Problems
139   Perceptual Problems

8
143   Applying a Systems-Management Approach
146   The Process and the Product
147   The "Systems Approach" to Instructional Programming
151   A Final Note

Part III
153   Techniques for Solving Some Common Problems

9
155   Screening and Diagnosis
157   The Nature of Screening Activities
162   Planning a Screening Program
166   Techniques, Procedures, and Instruments for Screening
182   Implementation and Follow-Up

10
185   Communicating Diagnostic-Prescriptive Information

11
200   Preparing and Selecting Remedial Materials
200   Basic Criteria for Remedial Materials
205   User Preparation
208   Identification of Remedial Material Areas
214   Choosing and Preparing Materials
219   Summary

12
220   Delivery of Service Alternatives
229   Specially Trained Personnel Models
230   Models that Restructure the School
232   Models Focusing on Internal Support Services
235   External Support Models
236   Models Conceived for Working with Special Groups
239   Summary

13

240   Handling Behavior Problems
242   Observable Behaviors
245   Situations in which Problem Behaviors Appear
247   Responses to Problem Behaviors
248   Effects of Others' Responses upon the Child
250   General Strategies for Alleviating Problem Behaviors
266   Summary

14

267   Counseling
268   Counseling the Learning Disabled Person
274   Counseling Family and Friends of the Learning Disabled
283   Counseling the Teacher of the Learning Disabled
287   Summary

Part IV
289   A Systematic Strategy for Remediation

15

291   Analysis of the Educational Task
294   Final Task Description
295   Assumptions Regarding Entering Behavior
296   Flowchart Task Analysis
302   Discrimination Task Analysis
310   Generalization Task Analysis
312   Combining Discrimination, Flowchart, and Generalization Analyses

16

314   Preparation of Criterion Measures
315   The Source of Criterion Measures
315   Subcriterion Measures
317   The Need for Direct Measurement
321   Covering the Range of Possible Situations
321   Criterion Measures Do Not Teach
323   Criterion Measures Must Be Relevant to the Task
324   A Final Note on Criterion Measures

17

326   Preparation of Objectives
327   Student Behavior in Objectives

328 Measurable Objectives
329 Describing the Conditions for Performance
331 Preparing Objectives from the Task Analysis
332 Preparing Objectives from Criterion Measures
334 A Final Note About Objectives

18
336 Preparation of Instructional Sequences
346 A Checklist for Instructional Sequences
350 Knowledge-of-Results, Feedback, or Reinforcement
351 A Final Note on Instructional Sequences

19
353 Implementation and Revision
354 Why Test and Revise?
354 Individual Testing
356 Group Testing
358 A Strategy and Checklist for Revision
361 Revise the Instruction or the Criterion Measure?
362 A Final Note about Program Implementation and Revision

20
364 An Illustration of the Systems Approach
364 The Case of Deborah L.

Part V
377 Appendixes

A
378 Examples of Task Analysis
378 From a Program Titled "Decoding Words"
379 From a Program Titled "Beginning Multiplication Concepts"
381 From a Program Titled "Place Values"
382 From a Program Titled "Map Studies"
383 From a Program Titled "Base Six Numeration"
385 From a Program Titled "Working with Sets"

B
388 A Glossary of Learning Disability Terms

C

391   A Suggested Library

D

394   Sources of Current Information

E

396   Major Sources of Learning Disability Materials

405   References
425   Author Index
431   Subject Index

Preface
to the First Edition

During the past few years we have come face to face with learning disabilities under a number of different guises and in several different contexts. In the early 1960s we shared the frustration of many of our clinical and teacher colleagues who recognized the distinctive problems and needs of the learning disabled child but found little help or guidance either in theory or applied techniques. In subsequent years we progressed—perhaps trudged is a better word—through a number of research experiences, trying to discriminate fact from fiction and perceive order in chaos. Throughout all this we continued to try to use our specialized training and interests as applied and educational psychologists to improve the learning efficiency of youngsters who were brought to us for help, many of whom might best be categorized as specific learning disabled children.

Our professional training, in almost every respect, has been as empiricists. We have been taught and shaped to seek evidence, to focus on defensible data, and to avoid "soft," "unpredictable," and "superstitious" assumptions and behavior. To some, such an approach or bias is often thought to exclude any concern for the humanity of people. We thoroughly reject such an assumption for we have witnessed and shared in the despair of the child who cannot learn; we have felt the surge of exaltation of the child who finds that he or she can also experience success. Indeed, it was this combination of our professional orientation and concern for children that led to this book. Our belief has given us hope and confidence that answers do exist and that solutions may be found.

We bring to this work assumptions about children and learning, about the process of remediation, and about those who would help in the process of remediation. These assumptions should be shared with the reader for they really exemplify the objectives we had in mind as we wrote.

First, we assume that the process of learning—acquiring new behaviors, skills, and information—is a process natural to the organism. Given a context and set of experiences that match the individual's capacities and allow the organism to make use of its inherent behavioral capacities, the child will learn and learning will be to a large extent a reinforcing thing in itself. We are personally committed to helping children discover the intrinsic joy of learning.

Second, we believe that the remedial process should be strongly and firmly directed toward the goal of helping the child, not to satisfying the practitioner or to matching the predetermined and perhaps unrelated tenets of a theoretical bias. Thus we encourage eclecticism if it is knowledgeably done and if it serves the principles of efficiency and economy. We consistently shape our own students to be aware of and sensitive to theoretical differences, whether as obvious viewpoints or as subtle nuances. But we most fondly hope that this knowledge and sensitivity will increase the likelihood of wise and pragmatic choices, not merely rigid and defensive biases. Therefore, we have deliberately chosen not to endorse any single polemic or theoretical stand in this text. Most positions have strengths; all have weaknesses. At best, in our view, they are incomplete estimates of a yet undefined reality. Instead we encourage study of these varied ideas, strongly support systematic research, and urge exploration that may advance the frontiers of our knowledge about behavior in general and specific learning disabilities in particular. We clearly endorse the presumption that the state of theory in learning disabilities is not yet well organized or maturely developed in most respects. We encourage those who are working diligently to develop more substantive theory but do not feel we are ready to espouse any of the existing theories firmly and exclusively as they now stand.

We do strongly advocate a systems approach to programming remedial activities. It seems to us that such an approach, usable in harmony with almost any theoretical emphasis, improves efficiency, clarifies decision making, and increases the probability of accountability in the sense of improving remedial efforts. However, we wish such an approach to be conceived simply as a tool, a means to an end. Our objective is *effectively learning children*. This technique has often helped us achieve that goal and we share it for that reason.

Finally, we feel that the processes of recognition, diagnosis, planning, treatment, and evaluation as applied to the learning disabled child can often be most effectively carried out when performed by one individual or a single team of individuals. It is sometimes necessary to compartmentalize responsibilities and to rely upon outside, relatively uninvolved help. But this should happen, in our opinion, only when absolutely necessary. Therefore we have tried to suggest to the reader that he or she may as an individual accomplish much of what is needed in each of these processes. Understandably, not everyone will perform equally well in each area, but the disadvantages of such unevenness can often be more than compensated for by the consistency, knowledge, and understanding that come with more complete and longitudinal involvement. We are attempting to convey the idea that with study and practice many are capable of becoming the "nearly compleat" practitioner. And, if such total competency seems beyond reach, at least a total awareness of what each process involves and demands increases the likelihood of effective interaction among members of any team.

We owe special gratitude and appreciation to a number of groups and people who have helped us in this task. Many of our students and colleagues, collectively and individually, have helped us evolve ideas, test techniques, evaluate materials, and weigh premises. We appreciate their interest, their contributions, their concerns, and most of all their patience.

Of specific note, Ms. Agnes Elizabeth Shine helped with many important and often tedious details. Ms. Carol DuBois and Ms. Joan Granoff also worked hard on some specialized clerical problems. Mrs. Judy Dashnaw helped assemble and hold the whole project together and is largely responsible for everyone managing to retain their sanity in the face of office crises, publisher's deadlines, and authors' recurrent spells of manic anxiety. Mr. Phil Cerone and Ms. Amy Patnode also were most helpful with details. To these, and others, we express our thanks.

S.W.J.
R.L.M.

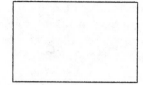

Preface
to the Second Edition

Preparing a second edition is like getting a second chance in any endeavor, except that in the case of a textbook the authors have the additional advantage of applying fresh insights, new and additional data, and building upon the often helpful constructive feedback of readers. This is a heady experience, and it is exciting in many ways to be able to act upon the new closures that came too late for the first edition. The danger is, of course, that new is not always better nor is old necessarily passé.

We have tried therefore to use care and good judgement in both excisions from and additions to the first edition manuscript. The substantive changes we have tried to effect in this edition include the following:

1. Updating the content to include consideration of contemporary trends and field-shaping events (e.g., the effect of P.L. 94–142)
2. Focusing more directly on the application of management techniques to the field by including a separate chapter devoted to that topic
3. Adding new material related to working with and counseling those affected either directly or indirectly by learning disabilities
4. Restructuring, in a simpler format, the complex array of orientations, approaches, and strategies as developed in remedial systems used in the field
5. Adding new material relating to an array of systems and approaches that focus on different important areas of learning disability problems

This has involved including much new information and some rearranging of the material contained in the first edition. In each instance these have been undertaken in response to clear feedback from readers and users of the text. It is our hope that we have clearly discerned and meaningfully responded to the needs of our readers, though we know it is impossible to equally satisfy or please all. Their communications have been invaluable.

As with the first edition, special thanks is owed to many—students, colleagues, and others. Without attempting to name them all, we extend our appreciation to each in turn.

S.W.J.
R.L.M.

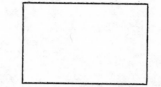

LEARNING DISABILITIES

Part I

An Introduction to Learning Disabilities

The four chapters of this initial section are designed to present the reader with a general introduction to the wide range of problem learning behaviors and professional activities typically subsumed under the category of *Specific Learning Disabilities*. Basically, these chapters represent an attempt to provide a general orientation for the potential practitioner more than an effort to define the field explicitly, for definition is a difficult area for all involved in learning disabilities.

Chapter 1 is a panoramic survey of the early beginnings of the field and of some important stages in its growth and development into its present complex status. Our intention is not to cover exhaustively all of the major events and important people contributing to the field or to explain the many complex inter-relationships that exist between them. Our intent, instead, is to provide a general awareness of where the field has been and where it is now so that details discussed later in the book can be integrated into a broad historical context.

Chapter 2 notes some characteristics that help discriminate learning disability behaviors from other childhood problem behaviors. For example, uninformed individuals frequently confuse learning deficit behaviors with "acting-out" behavior problems. This chapter provides some basis for making clearer inclusion-exclusion judgements where ample data can be found for this discrimination.

Chapter 3 presents certain major issues currently facing those who work in the learning disabilities field. Highlighted are some of the trends that seem to exemplify the directions in which new developments may be taking us, along with the needs we feel must be satisfied, at least in part, before the field can become all we would wish it to be. As chapter 1 provides a panorama of the field's development up to the present, chapter 3 provides a glimpse into its future.

Chapter 4 helps to orient the reader to learning disabilities from the standpoint of the different professional disciplines active in the field. Objects and events are frequently described as they are seen through the "eye of the beholder." The varying perceptions of learning disabilities and remedial role concepts are discussed in this chapter so that the practitioner will be better prepared to appreciate and work effectively with a variety of professional contributors.

1

Learning Disabilities — A Historical Survey

"Just what is a learning disability?" This is probably the query professionals encounter most frequently when they are speaking to concerned parents, service club members, school personnel, physicians, or others interested in helping remove this cause of so much unhappiness and learning inefficiency among school children.

The question is not easily answered.

First of all, an adequate description of behaviors contained in this generously broad diagnostic label is almost always relevant to the observer's intent, professional orientation, and personal biases. Like the classic tale of the three blind men's description of an elephant, a meaningful description of learning disabilities is primarily dependent upon what aspect of the problem the definer is attending to at the moment.

Second, in purely behavioral terms—that is, in terms of the actual things a child may be doing at a given moment of his or her learning experience—there may be no single kind of behavior that can with any degree of assurance *always* be labeled as a "learning disability behavior." The problems observed in learning disabled children can and do represent other categories of difficulty, such as emotional, physiological, or developmental problems. Much of the time, children experiencing learning disability difficulties will also be struggling with lowered motivation, social-behavior problems, and other frequently concurrent handicaps.

Finally, professional consensus on the definition of the term is simply not

3

present. This is due partly to some basic theoretical disagreements (the role of the central nervous system in learning disabilities, for example), and partly to the fact that contemporary working definitions are constantly being revised. Even where theoretical agreement is present or where differences have been deliberately laid aside, changes in defintions, such as those used by governmental funding agencies, add to the confusion as some adopt newly presented definitions more quickly than others.

As Bateman and Haring (Clements, 1969) clearly point out in the report of a task force established by the Public Health Service, formal descriptions have gone through a series of metamorphoses influenced by different disciplines and various professional and lay organizations. Throughout this evolving period no single inclusive defintion has been universally satisfying. Controversial topics, such as whether or not to orient the definition toward a particular diagnostic model, whether learning disabilities should be included as a subcategory of retardation and/or special education, whether neurological impairment is a discriminating variable, or even whether or not *any* cause or etiologically based taxonomy should be included in the term, have so confused the issue that a single consensual definition is nowhere to be found.

Having noted all these difficulties in arriving at a workable and acceptable definition, however, we do not want to suggest that the situation is hopelessly confused or that learning disabilities themselves, as discriminable behaviors, preclude adequate definition. Definitions *are* formed, adopted, and used successfully. The demand for workable definitions underlines an apparent need for such descriptions in helping workers focus their efforts. The most immediate concern is to arrive at a definition which, though perhaps not consensual, is at least functional for a large number of people. As Johnson and Myklebust (1967) have pointed out:

> The crux and focus of the definition and for the criteria (for differentiation) must be those features, symptoms, and characteristics that designate, circumscribe, and point out the group's homogeneity.

Despite the wide variety of behaviors and learning problems frequently listed under the umbrella of learning disabilities, there are some discriminative characteristics that separate children with learning disability problems from those experiencing other types of difficulties. A most common error is to assume that learning disabilities and learning problems encountered in everyday school experiences are identical. The two terms are not synonymous. "Learning disability is used to describe a specific type of exceptional child; it is not a generic term for all childrem who have learning problems in school" (Myers and Hammill, 1969).

The learning disabled child is experiencing a particular type of learning problem: difficulty with some discriminable characteristics that are sufficiently identifiable to lead to the deliberate use of the modifier *specific* in referring to problems of this type; hence the commonly applied phrase, *specific learning disabilities*.

Variously stated, these characteristics serve as identifying benchmarks: ·

- The L.D. child has average or above intelligence, adequate sensory acuity, but is achieving considerably less than a composite of his intelligence, age, and educational ability would predict (Gearheart, 1973).
- The L.D. child has specific difficulty in acquiring and using information or skills essential to problem solving (Valett, 1969a).
- The L.D. child has integrity emotionally, motorically, sensorially, and intellectually, but despite these integrities, cannot learn in the usual manner (Johnson and Myklebust, 1967).
- The L.D. child displays developmental discrepancies in ability, has a specific problem that is not a correlate of other primary handicapping conditions, and displays behavioral deficits (Kirk, 1972).
- The L.D. child exhibits an educationally significant discrepancy between apparent capacity and functioning (Bateman, 1964).

Characteristics
of the learning
disabled child

It is logical that these discriminating characteristics, broadly stated, should be both drawn from and reflected in the more frequently accepted definitions. Such is indeed the case, and as several authors (e.g., Myers and Hammill, 1976; Gearheart, 1973) have pointed out, there is a substantial amount of basic agreement among definitions. Most currently accepted definitions agree upon the following:

1. *Some principle of discrepancy or disparity.*
   Such a principle states that there is a significant difference between the level of a child's actual performance and his predicted potential or capacity. Identification of the disparity usually follows a pattern set by the theoretical approach of the assessor, but both breadth and depth of deficit are considered. Isolation of the deficit-disparity area is crucial to successful prescription and remediation.

Components
of learning
disability
definitions

2. *General role of the central nervous system.*
   As Gearheart (1973) states, "In many cases it is assumed that there is a central nervous system dysfunction; however, the means whereby this must be shown to exist vary greatly. In a similar manner it is generally assumed that one or more of the learning *abilities* must be malfunctioning, but proof of this is not often required for entrance into a program of special services." Since few if any learning disability specialists are pure dualists who assume that mind (thinking, learning, etc.) and body operate independently, there seems to be little attempt to totally rule out the possibility of central nervous system (CNS) involvement in any learning behavior. Few contemporary definitions, however, focus on the necessity for demonstrating neurological pathology or dysfunction for inclusion in a learning disability category. Remedial techniques, drawn in part from assumptions inferred from definitions, do vary greatly in their focus on CNS structure and function (a situation discussed elsewhere in this book).

3. *Primary physiological problems are excluded.*
   Learning problems or deficits attributed primarily to basic inadequacies or pathologies in specific physiological systems are generally excluded from the

category of learning disability. Thus, failure to read caused by a lack of visual acuity that could be corrected by glasses would not be considered a learning disability. Such an exclusion doesn't always apply in all cases of impaired vision or other physiological system dysfunctions. It is quite possible for a child to have both a problem of sensory acuity (e.g., inadequate vision) and a learning disability which actively interact. Such multifaceted problems are commonly encountered and typically are handled through team or cross-disciplinary efforts.

4. *Some special problem areas are excluded.*

Problems arising out of primary causes such as cultural disadvantage, mental retardation, and emotional disturbance are frequently excluded from the learning disability category by the more commonly accepted definitions. Specific exclusion decisions will vary from situation to situation, but definitions allow for specific exclusions if local policies dictate operating under such rules.

5. *The relevance of the problem to the learning process.*

Most definitions in current use either state or clearly imply that for a problem to be labeled as one of learning disability, it must involve the learning performance and be relevant to educational growth, development, and performance. Various authors categorize the learning process in different ways as we will note, but the assumption that a learning disability reflects the loss or retardation of such processes or interferes with the use of processes already adequately learned is included in almost all definitions.

Two frequently used definitions are good examples of the conditions listed above. In an attempt to resolve the problem of so many different definitions and interpretations, the U.S. Office of Education asked a newly formed committee to write a more universally acceptable definition. The committee presented the following definition (Kass and Myklebust, 1969).

Universal components of learning disability definitions

- Learning disability refers to one or more significant deficits in essential learning processes requiring special education techniques for remediation.
- Children with learning disability generally demonstrate a discrepancy between expected and actual achievement in one or more areas such as spoken, read, or written language, mathematics, and spatial orientation.
- The learning disability referred to is not primarily the result of sensory, motor, intellectual, or emotional handicap, or lack of opportunity to learn.
- *Significant deficits* are defined in terms of accepted diagnostic procedures in education and psychology.
- *Essential learning processes* are those currently referred to in behavioral science as involving perception, integration, and expression, either verbal or nonverbal.
- *Special education techniques for remediation* refers to educational planning based on the diagnostic procedures and results.

During the next few years, federally (and most state-) funded programs operating under specific legislation used the following definition. It was largely in harmony with the Office of Education Committee's subsequent report.

Children with special learning disabilities exhibit a disorder in one or more of the basic psychological processes involved in understanding or using spoken or written languages. These may be manifested in disorders of listening, thinking, talking, reading, writing, spelling, perceptual handicaps, brain injury, minimal brain dysfunction, dyslexia, developmental aphasia, etc. They do not include learning problems which are due primarily to visual, hearing, or motor handicaps, to mental retardation, emotional disturbance, or to environmental disadvantage.

When the Mainstreaming Act (P.L. 94–142) was enacted in the mid-1970s, the above definition was modified to read:

Specific learning disabilities means a disorder of one or more of the basic psychological processes involved in understanding or in using language, spoken or written, which may manifest itself in an imperfect ability to listen, think, speak, read, write, spell, or do arithmetic calculations. The term includes such conditions as perceptual handicaps, brain injury, minimal brain damage, dyslexia, and developmental aphasia. The term does not include children who have learning problems which are primarily the result of visual, hearing, or motor handicaps, of mental retardation, or environmental, cultural, or economic disadvantage.

Initially it was proposed that a formula be used to establish a cutoff point for severe (apparently as opposed to mild) ability-performance discrepancies. It was also proposed that, for allocation purposes, a 2% limit be established on the number of children who could be so allocated. Both the formula approach and the limit proposal were subsequently dropped in supplemental regulations.

The use of an exact equation to define a severe disability seemed unworkable for at least three reasons:

1. The behaviors of such a heterogeneous group of children simply does not meaningfully reduce to numbers, certainly not to a single formula for all ages and types.

   Problems in using an exact equation

2. Psychometric assessment methods and statistical analyses necessary for obtaining such a precise numerical definition are inadequate.
3. Such formulae are too easy to apply to the detriment of special children with important needs.

Both of these issues have relevance to an acceptance of any consensual definition. The Congress and federal agencies were influenced by the convincing testimony of workers in the field that (1) the L.D. area is a broad and complex one defying any simple explanation and definition and (2) no legislation, set of regulations, or practice in the field should be accepted that would at this point arbitrarily limit inclusion to certain age groups or population percentages.

As we noted earlier, there is no universal acceptance of these or any other definitions of learning disability. But the majority of professionals working in the field would not find it constricting to operate under the general principles of either of these two prototypes. The authors have found these two definitions quite functional in most practical situations. Only in largely theoretical or research-oriented situations might some disagreement or lack of precision be attenuating. Disagreements would most frequently center around the exclusion clauses or the CNS etiology aspects of the definitions. A substantial number of workers in the field feel that some children, largely excluded by these definitions, should receive more attention in the planning and delivery of learning disability services. Field workers primarily object to the exclusion of the mentally retarded and disadvantaged from the category of learning disability.

These objections are based in the first case upon the premise that the exclusion categorization is a false one: that the present status of the learning disabilities field is largely an outgrowth of earlier work in the field of retardation. Disagreement about excluding the disadvantaged centers around the current concern for improving the status of this segment of our population, and there is a theoretical objection to differentiating on the basis of cause what often appear to be quite similar behavioral deficits and problems.

Groups and individuals with heavy neurological orientation in etiological and treatment aspects stress CNS function and importance much more than either of these two definitions. As we stated previously, few workers in the field would espouse a dualism that would suggest the uninvolvement or lack of importance of neurological functions in any learning behavior. However, those who object to this apparent de-emphasis suggest that neurological aspects (CNS functions) are apt to be reduced to an insignificant role by those who follow the definition literally. In actuality, of course, local policies and individual theoretical preferences employ the definitions in ways which best fit their own specially defined needs and objectives. These two definitions find heavy use and general acceptance even with the groups who object to one or more parts of the overall statement. The objections raised are serious ones, though, and are important to basic decision making in planning and carrying out a program. We will discuss such issues in detail in later chapters.

At this point it may still be difficult for those new to learning disabilities to obtain a firm grasp of just *what is* and *what is not* a *specific learning disability*. Discussion and examination of many of the critical behaviors, those deficit areas demanding remediation, occupy a major portion of this work. When children are seen to fit the broad categorization outlined in the two prototype definitions, further work, which we will discuss subsequently, attempts to isolate, discriminate, and describe problem areas that can be attacked, lessened, or in many cases completely relieved.

These disagreements over focus or over the inclusion or exclusion of certain terms and ideas in working definitions and approaches, or disagreements that obscure understanding for the new worker, do not rise out of complete lack of structure, disharmony, or confusion. Divergent emphases come as a result of different experiences and involvement with actual cases; from the varying training and background of professional workers; and as a response to pleas for help and assistance from varying groups of involved laymen and others, often at different historical periods, and at different stages in the development of the field now being formally labeled as *learning disabilities*. There is, though, far more agreement and harmony than disagreement and confusion. And most experienced workers do not find it difficult to work around disagreements or to function satisfactorily alongside someone who emphasizes different approaches.

Historical Development of the L.D. Field

One way to start to bring structure and clarity to the many viewpoints and differences in focus and emphasis is to become aware of how they developed. Learning disabilities is a young field and its history is largely one of the past very few years. Fortunately, it is relatively easy to perceive how the field has developed, what the contributions of major professions have been, and what roles some of the pioneers (many of whom are still active workers) have played.

Essentially, all of the relevant history of learning disabilities took place within the twentieth century. The possible exception was the work of Morgan, an ophthalmologist, who wrote in a British medical journal in 1896 about what he called "word blindness."

In the late 1920s and 1930s some apparently independent events were producing ideas and data that were to provide important contributions to the nascent field of learning disabilities. Following World War I, clinical studies of the behavior of soldiers who had suffered various types of head wounds led to the recording and categorization of behaviors peculiar to those with a history of brain lesions (Goldstein, 1927, 1936). At the same time a neurologist (Orton, 1937) was studying the problems of children with developmental language difficulties. His work was also oriented in brain function as he explored the possible effect of cerebral dominance of the right or left lobes on certain learning-related behaviors. A very few others such as Fernald (1943) were beginning to initiate some programs aimed at remediation of problems later to be labeled learning disabilities.

The rise of Nazism toward the end of the 1930s and into the early 1940s caused two prominent researchers to flee Germany and ultimately relocate together at a training school for the mentally retarded in Michigan. There, Alfred Strauss, a neuropsychiatrist, and Heinz Werner, a psychologist, worked on isolating the behavior characteristics of brain injured children. Although their earlier independent work had been primarily with the severely retarded, together they focused on less severely handicapped children who were more apt to be subjected to attempts at remediation and rehabilitation. Firm groundwork for careful notation of developmental characteristics was concurrently being laid by others such as Gesell and Amatruda (1941) who were working on normative schedules of behavior for different age levels.

Werner and Strauss began to notice that children with *exogenous* brain damage (neurological damage not due to genetic or inherited factors) could sometimes be discriminated from those with *endogenous* (genetic and inherited problems) diagnoses. Among other characteristics they noted disorders of perception including figure-ground confusion, perseveration or difficulty in shifting to a different behavior once another behavior has been initiated, inability to organize and deal with abstract concepts in a normal manner, and some specific problem behaviors such as uninhibited, overly active (hyperkinetic) behavior (Strauss and Werner, 1942).

It was not long before the work of Strauss and Werner became the standard for most of those working in the same behavioral area. The writing of Strauss and Lehtinen (1947) focused further attention on their findings. Problems of overgeneralization became frequent, as the terms *brain-injured* and *exogenous* became more frequently used. Confusions and misunderstandings began to arise. Disagreements arose over what actually constituted *exogenous* as opposed to *endogenous* injury. Problems of inadequate description and diagnosis were encountered. Difficulty in finding descriptive terms that meant the same to all concerned—professionals in different fields and laymen alike—created further problems. Finally in the mid-fifties the problem crystallized and Stevens and Birch (1957) suggested a solution to what had become a greatly complicated problem. First of all they noted four objections to the use of the term *brain-injured child* and the related terms which had come to be paired with this descriptive phrase. These were:

Objections to the use of the term "brain-injured child"

1. The etiological term *brain-injured child* does not deal in behaviors or actual symptoms, yet cases of brain-injured patients invariably describe the situation in terms of behavior.
2. The term too often is generalized to other conditions (such as epilepsy) where the relationship is at best tenuous and in many cases completely unsupported.
3. The term does not aid in the development of good teaching techniques and approaches for children so labeled.
4. The term encourages oversimplification and is too imprecise to be useful descriptively.

Strauss syndrome behavior symptoms

Not wishing to destroy the valuable contribution of these pioneers, Stevens and Birch suggested substituting a new term, *Strauss Syndrome*, for the old term, *brain-injured child*. It was assumed, by definition, that the new term would be used to describe any child who displayed many or all of these specific problem behaviors:

1. Erratic and inappropriate behavior on mild provocation
2. Increased motor activity disproportionate to the stimulus

3. Poor organization of behavior
4. Distractibility of more than a normal degree under ordinary conditions
5. Persistent faulty perceptions
6. Persistent hyperactivity
7. Awkwardness and consistently poor motor performance

The new term quickly caught on and although it solved some of the labeling problems encountered with earlier terms, it was not long before it, too, was subject to similar errors of misinterpretation and overgeneralization. During this period, others were trying different terms. Doll (1951) was using the term *neurophrenia* early in the 1950s. Johnson (1962) was holding teacher training workshops under the label of *Marginal Children. Minimal brain dysfunction* was introduced by Clements (1966). Somewhat later Chalfant and Scheffelin (1969) suggested a broader term, *central processing dysfunctions,* as an umbrella phrase generalizing several more specific definitions relating to subsets of learning-problem behavior.

Hallahan and Cruickshank (1973) note that during this early formative period, up to about 1960, there was "paucity of research, very limited personnel, and no teacher education" specifically oriented to learning disabilities as a discrete field. Early in the 1960s the situation began to change drastically. Awareness of the existence of an identifiable group of children experiencing some specific learning problems began to grow. More attention began to be drawn to the important issues involved, including the initiation of some badly needed theoretical research. Belmont and Birch (1963), for example, initiated research into lateral dominance and the resulting behaviors in normal and underachieving children, an area of concern introduced years earlier by Orton (1937). This and similar empirical investigations in other areas grew into involved sequences of research and began to develop a bank of data and knowledge upon which to base important decisions of program planning and remediation.

In 1962 one of the first specific definitions of learning disabilities appeared in a college textbook dealing with special education (Kirk).

Pressure for more activity, and indirectly for better definition, really came largely from parents' groups, however. A number of states began to enact legislation for helping children with learning disability problems (although the characteristics were still variously labeled), and the majority of the legislation grew out of the efforts of a few interested professionals associated with groups of highly involved parents. In 1963 an event of historical importance for the whole field of learning disabilities took place in Chicago. A group of parents sponsored a conference to examine and explore the problems of the perceptually handicapped. Foremost in the minds of most of those attending the meeting was concern over the lack of definition of the problems involved and the resulting difficulty in organizing a homogeneous, recognizable group to foster support for training and treatment programs.

Dr. Samuel Kirk of the University of Illinois, a featured speaker at the conference, responded directly to the participants' pleas for help and guidance. As he had noted earlier in his book (1962), Kirk called the attention of the conference to the two major classifications of definitions: first, those dealing with causation and etiology involving labels such as *brain injury* and *minimal brain damage* and, second, those dealing primarily with "behavioral manifestations of the child" and involving such terms as *perceptual disorders* and *dyslexia*. Kirk put the issue squarely to the conference: ". . . the term you select should be dependent on your specific aims. . . ." He pointed out that the two major directions open lay toward research into etiology (largely a neurological and physiological psychology problem) or toward finding "effective methods of diagnosis, management and training of children." His own bias was made clear as he pointed out that he did not feel that attempts to closely correlate specific CNS etiology and resulting behavioral manifestations had been particularly fruitful and that the behavioral direction offered more tangible, functional rewards. He said:

> I often wonder why we tend to use technical and complex labels, when it is more accurate and meaningful to describe behavior. If we find a child who has not learned to talk, the most scientific description is that he has not yet learned to talk. The labels of aphasia or mentally retarded or emotionally disturbed are not as helpful as a description and may, in many instances, tend to confuse the issue. Instead of using the term hyperkinetic we would understand the child better if the observer states that he continually climbs walls or hangs on chandeliers.

At this point, Kirk introduced to the conference a term he had been using himself, *learning disabilities*, as a more workable, descriptive phrase.

The conference responded quickly to this positive descriptive approach and that very evening voted to organize itself as the *Association for Children with Learning Disabilities*. A Professional Advisory Board was formed and the organization began the world-wide growth it has achieved today: this group draws thousands to its annual convention.

Although there were tangible results from the conference, including the issuing of a specialized publication, the *Journal of Learning Disabilities*, and the appearance of texts dealing totally with learning disabilities, the problems were not over.

Kirk actually was trying both to simplify the issue for laymen and to establish a precedent for using behaviorally descriptive terms rather than labels. Unfortunately, popular use of the new term transformed *learning disabilities* into a labeled category again, one appearing to be more homogeneous than it was and guided by little research and few trained professional leaders. A functionally operational definition of the term was still lacking. Lay people, and too often professionals as well, tended to equate "learning disabilities" with "learning problems" of almost any type. Sensorially handicapped children, mentally retarded children, children with individual behavior problems—all became confused with the newly defined category. As Hallahan and Cruickshank (1973) point out, "the profession was unready and unable to meet the challenge of a new idea." They indicated the problems at a practical level:

> Reading problems, emotional problems, management problems, intellectual problems, speech problems, handwriting problems, and others, irrespective of their etiology or symptomatology, are found grouped together on the premise that each is a learning problem. While the latter point may be valid, the administrative decision regarding placement does not result in a positive intervention program when heterogeneity within a class exhausts the capacity of a teacher to encompass individual differences, particularly when the teacher lacks training in some very complex aspects of teaching.

The problem becomes more obvious in any review of the literature. Entire volumes approach the field from sometimes diametrically different approaches due to differences of orientation, professional background, inclusion-exclusion decisions, and similar factors. It is difficult for the neophyte to make adequate judgments, not only in terms of theoretical rights and wrongs, but in terms of specific applicability to an immediate problem.

Thus, even today as the level of sophistication in the field continues to grow, bulwarked by more research and organized study, there is still a great deal of confusion and disagreement over the actual boundaries which limit the field and the lack of a single, universally accepted definition. Discouraging as this may seem at times, it is our position that effective remediation and productive research are possible nevertheless. Those choosing to work in the field should orient themselves toward immediately demonstrable and defensible methods. They may actually benefit from the diversity of opinion gleaned through carefully planned and objective eclecticism, as long as they remain sensitive to the possible limitations as well as the advantages of different ideas and approaches.

Such newly enlisted workers can be helped by three things: first, a better understanding of the exact intent and nature of contributions attempted by various approaches and professions; second, by becoming familiar with specific problem or deficit learning behaviors as they may be observed in both formal assessment and informal learning situations; finally, the worker seeking to be practically productive is helped by developing an ability to relate his or her own professional orientation choices to practical problems. Quick identification of such problems and developed sensitivity to some solution options should provide a feeling of confidence for the practitioner regardless of his or her approach or profession. Considerable material directed to each of these three points will be found in later chapters of this book.

A Brief Outlook

As a summary note it seems that a primary task facing the writer of any text in the area of learning disabilities is to assure the newly enlisted worker, reading the text for guidance and help, that functional effectiveness is actually possible with reasonable amounts of work and training. The field *is* a viable one. Progress has been and is being made. Successful remediation is possible given the development of some basic insights and skills by practitioners. Involvement and participation is worthwhile. Looking for solutions to some of the major problems facing the field is in itself an exciting and rewarding pursuit.

The insight of Kass (1969) into some underlying ideas important in understanding the area of learning disabilities seems quite relevant here.

> Basic to an understanding of the area of learning disabilities within special education are several assumptions: (1) that there are children with a handicapping condition who can be so labeled; (2) that, although services for these children are scarce now, both public and private programs are growing in number; (3) that, while the understanding of learning disabilities is complex, behavioral science research indicates that the child with learning disabilities has psychological process deficits adequate for remediation purposes; and (4) that the handicapping condition known as learning disabilities can be diagnosed educationally and psychologically and that specialized remedial education programs can be prescribed.

In the remainder of this book we will outline and explain some important steps for successfully meeting the challenge of attacking and defeating the problem of learning disabilities.

2

Learning Disability
Behaviors

During the important conference in Chicago that led to the formation of the *Association for Children with Learning Disabilities* it became apparent that concerned parents, laymen, and professionals felt that they needed some type of meaningful label, name, or tag to hang on the peculiar learning difficulties that were occupying their attention. In his role as a recognized leader within this group, Kirk (1963, 1972) was quick to identify and emphasize the danger in labels.

> I have felt for some time that labels we give children are satisfying to us but of little help to the child himself. We seem to be satisfied when we give a technical name to a condition . . . I would like to caution you about being compulsively concerned about names and classification labels . . . I would prefer that people inform me that they have a child that does not talk instead of saying to me their child is dyspasic . . . This approach has led me and my colleagues to develop methods of assessing children or describing their communication skills in objective terms. . . .

Even now there seems to be little serious challenge to Kirk's position. The use of formal taxonomies, classifications, or categories often does little but produce problems, misunderstandings, and overgeneralizations.

But how, one might reasonably ask, can attention be correctly focused on relevant activities or pertinent behaviors if there are no means for discriminating the objects to be focused upon from others? And the criteria for discrimination **15** must have names. The answer lies within the question itself. The solution is to describe behaviors adequately rather than to fixate on groupings under some taxonomic label.

It is possible, for example, to group similar phenomena together by the behavioral activities themselves rather than by some categorical name. A child's failure to read, including a notation of the problem-contributing component behaviors (inability to discriminate letter forms, failure to scan left to right, or poor auditory discrimination of initial word sounds, for example), is much more meaningful than the categorical label *dyslexia,* which may or may not carry similar connotations for different readers.

As Kirk and other members of the newly formed Professional Advisory Board of the *Association for Children with Learning Disabilities* quickly perceived in 1962, the creation of a new and separate classification within special education, *learning disabilities,* was fraught with problems. Although that group, in its early leadership of the developing field, was able to agree generally on operational definitions of the new definition and use behavioral classifications rather than labels, such was not the case with many other groups of professionals and laymen. In subsequent years others have also been quick to see the problem despite the advantages of having a clear-cut classification scheme (such as ready interpretation to naive parties, useful tags for program areas, or for funding applications, starting points for frames of reference, etc.). Even acceptance of the general classification of *specific learning disability* has been viewed with some skepticism because of the developing misuse of Kirk's original term.

Hammill and Bartel (1971) clearly outline the objections raised to this special category of special education because of the reification that has developed:

Objections to the category "Learning Disability"

1. The recognition of commonly shared behavioral learning characteristics of groups of children invariably leads to their being christened with a label;
2. No matter how neutral the label is intended to be, it will rapidly acquire a stigma;
3. Negative labels may reduce teacher expectations and demands from these students, thus further depressing their opportunities for achievement;
4. It is easy to use labels as causes for conditions that the label is supposed to describe—a kind of tautological thinking in which one can reason that the child is not learning to read because he has a learning disability, and must have a learning disability because he is not learning to read;
5. These children differ so widely on intellectual, motor, perceptual, and behavioral traits that a common label—and more importantly, a common treatment—is meaningless and impossible.

Hammill and Bartel also point out that, in dealing with problems of assessment in learning disabilities, the end result of assessment can be more than a classification into some category such as "mental retardation." Sometimes descriptive data appropriately grouped under meaningful titles assist in proper placement of children or in receiving support and services for a child through providing evidence of his appropriate "classification." Still another end result of assessment (which is a form of classification procedure) can be to assist in planning educational prograns, remedial activities, and rehabilitative functions.

Orientation of this Book

The authors of this book assume that this last potential outcome of classification is the most important of all. Any description or listing of behavior must be in a form that is functionally effective in removing deficit learning behaviors, that provides information for remediation and for active intervention strategies. Thus, any summary listing of learning disability behaviors should produce a body of data that is directly interpretable in terms of what the individual child is doing or failing to do. Others have anticipated this distinctive aspect of classification and have noted its importance as well as its relevance to other classification outcomes. In outlining the scope of the field of learning disabilities, Bateman (1964) noted three broad descriptive dimensions: focus, orientation, and problem.

Under the dimension of focus Bateman listed the options of etiology, diagnosis, and remediation. The emphasis in this book is predominantly on remediation. Diagnosis is involved only to the extent that it provides necessary input information for effective decision making in planning remediation.

Under the dimension of orientation Bateman listed three predominant disciplines: education, psychology, and medicine. The authors' orientation (which necessarily is reflected in any listing of "behaviors") is primarily toward education and psychology, with medicine involved only in those areas where there is general consensus regarding the defined overlap across professional specializations. Such an orientation is not meant to exclude the importance or viability of medical contributions, but rather to reflect the nature of the authors' *expertise* and to focus on the problem in terms of its most noticeable context, the learning situation.

Finally, Bateman notes that some subdimension classification can be made of problem types. She includes three: reading, communication, and visual-motor. In chapters to follow we will note major problem areas, behaviorally defined whenever possible, as delineated by a number of important people and programs active in learning disabilities. The formation of any hierarchical standing of importance among problem areas must remain, however, primarily a product of the individual reader's own situation coupled with any emphasis that may result from any one of several theoretical biases the reader may adopt.

Incidence of Learning Disabilities

Because of the apparent lack of homogeneity among learning disability behaviors and resulting differences among criteria, there is considerable variance among estimates of the prevalence of the problem. An early study (Myklebust and Boshes, 1969) screened nearly 3,000 third- and forth-grade public school children for learning disabilities as part of a research project. As part of their study, the researchers wished to separate the children into two groups: those with and those without learning disabilities. To establish a cutoff point for making such a decision, they derived a learning quotient (LQ) by dividing the children's age scores on different psychological tests by their chronological age.

$$\frac{\text{Age Score}}{\text{CA}} \times 100 = \text{LQ}$$

Using an LQ of 90 as the division point, they found that 15 percent of the children fell into the lower group. Adding more tests and dropping the LQ cutoff point to 85, only 7 percent fell into the lower group. The latter figure, based on a more conservative estimate, is frequently quoted as a normative figure. Some concern for the validity of such generalization must be noted since the study, despite its large sample size, was not nearly representative of any cross-crountry population nor was the establishment of incidence norms a defined purpose of the study itself. The National Advisory Committe on Handicapped Children (1968) suggested, "A conservative estimate of the latter group (*more severe cases requiring special remedial procedures*) would include from 1 to 3 percent of the school population." The Committee further noted that definition of these 1 to 3 percent being labeled severe suggested that more cases, less severe in nature or extent, were probably handled routinely in the classroom by the average teacher using the typical curriculum without any special note or census.

Even using the more conservative estimate of 1 to 3 percent, the fact remains, as Lerner (1971) declares using the data of Mackie (1969), that this learning disabled group still ranks first among the different types of exceptionalities listed (including such classifications as mentally retarded, speech handicapped, and crippled).

Early specifications in the federal legislation dealing with mainstreaming, P.L. 94-142, indicated suggested quotas for the proportion of handicapped who might be designated as learning disabled. Fortunately, however, later regulations removed the quotas as they were unworkable both in terms of definition and application. Individual states have not always been as insightful and some still maintain quotas that control the allocation of funds, demonstrating closer attention to their own peculiar fiscal problems than to the genuine needs of children. For example, despite the almost total consensus of both formal and informal professional and lay groups in special education, the state of New York, as of early 1979, had still not removed the same type of quotas the federal government had dropped many months before.

Learning disabilities apparently occur frequently enough to be of concern to educators, and by inference such problems should be discernible using the appropriate identification procedures.

Consensus regarding the discernibility of these highly prevalent problem behaviors seems to center about three main concepts or ideas:

1. There are some general problem-type behaviors that occur sufficiently often in learning disabled children to warrant consideration of the possible presence of an L.D. problem when such behaviors are viewed in any elementary-level school child.
2. Given the initial discrimination cue offered by the presence of such general problem behaviors, the likelihood of a learning disability is increased when behaviors peculiar to the principle of disparity are also observable.
3. Given the presence of cues of the types mentioned in points one and two, some areas of learning behavior seem to be focal points of those special learning problems labeled as learning disabilities.

General Problem Behaviors

The first basis for discerning the probability of a learning disability being present is the appearance of some general problem behavior, a method that is frequently used as the starting point for screening programs (as noted in chapter 9). A number of writers, some reporting from their own anecdotal records of observation and some from more rigidly conducted research, note some of these general behaviors which may subsequently be identified as learning disabilities. Valett (1969b) lists seven general characteristics often found in learning disabled children.*

1. *A repeated history of academic failure in educational pursuits.* Such failure patterns, so often repeated, seem to establish an expectation of failure and a drop in attempts to achieve.

Valett's characteristics of L.D. children

2. *Physical, environmental limitations interacting with learning difficulties.* The presence of a physical or environmental anomaly, such as a relatively minor sight or hearing loss, can cause unproductive or incorrect learning habits to develop which in turn lead at some later point to a major learning disability beyond the scope of the original physical problem.
3. *Motivational abnormalities.* Repeated failure, rejection by teachers and peers, lack of reinforcement—all or any of these problems tend to lower the behavior rate, divert interest from normal educational pursuits, and generally lower or shift motivation.
4. *A vague, almost free-floating anxiety.* Probably stemming from their repeated failure history, learning disability children often develop an expectancy of failure in academic activities that generalizes to experiences of other types. Thus, the anticipation of forthcoming failure, of a still undefined specificity, may produce restlessness, uneasiness, and some types of shallow withdrawal such as daydreaming or inattentiveness.

---

5. *Erratic, uneven behavior.* The overall academic production record of the learning disabled child is apt to be uneven. The child's work in a given area often will fluctuate far beyond the variance expected of children his or her age. Interest and attention span will also fluctuate, sometimes at a normal and high quality level, sometimes short and flitting and more typical of children with other than learning disability problems. The irregularity and erratic nature of the changes are more important clues than the absolute levels and quality of the behaviors.

6. *Incomplete evaluation.* As Valett notes, many children who have been labeled with other designations (e.g., slow, disturbed, retarded) are seen to be suffering from a learning disability upon more thorough behavioral analysis. The clue which might alert the person dealing firsthand to the presence of such a mislabeling based upon incomplete evaluation might be bits of behavior that seem inappropriate to such diagnosis. For example, though a child has been labeled as "retarded," the presence of pieces of academic behavior inappropriately high for such a labeling may indicate that categorization has been made too quickly, based upon incomplete behavioral information, and too often in error.

7. *Inadequate education.* Since a basic assumption of the field of learning disabilities is that the child is capable of better performance than is being produced, this characteristic is an important one. By definition, the learning disabled child has not had the type, quality, extent, or sequences of learning experiences which he or she has needed to produce nondeficit behavior. The issue is not necessarily one of attack on the quality of the educational system or its components per se. Teachers often have all the necessary skills to provide the missing experiences if they are adequately alerted to the need for them. The problem is often one of a poor match between classroom activities and the individual child's needs. A common clue often comes from the teacher who says, "Somehow, what we're doing in class just doesn't seem to consistently work for this child."

Valett's seven characteristics are important ones and though some practice and experience is necessary to assure regular translation into observed behaviors, the ability to do so is rather quickly added to those many skills teachers, psychologists, and others working with children already possess.

Different behavioral indices have been developed by other experimenters. Meier (1971) reports on behaviors that teachers have identified in children correctly diagnosed as learning disabled. Two-thirds of these learning disabled children displayed unusually short attention spans, lack of concentration, significantly slower reading speeds, and word substitutions that distort meaning (e.g., *when* for *where*). Behaviors noted less consistently, but appearing frequently, are also listed (see the complete list and breakdown of frequency in Table 9–1, in chapter 9 on screening). General behaviors reported by many different practitioners include lack of auditory and visual attention, poor motor coordination, low frustration tolerance, mood fluctuation, and poor perceptual ability.

Although the examination of the cognitive aspects of learning disabilities is a newer focus than some others, it has drawn special interest to two common problem behaviors frequently observed in learning disabled individuals. Deficits in attention, both in degree and type, have been noted in research reports (Hallahan, Kauffman, and Ball, 1973; Tarver, Hallahan, Kauffman, and Ball, 1976; Tarver, Hallahan, Cohen and Kauffman, 1977) and elaborated on at length as a major component of nearly all learning disability problems (Ross, 1977). Others have noted that learning disabled children are frequently deficient in their levels or rates of active, productive behaviors (Flavell, 1970; Flavell, Beach, and Chinsky, 1966). Hallahan, Tarver, Kauffman, and Graybeal (1978) have reported that this deficiency is responsive to specifically applied reinforcement conditions, a finding congruent with the shaping of cognitive behaviors through common behavior modification procedures, as reported by Meichenbaum (1977). It has been categorically suggested by Torgeson (1977) that the learning disabled child is a passive rather than an active learner and that classroom approaches may be modified to raise the production level of these children as a step in remediation.

Principle of Disparity

The second concept upon which discrimination of learning disabilities is based is the *principle of disparity*. This principle, as observed in overt behavior, is probably most frequently and universally applied as the practitioner attempts to differentiate between learning disability problems and other types of difficulties. Bateman (1964) alluded to the principle when she stated, in an early definition, that the learning disabled child is "one who manifests an educationally significant discrepancy between his apparent capacity for language behaviors and his actual level of language functioning." Later, in 1965, she broadened the area of deficit areas to include a "significant discrepancy between their estimated intellectual potential and actual level of performance related to basic disorders of the learning process. . . ." Gallagher (1966) used uneven growth patterns as part of a proposed definition. Others (Gearheart, 1973; Kass, 1969; Kirk, 1962) have underlined the same principle.

Basically the principle assumes that the child in question is essentially a "normal" child with the capacity to operate at an "average" level—although normal and average may sometimes be defined idiosyncratically for each case. The problem behavior in question is assumed to be limited to a definable area(s) at a level which is disparate from or lower than the child's other behaviors. The discrepancy in behavior, noticeable and definable in a variety of ways ranging from established standard score differences (Kirk, McCarthy, and Kirk, 1968) to erratic fluctuations in behavior (Valett, 1969b), becomes the significant factor. An important corollary of the principle is that the child can and will profit and remove the deficit and/or disparity, given the correct or appropriate experience.

The learning disabled child behaves as he does due to forces beyond his control, and with proper attention has the potential for normal development and successful school achievement. This assumption removes the child from the ranks of the mentally retarded in perceived learning potential and social adaptability. The learning disabled child's condition is amenable to treatment and specialized instruction. This assumption proclaims that the condition is remediable and that there are persons with the knowledge and skill to accomplish this (Gearheart, 1973).

Working from their neurological orientation, Johnson and Myklebust (1967) focus on the factors that must be functioning adequately for learning to occur. They note that their "primary concern is that the integrities are optimum or at least average." Although their concern with the etiology of observed disparities and subsequent remediation may differ from some others, the principle of disparity is still present and of major importance to their theory.

A year year later Myklebust (1968) affirmed that, in addition to demonstrating certain neurological dysfunction (in harmony with his theoretical emphasis), it is necessary that a "specified deficiency in learning" be evidenced. But as Myk-

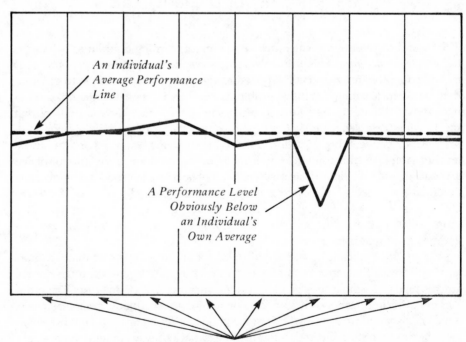

Identified Areas of Academic Behavior

FIGURE 2-1
Principle of Disparity

lebust indicates, the extent of the nature—both in range and intensity—is a difficult problem to gauge.

Naive approaches to measuring the deficit intensity or the cutoff point at which a slowness or lag becomes a problem deficit have included such simplistic criteria as grade level, or grade-months accumulated, in comparison to a child's peers. This method of measurement has proven grossly unsatisfactory. Certainly the uneven and erratic nature of the behavior of a learning disabled child in itself precludes the use of this simple measure. Deficits are apt to appear unevenly in separate aspects of behavior as well as appearing to be greater or lesser in a single area at different times. Solutions to this measurement problem have appeared in three primary areas.

Statistical Weights

There have been attempts to derive some sort of statistical weighting scheme whereby deficiencies can be given standardized numerical weights. Such a scheme would present evaluations of individual learning behaviors that might be compared the same way that subtests on intelligence tests are compared one against another and also with some overall measurement of global intelligence. One of the most publicized attempts at such a solution was produced by Myklebust (1968). According to his plan, three separate pre-established measures are assembled for a child: *mental age, chronological age,* and *grade age. Mental age* refers, of course, to the output of a typical intelligence test, also used for ultimate derivation of an IQ score (mental age divided by chronological age). *Chronological age* is simply the child's age. *Grade age* is a numerical expression at which the school has placed the child. The validity of this piece of data is, of course, dependent upon the sincerity and accuracy with which the school makes grade placements. "Passing students along" to keep them out of trouble would cause serious problems for this method, of course. In Myklebust's equation, these three measures are added and then divided by three to obtain an average that is labeled the *Expectancy Age* or *EA*.

$$\frac{MA + CA + GA}{3} = EA \text{ (Expectancy Age)}$$

The final statistic is an average of the child's position on three different normative continua: intelligence, physical age, and level in school. Various areas of learning are then examined. These might range from broad areas, such as the child's general reading ability, to more specifically defined behaviors that are narrower in scope, such as auditory receptive behaviors. The child's achievement is measured in terms of "level achieved in years." In order for such data to be available, of course, the assumption is that suitable measuring instruments are available and that the child's performance on these instruments can be expressed in age-level scores—an assumption not always easily supportable in practice, however. The child's level as achieved in years, designated in *achievement level,* is divided by his *expectancy level* (the same as expectancy age). Thus, a *learning quotient,* usable in much the same way as an intelligence quotient, is obtained.

$$\frac{\text{AL (Achievement Level)}}{\text{EL (Expectancy Level)}} \times 100 = \text{LQ (Learning Quotient)}$$

A major problem with this approach, as noted, is that many times the individual bits and pieces of behavior that need to be measured have not been adequately defined, isolated, and described. Consequently, satisfactory measuring instruments, devices, and techniques are often lacking.

Despite attempts to make them precise enough for practical application, such equations and weighting techniques have proven to be virtually useless and are seldom used now. A major part of the problem is, of course, that the preciseness of input data, both taxonomically and psychometrically, is highly questionable. Therefore both the reliability and validity of derived data is minimal.

Defining Behaviors

Because of such gaps in measurement, the second area in which solutions have begun to appear has been in the more specific definition of behaviors and sub-behaviors comprising the educational activity in question. Measurement specialists have begun to focus on this problem and have recognized the need for more specific measurement techniques and analysis procedures. Simple measures of behavior such as auditory discrimination (Wepman, 1958) have led to more sophisticated, more precise, and, most importantly, more detailed or molecular measurements of the same behavior (e.g., the *Test of Auditory Discrimination*, 1970). Even such general classroom achievement areas as reading are benefitting from attention to the need for more detailed and precise measurement of the behaviors involved.

Combining Approaches

The first two solution areas—(1) establishing some type of statistical summary of disparity and (2) providing more detailed behavioral analyses—have started to become combined into a third. It is now possible, in areas such as language, to measure discrepancy behaviors in terms of behaviorally defined subcategories of behavior (Kirk, McCarthy, and Kirk, 1968). Moreover, the scores obtained can be converted into a standard format. They can also be portrayed on an individual profile basis that is both graphic and functional and combines accurate behavior analysis with precise mathematical interpretation of behavioral data. For example, in the area of language, the *Illinois Test of Psycholinguistic Ability* defines a precise standard deviation for making significant deficit-disparity judgments.

Similar instruments are beginning to appear in varied areas such as reading, arithmetic, articulation, and other academic activities.

Types of Learning Disabilities

The discrimination of learning disabilities centers about behavioral areas in which the deficit behaviors we described appear most frequently. This does not imply that there is any general agreement on exactly what the areas are. Indeed, there is much disagreement about which taxonomy of problems is most useful or most important. But, almost universally, successful learning disability strategists offer some outline, list, or suggested hierarchy of most frequently encountered or most important problem areas. There seem to be at least two major reasons for the discrepancies among lists.

First, without any doubt there is some quite honest but nevertheless very real self-fulfilling prophecy present. Basic differences in theoretical orientation cause different individuals to search for certain syndromes and their searches are sufficiently successful to substantiate their own biases. Thus, those looking for perceptual problems tend to find them. Those looking for language difficulties tend to find them. It has been suggested that when two quite honest researchers discover defensible but contradictory results, then one of several things may be true. Either or both may be wrong. Both may be right, but may be observing different phenomena in the same event. Or, the phenomenon itself may not be stable and therefore appears differently at separate times, or under different analyses. There is probably some truth in each of these possibilities when it comes to learning disabilities. The field is still young and although research is much more intense than it was ten to fifteen years ago, it is still relatively new and much more centered about applied functions than theoretical concepts and structures. It is also quite possible that most specific learning disabilities contain several or perhaps many different types of deficit behaviors and that particular analytical techniques tend to uncover certain kinds of behaviors more than others. There has been relatively little factor-analytic research in the area to measure the amount of overlap and the congruency of different theories and models. This type of research is desperately needed. And it is quite possible that the erratic nature of learning-disability behavior itself may add to the difficulty, due to (1) the high proportion of normal behavior present in the individual, which allows at least momentary compensation for deficit areas, and (2) the difficulty of obtaining a meaningful static sample of an ongoing process at any one time.

A second major reason for such a variety of behavior lists found in learning disability texts and journals is that there is some evidence that certain behaviors can be almost epidemic in nature. This certainly may be true at least to the extent that children in a given geographical, social, or educational setting may be subjected to similar stimuli or the absence of certain necessary learning experiences. A simple example of this situation is often noted in localities where screening is performed for the first time. If a population of school children has not been screened for hearing deficits for a period of several years, then the first new screening will probably elicit an unusually high number of children with

Reasons for disagreement on types

hearing problems. A school system that has not been sensitive in its classroom activities to the need for directed development of adequate visual discrimination skills will be found to have large numbers of children with problems of this type. In most cases suggested listings and hierarchies represent actual experiences in real situations; and, because of the peculiar situations variables and/or the skills and talents and techniques of the investigators, the experiences tend to be repeated, thus giving birth to a particular schematic view of the field that may or may not always generalize to other situations and other individuals.

In a way, however, this diversity of viewpoints is an asset. It suggests that the field is being examined in many different ways and that, through eventual cross-validation of experience and observation by different viewers with different orientations and experiences, some common denominators of a very basic, substantial, and useful nature may be uncovered.

It is also useful to examine some of these behavioral breakdowns of the types of learning disabilities because they may suggest new or overlooked ways of analyzing such behavior. Gaps in our own understanding of the field, issues that remain confused despite our own experience, can sometimes be filled or clarified through an appreciation of how others perceive the same problems.

We have already noted Johnson and Myklebust's (1967) concern for the integrity of the individual, for the ability of the child to learn from "opportunities (which are) optimum or at least average." Projecting their presumption that "learning disabilities . . . are the result of minor disturbances of brain function," they categorize the necessary integrities into three types: psychodynamic, or what many might call *psychological* integrities; peripheral nervous system integrities; and central nervous system integrities. Deficit learning behavior might result from a dysfunction or inadequate level of functioning in any of these broad areas or the more specific subsets of behavior that they encompass. Specifically, Johnson and Myklebust categorize them in this way (1967):

Structural levels of deficit learning behavior

- *Psychodynamic Factors:* Processes of identification, imitation, and internalization.
- *Peripheral Nervous System Factors:* Overloading and underloading problems such as varying kinds and degrees of deafness and blindness, and cases of deprivation rather than inability (an input problem).
- *Central Nervous System Factors:* Problems that are manifested in children not displaying "gross neurological abnormalities," but having some dysfunction which interferes with normal or sometimes even superior learning capabilities. The concept here is one often subsumed under the more common label, *minimal brain damage.*

A number of prominent people in the field, notably those less concerned with neurological involvement than Johnson and Myklebust, prefer other ways of listing or categorizing problem areas of learning disability. As might be expected, many of the alternate models tend toward a more behavioral and less structural model. Bateman (1964) originally delineated three major subcategories of problem areas with recognized overlap:

1. *Dyslexia:* A term apparently meant to encompass any one of a number of reading difficulties with further specification depending upon finer behavioral analysis.
2. *Verbal Communication Disorder:* Primarily comprehension and expression problems in the spoken word. In some areas the term *aphasia* or *developmental aphasia* is used in place of this, though confusion may easily result from learning disability problems becoming confused with more clinical cases of aphasia resulting from or involving known emotional disturbances or demonstrated brain trauma, as in the case of cardiovascular accidents.
3. *Visual-Motor Integration Problems:* Bateman most often uses these within the context of reading, but notes the possibility of many other types as well.

Bateman's problem area categories

In a more recent text, Myers and Hammill (1969) outline the basic learning processes that must function satisfactorily if normal developmental learning progress is to be achieved. They list those processes necessary for *perception,* including decoding of information received in any and all sensory modes; those necessary for the formation of adequate *response behaviors,* including vocal, graphic, and presumably manual encoding or response production; and those necessary for adequate *connecting associations* including memory, recall, some types of associative recognition, the class of phenomena commonly referred to as closure, and various types of abstract and symbolic thinking.

The same authors (Myers and Hammill, 1969) categorize learning disabled children in terms of six major areas of disability:

1. *Disorders of Motor Activity:* including hyperactivity, hypoactivity, incoordination and perserveration
2. *Disorders of Emotionality:* including prolonged dependency, frustration, misinterpretation of reality (and the resulting bizarre behavior problems), disturbed impulse patterning which likely would also describe inability to delay or postpone gratification and reinforcement
3. *Disorders of Perception:* including problems of interpreting, identifying, discriminating, general decoding or receptive behaviors (as differentiated from problems of inadequate acuity; e.g., nearsightedness)
4. *Disorders of Symbolization:* including the integration of perception and memory, receptive skills in auditory and visual modes, expressive behaviors in vocal and motor modes
5. *Disorders of Attention:* including both too little and excessive attention
6. *Disorders of Memory:* including assimilation, storage, and recall behaviors

Hammill and Myers' areas of disability

In a later edition of their book, Myers and Hammill (1976) specifically reject the notion of "processes" as a result of their subsequent research. However, even if their rejection of processes is adopted, the initial list remains useful as long as the categorizations are accepted as integral behavior bits, functionally sequential in the typical child, but not organismically or developmentally necessary as prerequisites.

Valett (1969) has defined learning disabilities as "any specific difficulty in acquiring and using information or skills that are essential to problem solving." For his remedial program he has defined "specific disabilities" as referring to any one or more of six discriminable areas:

1. Gross-motor development
2. Sensory-motor integration
3. Perceptual-motor skills
4. Language development
5. Conceptual skills
6. Social skills

Valett further defines the specific behaviors involved in each of the six broader areas, compiling a list of fifty-three learning behaviors that may appear in deficit form as a specific learning disability. See Table 2-1 for Valett's Basic Learning Abilities lists.

TABLE 2-1
Basic Learning Abilities*

GROSS MOTOR DEVELOPMENT
The development and awareness of large muscle activity.
1. *Rolling:* the ability to roll one's body in a controlled manner.
2. *Sitting:* the ability to sit erect in a normal position without support or constant reminding.
3. *Crawling:* the ability to crawl on hands and knees in a smooth and coordinated way.
4. *Walking:* the ability to walk erect in a coordinated fashion without support.
5. *Running:* the ability to run a track or obstacle course without a change of pace.
6. *Throwing:* the ability to throw a ball with reasonable degree of accuracy.
7. *Jumping:* the ability to jump simple obstacles without falling.
8. *Skipping:* the ability to skip in normal play.
9. *Dancing:* the ability to move one's body in coordinated response to music.
10. *Self-identification:* the ability to identify one's self.
11. *Body Localization:* the ability to locate parts of one's body.
12. *Body Abstraction:* the ability to transfer and generalize self-concepts and body localizations.
13. *Muscular Strength:* the ability to use one's muscles to perform physical tasks.
14. *General Physical Health:* the ability to understand and apply principles of health and hygiene while demonstrating good general health.

SENSORY-MOTOR INTEGRATION
The psychophysical integration of fine and gross motor activities.
15. *Balance and Rhythm:* the ability to maintain gross and fine motor balance and to move rhythmically.

* From *Programming Learning Disabilities* by Robert E. Valett. Copyright © 1969 by Fearon-Pitman Publishers, Inc., 6 Davis Drive, Belmont, CA 94002. Reprinted by permission.

TABLE 2-1
Basic Learning Abilities (*Continued*)

16. *Body-Spatial Organization:* the ability to move one's body in an integrated way around and through objects in the spatial environment.
17. *Reaction Speed-Dexterity:* the ability to respond efficiently to general directions or assignments.
18. *Tactile Discrimination:* the ability to identify and match objects by touching and feeling.
19. *Directionality:* the ability to know right from left.
20. *Laterality:* the ability to integrate one's sensory-motor contact with the environment through establishment of homolateral hand, eye, and foot dominance.
21. *Time Orientation:* the ability to judge lapses in time and to be aware of time concepts.

PERCEPTUAL-MOTOR SKILLS
The functional utilization of primary auditory, visual, and visual-motor skills.
22. *Auditory Acuity:* the ability to receive and differentiate auditory stimuli.
23. *Auditory Decoding:* the ability to understand sounds or spoken words.
24. *Auditory-Vocal Association:* the ability to respond verbally in a meaningful way to auditory stimuli.
25. *Auditory Memory:* the ability to retain and recall general auditory information.
26. *Auditory Sequencing:* the ability to recall in correct sequence and detail prior auditory information.
27. *Visual Acuity:* the ability to see objects in one's visual field and to differentiate them meaningfully and accurately.
28. *Visual Coordination and Pursuit:* the ability to follow and track objects and symbols with coordinated eye movements.
29. *Visual-Form Discrimination:* the ability to differentiate visually the forms and symbols in one's environment.
30. *Visual Figure-Ground Differentiation:* the ability to perceive objects in foreground and background and to separate them meaningfully.
31. *Visual Memory:* the ability to recall accurately prior visual experiences.
32. *Visual-Motor Memory:* the ability to reproduce motor-wise prior visual experiences.
33. *Visual-Motor Fine Muscle Coordination:* the ability to coordinate fine muscles such as those required in eye-hand tasks.
34. *Visual-Motor Spatial-Form Manipulations:* the ability to move in space and to manipulate three-dimensional materials.
35. *Visual-Motor Speed of Learning:* the ability to learn visual-motor skills from repetitive experience.
36. *Visual-Motor Integration:* the ability to integrate total visual-motor skills in complex problem solving.

LANGUAGE DEVELOPMENT
The current and functional stage of total psycholinguistic development.
37. *Vocabulary:* the ability to understand words.
38. *Fluency and Encoding:* the ability to express oneself verbally.
39. *Articulation:* the ability to articulate words clearly without notable pronunciation on articulatory problems.

TABLE 2-1
Basic Learning Abilities (*Continued*)

40. *Word Attack Skills:* the ability to analyze words phonetically.
41. *Reading Comprehension:* the ability to understand what one reads.
42. *Writing:* the ability to express oneself through written language.
43. *Spelling:* the ability to spell in both oral and written form.

CONCEPTUAL SKILLS
The functional level of concept attainment and general reasoning ability.
44. *Number Concepts:* the ability to count and use simple numbers to represent quantity.
45. *Arithmetic Processes:* the ability to add, subtract, multiply, and divide.
46. *Arithmetic Reasoning:* the ability to apply basic arithmetic processes in personal and social usage of problem solving.
47. *General Information:* the ability to acquire and utilize general information from education and experience.
48. *Classification:* the ability to recognize class identities and to use them in establishing logical relationships.
49. *Comprehension:* the ability to use judgment and reasoning in common sense situations.

SOCIAL SKILLS
The skill involved in social problem solving.
50. *Social Acceptance:* the ability to get along with one's peers.
51. *Anticipatory Response:* the ability to anticipate the probable outcome of a social situation by logical inference.
52. *Value Judgments:* the ability to recognize and respond to moral and ethical issues.
53. *Social Maturity:* the ability to assume personal and social responsibility.

Other theorists and program builders present taxonomies that are primarily reflections of their own approaches. Thus, Kephart (1971), viewing all learning disabilities as a function of perceptual-motor difficulty, differentiates among problems as they are related to the developmental level of certain subareas of perceptual-motor behavior, like balance and posture, body image and differentiation, perceptual-motor match, ocular control and form perception. Lists of this type, somewhat less obviously related to actual learning activities at first contact, become more meaningful when viewed within the context of the individual theory, assessment, and remediation techniques from which they are derived. A similar example is found in the work of Kirk, McCarthy, and Kirk (1968), authors of the *Illinois Test of Psycholinguistic Abilities*, who delineate learning disabilities into deficits involving various combinations of sensory modes, certain input-association-output behaviors and automatic or habitual versus representational or conceptual levels of language functioning. Subscribing to Kephart's theories on perceptual-motor functions or Kirk, McCarthy, and Kirk's on language functions does not demand absolute acceptance of a theory that may limit the user to its orientations. Neither is it necessary to be a total convert in the case of other approaches that do not necessarily limit the range of possible disabilities to their own focus but strongly imply a hierarchy of importance or relevancy. Some authors and theorists are more rigid or lenient than others in this respect. The practitioner may use the lists in his or her own way, primarily accepting them at first as a useful vantage point from which to recognize and view the problem and leaving the development of any firm belief in absoluteness or relative importance to some later date.

It is also interesting to note that, even with those who at first reading may seem to be most exclusive of others' alternative categorizations, the first perception may be incorrect. No one, for example, could challenge that Johnson and Myklebust present more neurological material, emphasis, and theory than Kirk. And, upon first reading, it might seem that it would be difficult ever to resolve their separate listings. Yet, upon more careful examination, one finds Johnson and Myklebust suggesting that some of the common areas of deficit may be those of (1) input-output, (2) modality, and (3) integration. Apparently they feel that such a listing is not incongruous with their own approach: the similarity of this triad of areas to Kirk, McCarthy, and Kirk's (1968) ideas, as personified in their major assessment instrument, is obvious.

Delineating the broad areas in which learning disabilities are most commonly reported as interacting negatively with components of the elementary arithmetic curriculum, Johnson (1979) lists:

1. Memory
2. Visual and auditory discrimination
3. Visual and auditory association
·4. Perceptual-motor
5. Spatial awareness and orientation
6. Verbal expression
7. Closure and generalization
8. Attention

One final type of listing might be noted. The authors informally requested a group of elementary teachers, people experienced in working with learning-disabled children, to list the problem areas they seemed to encounter most frequently. This group, accustomed to dealing more with actual problems than theoretical orientations, listed these eleven behaviors—which they define operationally as being learning disabilities rather than something else—as occurring most frequently in their classrooms.

1. Atypical spelling errors
2. Auditory discrimination problems
3. Letter recognition problems
4. Initial sound-in-words confusion
5. Counting and number recognition difficulties
6. Auditory memory deficits

Problem areas reported as encountered most frequently

7. Visual memory deficits
8. Gross motor incoordination
9. Spatial disorientation
10. Articulation errors
11. Fine motor problems—usually perceived in handwriting.

The most defensible reason for any categorization strategy, of course, is simply to facilitate eventual remediation. Labels in and of themselves are largely useless. Smith and Neisworth (1969) remind us of the heterogeneity of the typical classroom. The usual classroom, they say, contains students who—

Smith's and Neisworth's description of students in the typical classroom

1. Do well in all school subjects by performing at a level that is consistent with their "predicted" ability;
2. Exhibit unequal achievement in certain subject areas which require similar skills for an effective performance;
3. Have developed the basic technical skills for a subject, but are deficient in applying these skills efficiently;
4. Have not developed basic precursive or technical skills for a subject, or apply the processes involved in the subject inconsistently;
5. Are intellectually superior and do well in all subjects, or are intellectually superior and underachieve in all subjects;
6. Are mentally retarded and do not understand regular classroom instruction;
7. Have emotional problems which impede adequate performance in academic areas or restrict effective interaction with classmates or authority figures;
8. Have other specific problems such as perceptual-motor difficulties; communication disorders, social difficulties, or physical disabilities that reduce their ability to perform effectively at a minimum level in all areas.

Summary

Learning disabilities has been developed as a specialized field (with admitted overlap in related areas such as the study of retardation) with the belief that there are children within this heterogeneous mass who have enough in common—either in the area of their difficulty or in the type of remediation to which they may most effectively respond—to be worth identifying and helping. The basic tenet of this belief is that learning-disabled individuals are suffering from problems that can be relieved. As Gearheart (1973) has so aptly written, the learning-disabled child's condition is amenable to treatment, he does have the potential for normal development, and he behaves as he does because of forces beyond his control.

The identification of typical categories of behavior that may make the practitioner aware of the possibility of a specific problem is only an initial step toward remediation. Knowledge of appropriate attack strategies, of techniques for more precise individual behavior assessment and analysis, and of the detailed aspects successful remediation procedures must follow are equally important.

3

Issues, Trends, and Needs

Learning disabilities is not a quiet, peaceful, and settled field of endeavor. During the approximate decade and a half since its formal recognition, it has gone through a tempestuous period of trying to define itself, to establish clear role identifications, and to articulate its mission and method. The 1970s have seen the field begin to come of age. This apparent growth in stature as well as magnitude is personified by a number of events. The field is beginning to move beyond first generation workers; and, although the work of the early stalwarts has lost none of its significance as pioneering and groundbreaking leadership, there is evidence that even better ideas, more complete concepts, and more effective techniques and methods are being developed by new rising figures.

This new growth does not come totally at the expense of early gains and contributions. Ideas that have stood the trial of repeated exposure and testing serve as the basis for many new theories. And a substantial number of the pioneer figures in the field today lead the cry for additional research, refinement, better definition, and improvement of techniques. Major contributors such as William Cruickshank, Maryanne Frostig, and Doris Johnson personify this unwillingness to settle for the concepts, techniques, and assumptions of the past. Cruickshank's conferences at the Institute for the Study of Mental Retardation and Related Disabilities, for example, have focused on the need for growth and development. In 1974, he reminded guest participants that they should not concentrate on achievements to date, but should instead "suggest realistic goals for meeting the needs of learning disabled children in the next ten years" (Krasnoff, 1974).

As old ideas and new have come together it is only natural that comparisons have been made and serious questions have been asked about the adequacy of some past concepts and the accuracy of some former assumptions. This reshaping process, a necessary step in the growth and refinement of any set of ideas, has not always been painless or without dispute. There are a number of active debates over important issues in the field today. Given the increasing desire of many in the field to substantiate their hypotheses in more concrete ways than public or private debate, it seems likely that in the long run nothing but progress can develop from such differences of opinion. Scanning the professional literature indicates that, in almost every segment of the field, workers of pratically every theoretical bent and espousing a wide variety of preferred methodologies are seeking firmer evidence of the efficacy and accuracy of their viewpoints and approaches. The cry for more, better conceived, and defined research permeates the field.

Black (1974) and Topaz (1973) have reminded us that there is still a great disparity between the material written on descriptive and remedial topics and the funding and reporting of research on the effectiveness of these remedial efforts. Blending a recognition for the need of research with a focus on the importance of remediation as our major objective, these writers and others emphasize the need to fund more studies on remedial efforts and to encourage better dissemination of the results. It is still difficult to discover how effective a particular program, technique, or delivery of service model has been. In part this is because many of our demonstration programs and models are so new that longitudinal data have not yet been gathered. In part it is also due to a less than rigorous approach to research design and data reporting by many practitioners in the field. However, professionals working in the field do seem to be moving in the right direction. Periodicals such as the *Journal of Learning Disabilities* and the *Learning Disability Quarterly* are publishing sophisticated articles dealing more with reported evidence and less with speculation or opinion. And it is encouraging to note that critical analysis includes more than single publication challenges. Increasingly, the field is finding monograph and even book length examination of important issues (Newcomer and Hammill, 1976) in an obvious attempt to refine and improve our understanding and practices.

High quality comparative evidence of this type is badly needed by those who are making major planning decisions in program building.

In the past, the quality of reported research in learning disabilities has been at best uneven. Kephart (1971) several years ago noted the need for better formulated hypotheses in basic designs. And Frostig (1974), in welcoming the research challenge to some of her own ideas, pinpointed some of the methodological and conceptual weaknesses obvious in too many current research studies. Some of the assumptions of the past need to be reconsidered and rechecked through more careful reseach. As Cratty (1974) points out, too many of our ideas are based on assumptions of causal relationships between variables and behavioral effects when all that has been demonstrated, and not strongly in too many cases, has been a tentative mathematical relationship. Some of our current debates center around such foundering assumptions, and the growing body of research evidence supporting or challenging some of these ideas is exceedingly healthy for all of the learning disabilities field.

Learning disabilities, as a special discipline, is well into its second decade. However, along with maturity has come a crystallizing of the various issues of the past, which, though yet to be totally resolved, have been the subject of much focused debate and some (though not enough) research. Because of this extra attention, practitioners in the field are not as naive about these issues as they once were. As a result, uncritical and naive adoption of basic assumptions is less commonly observed today than in the 1960s, though considerable attention is given to such questions as the following:

1. Are remedial reading and learning disabilities really the same thing? (Kirk, 1972; Lerner, 1976; Wiederholt, 1974b)
2. Does perceptual-motor training generalize to other academic areas and are current programs effective? (Hammill and Wiederholt, 1973; Larsen and Hammill, 1975; Pitcher-Baker, 1973)
3. How does cultural and economic deprivation interact with learning disabilties? (Deutsch, 1968, 1974; Hallahan and Cruickshank, 1973; Moss, 1973; Myers and Hammill, 1976; Redelheim, 1973)
4. What effect does nutrition have on learning? (Cravioto, 1972; Hawley and Buckley, 1974; Powers, 1973)
5. How effective is early preschool screening and diagnosis? (Keogh, 1970)

Identifying the Major Issues

While maturity has refined some old issues, it has also spawned some new ones. Those which face the field today seem to cluster in four major areas: problems of definition, a developing concern for consumer protection, research, and matters of professional training and preparation. These areas are worth examining in more detail before looking at developing general trends and some unresolved needs.

Questions of Definition

Like most adolescents, Learning Disabilities, as an independent field of study and specialization, is beginning to worry about its own identification as it comes of age. Its professionals are struggling with roles and self-concepts. The problem of who and what we are has progressed far beyond the earlier concern for a clear-cut definition of the nature of L.D. itself. That problem is still with us however and does not make role clarification any easier.

What Is L.D.?

As noted in previous chapters, learning disability workers and lay people working in the field have always had a difficult time with definitions. Every effort to arrive at a definition involving less labeling and categorization has resulted in exactly the opposite. All the pitfalls and errors of categorizing and classification have been demonstrated in this field (Siegel, 1968). Practitioners have had difficulty communicating to the public what types of problems they were encountering. Government agencies at both state and federal levels have been in a quandry over how to define the field for funding and licensing-certification legislation. In some cases these agencies have chosen not even to try to formulate definitions but to settle for lumping learning disabilities in with some other related area, usually special education for handicapped children, a logical but not very helpful solution. In 1974 the Advisory Board of the Association for Children with Learning Disabilities made their first recommendation, the inclusion of learning disabilities in the definition of "handicapped" in Congressional bills: evidence of the lack of clarity about the field in Washington (Wiederholt, 1974). As Cruickshank (1972) has declared, learning disabilities has had a "precocious maturation" and one vital issue is its failure to make an adequate operational definition of the behaviors it deals with and the population it serves. Cruickshank also feels that some major constitutional issues are involved, particularly in the matter of educational placement and labeling, an area where definition is functionally important. The need to sharpen and redefine our terms and refine our target population has drawn much attention. Hammill (1972) points out that these shaping efforts must provide a definition and description along several lines. These include a clear statement of intention, a useful application, specificity adaptable for research use, a syntactical clearness and straightforwardness that eliminates misinterpretation, a clear focus on educational relevancy, and a brevity which allows easy use.

Philosophical and theoretical differences in definitives

Given this criterion list, the mechanical task of finding the right words is not easy. But the major problems are not mechanical: they are philosophical and theoretical in nature. The single most important reason for the lack of a clear, concise, and consensual definition in the field today is that there is no clear, concise consensus present. Due in part to the many disciplines involved, each with its own vagaries of training, professional biases, and to some extent self-supporting defensiveness, common denominator words and concepts are difficult to find. The situation is complicated by the generally disorganized state of research in the field, which prevents those who would define issues better from relying on a discernible body of data for support on one side or another of a nonconsensual issue. One of the most important arguments for better organized data collection and research is that it would provide the field with data for establishing some of these badly needed definitions.

Finally, different individuals, each technically correct given his own particular vantage point, list of hierarchies, and theoretical premises, do not agree on what details should be included. Some progress is being made. Practically no one is satisfied with present definitions and this is a step in the right direction since it encourages individuals to resolve dissonance in favor of a more workable set of definitions.

Some constructive suggestions are being made. Ford (1971) suggests that:

> . . .it would seem more parsimonious in the long run to broaden the definition of learning disabilities to include any child of average intelligence, without sensory deficits, who is unable to learn within the regular curriculum whether the apparent basis for the difficulty be neurological impairment, emotional disturbance, or cultural deprivation. Furthermore, the concept of an "educationally significant discrepancy" (Bateman, 1964) between apparent capacity and actual level of performance should be made an explicit part of the definition.

Cruickshank (1974) feels strongly that new definitions should ignore age and IQ. Deutsch (1974) feels equally strongly that the disadvantaged and culturally deprived should be included. A national committee, established by federal funds and including some learning disability specialists among its members, has attacked the general issues of classification and offered suggestions for new definitions that include many of these proposals. The committee also focused on areas of inclusion rather than exclusion, an approach much more amenable to behavioral definition and refinement (Hobbs, 1974).

Much of the impetus for revision and sharpening the definition has arisen out of the need for including in federal legislation a definition that is workable in terms of allocating responsibility and focus for reseach, training, and demonstration projects.

Thus, the early National Advisory Committee's report became incorporated into law in the *Children with Specific Learning Disabilities Act of 1969* (and its amendments). This was also included in 1974 as part of Public Law 93–380. Subsequently, when Public Law 94–142, commonly known as the *Mainstreaming Act,* was drafted some changes ensued. These included a refined definition, more specific in some respects:

> *Specific learning disabilities* means a disorder of one or more of the basic psychological processes involved in understanding or in using language, spoken or written, which may manifest itself in an imperfect ability to listen, think, speak, read, write, spell, or do arithmetic calculations. The term includes such conditions as perceptual handicaps, brain injury, minimal brain damage, dyslexia, and developmental aphasia. The term does not include children who have learning problems which are primarily the result of visual, hearing, or motor handicaps, of mental retardation, or environmental, cultural, or economic disadvantage.

Redefinition stipulated by federal legislation

The act also added some additional requirements for establishing remedial teams and individualized educational programs. These included the following:

1. Inclusion of the child's regular teacher on the team.
2. More liberal criteria for determining the presence of L.D. (dropping any specific formula for inclusion).
   a. Presence of a specific learning disability shall be assumed when the child does not achieve commensurate with age, ability, when provided with appropriate educational experiences, or when
   b. There is a discrepancy between achievement and academic ability in one of the seven areas relevant to communication skills and mathematical ability.

The seven areas included in the act and referred to in the above criteria statement are oral expression, listening comprehension, written expression, basic reading skill, mathematical computation, and mathematical reasoning.

The trend in learning disabilities seems to be toward more and different definitions. It remains to be seen whether or not the new ones will resolve the criticisms leveled at the earlier ones. One can hope that each succeeding step will closer approximate the final ideal model. Nevertheless, present circumstances seem to suggest that until more hard information is on hand to resolve some of the issues, disputes, and personal points of emphases, the search for a genuine, workable definition that approaches consensus may be a long and difficult one.

Who Are the Learning Disabled?

This question has raised an interesting paradox. Two separate drives to better define the field come in direct conflict regarding this issue. While some strive to better isolate the varying types of deficit behaviors that comprise what most feel to be the too heterogeneous classification of *learning disabilities,* others seek to include an even broader range of problems and possible etiologies because of concern for the children involved.

Philosophically, there may be little basic difference. In practice, severe problems are created. For example, frustrated practitioners trying to better define what really is the nature of inadequate reading behavior (in itself being a far too broad classification) struggle with finer and finer analyses of behavior in an attempt to pinpoint the difficulty and its cause. These cry in despair at reports that speak glibly of "reading disorders" rather than more precise problems. At the same time, the need to work with children who are in contexts or diagnostic categories sometimes formally excluded from the area of learning disabilities (children suffering from environmental deprivation effects, for example) seems of paramount importance if the main concern is the welfare and future of children rather than the maintenance of a classification scheme. Unfortunately, these children do not represent any homogeneous syndrome of problems.

The issue is unresolved—perhaps unresolvable given the current context in which we work and the problems we and our society face. The field, already beleaguered by too many types of problems to treat, faces the probability of a steadily increasing range of learning difficulties and problem etiologies despite the exclusion statements in federal statutes. Some hope lies, of course, in the possibility that more systematic research will uncover meaningful and useful common denominators of behavior and/or treatment. Given the disorganized status of much of the current research effort, the solution does not appear to be hovering just over the horizon.

What is an L.D. Specialist?

Increased attention to the field, expanded identification and treatment capabilities (given a strong authoritarian push by P.L. 94-142 and similar measures) has increased the amount of training activities and programs resident in our schools and colleges. Training raises some issues of its own, which will be examined later. However, one of the most positive spin-offs of this increased sensitivity to the need for better training has been attention to what skills comprise the expertise required to be considered an L.D. specialist (Larsen, 1976; Sartain, 1976; Stick, 1976).

The need for defined skills has spurred some tangible results. Specialized programs are to be found in far more schools than were five years ago. Since the programs that these schools promote are not identical, a baseline of data is being compiled regarding the effectivness of differently trained graduates as they move out of academe and into positions of first-hand responsibility. Eventually, some clear-cut information suitable for role definition may ensue regarding the effectiveness of different role models.

The *Division for Children with Learning Disabilities of the Council for Exceptional Children* (DCLD) has prepared a code of ethics and competencies for teachers of learning-disabled children and youth (Larsen, 1978). By focusing on both ethics and competencies, they have underlined an important concept: that the L.D. practitioner acknowledges certain professional codes of behavior (ethics) as well as areas of specialized ability (competencies).

The major disagreement centers around the appropriateness of including professionals from related fields who have not been specifically trained as L.D. specialists.

Pioneer code of ethics in the L.D. field

Consumer Protection

Once eager to grab at any straw, to look in any direction for assistance, to promote any idea or practice that even hinted of success, the field and its representatives today have recognized the need for more care in the adoption and promotion of new ideas, techniques, and practices. Quite in harmony with the general times, learning disability professionals have come to recognize the need for consumer protection. Fortunately this increasing conservatism has seemed to rise spontaneously throughout the field. But had it not been naturally born of a growing sense of professionalism, the specific requirements for justifying and defending choices of treatment methods, as called for in Public Law 94-142, might well have forced a precipitous birth.

This growing awareness that not all techniques and materials are equally useful, nor all theories based in fact, has had a subtle but salubrious effect upon the field. The second generation of workers now establishing themselves are finding that there are challenging questions left for them to answer. Pioneers have led the way, but some older ideas are becoming suspect—in need of refinement or even replacement. New leaders and heroes are needed in the areas of theoretical and applied research, in the development and testing of materials having established validity and reliability, and in the development of new, functionally efficient and effective remediation techniques.

Increasingly, issues are being resolved by openly debating assumptions and data interpretation based on research instead of arguement. Apologists are turning to further research for support of their stand—an excellent development that will certainly be beneficial to the field.

Another benefit has been increased emphasis on better psychometric data in some of the newer assessment instruments. Manuals that used to consist of broad outline directions now are including measures of validity, reliability, evidence of ample sampling in developing norms, and similar indications of more sophistication and care.

More careful scrutiny of articles submitted to professional journals is further evidence of the entire field's sensitivity to this issue. And the code of ethics mentioned earlier (Larsen, 1978) points to areas where concern for standards is rising: professional competence, welfare of served individuals, research, publications, professional relationships, and delivery of services.

Research

Since college and university training programs have multiplied, the amount and legitimacy of research has also increased. More and more learning disability professionals are feeling that if there are answers that may serve to resolve the undecided issues which sometimes divide us, research that is superior because of sharper design, better sampling, and more careful data-gathering may be a major avenue for arriving at them.

Areas of Concern

A number of areas are receiving increasing research attention, even though many of them are not yet at the debatable issue stage, since we simply do not know enough about them to establish firm positions. In surveying the needs for the decade ahead Frostig (1974) has called attention to the importance of considering cultural differences in learning behaviors, both for the establishment of norms or average criterion behavior levels and in analyzing the behavior of deficit performing children. Hallahan and Cruickshank (1973) have devoted much of their text to consideration of ecologically, culturally, and environmentally related etiological factors. Though they report an impressive array of research, definitive information is lacking and wide gaps in available information are obvious.

Frostig (1974) has also noted that the field needs to examine carefully how individual personality variables may interact with normal and deficit behavior patterns and perhaps influence the progress of remediation. She calls for a reinitiation of the interaction work of Witkin (1962) and the study of personality effects on perception, language behavior, and the other areas so frequently affected in learning disabled children.

Operating from the assumption that *movement* behaviors will remain an important focus of attention for the learning disabilities field during the next ten years, Cratty (1974) calls for a wide research effort to establish some better baseline information relevant to movement and motor behaviors. He notes the need for better standards for movement-motor tests. He also points out that sophisticated examination of these behaviors, through such techniques as factor analysis, might supply valuable information about what we are viewing and attempting to work with in children with motor problems. He suggests that we should examine normal children–deficit children motor comparisons to see if there actually are discriminable differences. And he points out that studies should be examining the hypothesis that there are identifiable subgroups of motor handicapped children who lack the intergroup homogeneity which we now assume when we glibly use the collective phrase *perceptual-motor handicapped*. In the same area of motor behavior, Wedell (1974) suggests that we need to know if perceptual-motor skills are really intrinsically important to a child's development or whether they are important because of the tasks we ask a child to perform. This question of course opens a whole area of research where the appropriateness of curriculum and training demands to the nature of the developing organism is examined. It might, in some cases, be hypothesized that our school curricula and programs may help create predispositions to learning disabilities because they place inappropriate demands upon our children. It would seem worthwhile to mount wide research programs in many other areas of deficit learning behavior patterned after Cratty and Wedell's suggestion (relevant to motor areas).

Dunsing (1973) has raised a number of potential research topics. These include the need to clarify interdisciplinary roles and boundaries as they relate to all phases of diagnosis and treatment. Some specific questions which Dunsing feels need to be answered include:

1. What kinds of individuals are responsive to a particular remedial procedure?
2. What special remediator skills are required by a specific remedial procedure?
3. What outside factors accompanying remediation may support, inhibit, or increment positive change?
4. In what cases does spontaneous remission occur without, or in spite of, remedial efforts? When this happens, what variables are involved?

Potential research topics

The need for research is obviously great and the list of potential research areas is almost endless. Related research topic areas, such as the role of drugs in learning disabilities work (Walker, 1974; Kornetsky, 1974), are important. Neurological research regarding the efficacy of some present theories and even the possibility of the development of a new cross-discipline field of "neurometrics" (Denckla, 1973) is worth attention. Doris Johnson (1974) has pointed out that we know little about the interaction of an individual's strengths and weaknesses and we should indeed be knowledgeable about such important functions. In the same respect Wedell (1974) has called for study of specific transfer of skills within an individual with a view toward something like a planned prescriptive compensation technique where an individual learns to use his own strengths to combat his own weaknesses.

Some organization and collective focusing of these research gaps is needed. It seems apparent, from a review of the present research literature and from the comments of those who are drawing attention to this need, that some areas stand out above others. Four of these prominent areas are included here: identification of learning disability behaviors and populations, issues of training, technological needs, and curriculum and facilities topics.

It appears that researchers should strive for the fulfillment of at least two main objectives:

1. To resolve some of the confusion and lack of organization about the accuracy and efficacy of some of our present techniques and methods; and
2. To enlarge the depth and scope of our knowledge so that we progress into areas of insight and awareness presently beyond our grasp.

The training issue is not essentially one of debate. It is a matter of almost everyone in the field recognizing that our sophistication in diagnosis and treatment capabilities has not been equaled by the development of enough top-notch training programs that follow some well-established and effective training paradigm.

In 1972 Cruickshank was bemoaning, and quite justifiably so, the lack of qualified professors and trainers who had been specially trained in learning disabilities. He even suggested a corp of specially trained and nationally recognized university personnel to help relieve the shortage. When there is lack of trained personnel at the higher education level, then field programs eventually suffer in quality. As the demand for more and more programs grows and numerous school districts respond to the need by establishing their own programs, the end result is often a dilution of strength as schools are forced to settle for partially or poorly trained personnel. One must agree with Cruickshank (1974) when he pleads for the end of the instant specialist. As he says, we have too often sent people to brief summer sessions, or to weekend or evening workshops and then assumed that they have been magically transformed into learning disability specialists overnight.

Since so few really well-trained specialists can be found, those who do show some knowledge or ability are quickly tempted to respond to the press of the problem far beyond their real ability or depth of understanding. Learning disabilities, particularly in the popular literature and on local lecture circuit levels, has been the victim of the *ad hominem* argument much too often. Good intentions, expertise in some other semirelated field, and a smattering of first-hand acquaintance are no substitute for in-depth supervised training.

Good, solid training programs are beginning to develop and are turning out graduate-level workers quite capable of serving in an effective and professional manner. The trend seems to be toward a continued growth in this direction with increasingly stringent demands for evidenced ability and competency before licensing, certification, or other recognized credentials can be granted.

Several interesting approaches are evolving within this trend. In-service education receives a great deal of attention as recognition of the importance of learning disabilities as a major problem grows and as mainstreaming emphasis places greater demands on practicing personnel. Teachers and other people with established credentials in education are seeking to augment their capabilities through such programs. There is some indication that as the years pass this in-service emphasis will be increasingly supplanted by pre-service training, as institutions preparing regular classroom teachers add the area of learning disabilities to those already a part of the standard education curriculum. Teachers of the future should be trained to deal with learning disabilities before they leave school, not after they are on the job. Social intolerance of what is sometimes called "plateau placement," that is, being satisfied that a child who is not improving has reached his peak performance and can be allowed to continue to perform at his present level, is forcing the educational field to prepare teachers who can adequately evaluate students' capabilities and provide creative opportunities for developing individual potential.

Evolving approaches

At the same time, as Mann and McClung (1974) emphasize, there is an increasing sense that education must demonstrate accountability: there is less allowance for unchallenged failure in the classroom. Thus, the training of teachers is being directed toward a model less satisfied with the status quo and traditional lesson plans and subject areas and more directed toward developing the individual child's abilites. The field of learning disabilities has a positive contribution to make to this philosophy and the next few years should see this idea better integrated with teacher education in general.

The training of learning disability specialists or teachers who are capable of dealing with learning disabilities is undergoing some other changes. There is less of a tendency to deal with traditional categories, for example, the educable mentally retarded, and more of an emphasis on those needs of children which may group together behaviorally. Those who are focusing their training on limited areas rather than becoming generalists are proceeding along problem and needs lines rather than in accordance with artificial grouping and categorization taxonomies. Teachers and other school personnel are being taught, and should continue to be, more about the total developmental continuum of the child rather than about artificially exclusive age and stage categories. It is, for example, absolutely vital for junior high teachers to know a great deal about the young developing child, if they are to work successfully with the problems of early adolescence.

The ACLD advisory board has recommended continued funding of Child Service Demonstration Centers and Leadership Training Institutes (Wiederholt,

1974a). These are indeed vital programs. One hopes however that some better method of disseminating results and providing for effective models will be a prerequisite to such financial support. Although a myriad of "final reports" are available from past demonstration projects, and project directors are usually co-operative in providing them, it is exceedingly difficult to draw any meaningful generalizations from them. We need not only more training experiences, but also better training models that can be used by others across the nation.

Finally, it appears that there is a trend toward developing more finely focused specialties and specialists. This has been true of almost every other discipline and learning disabilities should prove no exception. Such specialties frequently become the vehicle for providing us with better and more precise information about some of the problems we face in the field. We hope that, as these specialties develop, the field will avoid noncommunicative compartmentalization and will develop a greater capacity for integrated team effort.

This last point should be restated and reemphasized in a slightly different form. Not only must closely related specialties communicate, but the field desperately needs to better improve interdisciplinary interaction and communication. Unfortunately, when asked about interdisciplinary programs one too easily thinks of classic learning disability feuds (such as that which exists among the vision-related disciplines) rather than smooth and mutually helpful cooperation. Perhaps if developing specialists could be specifically trained to communicate with those of other disciplines, the positive, pragmatic, as well as morale effects could be great.

Model Projects

Significant impetus has been given to learning disability research through the assignment of federal funds through Title VI-G of Public Law 91-230, administered by the Bureau of Education of the Handicapped. Historically, funds from this title have been directed toward Child Service Demonstration Centers, a clear representation of the early emphasis in the field. However, beginning in the fall of 1978, programmatic research efforts started at five different university centers (Columbia University Teachers College, University of Illinois-Chicago, University of Kansas, University of Minnesota, and the University of Virginia).

Designed to foster programmatic research lapping over into the 1980s, these funds support a wide variety of research goals. Among those being studied are the following:

• At Columbia—
  1. Conceptualization of learning disabilities in terms of meaningful functional tasks
  2. Development of specific component disability learning tasks
  3. Adaption and evaluation in varied school settings of those interventions developed in step 2
  4. Development and testing of a theoretical model that conceptualizes L.D. in terms of response to instruction, process dysfunctions revealed in spe-

cific learning tasks with specific learning procedures, and also in correlated measures and demographic variables (Bryant, 1978)
- At Chicago—
  1. Analysis of teacher and pupil verbal and nonverbal communication
  2. Linguistic analysis of oral reading and reading comprehension
  3. Social issues related to teacher and parent attribution to L.D. children and subsequent attitude development
  4. Further definition of L.D. by studying learning patterns, strategies, memory and other aspects of deficit and nondeficit learning
  5. Family networks in learning disabilities
  6. Various intervention strategies in education (Bryan and Eash, 1978)
- At Kansas—
  1. Definition and description of the characteristics and epidemiological factors related to learning disabilities
  2. Development and implementation of sound intervention procedures
  3. Replication and evaluation of the generality of interventions across different populations, settings and content (Meyan and Deshler, 1978)
- At Minnesota—
  1. Examination of assessment-intervention criteria and procedures as related to the characteristics of the child, characteristics of the teacher, nature of intervention, nature of behavior change sought, and nature of the social setting involved
  2. Identification and arrangement for optimal instructional arrangements for children needing alternative instructional environments (Ysseldyke, Shinn, and Thurlow, 1978)
- At Virginia—
  1. Determination of the appropriate educational procedures for enhancing academic performance of children with attentional deficits
  2. Creation and evaluation of suitable classroom and homebased procedures for use in such situations (Hallahan, 1978)

Training and Preparation

Public Law 94-142, with its mandate for providing appropriate situations and services for the handicapped, has mustered wide-spread support for broader and more inclusive training programs reaching even into the undergraduate teacher-preparation curricula.

Educators and trainers in the field are struggling for a workable outline of skills and competencies that can be supplied in the normal course of teacher preparation and still deliver adequate skill and performance levels for the wide range of children the learning disability specialist must face. The list of competencies compiled by a national committee of the Division for Children with Learning Disabilities of the Council for Exceptional Children (Larsen, 1978) represents one of the first formal steps in that direction. Currently under study and

TABLE 3-1
Competency Areas for Teachers of Learning Disabled Children and Youth—
Adopted by DCLD/CEC

Oral Language	Behavioral Management
Reading	Counseling and Consulting
Written Expression	Career/Vocational Education
Spelling	Education Operations
Mathematics	Historical-Theoretical Perspectives
Cognition	

revision, the list covers an extremely wide range of competencies related to this type of specialist (See Table 3-1).

Trends

The learning disabilities field is growing, and the growth is in the breadth of concern as much as in the number of approaches. Four important trends can be readily identified by studying new publications and topics of interest at conventions and institutes for learning disability workers. These are as follows: (1) a broadening of the age-range of the population served, (2) a shifting in emphasis on categorization, (3) vocational and life-skill preparation, and (4) new areas of special focus.

Broadened Age Range

The population first receiving the attention of this field during the early 1960s was the elementary-school child. Most of the earlier literature, assessment, and remediation procedures focused on the K to 6 range. The first indications of a broadening age range followed in the late 1960s and the early 1970s with more attention being paid to the preschool, early childhood population (Keogh, 1970). This emphasis has continued to the extent where broadly conceived and well organized state-wide programs can be found in a number of different states. The Massachusetts Early Childhood Program for Children with Special Needs is one example.

This was followed by increased attention to the special needs of the secondary-level learning disabled student. Some prominent contributions have strengthened the trend (Bailey, 1975; Goodman and Mann, 1976).

There seems to be a growing awareness that learning disabilities are not confined to a particular age group and that remediation is both possible and worthwhile at any age level. Considerable presure has been placed upon the field to develop the necessary specialized instruments and techniques for use with every age group. The trend appears to be toward an increasingly broad range of attack on learning problems, disregarding age limitations at either end of the scale.

Curry College in Massachusetts has pioneered in this area, particularly with secondary and college-level students.

Awareness of this trend is personified in the Association for Children with Learning Disabilities (ACLD) proposing to drop *Children* from their name and becoming the *Association for Learning Disabilities* (ALD).

Categorical versus Noncategorical Approaches

Though everyone realizes that categories are potentially dangerous stereotypes and present relatively little usefulness in any remediation or treatment program, the learning disability field has gone through its own categorization growing pains. First formulated as a definition to avoid the stigma of categorical labeling, the term *learning disabilities* soon became vested with many of the same disadvantages. Today's trend seems to be firmly away from categories. Mainstreaming efforts have reinforced such a trend by making labeling even less useful than it was in the past. Research programs are striving for common identification based upon needs and behaviors often held in common by many different categories of exceptionality. Training institutions in many states are adopting a noncategorical approach to training teachers and dealing with the problems of children. Except in those instances where there are attempts to maintain the medical model approach of naming and labeling etiological-treatment relationships for each problem, the trend is away from categorization.

Vocational and Life-Skill Preparation

One of the side effects of broadening the age range receiving treatment consideration to include secondary-school-age children has been an awareness that, disabled or not, these individuals need to be able to carry a responsible role in society. As a consequence, a trend has developed toward providing what might be called vocational back-up preparation along with specific remedial work at the secondary level. Preparation for specific vocational placement and general-life-skill capabilities has become a major part of the secondary program in many areas. Secondary school learning disabled individuals in the New York State Niagara-Orleans County system, for example, receive special remedial treatment programs parallel with vocational and on-the-job training. Reciprocally beneficial results have been noted with increased positive self-concept and heightened motivational levels. Mainstreaming has helped in this respect too since it has emphasized the necessity for highlighting the normal rather than the deficit aspects of the disabled person's behavior.

New Areas of Special Focus

Heralded perhaps by the diagnostic-clinical teaching approach, another trend toward focusing in first-hand on special problem areas can be currently observed. These efforts range from studies attempting to locate any possible caus- ative link between learning disabilities and delinquency (Kratoville, 1974) to scrutinization of a particular subject matter area, such as learning disabilities and arithmetic (Johnson, 1979).

Hyperactivity, both as related to diet (Lipton and Wender, 1977) and more complicated biochemical factors (Borschbaum, Coursey, and Murphy, 1976), and other physiologically oriented difficulties are receiving more attention with mixed and still nondefinitive results.

Assessment techniques, as well, show the trend toward isolating individual problem factors in special children. These include techniques and instruments for measuring language development (Newcomer and Hammill, 1977), reading comprehension (Brown, Hammill, and Wiederholt, 1978), and other subject mat- ter and academic areas.

In many cases, more sophistication and the demand for empirical anchoring is more evident. Every indication is that this trend toward requiring demonstrable validity and reliability in the development of new ideas and techniques will continue.

Needs

The field is beset by four substantial needs that as yet are largely unmet. Fulfill- ing these needs would solve a substantial number of the major problems facing the field today. They range from the quite esoteric to some very practical consid- erations.

Pure Basic Research

As has been noted previously, the research history of this field has not been particularly noted for a systematic and organized approach. To some extent this is being changed, partly because of the increase in the number of people inter- ested in doing learning disability research, and partly because of the support granted by the funding of special research projects at the five major universities. Still, most of the research effort is primarily applied in both intent and nature. Many of the major issues still debated in learning disability circles today, nearly two decades after the field became formerly recognized, could be moved toward resolvement through organized basic research.

Typical of these areas is the need for advanced research in neurological in- volvement in learning disabilities. While only the naive would assume that the central nervous system is totally disinvolved in a learning disability, no absolute pattern of interaction or involvment has yet been discovered that can provide any unified and meaningful interpretation for disparate behaviors. We need to know more about how and when the CNS is involved. All we have today, in actuality, are hypotheses, some well organized but still largely speculative. There are other areas where pure research would be most helpful, such as a determination of whether or not reading follows an inherent developmental stage pattern similar to language or if it is purely an acquired skill. Again, we have only hypotheses to satisfy our professional curiosity and practical needs.

Organizational Consolidation

Without any deliberate intention to have open conflict or to usurp roles, we find professional organizations not only proliferating in number and type but also to some extent diluting the efforts of those who wish to be involved in the best aspects of each but find insufficient time to do so. There probably are justifications for the variety of organizations that include in their purpose an emphasis on learning disabilities. But it would be helpful if some clarity of individual focus could be developed so that the activities and focus of one organization do not unnecessarily duplicate those of another. Time and financial support are both too precious to be wasted in such duplication. While the overlap is not quite chaos, it certainly is not conducive to a clear picture of the status of the field and current developments. Some type of organizational consolidation of, or clearing house for, ideas and events would be most helpful.

Legislative Congruence

It may be too much to hope for, but those in the field who must work within state consortia or who attempt to blend together the support and endorsement of local, state, and federal statutes, earnestly pray for more legislative congruence. A maze of definitions of learning disabilities is to be found through the legislation of different states. Some states define and regulate in harmony with federal statutes. Others do not. Some states avoid the conflict by not even including a definition of learning disabilities or the duties and competencies of a learning disability specialist within their procedures.

Efforts to resolve this confusion, such as those of the Governmental Relations Unit office of the Council for Exceptional Children are often heroic but the problem is still with us.

Perhaps the stability of common definitions and consensually accepted roles is a product of more maturity and age than the field has currently achieved. It is, nevertheless, a most urgent, and largely unmet need.

Some indications of the directions in which we seem to be moving can be gained from several sources. The Council for Exceptional Children has published a set of recommendations for model state statutes covering special education children in general (Weintraub, Abeson, and Braddock, 1975). The recommendations certainly apply to learning disability children as part of that general group and represent lines along which new developments may progress. Their recommendations include eleven main points:

1. Every child should have a right to education and even severely handicapped children should be required to attend schools. And schools should be required to provide effective services and facilities for such children.
2. Service should be provided from birth to twenty-one and stigmatizing labels that often provide *de facto* below-average services should be eliminated.
3. Screening and evaluation should be continual and on-going and individual differences in language and culture should be taken into consideration in testing, establishing norms, and compiling records.
4. Divisions of the handicapped should be established at state as well as federal levels and free education assured for the handicapped.
5. Special advisory planning councils should be provided for legislative and executive governmental bodies insuring adequacy and appropriateness of administrative planning.
6. Sufficient financing should be available to allow flexibility in educational programming to meet individual needs.
7. Administrative structure and organization should require and support cooperative services for greater effectiveness of delivery of services.
8. Services should provide a full continuum of offerings ranging from regular classrooms to full-time residential institutions.
9. Private schools should not be exempted from high standards and where necessary financial support should be provided to assure quality.
10. Personnel should be better trained and training programs should be available on a full-time, part-time and in-service basis.
11. Facilities should be designed with the specially handicapped in mind and building codes should be changed or adopted to permit appropriate exceptions to typical standards where needs exist and safety permits.

Technological Needs

Three major processes connected with attacking learning disabilities are intimately involved with the need for increased technological contribution. These are the identification and diagnosis of a specific deficit, the delivery of services, and remediation itself.

In the area of recognition and identification of specific deficits it goes almost without saying that we need to work on some of our techniques and instruments. Some of our most frequently used techniques are applied far above and beyond even the grandest claims for the capacity of the instrument. Almost every issue of the more popular learning disability periodicals, including state and district newsletter-type publications, contains pieces about new measuring devices, diagnosing techniques, discriminative behaviors, etc. Only rarely do these introductions to new methods contain sufficient information or evidence about psychometric characteristics necessary for functional effectiveness.

Careful surveys of the reliability and validity of the established relationship of certain methods or instruments to behavior areas yield little solid evidence that we approach the problem of psychometric evaluation with anything like a well-proven portfolio of instruments and techniques. Larsen and Hammil's (1975) review of correlational studies reporting the relationship of selected visual-perceptual abilities to school learning is an example of how sparse and indefinite our evidence really is. It is, of course, frustrating to the practitioner in the field, faced with a hundred or more cases crying for help, to be told that unusual care and caution must be taken with a favorite instrument due to its unestablished validity or reliability. But to do otherwise seems to demonstrate a willingness to gamble with a child's future—a chance no one should be willing to take.

The trend, of necessity, must be toward a more thorough analysis of current instruments and techniques and the establishment of better psychometric credentials for those being developed. The current press for better research (as we noted previously) moves in quite parallel directions, and the two needs should mutually support refereeing of journal publications. More careful consumer screening of published claims in necessary and must develop more actively if the field is to develop respectable instruments and techniques.

Need for consumer protection

Technology has something to offer in the delivery of services area too. Perhaps the most obvious demonstration of this is in the use of the computer. The magic black box is being used quite effectively in a number of different situations. The trend toward the development of better software programs as well as more capable hardware seems assured. Present computer assistance is available in several distinctive ways. In one program (Hall, Cartwright, and Mitzel, 1974) the computer is used to assist in-service education. As teachers seek to renew and supplement their skills, special mobile labs containing programmed computer terminals tour the schools so teachers may take advantage at first hand of several "renewal" curricula programs including work on the special child, preschool teaching, and working with specially handicapped children.

In another program operating in conjunction with Florida State University, a computer-managed instructional system provides an explicit delineation of target behaviors and measurable performance outcomes for clinical teachers in training and for exceptional children (Schwartz and Oseroff, 1974). A notable feature of this program is that its development has included an active alliance among several different disciplines including special education, school psychology, elementary education, computer-aided instruction, instructional media and television, and educational research and testing.

Some programs, such as the one available through the Cooperative Child Demonstration Program for Children with Learning Disabilities for the State of New Jersey, offer a computer-based state instructional and diagnostic information retrieval network. Stored information can be retrieved in a meaningful fashion for use by educators wishing to find or program remedial activities. A similar program is available through the University of Buffalo in the State University of New York system.

Computers are not the solution to all of our problems but they can assist in the storage and analysis of a great deal of information and greatly aid in assembling and integrating new data as we add it to the information we already have at hand.

Finally, there is some evidence that some widely diverse technologies may eventually offer contributions to the field. Braud, Lupin, and Braud (1975), for example, report on the possible use of the new field of biofeedback in dealing with problems of hyperactivity. This seems to offer some particular value as a possible substitute for the use of drugs that too often have unpredictable or undesirable side effects.

On the other hand, there is also evidence that some great expanses of needs remain largely unassailed by most of our current technological capabilities. If the learning disabilities field is to face up to some of these problems it will certainly need the help of technology as much as the involvement of highly motivated and competent personnel. These important gaps in our knowledge range all the way from highly sophisticated problems concerning the role of the nervous system in learning behaviors to broader and more common problems concerning effects of impoverished living conditions and of rigid, nonindividualized school curricula on the learning behaviors of children (Deutsch, 1974).

Sometimes those working on the firing line of learning disabilities, meeting children with large problems every day, find it difficult to take the time to enlist the support, invite the participation, or accept the contribution of technology. If the next decade or so is to witness significant progress in solving the many problems related to learning disabilities, such a blending of effort is necessary.

Curriculum and Facility Needs

As is apparent from the chapter in this text dealing with delivery of services, matters of curriculum and facilities are largely inseparable and are therefore considered together here. The problem may be approached initially by a single generalization: there is a clear need to evolve our concepts of curriculum and facility design to accommodate increasing knowledge about the learning process and about how the child integrates his capabilities with the context within which he operates.

Without knowing what new information may come to light it is impossible to say exactly what changes in curriculum and facilities we may face within the near future. However, it is certainly accurate to say that increased flexibility is demanded; and it is reasonable to suppose that growing sensitivity in the field and increased social pressure will insist upon some sort of functionally effective flexibility.

The advisory board of the Association for Children with Learning Disabilities (Wiederholt, 1974a) calls for a number of special service models including regular treatment centers and centers established in cooperation with schools and universities that include clinical services, research facilities, teacher preparation, and technical assistance and consultation for solving day-by-day problems.

New curricula and facility planning will probably take note of the multihandicapped. Those presently dealing with children falling solely within the narrow definition of learning disabilities will probably find themselves handling children with multiproblems and with learning deficits compounded by other handicaps and socioeconomic deprivation.

Speaking about the decade ahead, Cruickshank (1974) reminds workers in the field that the structure necessary for reducing learning deficits includes not only classroom control but also environmental and ecological factors, spatial structure, programmatic structure, planned adult-child relationships, and the carefully considered structure of specially prepared materials. Each of these structures requires special care in curriculum and facility planning. As the field grows to meet the challenge of these new vistas, workers may very well find themselves working in new and enlarged contexts that may be more socially relevant than today's parameters.

The "cascade" approach also seems to be part of the current trend. Curriculum and facility planning demand that the child be offered as much of a normal and typical learning environment as he or she can handle. However, the child should be able to move, according to his or her special needs, down a cascade of services that in turn offer more personal care, attention, structure, and protection from the demands that he or she may not be able to handle. Mann and McClung (1974) point out that within this approach there are some areas of concern. These include the need for the coordination of the forces of change, better formal and informal assessment, the development of a special education curriculum for children based upon an analysis of behavior in the total environment, flexibility in reaction to that environment, greater community involvement in the learning process, and effective application of the principles of behavior management.

New curricula may well take into consideration some of the developing technologies (such as the biofeedback techniques we mentioned earlier). They will almost certainly need to attack those sources of disability that arise out of cultural and economic deprivation. The no-longer-quite-so-new technique of behavior modification will probably see greater use, although it will probably be specifically adapted to the behaviors and capabilities of deficit children. Other individually effective approaches and areas will almost certainly be developed.

Summary

To say that learning disabilities is an unsettled and less than peaceful field is not necessarily a negative comment. It is indicative of a live and viable field that simply has not found a comfortable identity. The problems are many and in some cases distressingly real and large. But they do not seem insurmountable.

The prospects for an effective future seem bright: trends are in the right direction, and we are doing a better job today than we were ten years ago. However, it does appear that we are at a crucial point in our development. Significant changes, some of which place large professional and personal demands upon us, must occur. Hopefully, as new workers are trained and new leaders emerge, the needs and demands of the times will not go unheeded and a substantial number of these necessary changes and trends will follow.

4

Roles of
Different Professions
in Diagnosis
and Treatment

Deficit learning behaviors frequently do not fall neatly into problem categories representing the obvious domain of a single professional discipline with easily defined boundaries. As Lerner (1976) notes, cross-disciplinary approaches are so common that at least five professional categories are typically included in listing the professions working with learning disabilities. She includes medicine, language, education, psychology, and a fifth group of "other" professions including optometry, audiology, social service, physical therapy, genetics, biochemistry, guidance and counseling, systems analysis, clinical administration, etc. The inadequacy of considering learning disabilities as the province of a single approach or orientation becomes even more obvious when one observes, as Lerner has, that these five groupings divide and subdivide even further.

The probability of successfully combating learning disabilities would be increased if it could be demonstrated that these many disciplines actually represent a thoroughly comprehensive approach to the field. Unfortunately such a conclusion cannot be clearly drawn. In too many instances, enough serious interdisciplinary disagreement exists to contribute to conflict and dissonance in the organization and execution of remedial activities. In other instances, overlap and interdisciplinary ignorance cause expensive, wasteful, and inefficient duplication.

Many influential individuals and organizations active in learning disabilities are sensitive to the problem and there is a growing demand toward interprofessional communication, integration, and development. Some are even calling for the development of a "learning disability specialist" who could be somewhat of a trained professional hybrid prepared to gather and coordinate information from several disciplines.

As early as 1963, several agencies of the United States Department of Health, Education and Welfare along with the National Easter Seal Society assembled a coordinating committee to try to arrive at a better definition of the field, to outline in an integrated form the necessary program and services needed to help learning handicapped children, and to review and organize the existing research related to learning disabilities. The committee recommended the establishment of three task forces to work toward these goals. The publications produced by these groups became a significant step toward resolving the problem (Clements, 1966; Chalfant and Scheffelin, 1969; Paine, 1969).

It was apparent, however, emphasized in part by some substantial disagreement over sections of these task force reports, that special focus and fragmentation of interests remained significant problems. Bassler (1967) has pointed out the seriousness of such fragmentation:

> The reading consultant knows the child has a complex of reading problems. The teacher sees a phonic difficulty. The school nurse observes a hearing problem; the speech therapist, a lisp. The school psychologist, the family doctor, the optometrist, the opthalmologist, the parents, each has a different view of the child and his constellation of problems. We have so segmented and fragmented the child, we have atomized our approach to the educational problems so that we have lost the child in the labyrinth of professions and techniques.

Solutions to the dilemma lie in several possible directions. One approach would be to create still another specialist whose training would not necessarily supplement or replace the more fragmented disciplines but who would be, as Kirk (1969) says, "the responsible agent for obtaining information from other specialists." This is a role which every practitioner must play at least in part, as the necessity to assemble and integrate diverse and varied information arises. Some attention is given in a later chapter to facilitating the successful solicitation and gathering of such pertinent information.

Another solution is to try to bridge the gap between existing professions by improving communication and recognizing the inherent value in different focuses and orientations. Such an approach emphasizes interprofessional agreements and strives to find organizational and practical formats for cross-disciplinary cooperation. As Rabinovitch (1959), writing for psychiatrists, has stated, "No single disciplinary approach to learning problems is valid; neurological, psychological, psychiatric and educational emphasis must be brought together without preconceived bias in both clinical and research work."

In yet another direction, there is considerable evidence *within* individual disciplines of a growing discontent with fragmentation and the resulting professional isolation. Such discontent has led prominent individuals to encourage structured coordination on the one hand and informal recognition of the worth of different approaches on the other.

For example, special education—a field that knows firsthand the problems of conflicting disciplinary biases and the inefficiency and limiting effect of fragmentation—has historically led the battle for better coordination of the various agencies dealing with the handicapped, including the learning disabled. Such active lobbying eventually led in 1966 to the establishment of the *Bureau of Education of the Handicapped*, a major step toward integration and coordination. It was a step, incidentally, that also helped to pave the way for the significant *Learning Disabilities Act* of 1970.

Evidence for a movement toward integration and sharing is to be found in many different fields. Psycholinguists see the need to bridge the gap between their contributions and those of neurology (Whitcraft, 1971; McGrady, 1968). Neurologists point to the advantage of learning the more precise measurement techniques studied by psychologists and psychometricians (Denckla, 1973). Pediatricians emphasize the need for thorough evaluation of the learning disabled child in nonmedical areas (Ong, 1968). Movements toward such cross-disciplinary sharing have in some instances progressed well beyond the recommendation stage. Some school systems have already moved toward an organizational outline of programs for pupils with special learning problems that by its very nature defines not only the peculiar function of different professions but facilitates intercommunication and joint remedial programs. Table 4-1 outlines one such program.

As an initial step toward the goal of better interdisciplinary participation it is important to recognize some of the more prominent professions active in the field, to delineate their roles as their members perceive them, and to note as well some obvious areas of dissonance that frequently arise. So many different disciplines are involved and so much overlap occurs that it is difficult to establish any absolute taxonomy for listing them. With full awareness of the obvious diffculties involved and the arguments for including other categorizations, we have found it useful to consider the professions in terms of three major categories without ranking any of them within or among these categories.

- Category One: *Educational Disciplines*
  These are disciplines whose functioning primarily occurs or is oriented in the academic learning situation either by the nature of the work or the focus of the research. These include *Special Education, Remedial Teaching,* and *Language.* The latter discipline area is assumed to include both the remedial language instructor, the speech pathologist, and to some extent the psycholinguist.
- Category Two: *Medical Disciplines*
  These are disciplines whose function is primarily physical or biological even though the specialities may be directed toward amelioration or prevention of learning problems. These include *General Pediatrics, Neurology* (including *Neuro-*

Advocacy role
of special
education

Categories of
professions
in L.D. work

TABLE 4-1

An Organizational Outline of Programs for Pupils with Special Learning Problems

	BEHAVIORAL DISABILITIES *(Emotionally Handicapped)* *(Brain-Injured)*	COMMUNICATIVE DISABILITIES *(Aphasic) (Partially Hearing)* *(Language Disordered)* *(Speech Handicapped)* *(Remedial Reading)*	MENTAL LIMITATIONS *(Educable) (Trainable)*	PHYSICAL DISABILITIES *(Orthopedically Handicapped)* *(Chronic Physically Disabled)* *(Visually Impaired) (Home Bound and Hospitalized)*
PRIMARY CAUSES OF LEARNING PROBLEMS *(Traditional Classification of Programs)*				
PUPIL CHARACTERISTICS	Learning disability not attributable to intellectual limitation. Behavioral disability may or may not have been the result of neurologic damage or defect. Poor behavioral organization. Inappropriate and erratic behavior under ordinary circumstances or circumstances of mild provocation manifested in disinhibition, distractibility, and hyperirritability. Disorganized thinking reflected in perceptual disorders and faulty conceptual formation. Inadequate self concept. Inability to establish and/or maintain interpersonal relationships.	Learning disability not attributable to intellectual limitation. Inability to use and understand language may or may not have been the result of neurologic damage or defect. Inability to deal with symbols of communication, i.e., speech, language, reading, and writing as reflected in poor integration of sensory functions into experiential patterns of symbolization. Abnormal utilization of sound with normal sensitivity to sound.	General subnormal intellectual functioning. Presence of other disabilities which may further handicap. May or may not be capable of independent living. Greatly reduced rate of mental growth resulting in difficulty in learning the formal material of the regular curriculum including academic subjects and moral issues.	Learning disability not attributable to intellectual limitation. Presence of physical impairments which may or may not be accompanied by neurologic damage or defect. Educational retardation based upon the lack of normal experiences, absences from school, and the necessity of functioning at a reduced rate. Varying degree of abilities for independent living of a temporary or permanent nature.

PRIMARY CAUSES OF LEARNING PROBLEMS (Traditional Classification of Programs)	BEHAVIORAL DISABILITIES (Emotionally Handicapped) (Brain-Injured)	COMMUNICATIVE DISABILITIES (Aphasic) (Partially Hearing) (Language Disordered) (Speech Handicapped) (Remedial Reading)	MENTAL LIMITATIONS (Educable) (Trainable)	PHYSICAL DISABILITIES (Orthopedically Handicapped) (Chronic Physically Disabled) (Visually Impaired) (Home Bound and Hospitalized)
PROGRAM FOCUS	Development of integrative learning and thinking through experiences of conceptualization and perceptual training used as a basis for the acquisition of fundamental academic skills. Development of more appropriate personal and social behavior. Development of more satisfying interpersonal relations. Highly structured classroom environment reflected in small group enrollment, individuality of approach, physical design of the classroom, and use of special equipment and materials.	Development and remediation of communicative skills as a basis for the acquisition of fundamental academic skills. Development of organized receptive and expressive language. Development of acceptable speech. Stimulation and encouragement in the use of communicative skills by individualization of instruction through reduced group size and specialized equipment and materials.	Development of selected functional academic skills essential to areas of independent living. Development of personal, family, social, and civic skills. Development of work habits and work skills. Total sequential instructional program, elementary through secondary levels of education. Reduced group enrollment and utilization of special materials, equipment, and techniques to enable individuality of developmental and remedial instruction.	Development of academic, personal, and social skills leading to independent thinking, self direction, and the establishment of a worthy self-concept. Adaptation of teaching, equipment, materials, and methods to the physical capabilities of the pupil enabling achievement through substitution and compensation. Incorporation of appropriate occupational, physical, and speech therapies. Utilization of a variety of program plans including special class or special school placement and home-bound and hospital teaching. Modification of physical facilities. Small group size to allow for more individual attention and the fulfillment of the needs of children requiring a disproportionate amount of the teacher's time.

From "Complementary Roles of the Pediatrician and Educator in School Planning for Handicapped Children" by R. Clemmens and J. Davis *Journal of Learning Disabilities,* 1969, 2, 524-532. Reprinted with permission of Baltimore County Public Schools, Baltimore County, Maryland.

logical Pediatrics), *Pharmacology*, and *Vision Related* disciplines (including both *Ophthalmology* and *Optometry*).
• Category Three: *Clinical Disciplines*
  These are disciplines whose function deals more with the cause and effect of behavior (often other than pure biological functions), and also tend to focus frequently on the nature of abnormal, deficit, or pathological functions. These include *Psychiatry*, *Psychology*, and to an increasing extent *Sociology*.

Each of the professions within these major areas has its own characteristic involvement with learning disabilities, just as to a lesser extent the major categories themselves represent somewhat of a common orientation.

Educational Disciplines

Although much of the early background work for the developing learning disabilities field was done in medicine and related to brain damage, neurological involvement, and mental retardation, the entire problem of learning disabled children has never excluded the field of education. Since the behavioral problems of these deficit-evidencing children have always involved learning, we find that even the earliest approaches to the field have been concerned with education. The present focus is decidedly on educational goals with all but a small portion of the work on such diverse topics as differential diagnosis, etiology, and delivery of services being directed toward better achievement of educationally related behavioral objectives. Many of the most prominent people in the field today perceive themselves as educators first and as learning disability specialists second. The work these specialists do and the models and products they produce personify this role concept. Typical of this situation is the work of Bateman who has made significant contributions to the learning disability field, ranging from the establishment and identification of significant trends (1964), to the design and implementation of a basic diagnostic model (1965), and, along with Frankel, to endeavors involving the integration of education with the focus of medical child specialists (1972).

Within the general educational field, a number of separate disciplines have made significant contributions.

Special Education

The role of special education is to a large extent quite obvious. This is the discipline that has been most intimately involved with the final face-to-face delivery of services in working with the learning disabled child. Though today's learning disability specialist has, by virtue of this emphasis on specialization, become somewhat insulated from the broader scope of problems included under special education, the importance of the broader discipline remains unchallenged. The role of special education as related to learning disabilities has followed three broad tracks, each yielding a particular set of valuable accomplishments.

First of all, the majority of academic training and research regarding learning disabilities still falls within the province of this discipline. Although other disciplines offer courses and training experience in learning disabilities (school psychology, for example), the overwhelming majority of training is still done under the aegis of this discipline.

This training and exploratory-research role is not a new one. Historically, special education, in active cooperation with psychology and other related fields, has explored such basically important areas as psychometrics and all of its evaluative, diagnostic, and definitive implications. Special education has contributed significantly to the development of theory and to understanding the phenomenon of intelligence, its nature, its measurement, and its function in the problems of special children suffering from learning disabilities. The function of diagnostic screening, a necessary prerequisite for effective delivery of remedial services, has been a major focus of special education. Pupil placement and classroom and curricular adjustments, such as in the concept of mainstreaming, have all developed to a large part out of the concern and efforts of those active in the field.

A second major contribution of special educators has been a concerted effort to induce government to play an active role in supporting and to some extent fostering the development of meaningful programs related to the handicapped, including the learning disabled. As far back as the latter part of the 1800s, special educators began to encourage the initiation of organized programs of attack. Following World Wars I and II special educators were quick to take advantage of the government's increased awareness of the handicapped by helping to formulate and encouraging passage into law specific acts designed to attack the problem systematically. In the 1950s, for instance, special education groups were primarily responsible for the passage of federal acts establishing grants for training personnel in the education of the handicapped and for establishing and funding ongoing research problems in the same areas.

In the late 1960s the establishment of a Bureau for the Education of the Handicapped within the U.S. Office of Education and the enactment in 1970 of the *Learning Disabilities Act* were strongly supported by special educators.

The third role of special education, not so clearly defined but important nevertheless, has been to urge better coordination and integration of knowledge among various fields. Ranging from lobbying for the 1967 Bureau for Education of the Handicapped legislation (which had as one significant goal better coordination of several separate agencies) to the contribution of individual leaders such as Bateman, many people within this field have consistently worked toward more efficient interdisciplinary structure and function.

Contributions of professional periodicals

Periodicals such as *Exceptional Children* and the *Journal of Special Education* publish material related to all three learning-disability-related functions. For those who have chosen generally to reject the role of medicine in the field of learning disabilities, there has been concern about the predominance of medically related disciplines in this aspect of special education. In some ways the development of the Association for Children with Learning Disabilities (ACLD), with its exclusive focus on learning disabilities, as contrasted with the broader concerns of the Council for Exceptional Children (CEC) which has subdivisions in such areas as learning disabilities, has resulted in less effective instead of better communication across disciplines. Despite the groups' overlaps of members and leaders they are not particularly well integrated either in sharing information or in their orientation to problems in the field. Neither their goals nor their approaches are completely congruent. But there are some indications that these problems may be resolved as members of each group call for a breakdown in both the real and perceived barriers that have separated the two organizations. Certainly the formation of a special Division for Children with Learning Disabilities has largely answered the criticism that the CEC lacks focus on the learning disability area. Although this special division followed the formation of ACLD by several years, it has grown rapidly and has attracted many interested professionals.

Remedial Teaching

Educators involved in remedial teaching have consistently shown an interest in learning disabilities and have long been active in both the ACLD and the CEC. The involvement of those specializing in the teaching of reading is typical of these groups—both in an informal sense by those who include such activities as an adjunct of other teaching responsibilities and more formally by those who would describe themselves as primarily remedial reading teachers. Reading problems, commonly subsumed under the broad label of *dyslexia*, occupy a very visible, large, and important section of the learning disabilities spectrum. Scarcely is an issue of the *Journal of Learning Disabilities* published without an article referenced under this general heading. Other journals, designed more specifically for those working in reading, also carry frequent articles dealing with learning disabilities. *The Journal of Reading* and *The Reading Teacher* both function as professional periodicals with such supporting roles. *The Reading Research Quarterly* also contains much information highly relevant to learning disabilities. Book-length publications relating to learning disability reading problems are numerous as are many specific remedial programs. Subjects range from suggestions for specific remedial approaches (Kaluger and Kolson, 1969, for example) to highly comprehensive academic studies of language and reading behaviors as they operate in learning disability individuals (Bannatyne, 1971). Although no specific data are readily available, it would seem to be a reasonable assumption that those involved with remedial reading in some aspect or other probably make up one of the largest single professional subgroups of educational specialists working in learning disabilities.

Other subject matter remedial specialties are not as well represented in terms of the number of people involved but still include a wide range of subjects and curriculum areas. Many different types of useful publications are available. Mann and Suiter (1974) include spelling, handwriting, language, and arithmetic in their handbook, although reading receives most of their attention. Hammill and Bartel (1978) offer models and specific suggestions in reading, arithmetic, spelling, writing, language development, and perceptual-motor development. Still others, such as Arena (1968), devote entire books to various aspects of a single subject-matter area, in this case, spelling.

Language

Much of the work in this area might just as easily be listed under the subheading of *Remedial Teaching* since a significant proportion of language-related effort involves both remediation and an active teaching role. Bush and Giles' book (1977), which is directed toward paralleling the structure of the ITPA with grade-differentiated remedial activities, and Karnes' work (1968), an activity book for young children developing language skills, exemplify this overlap. But language specialists do differentiate at times between remedial teachers in other subject areas and their own specialty. The term *language clinician* is sometimes used to refer to the specialist who integrates a clinical-type approach to language with more typical remedial teaching activities. Publications such as the two mentioned above are often rather closely designed for these individuals even though they are also useful in many applied ways for others.

Speech pathologists are becoming more and more involved in learning disabilities and their level of sophistication in this subspecialty field is increasing proportionately. The difficulty in effectively accomplishing such integrated sophistication is underlined by speech pathologists like Pannbacker (1968) who make highly defensible pleas for better cross-discipline communication, more consensual nomenclature, and broader research.

Some point out (McGrady, 1968) that language and learning disabilities blended together as a multidisciplinary effort encourage the fusion of physical and behavioral sciences. The study of language pathology is essentially an interdisciplinary experience and a speech pathologist is by necessity somewhat of a generalist as he or she works with learning disabled children. The primary contribution of the language or speech pathologist focuses on disorders of symbolic behavior. The many levels and types of training emphases available to a student studying in the language field assure a wide range of trained professionals, including speech therapists, remedial specialists, research scientists, speech trainers, speech program builders, and remedial program administrators.

Speech specialists point out that disruption of the learning process in children with accompanying language development problems can come from any one or combination of these four cases:

Four cases
contributing
to language
development
problems

1. Sensory deprivation—such as a hearing loss
2. Experimental deprivation—such as hearing only a limited vocabulary spoken in the home
3. Emotional disorganization—such as those traumas which lead to or contribute to stammering and mutism
4. Neurological dysfunction—such as those disorders stemming from a physiological incapability to produce vital verbal responses

There are specialists who focus on each one of these four major types of speech problems. Certainly there seems to be no consensus that speech problems stem from one major cause or problem type alone. As McGrady (1968) says, "the process of learning is far too complex to infer that all disordered language or learning is the result of neurogenicity."

Language
models and L.D.

Those working in the language field, some of whom may be regarded as language specialists *per se* and others as different types of specialists, have contributed basic models and conceptualizations that have been of significant practical help. Such contributions have come from major names in the learning disability field such as Wepman (1960), Myklebust (1965), and Kirk, McCarthy, and Kirk (1968).

Due to the work of these professionals, even the casual worker in learning disabilities soon notes that language is not a simple, unitary construct but consists instead of several different categories of behavior, apparently sequential in development, with each step important for satisfactory verbal learning development. Problems exist and remedial activities must be programmed for inner language, comprehension of the spoken word, oral expression, comprehension of the written word, and written expression. Each of these areas brings special problems and characteristic behaviors that call for the help of the speech specialist.

Although less involved in everyday activities in learning disabilities, the research-scientist and theorist of language study, the psycholinguist, also makes a significant contribution. The linguist may bridge interdisciplinary gaps as he correlates neurological and developmental research with behavioral manifestations and verbal learning pathologies (Whitcraft, 1971).

Psycholinguists work in a wide range of areas that offer useful information for learning disability specialists. Such professionals study the influence of verbal and nonverbal antecedent conditions on behavior and verbal learning. They carefully examine the relationships of various verbal-stimulus categories of nonverbal behavior, including learning. They inquire into the role of verbal mediators in behavior. They research interrelationships among various dimensions of verbal responses and between verbal and nonverbal dimensions of behavior. And it is the psycholinguists who offer the most comprehensive information regarding language acquisition, language development, and normative language behavior (Rosenberg, 1965, Whitcraft and Allen, 1972).

Medical Disciplines

Medical professions have had a strong influence on special education and learning disabilities ever since the latter two fields developed. Unless one adopts some type of dualism which assumes that mind and mental problems operate independently from physiological considerations, such an involvement is not only to be expected but desirable as well. Some of the problems and philosophical splits that have arisen (reliance on the medical model alone, for instance) are more a function of the failure to develop new ideas and explore fresh hypotheses than an indictment of the limitations of medicine as a meaningful contributor to learning disability study.

Medicine, through both research and clinical efforts, has a long history of positive contributions to the physical and mental health of children. Today many medical professionals are active as members of interdisciplinary teams involved in searching for better explanations of specific learning disabilities and in the active remediation of existing problems in identified learning-disabled children. Educators and physicians together (Bateman and Frankel, 1972) are pointing toward the need for joint work on problems of mental retardation, reading problems, learning disabilities, and other problems associated with special education. The most common critique of medicine's position and contribution—that the approach is too limited and aimed too narrowly toward identification of cause (etiology) and too little toward successful remediation efforts—may be gradually losing its basis. More often teams of remedial specialists, including medical representatives, are directing major efforts in the field toward the definition of adequate treatment goals, useful and achievable behavioral objectives, and task-oriented activities. Even in those cases where the search is primarily for etiological clarification, a strong preventative motivation holds forth. The wide range of nutritional studies, many involving medical professionals (as reported by Hallahan and Cruickshank, 1973), typify this more creative orientation.

The major objection presented by those who view medicine's contribution with less than complete acceptance does not concern itself so much with the worth of etiological knowledge alone as it does the rigid tendency to try to fit such explanations within the framework of long existing constructs and established diagnostic categories. Current research, more applied involvement by those involved with medical research, and cross-disciplinary efforts are helping to soften this criticism and alleviate concern.

The broad medical field is subdivided into dozens of specialities, and many of these are involved with learning disabilities. Four groupings of professionals within the province of medicine may be viewed as most active and most easily defined: *General Pediatrics, Neurology, Pharmacology,* and the vision-related fields of *Ophthalmology* and *Optometry.*

General Pediatrics

The pediatrician's active role in the schools started in the late 1800s when some relatively large-scale medical screening work was initiated. The positive effect of World War I on this field was remarkable, as it was with other related fields such as psychometrics and psychology. The exceedingly large number of men who failed military physicals precipitated a dramatic rise in interest in and governmental support for investigating the general health status of the nation. Increasing the role of the pediatrician in the schools and the establishment of school health teams (even to the point of specially training school nurses) were logical steps.

The pediatrician is most apt to become initially involved with learning disability cases in two separate ways. The first is through the medical steps that are typically taken to assure that a child is physically and emotionally ready for school: a physical examination and interviews with the child and parents. The second is through subsequent examinations and team involvement during early school years. Pediatricians frequently pick up signs of potential learning disabilities early in a child's life as they note immaturity and developmental lag in normal growth patterns. Parental interviews in the course of normal preschool medical treatment may isolate syndrome signs that, though not definitive (sometimes called "soft" signs), are still signals that alert the examiner to the possibility of learning-related problems. Such symptoms include hyperactivity, unusual distractability, shortened attention span, unusual emotional lability, lowered frustration tolerance, motor awkwardness, and lack of cerebral inhibition. Although the same symptoms may appear in other problems, their existence as a cluster in a young child is often used by the pediatrician as a signal or warning of possible or potential learning disability problems. Presence of such signs may cause the pediatrician to take extra time in the standard medical examination, to seek more comprehensive parental information, and to suggest special examinations in such areas as psychological functioning, EEG, speech and hearing, vision, and others (Ong, 1968). The pediatrician's major function in this situation is to act as an initial screening source who identifies possible problems and may prescribe broader diagnostic and treatment activities.

In another sense the pediatrician is frequently viewed as the coordinator or integrator of diagnosis and treatment of children with special learning problems (DeLaCruz and LaVeck, 1965). In such instances, less commonly associated with learning disability teams in the schools than in clinic or special learning centers, the pediatrician still may be primarily looking for physical etiology even though his search may take him into broader areas such as nutrition, organicity, infectious disease, metabolism, and sometimes functional psychiatric behaviors.

The functions of the school pediatrician are not only varied but also have decided sequential and longitudinal aspects. The pediatrician is the team individual most apt to have a long-term picture of the child's development, including infant and preschool periods as well as school years. As part of this continuing responsibility he or she may become involved in several different roles and functions, each with its own particular potential relationship to school planning for the handicapped including the learning disabled child.

Clemmens and Davis (1969) have outlined some of this role involvement of the pediatrician in an attempt to show the complementary role of pediatrician and educator. They note that the pediatrician may function in each or all of these roles:

1. The detection of disease process or physical handicap or sensory impairment that might detract or deter from the learning activity of the child.

    The pediatrician as educator

2. Obtaining and coordinating all necessary studies and consultations in a manner that helps them to be used in a meaningful and organized way.
3. The interpretation, when necessary, of special findings to parents and other members of the school team.
4. The periodic assessment of development status to maintain an ongoing growth and development profile.
5. Providing counseling for parents to facilitate effective educational placement thus helping to avoid secondary emotional problems stemming from repeated and prolonged school failure.
6. Providing periodic re-evaluation, reassessment, and ongoing support, medical management, counseling, and such other services as may be helpful.

The present trend definitely seems to be away from an isolated, unitary, high-status leadership and administrator role. Current emphasis is upon team approaches that share mutually helpful information and expertise.

Neurology

Neurologists become involved with learning disability cases on a variety of fronts. Since it is a complex field with its own array of subspecialities, it is difficult to portray concisely the unitary role that neurology plays.

Neurologists are often called upon to assist in total child examinations when a complete and exhaustive diagnostic workup seems a necessary preliminary step to remedial planning and activities. But even in such a referral situation the role of the neurologist is not a consensual one. If the neurologist to whom the child is referred happens to specialize in *developmental* neurology, then the approach may be primarily one that correlates behavior with brain structure or function so as to assist in medical differentiation between mental retardation, emotional disturbances, or learning disabilities of the neurogenic type (Vuckovich, 1968).

Many neurological specialists who accept learning disability referrals are specifically trained as *pediatric* neurologists. In such instances the role of neurologist and pediatrician become interwoven and the specialist functions much as pediatrician with the additional insight and capabilities afforded by neurological specialization. The pediatric neurologist is apt to focus more on disease or pathological occurrences than is the developmental neurologist, although the differentiation is not a clear one and certainly is not easy to make in the case of individual neurologists.

The typical activities of the neurologist consist of completing a thorough neurological examination; looking for and identifying typical characteristic syndromes (patterns of symptoms), such as those commonly associated with hyperkinesis or visuo-motor control deficits or major CNS dysfunctions; and identifying the child's progress or lack of progress through the various apparently critical stages of development and neurological maturation. Neurologists sometimes refer to these critical periods of time as the child's "maturity zones" with the premise that normal development consists of accomplishing some essential maturational progress during each of these important sequential periods. The actual behavioral tasks representing progress include such activities as sitting, walking, hand manipulation, seeing and hearing behaviors, social interaction, and language usage. During these "maturity zones," the relationship of the child's development to the learning disability topics is quite obvious.

The work of most neurologists in this respect closely resembles that of Gesell and Thompson (1941) and Gesell and Ilg (1943). Some of the criticism of neurogical approaches to learning disabilities has been similar to that made regarding the Gesell contributions. The criticism pinpoints too much dependence on exact stages and on the isolated role of maturation as opposed to maturation-learning interaction. This criticism, legitimate as it may be in regard to a hard and fast maturational-stages approach to behavior, is not nearly as relevant when leveled against the neurological profession. The modern pediatric or developmental neurologist may represent this classical approach but is equally likely to be conversant with contemporary social learning contributions and the current emphasis on the importance of contingency and situational management.

In actuality the neurologist working regularly with learning disabilities is most apt to be concerned with central nervous system maturation and demonstrable developmental lag that may be related to minimal brain damage. The neurologist works most frequently in the area somewhere between evidenced brain-damage cases and normal-variance child behavior.

The *neurological examination* is central to the neurologist's contribution. In this function the neurological specialist is trying to contribute relevant information that may not be available through any other method; to underline or validate evidence obtained through other means; and often to provide the necessary medical background information for possible subsequent medical prescription. The neurologist is often involved with research related to this examination function as he or she tries to determine what proportion of learning disabled children exhibit significant neurological and/or pediatric signs and which specific learning disability types benefit from certain special evaluative or examining techniques (Keele, Keele, Huizinga, Bray, Estes, and Holland, 1975).

The examination procedure will vary depending upon the type of information requested of the neurologist and upon what information is obtained through the progressive steps of the examination itself. In addition to the classic neurological testing involving the assessment of the functioning level and relative intactness of different neural subsystems, the neurologist may, (and in the case of learning disability cases, frequently does) go on to more involved evaluations. The additional steps may include sensory system examination, gross- and fine-motor-function determination, evaluation of basic language abilities, visuo-spatial examination, evaluation of perceptual functions, memory tests, and the observation of specific behaviors involving behavioral strategies and control (Denckla, 1972). In some instances special techniques such as using the EEG will be involved. However the learning disability diagnosis itself does not yet seem to be sufficiently homogeneous to lead to much meaningful discriminative information from this procedure (Hughes, 1968). Use of the EEG and similar techniques still remains largely in the research and speculative aspects of neurology-learning disability interaction.

Some neurologists, such as Cohn (1964) and others in related disciplines, are openly skeptical of some of the "soft" signs of possible neurological and minimal brain dysfunction, sometimes used as the basis for diagnostic labeling and remediation planning. Cohn points out that "soft" signs are characterized only by an arbitrary definition that is too dependent upon the individual neurologist's basic philosophy and training. He also emphasizes that it is not clearly demonstrated neurologically that such minimal clinical signs are related in fact to minimal brain pathology. The relationship is a suggestion, not a fact, a suggestion followed in practice by many neurologists who feel that the largest single contribution of the neurological examination is to clearly establish and point out the relatively intact neural systems that can be best used in general intellectual and academic activities. Such information clearly may be relevant to the planning and organizing of remedial activities—particularly to those whose strategy is related to using compensatory skills to make up for deficit areas.

Cohn also feels that as far as the neurologist is concerned the emphasis should be away from correction of deficits and toward making a stronger contribution to knowledge regarding development and growth. Others, such as Gaddes (1968), make a plea for the synthesis of neurological, psychological, and educational knowledge, with an increased emphasis on acquiring more basic information about the normal neurological functioning of the child. Denckla (1972) argues that it is nonproductive to make any "unitary statement about the child with minimal brain dysfunction." He states further that although there are some recognizable syndrome clusters, such as those in specific language disabilities, specific visuo-spatial disabilities, and general dyscontrol in the functioning of the learning disabled child, the child frequently tagged with a label is not clearly identifiable within the parameters of any homogeneous neural or behavioral pattern.

Undependable-ness of soft neurological symptoms

Indications are that the neurological field is moving toward more interdisciplinary team involvement as far as learning disabilities is concerned and that there is a discernible movement away from the "organic, minimal brain damage" label. Movement can also be seen toward the detection of patterns of asymmetry and discrepancy, which are cues to the type of deviation from developmental norms that may be indicative of learning disability behaviors.

Denckla (1973) has outlined some goals for neurologists who are interested in doing research in the field of learning disabilities:

Denckla's goals for neurologists

1. Greater precision in classification and nomenclature regarding childhood syndromes.
2. Development of analogies between childhood syndromes and adult acquired neuropsychological deficits for anatomical localization.
3. Acquisition of more sophisticated measurement techniques in order to develop a "neurometrics" for normal and subsequently deficit children.

Just the listing of such goals is indicative of the increasing involvement of neurology in the area of learning disabilities. The profession's role is changing from a simple application of existing techniques and procedures for learning disabilities to a deeper research involvement, to development of new techniques of measurement and explanation of behavior, and to the involvement of the pediatric-developmental neurologist as part of a learning disability remedial team. Such growth suggests a changing and more deliberately involved role in learning disabilities for this aspect of medicine.

Pharmacology

It is very difficult to define adequately the precise role of pharmacology in the treatment of learning disabilities since the use of medication or drugs seldom occurs in isolation from other types of treatment, such as child and parental counseling, special environmental manipulation, and almost the entire range of academic remediation programs. As Carpenter and Sells (1974) state, ". . . little information is available showing a predictable effect of a particular psychoactive drug on a specific aspect of behavior in children with learning impediments."

Still, a considerable body of research is involved with studying this approach, often called *chemotherapy.* Freeman (1966) has summarized the effects of the use of drugs on children as evidenced in the research literature up through 1965, but subsequent findings have yet to be as well integrated. Information frequently incorporating conflicting data can be found across a wide range of professional literature.

The use of drugs in treating learning disability children is based upon the same premises as any medical treatment of such children. These suppositions are that

(1) the brain is involved in learning, behavior, and emotional control; (2) the brain is a physiological mechanism; and (3) the brain, as a physiological mechanism, is subject to pharmacological agents.

The numbers and types of drugs that have been used for treatment are large and varied. The lack of homogeneity in learning disability case types, a characteristic which causes problems in many different aspects of diagnosis and treatment, and the heterogeneity of drugs prescribed complicates any meaningful description and definition of results. In general the drugs most commonly used in treatment and experimental work with learning disability cases are tranquilizers, stimulants, and some drugs that have mixed effects but are commonly used for seizure control in epileptic cases. Several tranquilizers are prescribed: *Chloropromazine*, a major tranquilizer; *Librium* and *Valium*, minor tranquilizers. *Amphetamine*, a stimulant that tends to soothe and quiet hyperkinetic children in some cases, is representative of the stimulant drugs reported used. *Ritalin* and *Phenobarbital* are typical of the seizure-control drugs of the third category.

Unfortunately, it is impossible to discriminate precisely the specific effects of any one or group of these drugs upon learning-disabled children. Mixed findings are reported; many diagnosed cases involve multiple problems such as learning disabilities coupled with epileptic-type seizures. Very frequently, mixed dosages of drugs have been prescribed and used.

It should be noted too that the use of pharmacological agents for children with learning problems covers a much wider range than a simple one-to-one application similar to the use of common medication, such as an aspirin taken for relief of a headache. Although some usage involves direct attack on specific disabilities through control of related behavior (Stewart, 1971), other applications are much more far reaching and tend to approach the learning disability deficit behavior through attacking more basic physiological etiology. For example, Cott (1972) is researching megavitamin treatment with such agents as *niacin*; and early results, although not definitive, show some promise. Such work centers around the concept of neural cell malnutrition which ultimately denies the individual of potential normal neural functional capacity.

The effect of diet and the presence or absence of specific nutritional elements in the diets of diagnosed dyslexics and others is also being studied (Roberts, 1969). Hallahan and Cruickshank (1973) report at length on an extensive list of possible etiological factors, many of which directly or indirectly involve nutritional and pharmacological factors.

In general, when favorable results are reported, the trend is to explain them through better control factors (Comly, 1971), as were the results gained in the prepsychotherapy application of tranquilizers to the emotionally disturbed patient. The physiological locus of control affected apparently lies predominantly in higher critical factors mediated by the cerebral cortex. Researchers also note that the major change in learning-type behavior seems to be in the reduction of the latency of response more than a change in the quantity or amplitude of the response. Such changes would be in harmony with the increased control mentioned above and perhaps relevant to the attention and orienting behaviors reported improved in other drug studies.

Comly (1971), for example, reports that parental observations of improved behavior in children who have been under stimulant drug use most often found improvement in direction following, attention span, decrease in overactivity, better interpersonal play, less over-excitement, quieter hobby interests, and better planning of activities. All such behaviors, although not direct learning activities in and of themselves, can be viewed as necessary prerequisite or entering behaviors for many types and levels of academic activity. All seem to involve control, attention, and orienting factors.

The often successful use of behavior modification techniques to achieve the same results as drugs, along with other problems in arriving at meaningful conclusions in drug research (social reaction to the present drug culture for example), have led to some decrease in the popular appeal of active remediation through chemotherapy programs. As Solomons (1971) notes, there are some careful prerequisites that should be met before any drug prescription program is followed:

Solomons'
prerequisites
for drug
prescription
programs

1. There must be no parental objections.
2. No delinquent behaviors noted in the prospective subject.
3. No delinquent behaviors noted in other members of the household.
4. Parents must agree to becoming involved in any necessary psychotherapeutic plan.

The foresighted care exemplified by this list of prerequisites is evidence of the general concern the prescriber must have for the public's reaction to the use of pharmacological agents. The intense feelings currently present regarding the contemporary drug culture and the awareness that the prescription and use of such agents alone may be an inadequate treatment of learning disability somewhat limit the scope of drug treatment.

As a final note, we should mention that drug research has led to some interesting side benefits. One of these has been better definition of the research design characteristics necessary for obtaining meaningful research data. Current studies are better designed and use of such factors as the double-blind design, where neither the subject nor the person administering the treatment is aware of who is a control and who is a treatment subject, is increasing. More attention is being paid to the placebo effect not only of drug application but of all types of treatments. The need for objective measurement of the child's before-and-after treatment behavior has led to concern over the appropriateness of some commonly used techniques (Carpenter and Sells, 1974) and, in some cases, to the development of a better instrument (Comly, 1971). The checklist in Table 4–2 for assessing hyperkinetic behavior in children (Davids, 1971) is an example of a preliminary step in that direction.

TABLE 4-2
A Checklist for Assessing Hyperkinesis in Children

Please rate the child on each of the characteristics (or behavior) listed on the following scales. Place a check mark at the point on the scale indicative of your estimate of the degree to which the child possesses the particular characteristic.

As you make each rating, judge the child in comparison with other children of the same sex and age. That is, the ratings should indicate your estimate of the child's behavior in comparison with the behavior displayed by other "normal children."

For each of the characteristics, which are defined below, place a check mark at one of the six points on the scales running from "much less than most children" to "much more than most children." Do not mark the midpoint of any of the scales. Even though it may sometimes be difficult to make a judgment, please make a rating on one or the other side of the scale.

1. *Hyperactivity*—Involuntary and constant overactivity; advanced motor development (throwing things, walking, running, etc.); always on the move; rather run than walk; rarely sits still.

Much Less Than Most Children	Less	Slightly Less	Slightly More	More	Much More Than Most Children

2. *Short Attention Span and Poor Powers of Concentration*—Concentration on a single activity is usually short, with frequent shifting from one activity to another; rarely sticks to a single task very long.

Much Less Than Most Children	Less	Slightly Less	Slightly More	More	Much More Than Most Children

3. *Variability*—Behavior is unpredictable, with wide fluctuations in performance; "sometimes he (or she) is good and sometimes bad."

Much Less Than Most Children	Less	Slightly Less	Slightly More	More	Much More Than Most Children

4. *Impulsiveness and Inability to Delay Gratification*—Does things on the spur of the moment without thinking; seems unable to tolerate any delay in gratification of his (her) needs and demands; when wants anything, he (she) wants it immediately; does not look ahead or work toward future goals; thinks only of immediate present situation.

Much Less Than Most Children	Less	Slightly Less	Slightly More	More	Much More Than Most Children

5. *Irritability*—Frustration tolerance is low; frequently in an ugly mood, often unprovoked; easily upset if everything does not w rk out just the way he (she) desires.

Much Less Than Most Children	Less	Slightly Less	Slightly More	More	Much More Than Most Children

TABLE 4–2
A Checklist for Assessing Hyperkinesis in Children (*Continued*)

6. *Explosiveness*—Fits of anger are easily provoked; reactions are often almost volcanic in their intensity; shows explosive, temper-tantrum type of emotional outbursts.

Much Less Than Most Children	Less	Slightly Less	Slightly More	More	Much More Than Most Children

7. *Poor School Work*—Has difficulty participating successfully in school work; cannot concentrate on school work; has some specific learning difficulties or blocks (e.g., poor in arithmetic, poor in reading, etc.); poor visual-motor coordination (e.g., awkward gestures, irregular handwriting, poor in drawing, etc.).

Much Less Than Most Children	Less	Slightly Less	Slightly More	More	Much More Than Most Children

From "An Objective Instrument for Assessing Hyperkinesis in Children" by A. Davids, *Journal of Learning Disabilities*, 1971, 4, 499–501. Reprinted by special permission of Professional Press, Inc.

Vision-Related Fields

Vision-related professions have been active with learning disabilities as long as the medical field has been involved. Concern over specific vision-related deficits is easily traceable to such pioneers as Hinshelwood (1902) and Orton (1928). The effect on remedial programs now in use—such as the approach developed by Getman, Kane, Halgren, and McKee (1968)—is obvious. Unfortunately this area has also been the locus of major interdisciplinary disagreements, a debatable issue covered at some length in chapter 6. In essence, however, the disagreement involves conflict over the efficacy of the remedial procedures advocated by a number of learning-disability-oriented optometrists.

Ophthalmologists, tracing their work back largely to the early research of Hinshelwood (1902), see their contribution in the procedures assuring that the child has adequate sight, in physiologically healthy eyes, and in the treatment of physiologically definable diseases and malfunctions of the sight processes. The diagnosis and treatment of learning difficulties is, in the opinion of the ophthalmologist, best placed in the care of other specialists once a specific sight problem is corrected or ruled out (Rosner, 1968).

Optometrists, carefully distinguishing between sight and vision, are also concerned with correcting problems such as common refraction limitations that are treatable and remediable by corrective glasses. However, many optometrists involved with learning disabilities feel that "vision education," the remedial processes that focus on the training and development of visual behavior, is an important if not basic part of the remediation of many specific learning disabilities. Vision education or visual training attempts to arrange conditions so that a learning disabled child can improve or in some cases initially learn the primary visual abilities as eye movement, binocularity, eye-hand coordination, and visual form perception.

Ophthalmologists, on the other hand, view visual-motor disturbances as merely associated conditions and do not feel that they are by any means consistent factors in learning difficulties. Evidence in support of one or the other of these two positions is mixed and not yet sufficiently definitive to allow one to take an irrevocable empirical stand in favor of either side. Because of this disagreement the involvement of the vision specialist in learning disabilities varies greatly from discipline to discipline and from person to person.

Clinical Disciplines

To designate a field as a *clinical discipline* may be a bit misleading unless one is aware that these fields are often represented elsewhere as well. Psychiatry, for example, is also a medical discipline, and Psychology frequently is listed under applied educational headings as well.

The *clinical* label does have some usefulness, however, when one realizes that certain fields devote a significant proportion of their focus upon the functional problems of the deficit population as they are encountered in a patient-doctor or client-therapist mode. In such interactions, the professionals involved are in an advantageous position to offer insights that grow out of the combination of highly technical knowledge in a specialized field with on-the-scene awareness of what problems and difficulties mean in terms of planning and effecting efficient remediation.

Clinical disciplines are less apt to be found dealing in pure research speculation or technical description without including a portion of sensitivity to everyday problems as well. This combination of approach and interest is shaped by the nature of these disciplines' practical functions. The advantages of such a blending of theory, technical knowledge, and practical awareness to the study of learning disabilities is obvious.

Psychiatry

Psychiatry is a much more diversified field than most laymen realize. The involvement of psychiatrists in learning disabilities is more a reflection of the specialty, interests, and practice of the individual psychiatrist than a product of the general orientation and training available in the discipline.

Psychiatrists active in learning disabilities tend to be either those involved in the treatment of children as a general practice or those who work most closely with neurologists who are referral sources for learning disability cases. The dichotomy between what is purely neurological and what is purely psychiatric is rapidly breaking down. More and more, common developmental factors, which involve both the developmental pediatric neurologist and the child psychiatrist, are coming to the forefront. To some extent psychiatrists have tended to become oriented to the "ages and stages" point of view commonly associated with Ames (1968), particularly as it relates to school and learning readiness as explored by Ilg, Ames, and Apell (1965).

The psychiatric approach tends to be personally rather than environmentally or situationally oriented. Remedial efforts are commonly directed toward combating evidenced immaturity and anxiety. There is need, as Giffin (1968) has pointed out, for more quantifiable diagnostic data in the psychiatric-learning disabilities area and for further definitive research into how it "feels" to be a learning disabled child. Two of the *Learning Series* films, *"I'm Not Too Famous at It"* and *"It Feels Like You're Left Out of the World,"* relate to this affective side of learning disabilities, but only on an elementary level.

Much psychiatric work is related to determining psychological or behavioral concomitants of neurological deficits. In these cases it is based upon the same premise that Myklebust (1968) and other nonpsychiatric learning disabilities workers operating on a neurological model use: that learning disabilities are the result of minor disturbances of brain function. Such an approach, whether it portrays the brain function–behavior function as isomorphic or the brain as a transducer, is dependent upon the psychoneurological definitions upon which it is based. Child evaluation is likely, under such a model, to consist of assessing intraneurosensory function and interneurosensory function (after the manner of the neurologist) and the resulting neuropsychological integrative behaviors from a clinical, psychiatric viewpoint.

As is the case in many other medically related disciplines, however, an increasing emphasis on interdisciplinary and cross-disciplinary team efforts is apparent in psychiatry as it is applied to learning disabilities. Vuckovich (1968) lists the important facets of remedial programming in this general area:

Vuckovich's factors of remedial programming

1. The need for professional interchange in evaluation and diagnosis.
2. The necessity for program contacts to be multifaceted including such areas as psychometrics, trained observation and tutoring, formal therapy, counseling, etc.
3. Flexibility to reprogram and update remedial plans.
4. The inclusion of parents as part of the total remedial effort team.

Such a remedial programming approach, carried to its necessary conclusions, guarantees a functionally active role to those psychiatric professionals interested in becoming involved with learning disabilities.

Psychology

Like psychiatry, the term psychology is used to cover a wide variety of subdisciplines, some of which have already been discussed in this chapter under other headings. Many of those working in language study, assessment, and treatment are, by training and label, psychologists. Practically all professionals involved in psychometrics are also psychologists. The educational psychologist has been very active in learning disabilities through contributions to instructional planning, curriculum content, and similar activities. Many of those active in retardation, such as William Cruickshank, and those in special research centers, such as Donald Smith of the University of Michigan Center for Research on Language and Language Behavior, are also psychologists.

Psychologists like Gardner (1974) and Ross (1977) have made a substantial contribution to the handling of special cases, particularly in relationship to management strategies and behavioral problems. Both authors of this text are also educational psychologists, one specializing in the contribution of personality and measurement theory and the other in the preparation and utilization of educational strategies to learning disabilities.

The *American Psychological Association*, the national professional organization of the majority of U.S. psychologists, is also active in learning disabilities, particularly through the functions of Division 16 which specializes in the work of school psychologists.

Psychology, as a unitary profession, does not represent any single orientation or theoretical stance in regard to learning disabilities. Instead individual psychologists of varying persuasions and theoretical biases can be found active in almost every facet of the learning disability field.

Sociology

Sociology has been a relative newcomer to learning disabilities and is still only peripherally involved in comparison to some other disciplines. Hallahan and Cruickshank (1973) have integrated some important sociological work as it relates to the understanding of the demographic and environmental etiologies of learning disabilities in children. The relevance of such work is a clear reason for encouraging more detailed involvement by trained sociologists who may be able to produce valuable information about social and environmental factors. Up to this point the work of sociologists has focused on about three major areas. In one area, sociologists have studied the processes of education and rehabilitation in those who have experienced economic deprivation; and they have isolated some of the effects of different environmental contingencies and the varying levels and types of beneficial stimulation and related topics for such people (Hess, 1964). Second, sociology has also examined the developmental growth of infants and young children under varying environmental presses in cooperation with other disciplines. Finally, in a third area, sociology is largely responsible for what we know about the general effect of poverty and its concomitant effects on children, some of whom eventually become labeled as learning disabled (Birch and Gussow, 1970).

The information available is not yet well integrated with ongoing remedial strategies or with delivery-of-services models. However, the value of such information, most certainly the province of several sociological subdisciplines, is apparent and the use of such information by learning disability specialists is increasing. One of the major issues in learning disabilities today (see chapter 3) is whether or not culturally deprived and disadvantaged children should be included in the total clinical group served by learning disability programs.

Summary

It is obvious that the study and treatment of learning disabilities is not the province of a single discipline or even a small group of disciplines. Many different professional groups are involved and each has its own peculiar contribution to make. The overwhelming problem at the present is twofold: (1) the establishment of better lines of communication to facilitate a more efficient exchange of relevant information and data from members of one discipline to another; and (2) better coordination of research and study techniques, procedures, and actual investigations so that competing hypotheses may be examined, falacious ones discarded, incomplete ones added to, and apparently similar ones resolved into more meaningful and comprehensive statements about the status of our present knowledge in the field.

Movement toward such ends is apparent in many different professions and even the immediate rewards evident in such initial trends is encouraging and supportive of further endeavors along these lines.

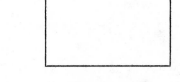

Part II

General Models and Strategies

Successfully attacking learning disability problems requires careful planning and attention to some highly important details. These details provide the practitioner with the input needed for effective decision making. A number of significant variables interact in any remedial effort. These include those that are particularly relevant to the nature and extent of the behavioral deficit being treated, the idiosyncratic characteristics of the problem learner, the distinctive skills and capability of the remediator, the type of physical facilities and materials available, and important questions regarding the hierarchy of treatment and objective preferences.

The four chapters in this section should help the reader identify the areas in which these significant details fall and provide some guidance for acquiring data helpful to programmatic decision making.

Chapter 5 outlines a taxonomy into which most remedial approaches and strategies may be fitted. Basic assumptions, potential strengths and weaknesses, and some implications of choosing a particular approach are discussed. Chapter 6 gives brief outlines of some actual theories or approaches that exemplify this taxonomy. Also included in that chapter are tangible examples of several different approaches highlighting the similarities and differences between strategies.

Chapter 7 presents further examples of some popular remedial approaches, viewed in this case from the standpoint of the particular problem areas they attack rather than the theoretical orientation they represent. Chapter 8 presents in some detail the rationale for and outline of the systems-management program espoused by the authors of this text.

Different Orientations, Approaches, and Strategies

Any attempt to describe different remedial programs or models adequately by classifying or labeling them is not very satisfactory. Categorization schemes never solve the problem of how to describe something that fits two different categories or something that doesn't seem to fit any distinct category exactly. This problem is exemplified in attempts to describe varying remedial programs in learning disabilities through categorization. Most remedial approaches can be equally well-described in more than one manner, depending upon how they are viewed. It is unfortunate that categorization is so unproductive. The availability of some efficient, quick, and precise referencing format would enable practitioners to select and use remedial programs more easily on the basis of their applicability to different kinds of situations and problems. Although some learning disability workers strongly adopt a single orientation and become fixed in their orientation and mode of response to problems, others do not. Instead, many choose to apply different approaches selectively where they seem to fit peculiar aspects of the situation, the problem, time-factors, the availability of personnel of one type or another, or other similar factors. Such an approach, if handled knowledgeably and with a sensitivity to the assets and limitations of different orientations and to the special opportunities and demands of each, seems to be an efficient and productive way to organize and carry out remediation.

The field of learning disabilities is not sufficiently crystallized to allow us to say that a single approach, orientation, or theory stands foremost to the exclusion of all others. Although there has been a considerable amount of effort expended **81** toward developing various theories of learning disabilities, the distance between theoretical formulations and demonstrations of remedial effectiveness (a type of criterion validation essential for long-term theory support) is still great. Many theoretical assumptions remain exactly that—both theoretical and assumptive— rather than having developed into demonstrable, lawful, and predictive relationships. As Strang (1968) has pointed out, the validating sides of the picture— remediation and treatment—have received much less attention than diagnostic activities, test instruments, and similar items. Much of the theory-validating evidence remains to be gathered.

Examining Approaches to Learning Disabilities

Rather than attempting to convert the reader to the detailed postulates and theorems of a particular theory, we will posit that any worthwhile learning disability practitioner should be able to demonstrate more than casual familiarity with a number of different approaches and theories. As the worker becomes increasingly sophisticated and experienced it is possible that he or she may develop a preference for some particular theory. But even then such leanings should only follow thorough exposure to a full spectrum of possibilities. They should never, even when finely developed into an individualistic, personal style and approach, operate to the total exclusion of alternative methods firm empirical evidence can support.

But these two assumptions—(1) that classifying various models and approaches is not very satisfying, and (2) that it is helpful for the developing learning disability practitioner to develop some type of framework for quick reference—seem paradoxical. How can the apparent contradictions be resolved?

Although aware of the difficulties involved, several authors who value having some conceptual framework have suggested some broad categories under which various programs might be loosely listed.

Myers' and Hammill's categories

Myers and Hammill (1969) first used a six-part conceptualization breaking the different systems into perceptual-motor, multisensory, language development, phonics, test-related, and specially structured types. More currently (1976), these same authors suggest that the field can be more meaningfully viewed through a spectrum of what they consider to be the most popularly adopted frames of reference (i.e., those of Guilford, Myers and Hammill, Osgood, Skinner, and Wepman) separated from a large variety of different remedial systems. The latter they classify into systems of language development, linguistics, psycholinguistic training, specialized reading, perceptual-motor, and a separate category dealing with teaching the demonstrably brain-damaged pupil.

Gearheart (1973) uses a breakdown similar to Myers' and Hammill's initial categorization but includes examples of a diagnostic approach and some environmental control systems. Kirk (1972) lists neurological, perceptual-motor, visual-perception, multisensory, and remedial-reading approaches. Lerner (1976) combines theories and teaching strategies and directs attention to five major areas: sensory-motor and perceptual-motor development, perception and memory, language, cognitive skills, and maturational-psychological-social factors.

Lerner's approach leans toward categorization of target problems rather than theoretical bases and is more closely allied with the approach of Hammill and Bartel (1978). They disregard categorization of basic theories and classify instead according to particular learning disability behavior problems in areas closely related to academic subject matter such as arithmetic and spelling. This approach is very helpful and can be useful in one's implementation of the different theories if the theories and models are equally applied to the problem behavior targets.

We have found that theories, models, orientations, and approaches (as they may variously be described depending upon their developed complexity and comprehensiveness) may be described by referring to the manner in which they are applied to various phases or aspects of any learning disability problem. There is no need to limit a theory to one particular problem or aspect of a problem since most theories either attack directly or can be applied against more than one such facet. But it is helpful to note the ways in which certain theories tend to emphasize heavily or become more involved with certain aspects than others. Such an approach is similar to one suggested by Hall and Lindzey (1970) in studying personality theories. They suggest that "substantive attributes" do not involve any particular implications about value or worth. Rather, such differences "merely reflect the particular assumptions concerning behavior which the theory embraces."

Five separate facets of learning disability problems seem to the authors to be discriminatively different and useful in demonstrating how theories and approaches vary in their basic emphases (substantive attributes). These are:

1. *Developmental Status.* Aspects focusing primarily on growth and development. The emphasis is on establishing a clear pattern of normal development and tracing the disruption or violation of such a pattern, which is then assumed to be the etiology of subsequent learning problems. The pattern may represent a single strata or segment of the organism but more typically is characterized by larger, generalized developmental segments. As a general rule, if the developmental focus is on a single aspect, the approach is more accurately described as fitting in the second category, *basic processes.*

2. *Basic Processes.* Aspects that focus on underlying etiology, upon behavior and systems prerequisite to the removal of current learning problem behaviors and to the elicitation of normal behaviors. Emphasis is typically upon a single system or process sometimes arbitrarily elected as "basic."

3. *Deficit Behaviors.* Aspects that center upon the symptomatic problem itself, and the production of missing behaviors or reshaping of nonproductive behaviors. Behaviorist techniques lend themselves well to this type of emphasis though

Five approaches to learning disabilities

the theoretical approach need not be limited to Skinnerian remedial activities. The focus is always on the successful accomplishment of specific behaviors; and this is sometimes labeled as a "task" approach.

4. *Assessment.* Aspects dealing with discrimination, the measurement of behaviors of both a criterion and deficit nature, and programs built upon such psychometric data and assumptions.

5. *Management.* Aspects dealing with the establishment of some structure, system, or situation that facilitates treatment activities of varied natures.

Each of these five facets carries with it some implicit assumptions, general techniques, and approaches that function differently as remedial activities are undertaken. Each also has some discernible advantages and problems or weaknesses. It is helpful for developing practitioners to acquire an awareness of the distinguishing characteristics of different approaches and a sensitivity to the potential assets and deficits of each regardless of which theory or program they are using.

Developmental Approach

It is a clear assumption in all developmental approaches that normal, healthy, and productive behavior is the natural sequential result for an operating organism that has evidenced a particular pattern of species-peculiar growth and development. Both growth and development are involved. Growth consists primarily of an increased magnitude and quantitative characteristic that, by virtue of increased size, strength, or perhaps newly added organs, limbs, or functions, increases the behavioral range of the organism. Such growth is an expected, only rarely aberrant, experience in most individuals' lives. On the other hand, development includes all the purely growth phenomena and additionally is concerned with the integration of parallel developing subsystems (speech and vision, for example), coordination of various behaviors and functions, and the production of behaviors that increase in complexity and sometimes change characteristics as well as simply grow in magnitude.

A developmental approach is interested in establishing the sequential characteristics of normal or typical development and identifying just what should be, as dictated by the nature of the species, the current behavior in the sequence. Adequate learning behaviors rest firmly and almost completely (in the opinion of advocates of this approach) upon healthy development. Absence of adequate learning behavior indicates a disruption or malfunction of some antecedent developmental stage or event.

Some distinctively characteristic emphases or techniques typify this approach. Developmental theorists and practitioners have a genuine concern for locating and defining the specific etiology behind a learning problem. The remedial attack is decidedly more apt to be directed toward causes rather than toward symptom reduction. Any one-to-one relationship between evidenced problem areas (such as letter reversals and actual treatment activities, which seem to have some face validity relationship to the problem, is not sought or expected. When such a similar relationship is found it is more apt to be due to coincidence than to any deliberate attempt to create such a relationship. The developmentalist would say, "The best way to get rid of a problem symptom is to go back and find what is causing it and then work on the cause." There are several fairly clear steps involved in such an orientation.

1. Adopt the premise that there are developmental patterns that have been established as healthy and normal.
2. Recognize that development is not capricious but lawful; it is regular in that it has definite sequential steps; and that adequate or normal development leads to some specific behavioral capacities in the individual.
3. Assume that the breaking or interruption of the sequential pattern leads to atypical, subaverage, or abnormal behavior.
4. When problems are present, retrace the sequential steps until an aberrant step, pattern, or disruption is located.
5. After an etiologically aberrant developmental point or stage is located, retrace far back enough to assure the presence of normal developmental behavior and then cause the individual to move through subsequent developmental stages, through and past the problem-causing stage, in a normal, healthy, typical fashion.

Developmental approach to treatment

Practitioners focus on what Baller and Charles (1968) call the "orderliness and coherent design" of the developmental sequences. A great deal of attention is paid to hierarchies of behavior in terms of what behavior "naturally" should come first or second or in some other position in a developmental series. The continuity of behavior, as one developmental stage and its consequent behaviors flow sequentially into another, is emphasized. Critical stages become points of attention as it is assumed that there are times (sometimes literally temporal periods in life, at other times more in terms of the congruence of a number of events or factors happening at the same time) when the organism is best "ready" to learn a certain behavior. The role of maturation, as development and the variables of experience interact, is an important issue as well. More physiologically inclined developmentalists are apt to stress relationships between changes in structure and changes in function.

The developmental approach is not a simplistic one and often involves a large amount of highly sophisticated theorizing and examining complicated behaviors and the complex developmental systems that either produce them or are necessary prerequisites.

Many different theorists identify with the developmental approach; and a significant range of interests and approaches, obviously developmental but very different from each other, are easily noted among learning disability and special education professionals. The variety is really very wide. Some approach the subject matter from the standpoint of changes and stabilities in behavior itself as Baller, Charles, and Miller (1967) have done in their longitudinal study of retarded individuals. Others focus more on specific aspects of behavior; Piaget (1952) does his work with cognitive development and his interest is in the individual's progressive adaptive and organizational behaviors.

Some researchers relate the developmental principle almost entirely to basic physical capability as it emerges and becomes active in social and cognitive behaviors. Typical of these approaches is Gesell's (1949) extensive work in the preparation of tables of typical sequential developmental behaviors. More specifically in the area of learning disabilities, Johnson and Myklebust (1967) postulate a number of developmental-type systems that must be functional for efficient learning to develop. Their approach is notable for its assumption of more than one "integrity for learning" area, each of which must show satisfactory developmental progress, even though not all of the areas are purely physiological or biological in nature.

There are pros and cons to this approach. One of its major assets seems to be that the approach provides some type of normative standard at different ages that may be useful in determining the relative status of a child's functioning. Another is that accurate discernment of critical periods or critical stages in a child's life can be very useful in helping decision making in remediation strategy. A common remediation goal is to maximize the advantages an individual may reap from some remedial activity. If such activities can be made to interrelate with special readiness, then maximizing is more or less assured. In a similar fashion general remedial planning is aided by the general structure, particularly the sequential characteristics, of a developmental approach. Deciding what step to take next in treating a problem is always a difficult decision. If sequential models are available the process is greatly simplified.

TABLE 5-1
Summary of the Developmental Approach

ASSUMPTIONS

There are established normal and healthy developmental patterns.

Development is a lawful, predictable process.

Interference with normal developmental patterns results in aberrations.

Aberrations are removed by re-establishing a normal developmental pattern through recapitulation of those segments that have been interfered with.

PROS

Normative standards for determining the status of development are provided.

This approach aids in discerning criterial periods or stages.

Sequential format is helpful in remedial planning.

CONS

This approach does not account for successful treatment which ignores developmental recapitulation.

There is sometimes an unnecessary and inefficient emphasis on tracing etiology.

Maturation, the interaction of development with growth, may be inadequately considered.

Of course, the potential of these assets rests largely on the practitioner's willingness to accept the basic premises of the approach. Not everyone is willing to adopt all developmental assumptions without qualifications or reservations. Some criticism is leveled against developmental emphasis as an "only" approach in that some problem behaviors seem to respond to treatment of symptoms alone and apparently disappear permanently. In such cases any retracing to an earlier developmental level would seem to be at least redundant and perhaps a complete waste of time. Other problems arise with developmental approaches that rely exclusively upon a single developmental system for etiological and problem explanations. Exceptions to the rule are very difficult to explain under such a paradigm. Cases of effective compensation behaviors or spontaneous remission of problem behaviors are equally difficult to fit into a single-system developmental approach. Finally, although most well-trained developmentalists are sensitive to the problem, the role of maturation—particularly as it is applied to the chance interaction of development and experience—is ambiguous and not clearly explained by any relatively simple developmental schema. The reaction to this problem is usually for the developmentalist to divide his or her focus between a rigid developmental orientation and some other, more experientially oriented approach.

It is an interesting development in the learning disability field that one of the newer focuses of research and study, the cognitive function of learning disabled children, blends well and lends support to the developmental approach, which is one of the oldest approaches.

Researchers such as Torgeson (1977), Ross (1977), and Case (1975) are pointing to the importance of broad, overall, developmental stages in learning. They are especially concerned with the disabilitating role that deficits in general learning styles and lags in developmental capacities can create for the child facing the high production, active involvement demands of a school system geared for normal, on-schedule styles and states of readiness.

The role of the cognitivists also emphasizes the difference between the broad developmental and narrower *basic process* approaches. Unless cognition is viewed as a single basic process (and its definition by those working in the field is much too broad to allow such an attenuating definition), their work personifies an emphasis upon progressive growth and expanding capabilities as necessary prerequisites to adequate classroom performance. The assumption of the contributing importance of cognition is in no way as susceptible to challenge as some of the processes spotlighted in different basic process approaches.

Basic Processes Approach

This approach to learning disabilities has much in common with a developmental approach. Both tend to agree that there are basic, established, healthy, and normal sequences of behaviors. Both endorse the concept of a lawful and progressive nature to these sequences. And finally, both approaches assume that the disruption of the "normal" progressive development process leads to problems in the form of ineffective behaviors or in some cases total inability of the organism to perform.

Almost everyone who adopts a basic process approach subscribes first of all to a developmental approach. However, the basic processes approach makes some additional assumptions that would not be found in all developmental theories. For the basic process advocate, the sequential, developmental focus is mostly on a single or narrow process rather than an orientation to all development. In most specific basic process theories or programs there is a fundamental assumption that the system or component of the system being studied is a *priority* prerequisite to other behaviors. The search is for a single or a limited set of systems that are basic in the organism when it comes to learning behaviors. There is the assumption of some type of functional priority in a particular system and other systems, and their correlative behaviors become subsets of that basic system.

This approach is aimed essentially at unifying all development and all behavior (as related to learning) under one important framework.

TABLE 5-2
Summary of the Basic Processes Approach

ASSUMPTIONS

This approach adopts the major assumptions of the developmental approach in addition to its own.

A certain organic system or subsystem is a necessary prerequisite to learning and/or other systems.

Different organic systems have a vital functional hierarchical priority in relationship to others.

The recapitulation of normal development need focus only on the component system considered basic.

PROS

Discernment of criterial stages of readiness are more precise when applied to a single system rather than to the entire organism.

Heavy focus on a single system discourages superficial holistic explanations.

Provision of a specific system model provides a useful framework for research and measuring treatment effectiveness.

CONS

The choice of which system is basic appears to be more arbitrarily than empirically based.

Research evidence tends not to support generalization of improved learning (or other behaviors) as a result of improvement within the system.

The various advocates' presentation of different systems as basic causes confusion and weakens the argument for any one as being primary.

Since in this approach the premise is established that all (most) behaviors are functional as a result of the operations of a more basic set of behaviors or systems, remedial approaches have some distinctive characteristics. Etiology is important to this approach although the search for cause is apt to be directed along a narrower line than would be true of other developmentalists. The establishment of remedial programs or activities for the purpose of alleviating an immediate problem or for the reduction of symptoms would not be typical. Remedial activities are more likely to center around reworking a developmental sequence in the system established as basic to the process. The philosophy that a normally developed system will yield normal behavior is paramount.

A significant question encountered within this processes approach is what system is most basic or most important. It is not difficult to find differences of opinion among basic process proponents on the answer. The range of systems or functions presented as basic includes many different types and levels. A common approach is to suggest that a primary sensory function such as vision (Getman and Kane, 1964) or the motor movement processes (Barsch, 1965) is the prime functional initiator of all other learning behaviors. Still another tack recognizes the equal importance of more than one system and concentrates instead on the process of basic integration between two or more, as in the interaction of visual and motor behaviors (Kephart, 1971).

In a strikingly fundamental approach to the issue some practitioners rely on CNS functions for *all* explanations and direct all remedial activities toward the primary neural connection-pathway level (Delacato, 1966). In a slightly less conservative approach others focus on a particular aspect of CNS function, such as integrative or reciprocal innervation and functioning through cross-model and intersensory transfer behaviors (Ayres, 1972).

The rigidity with which advocates push for the recognition of a single system as basic differs too. Some feel that the basic system is fundamental in an absolute way and there are no exceptions (Delacato, 1966). Others focus on what they consider to be a principle underlying process but take care to point out that other systems should not be ignored (Frostig and Maslow, 1968).

There is some difference of opinion too, especially in the applied aspect, about whether or not remediation activities are directed at actually building or rebuilding a basic system (Delacato, 1966) or at merely learning to use the pre-existing machinery of a system more effectively (Getman and Kane, 1964).

Almost all of the pros and cons of the developmental approach can be applied to this approach as well, due to the high similarity of basic assumptions and many similar techniques. Workers favoring this approach additionally note that it provides better explanations of and means for discerning the status of readiness periods and critical stages, since these relate to a single system rather than the entire organism or a maze of partially integrated and partially independent systems. Since so much attention is given to a single system process or a smaller number of processes, this approach tends to discourage the superficiality that can be found in approaches demanding less specific explanation and analysis. A few basic process-oriented theorists have published a great deal of research information about their work through this empirical approach, but this is by no means true of all basic-process advocates. Like the developmental approach, the basic process approach encourages ongoing sequential research and study and, by providing a model for correct or normal behavior, aids the practitioner in establishing criteria and in measuring progress toward goals.

The approach also presents some problems. At present there is no really defensible way to appraise which theorist is correct in his assumption that the system or process he emphasizes is the most basic one. Neither is there clear evidence as to which of these systems, when remedially applied, yields the most effective results in removing learning disabilities. The research evidence simply is not strong enough at this point to clearly support any one theorist. It does raise enough questions to suggest care and caution in unreservedly adopting all claims as equal. The generalization of results from basic process remediation to day-by-day academic learning activities is not always clearly demonstrated. A great deal more research, better organized, controlled, and longitudinal in nature is needed before this limitation can be removed. Finally, there seems to be no simple way to resolve the paradox that arises when two programs, each advocating a different basic process or system, seem to get large, equally successful results. The problem is more than one of being able to say which is correct. It is also a matter of needing to know more about how different subsystems interrelate and interfunction. Some of the reciprocal interaction hypotheses suggested by followers of this approach show more ingenuity than empirically supported physiological evidence.

Deficit-Behavior or Task Approach

This orientation is first and foremost an intervention strategy. The intent and practice is to strike directly at the problem behavior itself in an attempt to break a nonproductive pattern and substitute more effective or efficient learning behaviors. The two most important assumptions seem to be: (1) that there is some definable criterion behavior which should be displayed by an effectively learning child; and (2) that given the right type of educational intervention (remediation) the average child can be expected to achieve the expected criterion level of performance. Some rejection of other assumptions is implicit in this approach. One is that knowledge of or attention to basic causes is important. As Kirk, one of the leading proponents of this approach (which he calls the "learning disability strategy") has said (1972), "The knowledge of the etiology of the disability in most instances is not helpful to the organization of remedial procedures." This approach also tends to place less importance on the assumption that underlying processes or developmental stages in and of themselves are necessary considerations in planning a remedial program.

The behavioral deficit approach is often called "child centered" due to its heavy emphasis on the planning of individualized programs of remediation rather than dependence on some generalized, predetermined structure or sequence which might be more true of a developmental or basic process approach. The proponents for working directly on problem behaviors rather than on some etiological target do not necessarily deny or assume the presence of some underlying systematic deficit. Rather, the approach orients on accurately assessing or observing a child's actual behavior; comparing of this behavior against the criterion behavior already defined, noting any disparity which exists; and then specifically working on removing the disparity.

This dependency upon accurate determination of an individual's psychological abilities and disabilities, as Kirk points out, is largely responsible for the qualifier "specific" being added to the diagnostic label of learning disability. Thus, the term that is currently used most often in noting children with such problems is *specific learning disability.*

This approach stresses the concept of "normalcy" in reference to general functioning level, sensory functioning, and the overall physiological status of the child. The observer assumes that learning disabled children are "normal" children with a specific or isolatable learning problem that can be attacked directly.

Adopting a behavioral deficit approach does not necessarily limit the proponent to one specific program or tight theoretical system. Instead, as those working within such a conceptual framework would point out, the orientation encourages shifting from one remedial program or activity to another as analysis indicates the existence of different deficit behaviors. Although some behavioral deficit practitioners limit themselves to a fairly closed remedial or conceptual system, a reasonable eclecticism would be more typical.

Moderately formalized systems of remediation representing this orientation can be found for most school subjects, including the major problem areas of reading and arithmetic. There are also other programs that have a broader scope than single subject matter. These include rather comprehensive coverage of wider areas of behavior such as language.

Users of the deficit behavior approach indicate several important strengths in this strategy. Because of its direct approach to problem learning behaviors, it is a fairly straightforward process to relate remedial activities and remedial goals to curriculum activities and goals. The presence of remedial activities that have face validity, which actually "look" like they are directed toward the problem, seems to be helpful in sustaining the motivation of learner and instructor alike. Such apparent validity is especially helpful when dealing with parents or others who are particularly anxious about "getting right at the problem."

Proponents maintain that a major asset is that directly working on the problem tends to avoid compensation activities. They point out that such compensation activities, while apparently helpful in a substitution sort of way, do not actually remove the deficit or problem behaviors themselves and thus over the long run tend to perpetuate causes of frustration, disappointment over failure to achieve, and similar negative effects.

Another asset seems to be that a generalization of results does not have to be established. In some approaches it is necessary to demonstrate that remedial activities generalize to the problem itself. Since the problem behavior is being worked with directly, such generalization proof is unnecessary in the behavioral deficit approach.

Those who have reservations about the behavioral deficit approach list several concerns. Since the learning disabled child is frequently suffering frustration and worry over failure in addition to the anxiety generated by the actual problem in learning, direct focus on problems tends to raise anxiety even further. Some suggest that using compensating behaviors as evidence of success and encouraging the behaviors for the positive reward feelings they engender is very helpful in any remediation activity.

On a more theoretical basis, those who emphasize the fundamental importance of developmental aspects and those who stress the importance of some underlying or more basic process would disagree with the whole orientation of this behavioral deficit approach. Their criticism centers around something like

TABLE 5-3
Summary of the Deficit-Behavior or Task Approach

ASSUMPTIONS

Intervention in problem behavior is more important than etiology.

There are definable criterion behaviors that should be displayed by an effectively learning child.

The critical variable in the child's achievement of these criterion behaviors is effective educational experiences.

Remediation should focus on experience rather than organic systems.

Defining the etiology of deficits is helpful only in preventing future problems not in planning or implementing remediation.

PROS

Remedial activities and goals correlate easily with school curricula and classroom learning activities.

A direct attack on problem behaviors avoids formation of often nonproductive compensation behaviors.

The generalization of results is easily demonstrated since there is a direct relationship.

CONS

A direct attack on the problem area may increase anxiety and maximize frustration effects.

Blocking out compensation behaviors eliminates those that are helpful as well as others.

Working on only the deficit behaviors is like treating symptoms while ignoring cause.

Children may experience motivational problems when faced with focusing on materials well below their age-grade level.

saying, "Taking an aspirin may get rid of the headache but it is better in the long run to get rid of what causes the headache."

From the standpoint of day-by-day activities in the school, the teacher often encounters problems connected with this approach when a child has to regress behaviorally to some earlier grade level in order to redevelop or reshape a presently deficit behavior. If, for example, letter recognition is the problem with reading in a third grader, then it might be necessary under this approach for the child to become involved in elementary discrimination activities more akin to those performed by a kindergartener. This can cause motivational problems in the learner and practical planning problems for a teacher involved with many pupils in an already well-structured curriculum program.

As with the other approaches, pros and cons are often unresolved in any absolute way as long as basic assumptions are unchallenged. Decisions about which approach to follow are more apt to be based on familiarity, a personal sense of fitting in with the technique, and other immediate practical concerns.

Assessment Approach

Assessment-oriented approaches usually are highly formalized and structured. Since the concept of assessment carries with it the implicit question, "Assessment of what and for what?" those who align their efforts with an assessment approach must be prepared to answer these questions in some detail. Indeed, it is usually the attempt to supply accurate and reliable data for such answers that leads to the formal articulation of such an approach. Certain behaviors are observed and appear to fit some pattern or model. A theoretical model is built and data are needed to evaulate it. Assessment instruments are then designed to supply the necessary data. Subsequent shaping and reshaping of techniques, tools, and structure follow until a model is formed for which data can be drawn and for which some type of statistical validity can be shown.

All assessment approaches follow some model that to some extent (more carefully in some cases than others) has been proven to be a valid representation of behavior and behavioral interrelationships. The model may be of an overall system, as in the Wepman, Jones, Bock, and Van Pelt (1960) description of the levels of function in the central nervous system, even though the program itself is focused on speech aberrations (Figure 5-1, page 95). Or the model may be of an assessment instrument itself as a representation of the nature of behavior within the organism, as Kirk, McCarthy, and Kirk (1968) propose for the Illinois Test of Psycholinguistic Abilities (see Figure 5-2 on page 96). In some cases the model is much less formalized but still results in a particular evaluative instrument that is designed to reflect behaviors pertinent to important facets of the model. Frostig, Lefever, and Whittlesey's (1964) *Developmental Test of Visual Perception* is an example of this latter type of model.

What essentially characterizes this approach is the close tie between a theoretical model and an assessment schema or instrument claiming construct validity. It might be said that every approach is concerned with assessment ranging from naturalistic observation on the one extreme to careful psychometric techniques on the other. This is true, but not every approach depends upon this parallel between a specific model personified and a related, often derived, instrumentation.

Assumptions include those prerequisites to any psychometric approach including the premise that there are discrete behaviors that can be measured and that this evaluative knowledge is meaningful. The meaning for these approaches is usually derived in a normative form rather than against some criterion behavior level but this is not always the case. It is usually further assumed and in some cases statistically demonstrated that factors involving sets of behaviors are identifiable and measurable.

To be technically sound any such approach should be concerned with determining and proving statistical reliability and validity, some stability of scaling

TABLE 5-4
Summary of the Assessment Approach

ASSUMPTIONS

There are discrete learning behaviors that can be psychometrically assessed with accuracy.

Data derived from such assessment is meaningful in planning and evaluating remediation.

Using a normative-actuarial structure for remediation decisions helps maintain focus and effectiveness.

PROS*

Data is always available for evaluating progress and to aid decision making.

Assessment and remediation models are parallel thus avoiding misapplication of data and concepts.

CONS

Psychometric quality (e.g. reliability and validity) is difficult to achieve and is more frequently ignored or accepted at lower standards than desirable.

The presence of a formalized assessment system lends a sense of false security and validity that tends to decrease the critical self-evaluation of method and activities.

Assessment systems, to maintain validity and reliability, must often focus on narrow bands of discrete behaviors, thus discouraging varied and diversified program application in practitioners.

Dependence upon an assessment model encourages "self-fulfilling prophesy" behaviors.

* Additional pros and cons may be added from other approaches as different assessment model programs may use this technique within another approach. For example, one could build an assessment instrument/program designed to measure/treat a single system within the *Basic Process* approach.

aspects within the instrument, and the establishment of some demonstrable relationship between model, instrument, and actual behavior parameters. Unfortunately these very critical technical aspects are too often violated, ignored, or overlooked, and the result is that claims are made for and responsibility placed upon instruments and techniques that may not have the characteristics necessary to produce accurate information.

Once an instrument or evaluative technique has been formulated and technical security established, normative profiles are frequently established with varying degrees of sophistication and complexity. Some profiles like the ITPA system (Kirk, McCarthy, and Kirk, 1968) emphasize attention to statistical detail, including error-terms and subscale variances. Others, such as the *Purdue Perceptual-Motor Survey* (Roach and Kephart, 1966), stress that the instrument is only a survey and not a definitive test instrument and, therefore, should not be used in the precise way that a more technically detailed instrument might be.

Different approaches vary in the degree to which they are dependent upon formal testing. However, almost all programs favoring this assessment approach

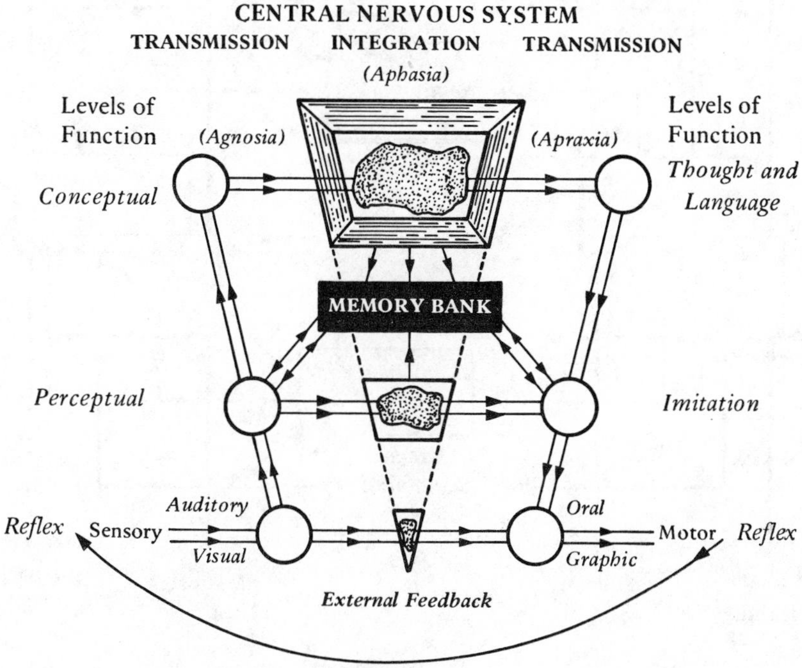

FIGURE 5-1

Wepman's Diagram of Level of Function in the Central Nervous System (From "Auditory Discrimination, Speech and Reading" by J. Wepman, *Elementary School Journal*, 1960, *60*, 325-333. Reprinted by permission of The University of Chicago Press.)

include gathering some type of data and then using some remedial activities paralleling the assessment instrument for the purpose of remedying problems. Within the remediation activities themselves, the approach may include a behavioral-deficit, basic-process, or some other emphasis.

Assets of this approach largely involve the structure and hard data supplied by

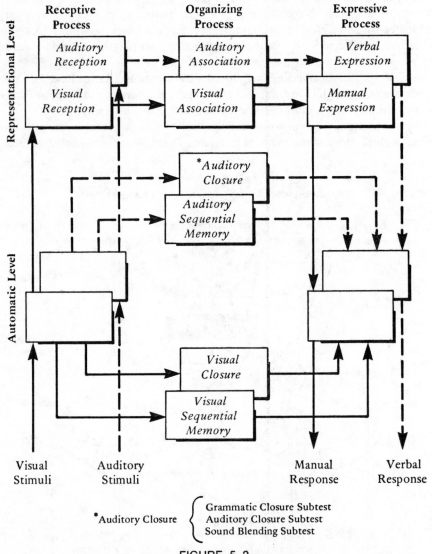

FIGURE 5-2

The Model of Psycholinguistic Behaviors upon which the ITPA Is Based (From *Psycholinguistic Learning Disabilities: Diagnosis and Remediation* by S. Kirk and W. Kirk. Copyright © 1971 by the Board of Trustees of the University of Illinois. Reprinted by permission of the University of Illinois Press.)

the instrument and program together. The ready availability of data lends itself to easier evaluation of pupil progress and the effectiveness of remedial prescriptions if the instrument is properly representative of the behavioral model applied in remediation activities—an assumption that cannot be made as easily when trying to adapt some other instrument for the same use. Although it would be possible to move in either direction, most learning disability programs of this approach do tend to categorize more in terms of *behaviors* (as defined by the assessment instrument) and less in terms of *meaningless categories.* It is vital however that the user of such instruments be thoroughly aware of the fine implications and assumptions resident in any arbitrarily selected operational definition of behaviors. Depending upon the reputation of the test without knowing what is implied in its definitions is like defining intelligence as that which an intelligence test measures—a true but largely useless statement.

There are many potential problems in this approach. The most dangerous ones seem to be those that may not be readily obvious to the untrained or psychometrically naive worker. Reliability and validity are too easily assumed to be present without evidence and the unsophisticated practitioner may be misled about the value of the data with which he or she is working. Unfortunately, this is often true despite the repeated warnings of those who have designed and built the instrument and program. Many test authors, as highly trained psychometricians, are thoroughly aware of and take care to publish the limitations of their own instruments. There is no way that author or publisher can be sure that such warnings will be read and heeded.

Criticism of this approach often centers around its tendency to foster a tight and closed system approach to varied and diversified problems. Too much dependence upon a single assessment model easily leads to failure to recognize or deal with other problems. Still other doubts about the total worth of this approach arise from the fact that assessment is often overused without any particular strategy. Also, research designed to measure the efficiency of an assessment approach is susceptible to a type of "self-fulfilling prophecy" in that only a certain type and range of data can be drawn from any subject if the evaluation always uses but one model and one measuring device. Adequate research design evaluating the outcomes of the approach should include measuring effects against different models, with other instruments, and in terms of actual on-site rather than test-defined behaviors.

Management Approaches

Management approaches differ in some very clear ways from the previous four orientations covered in this chapter. The most obvious difference is that these approaches often do not make any assumptions about models of behavior, systems of function, or similar aspects of learning disabilities. This approach is almost entirely caught up in the problem of how to make what the practitioner does more effective and more functionally productive. Exactly what is to be remedied, what criteria are to be used, and what techniques are to be involved need not be considered as part of this approach. This is not to say that practitioners who espouse a management approach have no ideas about models or techniques or these other things but rather that, to a large extent, an effectively designed mangement approach is usually considered applicable to almost any model or technique.

The most important assumption here is that good decision making rests upon clarity of intent, adequacy of data, and efficiency in the handling and processing of information. Whether the approach is conceived as being educational programming, engineered learning, or merely as an example of applied learning, theory seems immaterial. The purpose is clear: to organize or establish managerial procedures in such a fashion that the processes are prepared and followed logically, efficiently, and as precisely as possible. This behavioral engineering approach to instructional or remedial design is very congruent with much of the

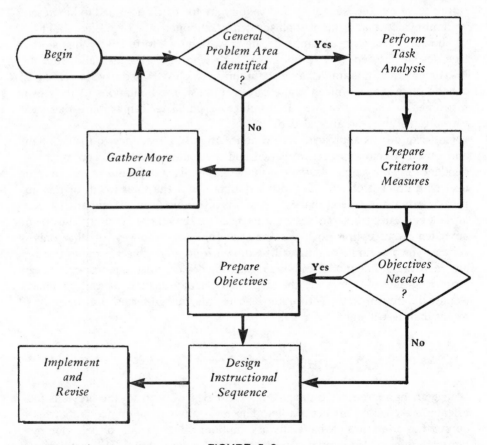

FIGURE 5-3
A Decision Plan Flow Chart for Programming Remedial Learning Disabilities Activities

contemporary work in behavior modification and other similar approaches. It is not limited to these models however and seems to have implications for a variety of other approaches.

The range of application of these principles is quite wide. Hewett (1968) has suggested the planned engineering of classrooms including physical components as well as curriculum content and teaching techniques to increase the efficacy of handling special problems. His theoretical orientation is largely developmental. Some years ago Cruickshank (1961) suggested changes in environmental situations and the management of external stimuli as an aid to working with learning disabled and hyperative children. Morasky (1973) applies systems theory to instructional design and has also demonstrated the application of these principles to the design of programs for the learning disabled to be used by paraprofessional teams. A characteristic of this approach, when well formalized, is the laying out of a decision-making plan which is easily used by all practitioners wishing to apply this system (see Figure 5-3). The last section of this text deals with an application of this approach through the media of instructional design to the problem of building remedial programs in learning disabilities.

The advantages of this approach center primarily about its organizational aspects. It aids in decision making, it helps avoid or weed out "superstitious" behavior (those activities which are done without any evidence of their effect); it aids communication between individuals of different orientations and disciplines; and it helps maintain efforts along a defined activity plan, thus avoiding loss of focus or unnoticed changes in emphasis or design.

Disadvantages are encountered because this is an approach that must be done well and consistently if it is to function effectively. Such procedures can and often are time consuming, especially in the initial stages. The time problem is lessened if opportunity exists to build a new program from scratch and the program can be first "engineered" on paper. Often though, the first step is an analysis of what is currently being done. It must be followed by evaluation and finally the establishment and testing of whatever changes seem appropriate. All of these steps are time consuming. Another concern is that the effective operation of such a system requires consistency—literally, sticking to the system design. Such consistency is often difficult to maintain, particularly among personnel who are not fully acquainted with the "game plan" or perhaps not philosophically supportive of the approach. This can be a problem with any approach, of course, but it has particularly negative effects on an approach that has predictable consistency as one of its major virtues.

Anytime a management program or an organizational scheme must be imposed on some other program or scheme, problems arise. Some teachers say that behavioral engineering in the classroom is difficult to mesh with other activities and demands additional time and/or personnel. At times there is no question but that this is a legitimate criticism. It is not always necessary though and does not cause problems as frequently, apparently, as the inexperienced would expect. Since this approach is not concerned with the content of a program *per se*, it is

TABLE 5-5
Summary of the Management Approach

ASSUMPTIONS

The efficacy of all diagnostic and remedial practices rests upon the clarity of intent, adequacy of data, and the efficiency in processing information.

Practitioners will accept useful and reject unuseful aspects of any model or program if they become well-informed of these.

Eclecticism, carefully practiced under organized managerial procedures, is preferable to more narrowly defined procedures.

PROS

This approach greatly facilitates decision making in prescriptive-diagnosis and program evaluation.

"Superstition" and nonproductive activity can be minimized or weeded out.

Communication is improved.

The best aspects of many programs and approaches can be blended into an effective, individualized remediation program.

CONS

The internal quality upon which this approach depends is difficult to consistently maintain without heavy effort.

Practitioners must be both technically capable and philosophically supportive or the entire approach breaks down.

It may be difficult to easily mesh this approach with other programs or institutional systems already functioning.

necessary for the user to supply a background of knowledge. This additional demand is seen by some as a negative factor.

Since the strategy applied in the later chapters of this book are strongly management oriented, a more detailed presentation of this approach is included in chapter 9.

Summary

It is important to reiterate that the five approaches mentioned above are simply that—approaches. They do not represent total systems, complete theories, full models, or completed designs by themselves. Many different theories and programs will make use of two or more different approaches. There is no particular advantage in trying to fit anyone's theory or program into a single approach. It is useful, though, to understand how approaches become personified in actual theories and practices and how they may be categorized in different ways. The following two chapters present a number of example theory-programs that exemplify these approaches in action. Chapter 6 views several remedial approaches as they exemplify different theoretical models. Chapter 7 looks at still other remedial approaches as they represent focus on areas of learning disabilities instead of theoretical orientations. Either type of categorization is valid, but a specific position on one factor (e.g., theoretical model used) does not relegate the approach to any predefined area on another (e.g., problems attacked). Many of the examples could have been interchanged. For example, though the Frostig system is used as an example of an assessment related theory, it could also have been used as an example of a program designed to attack perceptual problems.

6

Remedial Approaches Representing Different Theoretical Positions

As we noted in chapter 2, the wide range of behaviors that comprise the field of behavior disorders commonly labeled *learning disabilities* are viewed in a number of different ways and remediation is approached from a variety of orientations.

One way to conceptualize the historical development of the field of learning disabilities is to denote three major periods: an early *foundation* phase, followed by a program-developing *transition* phase, and finally the contemporary era, which might be labeled an *integration* phase (Wiederholt, 1974b). The transition phase, which ended about 1960, was marked by the development of a number of approaches directed specifically at remediation. While these program-building activities were created on theoretical frameworks, sometimes using an established theory and sometimes demonstrating theoretical creativity, they decidedly emphasized the production of remedial services and activities.

While the developmental and process models outlined are generally products of this transition phase, they are still quite theory-oriented to an extent and their conceptual basis focuses in varying amounts on the absolute importance of some underlying theoretical foundation. As we have noted, sometimes this foundation is totally neurological and in other examples an interacting environmental-developmental model is used, but the connection to a basic explanatory theory model is apparent and functional.

At the same time, other approaches were developing that were not as primarily theory-oriented, although they were still based upon and true to some theoretical models and assumptions. These latter approaches, perhaps more generally characteristic of the transitional historical period in which they were generated, were more problem-directed and encompassed an applied emphasis more clearly established than some other models.

As emphasis and strategies in some developing programs shifted from theoretical and etiological concerns to everyday problems of diagnosis, remedial activities, and delivery of ameliorative services, some substantial and well-known programs developed rivaling the popularity and visibility of the developmental and process models.

Finding a model that is discriminately representative of a particular approach is not a simple task. The teacher encounters at least two major problems. First, general categories of approaches are difficult to classify because of overlapping similarities in certain cases and the assigning of different concepts and meanings to identical terminology in others. Although this text uses an arbitrary breakdown of five separate approaches (developmental, basic-processes, task-focused, assessment-correlated, and management-systems-oriented), some emphasis should be placed on the word *arbitrary* since it is quite possible to categorize in other ways as different authors do. This, of course, compounds the difficulty in selecting representative models that will receive consensual agreement.

Major problems in a model-approach match

Second, although certain approaches developed by specific professionals in the field may lean strongly toward a given approach or set of theoretical constructs, it is very difficult to find theories or remedial programs that purely and exclusively portray a single approach. Most programs or models appear to fit a particular approach or emphasize a single orientation, but upon close examination—particularly when viewed in applied situations where the program is put to work—they are found to also contain elements of other approaches or orientations.

It is extremely difficult to categorize these models clearly enough to avoid overlap, confusion, or misdirection regarding the exact intent and nature of each program. Once again, the reader is reminded that these example programs or models share characteristics with others and might be logically classified in different ways. But they may also be viewed as good examples of general models and thus provide a useful frame of reference for the prospective user to apply in making strategy and program choices. Being able to apply a frame of reference, as Myers and Hammill (1969) point out, "permits the examiner to assess systematically the behavior of children who exhibit learning disorders and allows the teacher to plan a systematic and appropriate program of instruction."

Despite these difficulties, it is worthwhile to view some of the major programmatic models in learning disabilities as they seem to represent the five categories chosen for use here. Developing a sensitivity to how certain involved, complex programs are really extensions and applications of broader and more general theoretical approaches, which by implication encompass acceptance of the assumptions inherent in the adopted theoretical approach, is a valuable exercise and acquisition for the practitioner. We caution the reader to note that programs chosen as models of a certain approach might also be used as models of a different approach simply by making small shifts in emphasis or by stressing different parts of the program. Confusing as this may be to the beginner in the field, it may in actuality be an asset since it leads to flexibility in application and the availability of an eclectic approach for the trained professional working on the remediation of actual learning disorders. Such an eclectic capability seems to be characteristic of the current phase of learning disability work, a phase which was described as focusing on effective *integration* in Wiederholt's (1974b) review of historical perspectives in the field.

The examples included here have been selected because they effectively portray a certain approach. Evaluations of their substantive worth should be conducted separately.

A General Developmental Approach

A general developmental approach has two distinguishing characteristics. Obviously it must be a developmental orientation that emphasizes normal behavior based on the adequate development of a series of sequential and hierarchial events. And, if it is to be viewed as a true *general* developmental approach, it must stress and build all diagnostic and remedial activities on the universal presumption that *all* behavior is based on a single (though often complex) systematic operation that is biologically characteristic of the organism. This is in contrast to other less general approaches that, although developmental in emphasis, limit the application of such principles to a less than total view of behavior and base the studied behavior on some system that may not be basic to all aspects of behavior. An example of this less broad approach is found later in this chapter.

Patterning Theory

One of the clearest examples of a general developmental approach to working with learning disabilities is the *Patterning Theory* of Doman and Delacato (Delacato, 1959, 1963, 1966). Although quite controversial, this approach has been used by many working in the fields of learning disability or mental retardation.

According to patterning theory, all behavior is based upon the successful establishment of an identifiable series of developmental stages of normal neurological activity. The neurological organization underlying normal behaviors is assumed to be the system responsible for all adequate behaviors and when inadequacy, deviance, or dysfunction is identified, the etiology is assumed to be inadequate neurological development.

Such inadequate neurological development often leads to problems of mobility, communication, or both, according to this model. Workers pay a great deal of attention, first of all, to developing knowledge about the sequence of stages in normal development; then, to devising means for diagnosing an individual's status in regard to progress along these developmental stages; and, finally, to preparing remedial programs and activities that allow the deficit individual to recover function through the establishment of missing neurological organizational patterns.

For example, the attainment of functional mobility is conceived as consisting of thirteen sequential stages: (1) rolling over, (2) crawling in a circle or crawling backwards, (3) crawling without a pattern, (4) homologous crawling, (5) crawling homolaterally, (6) cross-patterned crawling, (7) creeping without a pattern, (8) homologous creeping, (9) creeping homolaterally, (10) cross-patterned creeping, (11) walking while holding on, (12) walking without a pattern, and (13) cross-patterned walking (Doman, Delacato, and Doman, 1964).

When a child's problem is brought to the attention of specialists following this theory, the diagnostic procedure consists of an involved examination incorporating many of the procedures used by other programs but focusing distinctively on the measurement of neurological development. The *Doman-Delacato Developmental Profile* (Doman, Delacato, and Doman, 1964), a series of tables of various stages of growth through which a normal child passes in the course of achieving normal mobility and language development, is used to assess the child's position. A treatment program prescribes activities to establish the necessary neurological patterns prerequisite to normal behavior.

Although the entire Doman-Delacato program is congruent with a general developmental approach, it is in the area of remediation that the distinctive characteristics of such an approach can most clearly be seen.

The *patterning* approach operates on the principle that "ontogeny recapitulates phylogeny," in essence the belief that maturation proceeds through stages paralleling or recapitulating the stages through which the species has evolved through the centuries (Delacato, 1959, 1963). Developmental growth for the individual proceeds through sequential development of the functions of the spinal cord-medulla, the pons, the midbrain, the cortex, and finally—last in the stages—the full neurological organization possible through the establishment of cortical hemispheric dominance (Delacato, 1963).

Failure to produce effective, normal behaviors is due to an inability to have established adequate neurological organization at one of these specific levels. Examination of existing behaviors allows for identification of the level at which the neurological organization is presumed to be inadequate. Remediation then proceeds upon the all-important assumption that a specific therapeutic experience will affect the development of a specific brain level. The focus of attack is toward that level where the child has been diagnosed as first lacking adequate neurological development. Remediation consists of following three basic treatment principles: presenting the child with normal developmental opportunities in areas where the relevant brain level is adequately organized or undamaged; externally imposing patterning activities relevant to behaviors dependent upon the yet to be developed neurological organization; and utilizing additional factors that will enhance neurological organization both in general and at the specific area involved (Doman, Spitz, Zucman, Delacato, and Doman 1960).

Advocates assume that as the organism is forced through certain behavior activities, the neurological development necessary for self-initiated activity will develop. This *patterning* approach, rigidly followed even to the extent of exactly prescribed limb movements performed for designated periods of time each day (often necessitating use of volunteer help to provide the necessary staff to maintain a demanding treatment schedule) is used in every case of treatment. Delacato (1966) defends the approach from a strategy point of view by stating that this is a matter of attacking the problem right where it is, in the nervous system, rather than by working on symptoms or peripherally related activities.

Followers of this approach assert that learning problems center around two primary areas, physical mobility and language or communication. Various parts of the program deal with functional attainments in six aspects of behavior, each of which has an obvious relationship to the learning behavior of the typical school child. These aspects include motor skills, speech, writing, reading, understanding speech, and stereognosis or tactile abilities. Regardless of the aspect involved or the level at which dysfunction is suspected, the patterning approach, based upon the general developmental principle of prerequisite sequential systems, is followed in all remediation activities.

Even though it is a substantial example of a general development approach, the Doman-Delacato patterning theory has been the subject of much criticism based upon its specific theoretical stance and therapeutic claims. Such criticism should not be considered as being directed at a general developmental approach since some of the strongest critics are themselves supporters of a general developmental approach. Most critics direct themselves specifically to a possible weakness in certain theoretical assumptions, to certain principles of remediation, and to some of the actual practices applied in the process of remediation. Criticism has stemmed from physician and educator alike. Cohen, Birch, and Taft (1970) summarize their conclusions after reviewing a number of pro and con research publications by saying, "It has been concluded that the data thus far advanced are insufficient to justify affirmative conclusions about the system of treatment." Freeman (1967) has listed the major objections most often noted by professionals of varying disciplines:

Major objections to the Doman-Delacato patterning theory

1. A tendency to ignore the natural clinical course of some patients with brain injury.
2. An assumption that this approach's methods treat the brain itself while other methods treat problems only.
3. The assumption that all not "genetically defective" may have above-average intellectual potential.
4. Making parents therapists.
5. Forceful prevention of self-motivated activities of the child.
6. Assertions about the child which increase parent's anxiety. These include

threat of the child's death, implications that universal childrearing practices may harm the child, and forcing of rigid absolute performance of patterning treatments to assure progress toward health.

7. The assumption that improvements noted are due to specific treatment factors.
8. Technical problems in the profile used in diagnosis.
9. Statistical problems overlooked in studies reporting effective treatment.

Despite these criticisms and similar questions such as those raised by prominent individuals in special education and learning disability (Cruickshank, 1968), many parents have followed this program. However, the efficacy of the patterning approach does not seem to be clearly demonstrated. We offer it here primarily as an example of a well-organized general development approach. The following example, a developmental approach oriented toward a narrower area, demonstrates many of the same principles although not in such a basic neurological context. It is also less criticized than patterning and may allow for a more unbiased consideration of the developmental orientation.

A General Basic Process Model

In his book, *The Slow Learner in the Classroom* (1971a), Newell Kephart outlined one of the most widely recognized remedial programs in learning disabilities. Although strongly developmental and easily representative of that type of model, Kephart's approach is also typical of those that stress the vital, underlying importance of some basic process that generalizes to all learning experiences.

In Kephart's program, all theoretical and applied aspects are based on a fundamental assumption: if a child has normal perceptual and motor development, he will find it easier to establish a better and more realistic relationship with the actual world in which he must perform and to which he must respond. Proponents of this program stress the broad generalization of perceptual-motor activities to learning activities of all types. As Gearheart (1973) points out in analyzing Kephart's approach, "Higher-level mental processes develop out of and after adequate development of the motor system and the perceptual system."

The Kephart approach is similar to that of more specifically neurologically oriented programs, such as Delacato's, but the emphasis is placed on a process rather than on the integrity of a specific system. Thus, the Kephart program works on many facets of perceptual-motor behavior rather than upon the establishment or reshaping of a more primitive or basic neurological system. It should not be assumed that focus on a process rather than biological system or subsystem precludes the importance or involvement of such biological aspects. The opposite is true in Kephart's approach and equally so with many other basic process models.

Kephart points out (1971a) that his work is based on a hypothetical construct of the functional operation of the human nervous system, a conception drawn from the work of Hebb (1949), but he also indicates that the construct is for use only if the practitioner finds it applies and that it should not be used if it causes problems. The emphasis and attention is directed at the process rather than the biological system or systems involved.

Proponents of this basic process model are apt to place just as much importance on the adequate functioning of the process, however, as biological developmentalists would on a biological system. Kephart has written, "It is logical to assume that all behavior is basically motor, that the prerequisites of any kind of behavior are muscular and motor responses" (1971a). Drawing upon the opinion of Piaget (1952) that overt motor learning apparently occurs before problem solving and more covert "internal" types of behavior, and upon the early works of Sherrington (1948) identifying the motor system as the initial neurological system to develop, Kephart has chosen to emphasize motor activities, broadly generalized, as the basis for all learning.

Used in the sense of this program, *motor* should be considered to mean an internalized neurophysiological event that relates to the output (external movement or body involvement) system (Dunsing and Kephart, 1965). Movement, on the other hand, is the observable, overt behavior that follows as a result of motor functioning.

The Kephart program itself (1971a) is an outgrowth of the author's extensive experience with handicapped and retarded children. After having coauthored an early work on brain-injured children with Strauss (Strauss and Kephart, 1955), Kephart worked in learning disabilities and related fields for many years. The conviction that there is a normal sequence of development in motor patterns and that learning is essentially a generalization of motor functions grew out of that experience. Kephart felt that the average child should demonstrate the types of behavior that give evidence of such normal development by about six years of age.

Too often, according to proponents of the perceptual-motor approach, children with learning problems are subjected to remedial activities or educational experiences that assume the operation of basic, functionally effective behaviors before they are actually present. Under such circumstances, remedial activities are not only nonproductive, they argue, but actually compound the problem by making further unanswerable demands on the already frustrated and handicapped child. What is needed instead, according to the Kephart orientation, is an approach that initially assesses the individual child's functional motor capability and then, where a need is demonstrated, supplies activities that help provide for the development of necessary basic motor patterns. It is important that remediation should provide for the establishment of basic patterns, not specific motor skills, since it is the absence or malfunctioning of the basic pattern that prevents normal behavior. An important part of the early development of the Kephart program was the establishment of what basic motor patterns seem to generalize to the majority of learning experiences.

Kephart presented four motor generalizations that he felt lead to the integration of basic motor patterns into functional learning capabilities. These four generalizations include:

- *Posture and balance:* Those activities that involve becoming aware of and maintaining one's relationship to the force of gravity.
- *Contract:* Those activities, such as reaching, touching, grasping, that provide information about the characteristics of the real world and possible manipulation of things and objects.
- *Locomotion:* Those activities, such as walking, that provide for the development of spacial relationships between separate objects.
- *Receipt and propulsion:* Those activities that involve some of the same aspects as the first three generalizations but deal also with objects and relationships that are not static but moving. These would include such activities as throwing, catching, pulling, and pushing.

Kephart's basic motor patterns for learning

As these motor generalizations are achieved the child gains information about the world and his or her capability to move and operate as a part of that world. Such generalizations are built in two essential ways, according to Kephart (1971): first, by increasing the differentiation of gross movement so that movements are integrated into patterns of behavior; and second, by integrating reflex activities to the point where muscle activity is purposeful rather than either random or purely reflexive.

A necessary component of such developmental progress is the organization of an effective and accurate *perceptual-motor match.* This process, a term coined by Kephart, consists of gathering and collecting more than one kind of input data about the world, collating and comparing the information, and then acting accordingly. It is necessary, Kephart practitioners say, for the child to be able to match data inputing from both motor and perceptual systems in order to function effectively in the world. At first this is done haltingly with much testing and retesting of relationships as a child will closely examine a new toy, handling and looking at it from every angle and perspective. As the skill progresses and the motor generalizations develop, the behavior becomes automatic or habitual and redundant input often is not needed. The individual learns to transfer information from one input source to another. Things "seen" may not always need to be "touched" and vice versa. Although a variety of biological systems provide perceptual-motor match information, Kephart's approach emphasizes matching visual input with motor experience.

Kephart makes an important contribution when he stresses the importance of corrective feedback, a point developed at some length by those who advocate a *systems* approach model.

In his blending of the developmental model with the basic processes model, Kephart denotes specific stages of learning development based upon the four motor generalizations. These include the *practical stage,* which is personified by the undifferentiated handling of objects and almost accidental manipulation of things by the infant who displays no evidence of these things being differentiated from himself; the *subjective stage*, where "self" becomes a visible entity and activities and relationships take place in reference to this newly formed concept; and, finally, the *objective stage*, where perception (particularly visual perception) is primary and complex and where advanced motor generalizations are demonstrated.

There are many similarities in therapy and program among Kephart and other perceptual-motor advocates who also postulate a type of basic process model (Barsch, 1965; Getman and Kane, 1964; Cratty, 1971). All seem to be developmentally oriented and stress the importance of a basic process rather than a biological system or some specific end task. Many, like Kephart, seem to place very heavy emphasis on one sensory input mode to the relative exclusion or ignoring of others—frequently stressing vision over auditory input as being most important or at least stressed heavily.

But Kephart is distinguishable for several reasons. The most prominent of these distinctions was his development of a large body of practical application materials, many books, pamphlets and other literature contributions, and the development of an assessment instrument, *Purdue Perceptual-Motor Survey* (Roach and Kephart, 1966). Kephart served for some time as editor of a series of special education publications, many of which related to his theoretical approach (i.e., the *Slow Learner Series*, published by the Charles E. Merrill Publishing Company). His own writings were involved with both assessment and treatment. The assessment instrument mentioned earlier deals with evaluation of motor generalizations in five areas: balance and posture, body image and differentiation, perceptual-motor match, ocular control, and form perception.

Kephart and his followers have prepared a large variety of training suggestions, techniques, and materials for those children thought to be deficient in motor generalization. They are usually identified by use of assessment techniques such as those encompassed by the *Purdue Perceptual-Motor Survey*. These activities include training relevant to perceptual-motor behaviors and encompass use of a walking board, a balance beam, a trampoline, angels-in-the-snow (an exercise similar to the activity of children lying in the snow making patterns by moving arms and legs), and a number of other games, stunts, and rhythm activities. Perceptual-motor match training activities include suggestions for improving gross motor behavior, fine motor behavior, visualization and auditory-motor match, with some brief mention of intersensory integration. Ocular control training suggestions involve working on visual fixation, ocular pursuit, and many classroom activities involving use of the blackboard and other equipment in games and functions using sequential control and visual search behaviors. Form perception is also included as an area for training and there are suggestions for activities relevant to differentiation of elements, matching, symbol, recognition, identification of missing parts, manipulation of items and subforms, figure-ground relationships, basic position concepts, cutting and pasting, and scanning activities.

Evaluation of this program centers primarily around the decision of whether or not to adopt the premises of the importance of the basic processes Kephart advances. If such a premise is adopted, the program stands as a good example of such an approach with well-organized assessment and training techniques and a highly explanatory body of literature with good construct validity. Major criticism of this type of approach in general has centered around the lack of a demonstration of the exclusive importance of a single basic process. Specific criticism of Kephart focuses generally on his failure to note the importance of auditory input systems and some tendency to make generalized assumptions about program effectiveness without firm empirical evidence in hand. Many learning disability practitioners are advocates of some type of perceptual-motor basic process approach and current research is directed at a clearer definition of the viability of certain specific basic processes and a better definition of program efficacy.

A Deficit-Behavior Task Model

Probably the most familiar learning disability model is Kirk and Kirk's (1971) approach to the diagnosis and remediation of psycholinguistic learning disabilities. The model is popular for several reasons. First of all, Kirk has been one of the historical leaders in the field and his influence on defining the problem and subsequent organizational and legislative events has been strong. Second, the diagnostic instrument intimately connected with this approach to working with learning disabilities, the *Illinois Test of Psycholinguistic Abilities* (Kirk, McCarthy, and Kirk, 1968), has been very widely used in both its original experimental and current revised form. And, finally, the part of the learning disability spectrum attacked by Kirk's model, language-communication behavior, represents a substantial proportion of those problems faced by workers in the field. The model arrived at the right time and place for popular adoption.

The conceptual basis for the ITPA is derived directly from the more theoretical work of some psycholinguists and others who earlier attempted to establish a model for language-communication behaviors. In the 1950s and 1960s, Osgood and others (Osgood, 1953, 1957; Osgood and Miron, 1963) formulated a communication model that combined with a similar model by Wepman, Jones, Bock, and Van Pelt (1960) to provide the basis for the ITPA and this general task approach to learning disabilities.

Using essentially an integration or mediation theory, Osgood's theoretical model attempts to account for what happens in the organism between the stimulus and the response while retaining Skinner's S—R paradigm. The Osgood model also suggested different levels of action or behavior, which later became incorporated into the Kirk mode. Wepman and his colleagues added some factors of memory, feedback, and different modalities of behavior to Osgood's conception and the combined results were also incorporated into the Kirk-ITPA model.

It may be worth noting parenthetically that some confusion has developed

PROFILE OF ABILITIES

DEVELOPMENTAL AGES

CA MA PLA — OTHER

YEARS AND MONTHS

10-0, 9-6, 9-0, 8-6, 8-0, 7-6, 7-0, 6-6, 6-0, 5-6, 5-0, 4-6, 4-0, 3-6, 3-0, 2-6

ITPA SCORES

SCALED SCORES: 64, 60, 56, 52, 48, 44, 40, 36, 32, 28, 24, 20, 16, 12, 8, 4

REPRESENTATIONAL LEVEL						AUTOMATIC LEVEL					
Reception		Association		Expression		Closure		Sequential Memory		Supplementary Tests	
Auditory	Visual	Auditory	Visual	Verbal	Manual	Grammatic	Visual	Auditory	Visual	Auditory Closure	Sound Blending

FIGURE 6-1

Profile of Abilities from the ITPA (From the *Illinois Test of Psycholinguistic Abilities, Revised Edition*, by S. Kirk, J. McCarthy, and W. Kirk. Copyright © 1968 by the Board of Trustees of the University of Illinois. Reprinted by permission of the University of Illinois Press.)

over the use of "psycholinguistic" in the model and the test title since psycholinguistics as a field of study involves much more than the language usage covered by Kirk and the ITPA. To clarify the use of the term, psycholinguistics should be operationally defined to mean *symbolic* or *linguistic* functions in the Kirk-ITPA model. It does not deal specifically with, nor is it meant to include, language development or some of the more esoteric nuances peculiar to the science of psycholinguistics.

Focusing on the functional use of language, the ITPA, as developed by Kirk *et al.*, attempts to delineate possible deficit areas by the use of three cross-referencing vectors or dimensions. These three dimensions include a set of three psycholinguistic *processes*, two *levels of organization* in language behavior, and the different *channels or modalities* of language input and output.

Psycholinguistic Processes

Normal language usage, symbolic behavior, is assumed under this model (as adopted from Osgood and others) to incorporate three major processes. These are the reception (decoding) of information or symbolic data, the expression (encoding) of the same type of data, and association (integration or organization) of symbolic material. The Kirk model denotes that learning disability behaviors or learning behavior deficits may be characterized in part by specifying the process or processes that are involved. Thus an individual who has trouble producing appropriate symbolic behavior can be said to be experiencing an expressive process problem. One experiencing difficulty understanding what someone says may be having receptive problems.

Levels of Organization

Osgood originally postulated three progressively complex levels of organization of language behavior. The first was the *projection level,* at which stimuli are conveyed to the brain primarily by established neural reflexes not requiring learning or the acquisition of adaptive behaviors. Second, Osgood suggested that behavior operates on an *integration evel,* where inputs and outputs are received, organized, and fitted together. Finally, the third and the most complex level, the *representational level,* is where meaningful mediation, communication, language, and symbolic functions operate.

Since the Kirk program is concerned with deficits due to the absence or malfunctioning of some learning-involved behaviors, his model incorporates only the higher two of Osgood's three levels. The lowest level in the Kirk model is called the *automatic level.* It deals with activities involving a memory function for language in terms of sequences and chains of behavior (e.g., letters in words and words in sentences) that are so incorporated into the organism's habit pattern that they become automatic. This level is virtually identical to Osgood's *integra-*

tion level. As Kirk and Kirk (1971) explain, such automatic behaviors, although highly organized and integrated, are less voluntary in nature and tend to involve rote learning, habitual sequencing, the synthesizing of sounds within a word and sequences of words within a standard phrase, and similar behaviors.

The higher and more complex level in the Kirk model, the *representational level*, parallels Osgood's level of the same name. Here communication behavior, which requires mediation and the use of complex and deliberate symbolic content, is organized. Deliberate interpretation and the conveying of meaning is involved.

Using the Kirk model then, it is possible to delineate a deficit behavior area by the level of communication behavior involved, whether it is automatic or representational.

Channels or Modes of Communication Behavior

By denoting differing channels of communication, Kirk invokes a third dimension or frame of reference to discriminate the deficit area to be remediated. Although language input and output may flow through a number of different combined modes or channels, Kirk's approach and the areas tested by the ITPA deal with two channels: the auditory-vocal channel, which incorporates aural inputs and vocal outputs (see the dotted line on Figure 6-2), and the visual-motor channel, where input is by vision and expression is through movement (see the solid lines on Figure 6-2).

By using all three of these dimensions, Kirk feels it is possible to define the deficit area so carefully in terms of process (receptive-organizing-expressive), level (automatic or representational), and channel (auditory-vocal or visual-motor) that remediation can be parsimoniously directed toward the specific task where the organism is having problems.

The Kirk model assists diagnosis by use of the ITPA, which includes twelve subtests that sample behavior representing the interactions of all of these dimensions with the exception of automatic-reception and automatic-expressive (again see Figure 6-2). A list of these subtests follows:

ITPA Behavior Sample Subtests

1. *Auditory Reception* assesses the ability to comprehend auditory stimuli of a symbolic nature.
2. *Visual Reception* assesses the ability to obtain meaning from visual stimuli of a symbolic nature.
3. *Auditory Association* assesses the ability to relate concepts when stimuli are presented orally.
4. *Visual Association* assesses the ability to relate concepts when stimuli are presented visually.
5. *Verbal Expression* assesses the ability to conceptually communicate vocally.
6. *Manual Expression* assesses the ability to communicate conceptions manually.
7. *Grammatic Closure* assesses the ability to make use of automatic language patterns and habits in dealing with syntax and grammatic inflections.

8. *Visual Closure* assesses the ability to identify commonly visualized objects when incomplete visual stimuli are presented.
9. *Auditory Sequential Memory* assesses the ability to reproduce orally presented symbolic sequences (numbers) from memory.
10. *Visual Sequential Memory* assesses the ability to reproduce visually presented symbolic sequences (designs) from memory.
11. *Auditory Closure* (a supplementary subtest) assesses the ability to fill in missing parts of orally presented words.
12. *Sound Blending* (a supplementary subtest) assesses the ability to group isolated, sequentially presented sounds into the words they represent.

By analyzing an individual's performance on these ten or twelve subtests the tester can draw a profile (see Figure 6-1) and inferences for remedial work. It is possible to read the profile in a number of ways. An individual's performance of

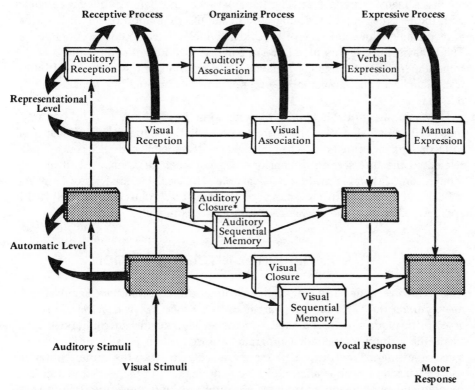

*Auditory Closure, Grammatic Closure, and Sound Blending subtests

FIGURE 6-2

Three-Dimensional Model of the ITPA (From the *Illinois Test of Psycholinguistic Abilities,* Revised Edition, by S. Kirk, J. McCarthy, and W. Kirk. Copyright © 1968 by the Board of Trustees of the University of Illinois. Reprinted by permission of the University of Illinois Press.)

language tasks can be analyzed generally on the basis of each of the three dimensions by obtaining part scores that are comprised of average scores for subtests representing a particular dimension. Or, interactions may be noted. For example, *Auditory Sequential Memory* is assessing the performance of a task that involves the association *process*, the auditory-vocal *channel*, and the automatic *level* of behavior. The ITPA also yields several other scores in addition to the profile dimensions mentioned above. The tester can obtain a composite psycholinguistic age score (PLA) which is an overall index of the level of psycholinguistic development of the child. A psycholinguistic quotient score (PLQ) may also be computed. The PLQ indicates the general rate, not level, of the psycholinguistic development of the child. Some estimate of the mental age (as would be represented on the Standford-Binet intelligence test) may also be derived from the ITPA score, using the original normative group as a basis for the conversion.

Although the ITPA occupies a prominent position in the Kirk model, the emphasis really is upon attacking demonstrated and defined language deficits with the test instrument assisting only in the discrimination of the deficit area. Remediation follows the line of specific activities related to criterion behaviors. The behaviors are represented in tasks comprising different combinations of the three dimensions of language behavior. An extension of the Kirk model into a test-related remedial-preventative program will be explored in a later section of this chapter.

The major asset of this approach seems to be in its ability to delineate areas that need remedial work. There are some limitations due to the almost total focus on language functions. The effectiveness of remedial activities conceptually related to the intersecting dimensions has not been demonstrated firmly, although some favorable evidence is available. The clear-cut analysis of language deficits and the direct, focused attack on the deficit task most clearly mark Kirk's approach as an example of the *task or deficit-oriented* model.

An Assessment-Correlated Model

Most remedial models use diagnostic instruments and techniques. Kirk depends heavily upon the ITPA and Kephart upon the *Purdue Perceptual-Motor Survey*. In assessment models, or test-related systems as Myers and Hammill (1969) label them, the training or remedial programs are more than parallel projections of some assessment procedure or items merely drawn from the same theoretical conceptualization as an evaluation instrument. Instead, in the assessment model, training and remediation procedures are intimately interwoven with an assessment instrument or procedure that is vital to the progress of remediation.

One of the most famous assessment models was developed by Marianne Frostig and involves the *Developmental Test of Visual Perception* (Frostig and Horne, 1964; 1966a, 1966b; Frostig and Maslow, 1968; Frostig, Lefever, and Whittlesey, 1964). Frostig's work, heavily influenced by Piaget, Hebb, Skinner, and Montessori (Frostig and Horne, 1968), is extremely well known to workers in learning disabilities as an example of a test-related approach. Frostig is also well-known for her own creative involvement in the founding and operation of the Marianne Frostig Center for Educational Therapy in Los Angeles, California. Coming from an extensive background of clinical observation of young children with problems, and shaped in part by the work of those dealing historically with problems of brain damage (such as Werner, Strauss, and Lehtinen), Frostig has become noted almost exclusively for remedial approaches centered around problems of visual perception in children. The work of the center deals with research, professional training, and a variety of remedial programs for individuals and small groups of preschool, elementary, and junior-high-age children. Although not exclusively visual-perceptual in content, the program's emphasis is upon those skills and activities usually considered to be visual-perceptual in nature.

As an example of a test-related program, Frostig's work in the center, in remedial programming, and in the *Developmental Test of Visual Perception* (Frostig, Lefever, and Whittlesey, 1964) is almost without equal. First published in 1961, the assessment instrument (DTVP) and related programmatic materials, commonly referred to in the field as "The Frostig," are based upon the perceptual work of Thurstone (1944), Wedell (1960), and Cruickshank, Bice, Wallen, and Lynch (1965). Influenced by many practical experiences and the professional contributions of some of those mentioned earlier, Frostig finally came to the conclusion that visual-perceptual problems represent a significant, perhaps the *most* significant segment of all learning disabilities. Following this conclusion, she structured the DTVP to measure five specific visual-perceptual subtask areas.

1. *Eye-motor coordination:* Primarily involving drawing, this subtest proposes to measure the integration of body movements and visual skills held to be important to reading and writing.
2. *Figure-ground:* This subtest involves discovery (in imbedded figures), discrimination, and outlining of specific selected figures intersected or overlapped with other figures. Here too the assumption is that the skill is directly related to reading ability.
3. *Form constancy:* Consisting of recognizing and then outlining various figures regardless of portion or size or texture, this subtest attempts to assess the individual's ability to recognize familiar figures out of typical positional or size context.
4. *Position in space:* On the surface this subtest seems somewhat similar to *form constancy* in that the individual is required to recognize specific forms in different positions. However, the emphasis here is upon rotation and reversals rather than size, position, or texture. It is assumed that such skills are related to various tasks in reading, such as recognizing that *b* and *d* or *p* and *q* differ only by virtue of their reversal or rotation aspects.
5. *Spatial relations:* A type of dot-to-dot performance is required in this subtest as the individual is required to connect dots with a drawn line to match a stimulus pattern presented by the administrator. A relationship is assumed between this behavior and word and sentence sequencing.

Frostig's
subtask areas

The grouping together of these various visual-perceptual tasks is not particularly based on any empirical model relating them in some type of cluster or hierarchy or through any such sophisticated grouping technique as factor analysis. Instead Frostig (1961) states that the reason these particular subtasks were chosen was that they all represent skills necessary for academic performance; they are all generalized rather than specific tasks, they are all developed early in the developmental process; they are areas of frequent deficit behavior in the neurologically impaired children; they may be assessed in groups; and all are areas where remediation efforts have been effective.

The DTVP yields a number of separate pieces of data. These include a perceptual quotient (PQ) which like the IQ is a comparison ratio of performance to age. A perceptual age (PA) is also presented. This is an estimate of the developmental level that may be compared to chronological age for interpretation. Subtest scores for the various subtests may be converted to scaled scores for intertest comparison to facilitate remediation planning. The DTVP is closely allied with an instructional-remedial program, the Frostig-Horne training program (1964), which is also designed for kindergarteners and first-graders. The emphasis is on practical, clear-cut worksheets and exercises that may be easily used even by those inexperienced in visual-perceptual remediation. The program includes exercises, activities, worksheets (see Figure 6-3), and procedures for evaluating and

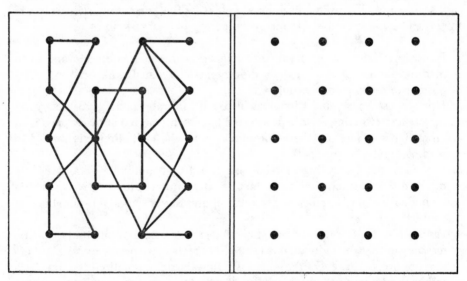

SR: Exercise 50

FIGURE 6-3

A Sample Worksheet from Materials for Use with the DTVP (From *Frostig Program for the Development of Visual Perception, Teacher's Guide,* by Marianne Frostig and David Horne. Copyright © 1973 by Follett Publishing Company, a division of Follett Corporation. Reprinted by permission.)

re-evaluating the progress of the children involved. The Frostig-Horne program deals primarily with the five areas covered by the DTVP in addition to some body concepts.

Every remedial task is directly associated with a prior or ongoing evaluation of a child's performance, using the DTVP mostly to provide the necessary assessment data. Due to its heavy emphasis on the visual mode, the Frostig-Horne program has been criticized for its relative inefficiency with children displaying problems involving the auditory channel. Although not rigidly bound to the visual mode, both the program and the assessment instrument—as well as the published interests and emphases of Frostig herself—are heavily oriented toward the visual field as personified in the selected subtasks of the assessment instrument.

In practice, the Frostig Treatment Center makes use of a broader evaluative process including use of such instruments as the ITPA, the *Wepman Auditory Discrimination Test*, the *Wechsler Intelligence Scales*, and other measurement tests. And Frostig had stated publicly that "test results should always be taken with a tablespoon of salt" (Frostig, 1967). Still, the most common use of the Frostig-Horne program is in connection with the DTVP, and the two are so closely intertwined as to be difficult to separate. The effectiveness of the program remains to be demonstrated substantially. Research results are at best mixed with little clear-cut demonstration of results attributable directly to the program materials.

Management Models

A management model is any approach that equally or more strongly emphasizes the manipulation of environment, personnel, planning, or materials as the actual content of program materials and activities. Obviously, however, it is also possible to pay close attention to content and still follow a management approach. The degree to which management is stressed as a technique in itself varies widely among the many learning disability programs. Some approaches center almost totally on the technique involved, the experiences gained, and the value of certain methods of attack with the feeling that different practitioners may then select the material and content they find relevant to the problem at hand. The work of Morasky (1973, and also as seen in later chapters in this text) exemplifies this approach. Others such as Freidus (1964) involve content considerably but place heavy emphasis on some systematic model that encorporates contemporary systems or management principles. Others, such as Cruickshank (1961), blend a specific set of content and activity concepts with highly specific ideas about physical management of individual personnel or environmental classroom space. Finally, there is a perceptable movement toward compiling and arranging remedial materials themselves in a form that lends itself to operational management techniques either specifically as directed (Valett, 1969b) or by implication and arrangement (Ashlock and Grant, 1972; Blanco, 1972; Mann and Suiter, 1974).

A Systems-Programming
Approach

The Morasky approach represents the most polemical of the systems-management approaches. It is based upon a systems analysis model that attempts carefully to define the desired criterion behaviors and then sets out to establish instructional steps or "frames" that will lead the participant from a deficit behavior position to criterion performances. Criterion-level performances are evidenced by the presence of desired behaviors and the absence of undesired or noncontributing behaviors. No emphasis is placed on content biases or theoretical issues relevant to what are or are not desirable behaviors. It is assumed that such choices are the province of the practitioner and once such decisions are made the technique may then be effectively applied to the material and behavioral goals chosen. The philosophy behind such an approach has kinship, though not necessarily direct involvement, with Skinnerian principles personified in behavior modification techniques. It is representative of current systems analysis trends.

Specific steps relevant to such an approach vary somewhat from author to author, but one such approach is outlined in detail in chapters 15 through 20.

Limited Management Approaches

Two prominent workers in the learning disability field have made limited contributions of quite different sorts related to management principles and techniques.

Freidus (1964), whose work is primarily noted for its connection with perceptual-motor remediation similar to that of Barsch or Kephart, very early suggested a theoretical model outlining a series of seven stages regarding the processing of information, which parallels modern systems theory. She postulates a potentially self-correcting servomechanism or servosystem that allows the individual, when provided with adequate information, to self-correct and successively approximate a desired or "correct" response until criterion-level behavior is reached. Freidus has proposed that the system be conceptualized as having seven stages:

Freidus's limited
management
model

1. Information is received through sensory systems.
2. Attention is paid to the information by the receiving organism.
3. Received information is compared and associated with other data previously received, stored, or associated.
4. An appropriate response is then assembled or organized.
5. The behavior is produced or a response made.
6. The organism monitors its own response for appropriateness.
7. The monitoring results are noted and stored for use with steps 3 and 4 in future behaviors.

Such a conceptual outline is a logical forerunner to most systems-management programs where efficient, consistent, and accurate monitoring and information feedback regarding correctness of response is deemed vital. Freidus chooses to analyze communication difficulties and other learning disabilities further in terms of breakdowns or hindrances to the effective functioning of this seven-stage system.

Cruickshank, long associated with research and remediation in the field of mental retardation as well as for his activity in learning disabilities, has contributed a management aspect to the field with his specific selection and outline of those principles and techniques associated with a good physical teaching environment. Cruickshank bases his theory primarily upon the behavior syndrome listed for the typical brain damage case as outlined by Lehtinen and others, commonly referred to as the Strauss syndrome. He suggests that the effective classroom environment is one in which physical aspects are carefully managed. He lists the following principles:

1. Unnecessary stimuli of both auditory and visual nature should be reduced or eliminated.
2. Environmental space should be reduced.
3. Programmed activities should be highly structured.
4. Instructional materials should have maximized stimulus value.

Aspects of a good teaching environment

This final principle is carried in some instances even to the extent of heavy use of color instead of black and white in written materials.

Details of Cruickshank's remedial programs all evidence these principles in action. The implied relationship to more broadly conceived management approaches is that by specifically structured control of physical environment, literally the management of space and things, learning is maximized.

A Program Displaying Management-Arranged Materials

The extensive work and publication of Valett (1966a, 1966b, 1967, 1968, 1969b) is a good example of a basically systems-management or programming-oriented approach where the most visible example of practice lies in the arrangement of written materials themselves.

Valett has outlined six major areas of psychoeducational growth: gross motor development, sensory-motor integration, perceptual-motor skills, language development, conceptual skills, and social skills (1967). These six areas are further subdivided into fifty-three separate tasks (see Table 2–2). Each of the major areas is defined operationally and is illustrated along with a presentation of an educational rationale. Remedial materials are presented in a looseleaf workbook format (1967) and are number keyed to these basic areas and subtasks.

Along with this general conceptualization of the range of behaviors relevant to learning disability work, Valett has contributed several psychometric instruments or profiles that lend themselves to a systematic delineation of deficit areas and the necessary subtasks relevant to remedial work in approaching criterion levels—an approach most consistent with a systems-management orientation. He has published a *Psychoeducational Profile of Basic Learning Abilities* (1966a) to be used by psychologists for coordinating and integrating both normative and clinical data regarding a child, to help in the planning of remedial activities for the individual, and for use in grouping children of similar remedial needs together.

The *Valett Developmental Survey of Basic Learning Abilities* (1966b), designed for use with preschoolers and kindergarteners, does much the same thing for the classroom teacher. A number of areas including motor integration, physical development, tactile discrimination, auditory discrimination, visual-motor coordination, visual discrimination, language development/verbal fluency, and concept developmental are assessed in a semiformal manner with some age norms for ages two to seven. Identified needs are then correlated with the fifty-three remedial subtask areas. Some, such as Gearheart (1973), feel that effective use of this instrument depends upon some specialized consultant work being readily available. However the intent to tie the data obtained from this survey to the remedial programming conceptualization is obvious.

Valett's (1968) *Psychoeducational Resource Program* relates the fifty-three items directly to a series of activities and program suggestions. Tasks are presented for teacher-classroom use at three progressive levels of difficulty designed for children from five to twelve years of age.

Valett has stated that learning disabled children especially need personal acceptance and understanding, specific psychoeducational evaluation and diagnosis, specific instruction, and success in learning (1969a, b); and his programmed materials are designed to assure that steps are taken to satisfy these needs. His use of Bloom's taxonomies (Bloom, 1956; Bloom, Krathwohl, and Masia, 1964) to identify remedially related areas and appropriate educational activities is further evidence of his involvement with a systems-management approach. His use of operationally defined goals, educational programming techniques, and detailed outlines of scheduling needs, class, and classroom organization and appropriate remedial materials also fit the management paradigm.

Summary

The programs presented here as examples perhaps share more concepts than they differ about. Still, the finer nuances of differences, the consequences of remedial material selection and techniques that must necessarily follow certain adoptions, the basic assumptions about the nature of the organism and of learning disabilities make discrimination between the five major model types a desirable component of the skills of the professional practitioner. Such knowledge has more than academic value. It has specific application in helping the worker fit the best remedial activity to the identified needs of the individual child. Such a goal has both pragmatic and moral worth.

7

Remedial Approaches to Different Problem Areas

As has already been mentioned, the range of remedial approaches available to the learning disability practitioner do not readily lend themselves to any simple classification scheme. Any attempt to relegate a particular approach to one category or another inevitably results in classification errors because of the overlap among categories themselves, and because remedial approaches tend to produce broad, general programs.

However, when faced with the need to attack deficit behaviors that appear to be localized in one definable aspect of learning behavior, it is helpful to be able to choose and select remedial approaches that offer strengths congruent with the needs observed. This chapter outlines a number of prominent remedial programs, viewed from the standpoint of offering specific assets for the remediation of certain types of problems. In contrast with the previous chapter, no attempt is made here to note how these programs might be described theoretically or to underline the basic, academic assumptions inherent in each. Obviously, orientations and basic assumptions are present, but the emphasis here is upon their application to a defined problem area.

Even within such an applied context, a word of caution must be introjected. The programs noted may, in some cases, be applied equally as well to problem types other than those described in this chapter. (The exceptions would be approaches categorically denoted as "arithmetic" or "reading" programs.) Those presented here have been chosen solely as examples of how program strengths can be mustered to solve a specific problem. It is not intended that the examples encourage the practitioner to always categorize a defined program in the ways presented here. Extended experience with many remedial programs can develop a most valuable asset in the practitioner—the ability to recognize how aspects and segments of many different programs may be applied in a practical way to successful remediation in a particular case. Such careful, selective eclecticism is to be encouraged if it is based on experience and not on unproven *a priori* assumptions.

The four major problem areas presented have been selected primarily because they represent areas of high concern in the field for which example remedial programs are readily available. Obviously, other or additional examples might have been selected. The four areas included are: language problems, reading problems, arithmetic problems, and problems in the perceptual-motor area.

Language Problems

Like so many diagnostic areas, this label represents an impossibly broad classification. In practice, one must divide and subdivide the area before finally achieving a defined segment of behavior small enough to meaningfully handle in remedial efforts. As an initial step, the area of language problems has been divided here into three subcategories: problems primarily concerned with linguistic development, problems primarily concerned with language training, and problems primarily concerned with communication skills. The reader should keep in mind that the division is arbitrary, and that differentiations are often fuzzy and program overlaps frequently encountered.

A Linguistic-Development–Focused Program

An important aspect of contemporary development in the learning disability field has been the involvement of scientific research and application from a variety of fields. The example presented here is a good example of such a cross-disciplinary contribution.

Developed at the Behavioral Sciences Institute in Monterey, California, the Programmed Conditioning for Language system (popularly known as PCL) is the result of the combined work of professionals from the fields of behavior modification and speech pathology. It draws heavily upon several established relationships within the province of speech and language development as denoted by psycholinguistic researchers.

The PCL program is designed to be used with nonverbal children, those demonstrating little evidence of possessing overt speech production. Primarily the work of Gray and Ryan (1973) and their colleagues at the Institute, this approach focuses on providing a sequential teaching program designed to establish overt speech, spoken language, in nonverbal children. The approach is channeled through the grammatic content of language (instead of using phonological or other aspects). It is based upon the assumption that grammar, apart from being the "rules" of a language, is in essence the tool that allows the speaker to generate speech, to create new sentences, and to go beyond mere rote and imitative vocalization.

Goals of PCL developers

The developers of PCL set about to accomplish two basic tasks in their initial work: first, to select those grammatical speech forms most important for the development of spoken language, and second, to establish a demonstrably effective sequence of grammatical forms for teaching purposes.

Although linguistic research has established the developmental sequence in which grammatical forms are acquired by the young child, this program elected to build teaching sequences upon the basis of teaching values rather than upon a recapitulation of the developmental acquisition of speech. That is, the sequences were selected for the ease in which they could be successfully taught and learned. In all, thirteen basic core sequences were built, designed to be followed by ten secondary sequences, and, if necessary or desirable, by a third series of eighteen sequences (Table 7–1). A glance at the first three sequences in the core portion of the program demonstrates how the choice of sequences functions.

TABLE 7-1
Sequences in the PCL Language Curriculum

CORE SEQUENCES	SECONDARY SEQUENCES	OPTIONAL SEQUENCES
1. Identification of nouns	14. Plural nouns/are	24. Was/were
2. Naming nouns	15. Are interrogative	25. Was/were
3. In/on	16. What are	interrogative
4. Is	17. You/they/we	26. What was/were
5. Is verbing	18. Cumulative pronouns	27. Does/do
6. Is interrogative	19. Cumulative is/are/am	28. Did
7. What is	20. Cumulative is/are/am	29. Do/does/did
8. He/she/it	interrogative	interrogative
9. I am	21. Cumulative what	30. What is/are doing
10. Singular noun, present	is/are/am	31. What do/does/did
tense	22. Cumulative	32. Negatives not
11. Plural nouns, present	noun/pronoun/verb/	33. Conjunction and
tense	verbing	34. Infinitive to
12. Cumulative	23. Singular and plural	35. Future tense to
plural/singular present	past tense (t and d)	36. Future tense will
tense		37. Perfect tense has/have
		38. Adjectives
		39. Possessives
		40. This/that/a
		41. Articulation

After a child has learned to (1) identify and (2) name nouns, the third sequence is to establish speech using the in/on prepositional forms. These forms do not developmentally follow noun naming; but they do lend themselves well to teaching sequences, since they allow the learning speaker to subsequently combine noun forms and verb forms. (E.g.; The *ball is* round.)

Included in the PCL are sequences that attempt to meet the multiple criteria of representing a cross section of the different forms necessary for oral speech, those most frequently used in the language, and those most useful as building blocks for further speech forms. Coupling these factors with teaching value resulted in the selection and sequence established in the program.

The program is administered following the basic behavior modification principles of presenting defined stimuli, noting carefully the resulting responses, and presenting a predefined consequence as a result of the quality of response. However, considerable effort has been made to further aid the practitioner by outlining specific administration steps as they relate to further variables affecting the successful acquisition of oral speech (Gray and Fygetakis, 1968). These additional steps include consideration of the form and nature of the model used, the nature and use of reinforcement, the scheduling of reinforcement, criterion models, stimulus modes applied, response modes to be observed, and the complexity of the task (primarily a matter of the number of units presented in the model and expected in the response).

One of the major advantages of the PCL is that it provides a carefully outlined, sequential, step-by-step program that may be specifically applied—a virtue inherited from its involvement with a typical behavior modification paradigm. It also offers a workable format in a problem area, the nonverbal child, where many practitioners experience frustration and despair. As additional assets, PCL offers some ancillary aspects that are useful and helpful. These include specific suggestions for initial evaluation, a test (Programmed Conditioning for Language Test) for measuring the parameters of language development paralleled by the PCL, directions for recording and evaluating response data, guidelines for establishing the teaching setting, and steps for involving parents in a home carry-over program. Although most often applied to severely aphasic children, the materials have been generalized to language development in the learning-disabled child.

As the authors themselves have stated, research results on the effectiveness of the program are still sparse, but the clear definition of variables and behavior involved makes the PCL a highly researchable approach. Clear, evaluative research data should become available soon.

A Language Training Program

A good example of an approach focused upon the specific area of language training is the *Preschool Diagnostic Language Program* (Hartman, 1966). This program was developed primarily for culturally disadvantaged children and based upon the ITPA both as an assessment instrument and as a model for analyzing language behavior. Hartman (1966) lists the intentions of the program:

Intentions of the
PDL program

1. To be used in compensatory preschool programs
2. To proceed from a specific diagnosis of deficit or malfunctioning behaviors
3. To provide sequential remedial programming
4. To be practical for use by preschool teachers

The program is built upon the clinical model of the ITPA (see Figure 6-2). The program itself is processed through two stages: developmental and remedial. The developmental stage, which ranges from but a few weeks to several months in length, uses ITPA profiles (see Figure 6-1) for possible intraclass groupings according to the types of deficits classified by the three ITPA dimensions. During this initial stage, the teacher informally cross-validates ITPA results through observation and also attempts to determine the severity of the deficit areas. Materials and rooms are prepared for remediation, and groupings are tried out to determine their practicality and effectiveness. The teacher establishes work routines and gives children an opportunity to become oriented to what will be demanded of them in the subsequent remedial stage.

During this stage, the teacher further assesses the child's behavior informally, attempting to cross-validate the ITPA results, while at the same time rating the severity of the problem and the areas of disabilities amenable to the formulation of subsequent remedial groups.

Hartman's materials provide guidance in learning both how to form remedial groupings and how to structure the physical classroom to accomodate such groupings.

Remedial activities call for a thoroughly structured classroom and class day that provide for maximum exposure and involvment with situations and materials relevant to an individual child's deficits. Groupings and activities directly replicate the areas assessed by the ITPA (e.g., auditory decoding, visual-motor association, etc.). Specific training procedures involve materials and programs such as those first suggested by Kirk (1966) and activities later outlined by such authors as Bush and Giles (1977). Materials prepared by Wiseman (1965), particularly in the area of language activities, are also used. Students are placed on a fairly complex schedule that assures that they flow from classroom station to station and from activity to activity as their own diagnosed deficits seem to necessitate. Mean ingful grouping according to deficit is obviously necessary to avoid chaos and confusion.

Although this program is still considered only experimental and research data are scarce, there is considerable evidence that some meaningful changes in language behavior (as measured by the ITPA) can be achieved through the use of these materials. The major problem, in interpreting and using such positive results, is one that is encountered with all test-related programs: there is a risk of a certain amount of circular validation when a particular assessment instrument is the major means to check on the effectiveness of a program built to use materials derived from that *same* test instrument or its theoretical model. Further evidence must demonstrate that not only ITPA test behaviors but other generalized language behaviors are positively affected.

Helmer R. Myklebust has also developed a general theory of learning disorders and a subsequent program of remediation. These have a narrower scope and deal primarily with language and language-related problems as they are involved in communication and effective social interaction in the learning contest (Boshes and Myklebust, 1964; Myklebust, 1964, 1968; Myklebust and Boshes, 1969; Myklebust and Johnson, 1962). Growing out of his extensive work and experience with speech and language pathology cases Myklebust's work presents a theoretical approach that is distinctly developmental in nature, but has aspects directly applicable to a wide variety of learning disorders. One of its most useful applications lies in its heavy emphasis on the need for the individual child to adequately communicate with the learning environment, to both receive and transmit meaningful information essential to effective learning. In this sense, its approach to problems of language is quite different from the two preceeding programs.

Myklebust has adopted the term *psychoneurological* to describe the type of problems typically subsumed under the more general term of learning disabilities. His assumption is that although the observed disorder or dysfunction is behavioral, the causation is neurological; and remediation should consider the developmental aspects of behavior as correlated with neurological function. He defines learning disorders or disabled children as those who evidence a *deficiency in learning* despite adequate motor ability, intelligence, hearing and vision, and emotional adjustment. This type of child is assumed to have a normal capacity for learning and, given appropriate remedial experiences, a normal outcome is expected (Myklebust, 1968). It is assumed that certain integrities are present since they are essential for learning and eventual normal outcomes are anticipated following remediation. The integrities are of three broad types related to the psychodynamic factors of motivation and adjustment, peripheral nervous system operation including sensory capabilities, and complex central nervous system functions. Specifically, the integrities include: (1) emotional adjustment as characterized by the absence of unusual acting-out or withdrawal type behaviors; (2) sensory capacities within essential normal or average limits; and (3) intellectual capacities as demonstrated by *either* a verbal or a performance IQ of 90 or above.

A deficit in learning is defined operationally as a *Learning Quotient* (achievement age divided by mental age multiplied by 100) of approximately 89 or less with some special attention given to unusual variances that appear in children younger than ten or eleven due to life-age and school experience (Johnson and Myklebust, 1967).

In a sense the Myklebust program orientation is as neurological as Delacato's but the emphasis differs greatly. All learning disorders are seen as neurogenic in origin. But, since the concept of *integrities* is assumed, the stress is on dysfunction of the neurological system (largely the brain) rather than on incompleteness or

Major assumptions of the Myklebust program

damage. The term damage implies "once but no longer complete," and this implication is not made by this program. The concept and resulting terminology of "brain damage" or "minimal brain damage" is not seen to be useful since, as Myklebust and Johnson (1962) point out, brain dysfunctions resulting in learning disabilities are not necessarily due to damage. They may be hereditary, endogenous, or *developmental* in etiology. This program focuses on problems that stem from developmental causes. Since some children with learning deficiencies show clear neurological anomalies while others do not, the presence or absence of such signs is not a discriminative factor in this approach. However, neurological correlates to disordered learning behavior are not ignored. The program assumes that a greater correlation between neurological signs and behavioral data will be established once properly sensitive discriminative evaluation techniques have been developed.

Ways of Examining Learning Disorders

The program focuses upon deficits of verbal or language usage since these seem to predominate both in terms of numbers and clearly conceptualized behavior patterns. In a manner similar to that used with the Illinois Test of Psycholinguistic Abilities, such disabilities are viewed and analyzed from several possible and different perspectives (Kirk and Kirk, 1971). First, the problem may be studied in terms of difficulties in obtaining and understanding information (input) and problems in using information (output). Viewed from this perspective, Myklebust and Johnson's (1962) developmental emphasis is obvious. They note that the "presumption is that learning is systematic and sequential and that the order of events is for output to follow, not to precede, input . . .," so that the child learns to speak after he or she learns to comprehend. Other learning behaviors are viewed in an equally sequential, developmental manner.

From a second point of view, this approach considers any learning disability from the standpoint of the sensory modalities that are involved in the relevant learning activities and any deficiencies that might be noticed. A developmental emphasis is apparent here too. Both theoretical concepts and remedial activities used by followers of the Myklebust approach assume some progressive and sequential activities. Such activities or behaviors are assumed to develop along certain patterns with some behaviors necessarily preceding others. Any failure to adequately develop prerequisite behaviors may be seen to result in subsequent deficit learning behaviors. Diagnostic searches are always directed toward pinpointing the exact level and place at which a dysfunction first appears.

Finally, Myklebust and Johnson note that learning disabilities also involve the appropriate connection of input-output experiences and behaviors and this process of *integration*, sometimes called *association* in other approaches, is the focus of a third possible way of examining learning disorders. Integration behaviors are seen to be those that involve the meaning and symbolic significance of words and ideas rather than simple rote behaviors. Since integration represents a higher order function, any deficient behaviors in this area are carefully examined not only for specific integration inadequacies but also for the possibility that more basic, necessary prerequisite behaviors may not be properly functioning.

This program directs remedial attention toward a wide range of learning disabilities that are categorized behaviorally since they are seen as related to hierarchical brain dysfunctions. These basic categories of learning disorders represent a continuum of behaviors starting with low-level, simple behaviors, and ending with very complex behaviors. An organism's normal growth and experience moves progressively through these developmental levels, and it is in this categorization and the resulting treatment and strategy scheme that the developmental emphasis can be seen most clearly.

The classifications, sometimes described as "levels of learning," are listed below:

1. *Sensation.* The adequate reception of stimuli through the sensory organs. Disorders involve the peripheral nervous system.
2. *Perception.* The conversion of sensation into some meaningful signal. Disorders involve the central nervous system at a relatively primitive level.
3. *Imagery.* The ability to retain and use perceptions even after the ongoing sensation has ceased; the addition of a memory component to perception. Disorders involve primarily the central nervous system, though in some social applications some psychodynamic factors may interact.
4. *Symbolization.* The ability (apparently present only in humans) to represent experience in both verbal and nonverbal behavior. This broad area is subdivided into areas of *inner language* (the foundation of language through understanding the meaning and intent of words), *receptive language* (ability to understand the spoken or written word, thus involving both visual and auditory modalities), and *expressive language* (a developmentally sequential behavior—first motor, then auditory, then visual—involving reciprocal communication with others).
5. *Conceptualization.* The ability to abstract and categorize. The highest level and most complex of language behaviors. Disorders are primarily integrative in nature.

Classifications
of levels of
learning

It should be clearly noted that this developmental approach firmly assumes that these behaviors are sequential in nature with more complex behaviors developing out of less complex behaviors. However, it is equally important to understand that such developmental steps or stages do not operate in isolation from each other but do indeed often overlap. Boundaries between levels are not clearly discrete.

One of the apparent strengths of this program is that its applications clearly parallel its theory so that the practitioner is not forced to generate activities and approaches based only upon implications or vague generalization.

All educational planning, according to Johnson and Myklebust (1967), must first involve a thorough diagnostic study that is designed to yield a multidimensional definition of the disability. From this multidimensional definition the teacher can develop an individualized remedial program. Such multidimensional definitions should always involve certain specific facets. These include the following:

Dimensions of multifaceted definitions

1. Whether the disability involves only one or more than one sensory modality.
2. The hierarchy-of-learning experience level at which the deficiency seems to rest.
3. Whether sensations are meaningful or nonmeaningful to the subject and whether the involved deficiency area is verbal or nonverbal.
4. The effect of the disability on various academic achievement areas such as reading and writing.
5. The effect of the deficiency on social maturity and functioning.

Through the use of a "clinical testing approach" the educator develops a comprehensive concept of readiness so that the deficient child can be approached at a variety of levels depending upon his or her readiness in each area. Since dysfunctions may occur at different levels in separate areas of behavior, it is obviously necessary to have a clear picture of the developmental growth of the child relative to individual tasks and areas of behavior rather than a unitary overall concept of readiness. Thus the clinical teacher tries to develop a program and approach that is shaped to meet the specifically individual needs of each child. The role of such a teacher is to blend knowledge of the developmental nature of learning, awareness of the specific deficiencies of the individual child, and sensitivity to the demands of the curriculum and the limits imposed by the established learning dysfunction present. Using such a blend, the teacher seeks to construct a meaningful program of educational remediation (see Figure 7–1 for the schema used by Johnson and Myklebust (1967) to illustrate such an approach).

Utilizing the developmental approach, this program presents specific ideas and suggestions for dealing with problems of auditory language, reading, written language, arithmetic, and some nonverbal disorders such as body-image problems and right-left orientation difficulties. The specific principles for remediation are listed below. They tend to underline the developmental and neurogenic emphasis.

Johnson and Myklebust's principles for remediation

1. Programs for learning disability children must be highly individualized.
2. Remediation and teaching must be directed toward the developmental level of involvement.
3. Remediation and teaching must also be directed at the type of involvement present.
4. Remedial activities must operate in harmony with multiple readiness levels.
5. Certain sequential hierarchies of behavior, such as input preceding output, must be incorporated in teaching and remediation.
6. Teaching and remediation must take into consideration the individual tolerance levels of learning disabled children.

7. Multisensory or unisensory stimulation should not be given automatically and indiscriminately but should follow careful consideration of the individual's ability to handle multisensory or to profit from unisensory inputs.
8. Teaching to the deficit should be used carefully in order to avoid proceeding past the disability area tolerance level of an individual child.
9. Teaching to the integrities should be used equally as carefully since disproportionate development can result.
10. Training in perception should be used only when specific perceptual deficits are demonstrated and not upon the presumption that all dysfunctioning individuals suffer from such deficiencies.
11. For effective teaching and remediation, different variables may need to be controlled for individual children. These include such common variables as rate, proximity, and structuring of materials.
12. A program involving both verbal and nonverbal areas of experience should be established.

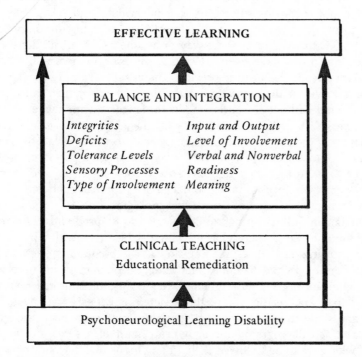

FIGURE 7–1

Schema Illustrating the Clinical Teaching Approach to Remediation of Psychoneurological Learning Disabilities (From *Learning Disabilities: Educational Principles And Practices* by D. Johnson and H. Myklebust. Copyright 1967 by Grune and Stratton, Inc., publishers. Reprinted by permission.)

All these principles emphasize the importance of considering the learning disabled child as an individual. Detailed ideas and suggestions presented in the program also stress the importance of thorough diagnosis and planning based upon the developmental, sequential, hierarchy-of-behavior concept. The Myklebust approach might also be said to represent a neurological basic process program since it is certainly true that there is a strong neurophysiological basis for the entire approach. However, remedial activities are directed toward the developmental level of observed behavior and neurogenic etiology is involved at this point only in the form of a theoretical, yet-to-be defined assumption. The program in action clearly portrays a developmental model applied to the remediation of learning disabilities.

Reading Problems

Historically, the field of learning disabilities has pinpointed reading as one of the two problem areas to receive the most attention (perceptual-motor problems constitute the other and they in themselves are often equated with reading difficulties). It is not surprising, therefore, that one would find a large number of programs focusing on reading. Indeed, almost every learning disability program involves itself with reading in some way or another. One of the more popular approaches that might have been selected as an example here is the Kirk and Kirk program already used in the previous chapter to exemplify the *deficit behaviors-specific task* systematic orientation, particularly as exemplified in the work of Hegge, Kirk, and Kirk (1970). Kirk's model deals with a wide range of language behaviors; yet, Kirk places the emphasis for diagnosis upon achieving careful discrimination of the particular language task that needs remedial attention. Gillingham and Stillman (1936, 1946, 1965) have formulated a program based upon Orton's (1937, 1939) hemispheric dominance theory, which is an example of a much more narrowly focused task and deficit area approach and is used here to exemplify an approach focusing on reading problems.

The Gillingham-Stillman program is designed to be used with third-to-sixth-grade children who are diagnosed as learning disabled (i.e., with normal sensory acuity but showing disparity in reading skills). The program is oriented toward helping the disabled child to understand and use phonics in learning to read.

The program is very highly structured. Remedial directions call for the deficient child to do no reading or reading-related activities except when in the presence and under the direction of a specially trained remedial teacher or instructor. The actual programmatic activities consist of a series of "logical sequences" which are to be followed without any individual deviance or variation. The guidelines for remediation, first published in the 1930s and republished in a number of editions since, call for an instructional program to be established in three parts: preremedial activities for the child and teacher that will help define some of the reasons the child may be having trouble; work on reading and spelling with phonetic words; and work on word phonetics for reading but not spelling.

The program's major assumption about remedial activities is that the child has been unable to learn to read, spell, and (to some extent) write by usual classroom methods and that a special program is necessary. The basis for the prescribed special programming is the belief that properly learned phonetic skills will alleviate most learning-to-read and pronunciation difficulties. The program moves through a series of progressively complex phonetic experiences and activities. It starts with simple letters, moves onto words, and then combines short words into brief sentences and simple stories. The child becomes involved with lesson activities such as reading (both silently and aloud), dictation, consonant blend work, spelling, working on syllable concepts and accenting. Some rules of spelling and pronunciation are taught along with phonetic generalization. Both visual and aural aids, like flash cards and dictation or pronunciation help, are offered but in almost every case the emphasis is upon phonetic interpretation and application of the material. Although some implications regarding cerebral dominance are present, as in Orton's theory, and were originally noted by the authors, the program is really in no way a basic-process model. The emphasis, focus, and attention of the pupil and teacher are directed toward the successful achievement of a specific task: the use of phonics in learning to read.

Assumptions of the Gillingham-Stillman approach

The program is of some distinctive interest apart from being an example of a specific task model since it was one of the earliest to stress integration among the sensory modalities as being important, an area more thoroughly explored by Ayres (1972) and others.

The Gillingham-Stillman approach uses six combinations of visual-auditory and kinesthetic (movement rather than touch) modalities. These utilize all possible combinations of the three modalities in the translation of symbols in one mode into meaning in another. The *V-A* combination, for example, involves the translation of visual symbols into sound and the *A-V* combination does the opposite.

In general this program has been rather seriously criticized for its rigidity and apparent ignorance of the actual role of auditory as opposed to visual learning and of the young child's capabilities in these areas. Critics also say that most of the remedial activities are so meaningless to a child that motivation is frequently lost or diminished.

However valid these criticisms may be, they are not related to the program's personification of a model that focuses upon a deficit task area. This model is much more limited than any basic process approach or even the general area of tasks model such as that used in Kirk's approach. The Gillingham-Stillman model attacks the area of inadequate phonetic performance in reading and this is done specifically and almost exclusively through the use of phonics training.

The work of Grace Fernald (1943) has led to a variety of reading programs somewhat different from those of either Gillingham-Stillman or the efforts of

Hegge, Kirk, and Kirk. One of the earliest pioneers in working with disabled readers, Fernald began to focus on the problems of these children early in the 1920s. Her approach, usually referred to as the VAKT method (the letters standing for visual-auditory-kinesthetic-tactile), focuses on techniques involving whole words rather than parts of words and puts more emphasis upon specific methodology than some others.

Stressing a multisensory approach, perhaps even more than Gillingham-Stillman, Fernald provides the learning reader with input through several sensory modes, utilizing tracing as an essential step in the learning-to-read process. As utilized by Harris (1970), the VAKT technique involves eight separate steps: The reader—

Steps in the VAKT technique

1. sees the printed or written word;
2. hears the word pronounced by the teacher;
3. says the word in response;
4. hears himself say the word;
5. feels the muscle involvement as the word is traced;
6. feels the tactile stimuli from fingertips while tracing;
7. sees his own hand and fingers move in tracing the word;
8. hears himself pronounce the word while tracing it.

This stimulus redundancy is assumed to assist in the cognitive implanting of the word, a neuropsychological concept as yet not firmly established but in harmony with the conclusions presented by Rood (1962) and Ayres (1964, 1972).

Fernald was one of the first to begin to characterize different types as well as levels of reading problems. Her early discrimination between severe and partial reading disability further noted that those partially disabled could be observed presenting problems such as an inability to recognize certain commonly used words, labored reading, or failure to comprehend the content of the material read. Her method also emphasizes the need for an individualization of learning methods with different pupils and utilizes the highly desirable process of informative feedback to establish such methods.

One other aspect of the Fernald work is especially worthy of notice. From her work in the Clinic School at the University of California she became sensitive to the negative effect of emotional upsets or maladjustment occurring prior to the learning experience, especially those upsets rooted in the pre-school years. Two general methods are proposed for dealing with maladjustment in order to improve the success probability of instructional experiences. The *analytic method* seeks to establish the etiology of the upset and, through insight and increased awareness by the reader, relieve the pressure they create—a classic analytical therapy approach. When such analysis proves too difficult or time consuming or ineffective, a second method—which Fernald called the *reconditioning method*—is to be applied. This second method consists of ecological and situational manipulation so that contexts and stimuli that precipitate emotional concern can be avoided. In this sense, Fernald anticipated the more contemporary management approach as expressed by Myklebust, Morasky, and many others.

Although the basic theoretical premises of the Fernald approach remain to be substantiated, it is a good example of a program that focuses on a specific problem, attempting to alleviate defined deficits by a combination of applied technique and basic theoretical assumptions.

Arithmetic Problems

Though arithmetic is one of the areas in which learning problems are most frequently encountered, the relationship of arithmetic performance to learning disabilities has been largely overlooked in favor of emphasizing reading and other areas. Brown (1975) states:

> Instruction in mathematics for the child labeled learning disabled is an area about which little has been written except that, "little has been written. . . ." Few pages are allotted to it in special education methods books, and instructional personnel seem to be on their own when trying to evaluate children or to select methodologies and materials.

A number of works such as those written by Hammill and Bartel (1978) and Mann, Suiter, and McClung (1979) include arithmetic along with several other academic curriculum areas. However only one or two programs are devoted totally to arithmetic.

Johnson (1979) has presented a behavioral task analysis strategy for relating arithmetic difficulties to learning disabilities and undertaking informal diagnosis

A behavioral task analysis strategy applied to arithmetic and L.D.

TABLE 7-2
Curriculum Content Areas Included on Cross-Referencing Charts

PRE-SCHOOL READINESS LEVEL	INTRODUCTORY LEVEL	POST-INTRODUCTORY LEVEL
1. Number Recognition	1. Vocabulary	1. Operations (multiplication and division)
2. Counting	2. Relationships, Sets	2. Rule Application
3. Grouping	3. Operations (addition and subtraction)	3. Written Problem Solving and Expression
4. Relationships Vocabulary	4. Grouping	4. Nonwritten Problem Solving and Expression
5. Verbal Expression	5. Problem Solving	
	6. Verbal Expression	

CURRICULUM AREA:
Grouping

LEARNING DISABILITY TYPE:
Closure and Generalization   Introductory **I-7**

Problem-free behavior

The child can identify missing elements in a group necessary to make it equal to another group.

Sample task where deficit child may display difficulty

Ask the child to answer such questions as: "How many nickels does it take to equal a dime?" or "How many pennies equal a nickel?" Also, pictorial problems may be used. Ask the child, "What must be added to the second group to make it equal to the first group?"

Do-it-yourself diagnostic activities

Prepare a worksheet and ask the child to tell you or draw in what must be added to the box on the right to make it the same as the box on the left.

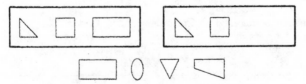

FIGURE 7-2
Sample material from the *Arithmetic and Learning Disabilities* handbook by Stanley W. Johnson. (Copyright 1979 by Allyn and Bacon, Inc.)

and remediation. The approach is based on an analysis of a variety of arithmetic curriculum areas as they interact with a number of the more commonly encountered learning disability types. The arithmetic curriculum is stratified into three levels: a pre-school readiness level representing nursery and kindergarten years;

Non-arithmetic situations where similar behaviors are required

Rigid, consistent habit-bound behavior even in the face of obvious reward for doing something different or new may be a warning. To move beyond the concrete here and now is not a typical part of the deficit child's behavioral repertoire. New solutions to old problems are more frightening than rewarding; therefore, they are frequently resisted.

Remedial objective for confirmed problems

The child will be provided with practice in completing the steps in measurement grouping which will achieve equality in number, size, etc.

Sample remedial activity

Many worksheet examples can readily be found for this area. Pictures cut from catalogs or food ads can also be used. Sample problems may include:

1 How many more pennies will it take to make the two groups the same?

2 How many more hours until 12 o'clock?

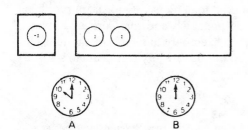

A   B

FIGURE 7-2 *(Continued)*

an introductory level paralleling the first year or two of elementary school; and a post-introductory level, which in most schools probably corresponds to the latter part of the second grade, the third grade, and in some instances the early parts of the fourth grade. Within each of these levels, the curriculum content areas most consensually included in school curricula are used (Table 7-2).

The list of included learning disabilities (Table 7-3) was drawn from applied experience in school and clinic situations and represents common labels applied by practitioners rather than definitive behavior areas.

Using a handbook format, the approach provides the practitioner with sets of materials for every combination of the eight learning disability types and the different curriculum content areas, 120 different sets in all. Each set provides examples of "problem free" behavior that the nondeficit child should be able to perform up to criterion, sample classroom tasks where deficit children may be most commonly expected to display inadequate behaviors, some informal diagnostic activities, examples of non-arithmetic behaviors where generalized problems may be expected to appear, remedial objectives for children confirmed as deficit in an interrelated learning disability/curriculum content area, and, finally, sample remedial activities designed to help achieve stated remedial objectives.

The approach is strictly behavioral with no assumptions about underlying processes or etiologies. The remedial efforts are designed to shape and elicit behaviors at established criterion levels.

No claims for concurrent or predictive validity or reliability are made since only informal diagnosis is suggested and behavior is assessed in terms of observable characteristics rather than constructs. Research is in progress designed to provide an empirical cross-validation instrument possessing the necessary psychometric characteristics, but such data are not yet available.

Perceptual-Motor Problems

The significant amount of research and applied effort in the learning disability field is devoted to perceptual-motor problems, though the proportion is probably somewhat less than it was 15 to 20 years ago. Several major programs, well known to all active in the field, might be used to demonstrate focus on problems in the perceptual-motor area. The Frostig approach and the work of Kephart, both presented in the preceeding chapter to exemplify different orientations and theoretical approaches, might well be used in this category too. Getman's Visuo-

TABLE 7-3
Specific Learning Disabilities Types Included on All Cross-Referencing Charts

1. *Memory Disabilities:* problems in recalling on demand bits of information perceived or learned a few moments before
2. *Visual and Auditory Discrimination Disabilities:* problems in recognizing that two separate auditory or visual stimuli or patterns of stimuli are the same or different
3. *Visual and Auditory Association Disabilities:* problems in relating separately perceived visual or auditory stimuli or sets of stimuli to each other
4. *Perceptual-Motor Disabilities:* problems in performing or in recognizing the need for specific eye-motor behaviors and in relating visual cues to motor responses or motor cues to visual stimuli
5. *Spatial Awareness and Orientation Disabilities:* problems in recognizing or adequately using temporal or spatial relationships between objects
6. *Verbal Expression Disabilities:* problems in communicating information to others (either by speaking or writing)
7. *Closure and Generalization (convergence-divergence) Disabilities:* problems in interpolating parts from wholes or extrapolating to wholes from parts
8. *Attending Disabilities:* problems in keeping sustained focus of attention on a problem solving task over a space of several minutes

motor program (Getman, 1965; Getman and Kane, 1964; Getman, Kane, Halgren, and McKee, 1968) is sometimes used as an example of a basic process model where the process is quite specific, less broad in nature. It is an equally good example of focus on a specific area, further narrowed by heavy dependency upon a single sensory modality.

Getman, an optometrist, worked with Kephart for a time and was exposed to much of the same formative influence of Strauss as was Kephart. In a sense it is unfair to consider Getman's program more narrow than Kephart's since it was Getman's intent that his program be applied as a supplement to normal kindergarten and first grade work, while the Kephart program is essentially for children with problems.

The limited scope of this approach is evident more in the narrowing of the basic process itself than in its application effects. Getman, who worked with the famed developmentalist, Gesell, at the Child Development Clinic at Yale, is basically a perceptual-motor theorist similar to Kephart but limits his focus and treatment procedures severely to visually oriented activities. Just as strongly developmentally and basic-process-oriented as Kephart, Getman nevertheless sees learning as functioning primarily around the *visual* perception area—an area he labels as "perception." Whereas Kephart, criticized for too much focus on vision and motor to the exclusion of auditory inputs, does generalize from a wide base of motor behaviors, Getman limits his application of the basic process model almost exclusively to visual perception alone.

The Visuomotor System has developed through five sequential developmental patterns:

- *General motor patterns:* learning by moving with the eyes providing the primary source of information and direction and guidance for exploring
- *Special movement patterns:* eye-hand coordination and all integrated body-sensory skills—again seen as primarily influenced by sight
- *Eye-movement patterns:* the replacement of touch with vision for all exploration with less one-to-one manipulatory contact necessary for inputing information
- *Visual language patterns:* the acquisition of oral language but with an emphasized role of perception in the learning of oral skills
- *Visualization patterns:* visual memory, recall, integration of old and new information, and the interpretation of new experiences on the basis of past experiences and information

Sequential patterns of the visuomotor system

Behavior can be described, according to Getman (1965), as consisting of a visuomotor complex made up of a number of different sequential developmental sequences as the individual acquires motor and perceptual ability. The human organism develops from a basic innate response mode comprised primarily of reflexes up through increasingly complex stages leading to peculiarly human, sophisticated level cognitions. Cognition is seen as the acquisition, transformation, and elaboration of information received and stored through earlier prerequisite stages, all of which strongly involve (seemingly almost to the exclusion of other modes at times, according to Getman's approach) heavy use of visual perception behaviors and abilities.

Like Kephart, Getman is criticized for underestimating the role of auditory systems in obtaining and using information vital to the learning experience. Since the basic process he emphasizes is even narrower than that of Kephart, the criticism becomes more focused. He also seems to overlook the vital role of the feedback of different sensory systems in learning. As he emphasizes vision, he is thus faced with such obvious questions as, "How do blind children learn?" Additionally, like many other program authors in learning disabilities, he seems to advocate a remedial approach without much demonstrated empirical evidence of its efficacy.

Remediation under the Getman approach largely follows the outline of his major work regarding reading readiness (Getman, Kane, Halgren, and McKee, 1968). Sequenced teacher instructions are offered along with specific exercises and activities for six major programs, including practice in general coordination, balance, eye-hand coordination, eye movement, form recognition, and visual memory. The focus is on developmental activities increasing in precision and complexity.

Another prominent approach is the Movigenic program of Barsch (1962, 1965a, 1965b, 1967). Barsch (1965a) focuses totally on man as a visual-spatial being: "At birth he is surrounded by space and 'makes his living' in space from one end of life's cycle to the other. . . ." Barsch derives or borrows a series of postulates dealing with man moving in a spatial world, and from these he establishes a list of twelve dimensions pertaining to learning. These range from the first dimension of muscular strength encountered during the early postural-transport orientations of learning to complex motor planning, which involves cognitive rehearsal, planning, and adaptive flexibility of the more mature organism.

The Movigenic Curriculum is based upon a complex series of instruction relating to the twelve dimensions. Highly developmental in his approach, Barsch allows for no individual deviation from the sequential flow of instruction through the twelve dimensions, but he instead maintains that every child should be progressed through each and every step without regard for differential deficits or presumed individual needs—a lack of flexibility for which the program has been criticized. The Movigenic Program is a particularly good example of a highly focused approach since it does not deal in any way with language or auditory-visual/reception-expression problems, being totally centered instead upon perceptual-motor problems.

8

Applying a
Systems-Management
Approach

The decade of the 1970s has witnessed a marked increase in the use of systems theory as a basis for structuring human services delivery programs. As a result, one can find numerous references to the "systems approach" in a variety of areas. (For instance, see Alexander, Barton, Schiavo, and Parsons, 1976; Case, 1976; Eaves and McLaughlin, 1977; Fleck, 1976; Nacman, 1975; and Orgurzsoff, Pennock, Sykes, and Vogel-Sprott, 1976.) In spite of its widespread utilization, there is little uniformity in what is meant by a "systems approach." However, the various applications of this approach can be categorized into two main themes. The first emphasizes the holistic or integrated conceptualization of systems. Within such a framework one is especially sensitive to the network of interacting and hierarchical units associated with any phenomenon. The second meaning for systems approach implies a methodological orientation that generally begins with an analysis of the final circumstances desired and works backward to develop the situation required to produce them.

It is the latter definition of systems approach that is being applied to the development of programs for the learning disabled. Sometimes this approach is called problem-solution oriented or centered and, although that label offers an overly simplified explanation of the methodology, the overall assumption is quite correct.

The basic premise of management approaches is that resources, both physical and human, can be assembled and applied toward the resolvement of a defined **143** problem—in this case learning behavior that fails to produce desired ends. Under the aegis of such an approach eclecticism becomes a careful selection process with choice and application highly correlated in a demonstrable cause-and-effect way with improved learning behaviors. It allows utilization of the best in materials and concepts and rejection of less defensible techniques and ideas without placing the user under the constraints of a narrow, theoretically limited system.

If current systematic approaches to learning disability problems were more firmly established in empirical bases, such constraints would be less severe in their effect. However as has been noted in previous chapters, such is not the case. The field abounds with speculation, primitive theorization, and remedial approaches based on highly tentative and poorly demonstrated assumptions.

Given such a current state of affairs, the authors of this text feel that the less limiting approach to the utilization of available materials and ideas is highly desirable. A management-systems approach offers valuable freedom of choice and application.

Foregoing chapters have provided basic information about learning disabilities in general, various approaches to the problems, theories attempting to explain or describe the problems, and some research relevant to theoretical positions.

The following six chapters deal with practical, not theoretical, techniques for dealing with some general, common problems. These are all approached, implicitly, from the viewpoint of a "desirable objective" analysis characteristic of the systems-management approach, though the relationship is not always categorically stated.

However, the chapters included in Part IV are intended to provide a specific "how to" format for those who must prepare means for remediating specific learning disabilities. This format clearly, and by intent, represents the systems approach favored by the authors of this text. The format offered in chapters 15 through 20 is general in nature, yet can be directly applied to the specialized problem areas of learning disabilities. Historically the approach illustrated in these chapters is related to the educational endeavor known as "programmed instruction."

"Superstitions" regarding programmed instruction

Over the years since the first programs came off the publishers' presses, rumors, supersititions, and expectations about "programmed instruction" have blossomed in many areas (Gotkin and Goldstein, 1967; Schramm, 1964; Skinner, 1961). There were comments like: "It's the greatest technological contribution ever made to education" and "This is the ultimate answer to requests for individualized instruction in regular classrooms and for special problems." In retrospect, maybe we should say that the authors of these comments should have known better, but the issue was complicated because one could also hear comments like "Programming exemplifies the ultimate in thought control" and "Using such rigid methods as programming, we will produce a culture of look-alike, think-alike robots." Looking back once again, we can say that these people, too, should have known better because none of these statements proved to be true.

The comments made by educators when programmed instruction was in its infancy were based on the limited evaluations of the programs available and the professional literature describing the fledgling technology. The positive instances from which one could form the concept of "a program" were limited, of course, but as time went by more programs were written and more information for evaluation became available. Educators discovered that it wasn't a new-found panacea for curing all instructional pains and illnesses, nor did the students always turn into robots after completing a few hours of programmed instruction. Indeed, a variety of events occured. For one thing some students who had difficulty in school appeared to enjoy learning from self-instructional programs, and their teachers were relieved to find a tool for reaching the problem student. For another thing, some teachers plunged headlong into "programmed this" and "programmed that," only to discover that many students regarded the materials as unstimulating and unrewarding. The behaviors the students exhibited led teachers to state, "Programs are boring—they don't work."

Another event had more to do with manufacturers than with educators; namely, machines for programmed instruction were developed and marketed with a rapidity common to modern American industry. These mechanical marvels in their various forms were called "teaching machines;" and like any productive tool they needed a plan or procedure, something to make them operable. They needed programs (Markle, 1962). About this time, however, the people who were building programs were discovering that a few simple concepts derived from experimental psychology labs did not account for all the intricacies of the learning process. In fact, in order to produce some instructional material that really worked, one had to devote an incredible number of hours and hard work to the task. So people began to say, "The hardware (teaching machines) has advanced far beyond the software (the instructional materials)."

This is not to say, however, that there were no programs whatsoever for the teaching machines. Companies could provide catalogs full of instructional programs, many of which were remarkably successful at teaching what they were supposed to teach (Hendershot, 1967). The best that could be said for others, unfortunately, was that they conformed to the standards programs were supposed to meet regardless of their effectiveness. They had all the characteristics experts said a program should have, but many of them didn't teach very well. In fact some people who were willing to create programs that *did not* conform to prescribed characteristics were experiencing unusual success. It was about this time that some educational technologists began to perceive that the *process* of preparing an instructional program might be more critical than the physical characteristics of the final product (Brethower, Markle, Rummler and Schrader, 1964; Corey, 1967; Gilbert 1962a, 1962b; Markle and Tiemann, 1967; Thiagarajan, 1971).

The Process and the Product

How can you separate the product of the instructional programming process from the process itself? It can be done by concentrating all efforts on identifying the characteristics a program (the product) must possess and ignoring the step-by-step sequence for developing that program. For example, if a program or any other product must meet specifications A, B, and C, which are physical properties, then it might not matter how you produce the product as long as it looks like other products with A, B, and C properties. Furthermore, if A, B, and C characteristics are tangible items, then intangible characteristics, such as function, can be missing without any critical effect on the evaluation of the product. And that was what instructional programmers were doing after the early professional writers told them what an educational program should look like. They were producing programs that had specific characteristics, and those characteristics were often physical, tangible properties that, at times, served inappropriate functions. For the classroom teacher this meant that materials on beginning math concepts, for instance, were made available and identified as programmed instruction. The materials looked like self-instructional materials were supposed to look, but because of that very structure they often taught a student to spell words associated with math instead of teaching the conceptualizations that the words denoted.

But as time passed it became more apparent that the product could have various characteristics and properties, and that the process of programming used would dictate the configuration of the final product.

The last six chapters of this book are designed to illustrate and teach a particular process of programming instruction rather than the characteristics of a program. That process has come to be known as the "systems approach" (Heimstra and Ellingstad, 1972; Lerner, 1976; Stolurow, 1971; Vaughn and Duncan, 1974). The reader may very well ask the question: "What is a program?" The only answer offered in this book will be: "Look at the examples—they are the result of the systems approach to instructional programming—they are programs." It is our hope that readers will learn the sequential order of the steps in the systems approach and the operations within the steps as they apply to preparing materials for learning disability problems. A program of instruction will logically flow from that process, but it need not conform to predetermined physical standards. The authors admittedly are offering an ambiguous, circular definition by implying that a program is simply the product of the programming progress, but as the reader becomes more cognizant of the steps and functions of the process he or she will be able to recognize the variety of program formats available, and, perhaps, understand the impossibility and undesirability of providing a definition. Be that as it may, the remainder of this book is devoted to the explanation, illustration, and teaching of the systems approach to instructional programming for learning disability problems.

Before delving into the matter of what the systems approach actually is, it is important to explain the use of several terms that will frequently appear in following pages. "Program," "sequence of instruction," "instructional program," and similar descriptions will be used variously to describe the same thing: the product resulting from the systems approach process. Anyone can employ that approach, but since this book deals with a specific educational problem, the person preparing the program for a learning disabilities problem has been referred to as the "teacher," "instructor," "programmer," or "practitioner." No matter what the name, it is all the same individual: the person who assumes responsibility for remediating a learning deficiency and follows the systems approach.

The "Systems Approach" to Instructional Programming

The development of a unit of instruction prepared in a systematic manner follows a sequentially ordered, step-by-step procedure in which the output of each individual step is linked to the succeeding steps. It is this step-wise, systematic progression that is called the "systems process of programming."

Within the process there are five major steps that have (Morasky, 1971, 1973) been labeled "phases." In order, the steps are listed below:

- *Step 1:* Task analysis
- *Step 2:* Preparation of criterion measures
- *Step 3:* Preparation of objectives
- *Step 4:* Preparation of instructional sequences
- *Step 5:* Implementation, testing, and revision

Steps in
instructional
programming

Each of the five major steps has numerous substeps, some of which are employed each time instruction is programmed, others of which are used only in particular circumstances. Regardless of whether some or all of the process steps are utilized, there is one major assumption that must be made before the process is initiated. The programmer must assume that *the disability to be remediated can be identified behaviorally to a degree sufficient to permit reliable assessment.* The logic of the entire systems approach depends on the acceptance of this assumption. This is, of course, closely related to the deficit-problem approach of Kirk and others that we have noted previously.

In subsequent chapters of this book each major step is dealt with in some detail so the reader can utilize either the discrete steps or the entire process. But before we launch into an extensive discussion of the intricacies of each major step, it might be profitable to preview the objectives and general activities associated with the steps.

Step 1: Task Analysis

The analysis of the task to be taught is the initial and most important aspect of the entire systems approach to programming instruction. The objective or purpost of doing a task analysis is to identify in some detail the behaviors, subtasks, discriminations, etc., which the *expert* must or does possess in order to perform the task successfully. We make the assumption here that the programmer must recognize exactly how the task is done *before* beginning to think about teaching it. One must strongly resist the temptation to assume that because the student can perform tasks, long division problems, for example, one need not analyze how to do them. It is quite common for teachers to begin immediately to consider how the task will be taught instead of considering exactly what goes into performing the task. Consider, for example, classroom behaviors like identifying colors or following a sequence of three instructions or identifying what syllables are. These are all tasks that can be broken down and analyzed for component parts before they are taught.

Another common error made by instructors at this stage is concentrating on determining what Jimmy or Sally or any other student with a learning disability will have to learn in order to do the task, rather than setting the student aside and concentrating on an analysis of the experts' knowledge and behaviors while doing the task. An expert, by the way, is anyone who can perform the task adequately. A good task analyst can observe someone doing a task, ask a few questions about the task, and derive a set of specifications regarding the performance of that task.

While completing a task analysis, the analyst or programmer can use one or more of a variety of strategies and principles. In this book the reader will be exposed to three approaches for analyzing a task: (1) discrimination, (2) flowchart, and (3) generalization task analysis techniques. Each has distinguishable characteristics; each has a separate function; each technique results in a distinctive product. The product of a task analysis is a set of behavioral specifications that must be met if the larger task is to be performed adequately and the specific disability alleviated. These behavioral specifications are the basis for the development of criterion measures.

Step 2: Preparation of Criterion Measures

If you have a set of behavioral specifications that are the result of a task analysis, then you can use those specifications quite readily to prepare tests or evaluative situations that will measure the student's ability to meet the specifications (Gallegos and Phelan, 1974). Such tests are called criterion and subcriterion measures. Let us state this another way: if the task analysis tells what one needs to be able to do in order to perform a task, then the criterion measures are designed to tell the programmer whether or not a student is able to do those things and hence perform the task. If a student can complete each subcriterion and criterion measure adequately, then he or she has the skills that are necessary for the overall task. Criterion measures play an essential role for the programmer because they can be used to indicate whether or not he has succeeded in his instructional goal. The word "criterion" is important to note here because the measures that the programmer develops represent the level of performance that is acceptable, the "criterion" level.

In order for the teacher to be confident that he or she can accurately measure the tasks and its subparts, the teacher must evaluate the criterion measure from a number of different approaches. The teacher's aim is to develop measures that come as close as possible to simulating the actual task or tasks that the student is to perform after training. A question often posed to programmers regarding a criterion measure is: "Will you accept a correct response on this criterion measure as evidence that your instructional goal has been achieved?" If the answer is "no," then the criterion measure should be revised. If the answer is "yes," then the programmer should consider whether or not behavioral objectives are necessary.

Step 3: Preparation of Objectives

Objectives typically are descriptive statements that designate where a system is or should be going. The classroom teacher often has implicit but specific teaching/learning goals such as writing one's own name, reciting the multiplication tables, or naming one's street, city, and state.

Behavioral objectives are essentially the same goals with the additional provision that the statement is an adequate description of the student's behavior after instruction. Such statements by necessity must include some mention of the conditions under which the behavior will be performed.

Any objective that meets all three criteria will serve as a means of communicating in a clear, unambiguous fashion the goals of the instruction. Behavioral objectives often serve only this communicative function, but on occasion a programmer might wish to use objective writing as a means of furthering the analysis and behavioral definition of the task (Markle, 1973). In this sense the programmer is relying on the rigor of objective writing as a help in identifying more clearly what tasks the student will perform and under what conditions they will occur. If a programmer utilizes objective writing for this analytic purpose, then he or she will probably prepare objectives directly after the task analysis and leave the preparation of criterion measure until after the objectives are completed. On the other hand, if objectives are to serve primarily a communicative function, then a programmer might wish to prepare criterion measures before writing objectives. It should be kept in mind that a well-written objective is simply a descriptive statement of what a student will be able to do after instruction is complete, and a criterion measure is the tool for evaluating what the student can do, so therefore, objectives describe the behavior a student will perform in a criterion measure. Regardless of when the objectives are written, it would be misleading to test the student's ability to do one thing in a criterion measure and to describe him or her as being able to do something else in an objective, so the correspondence between the behavior occurring in the criterion measure and that described in the objective must be exact.

The "how to" and the "when" of writing objectives is dealt with extensively in chapter 17 along with some discussion of methods for using objective writing as an analysis technique.

Having completed the task analysis, the preparation of criterion measures, and the writing of objectives, the reader should be quite ready to begin on instructional procedures in chapter 18.

Step 4: Preparation of Instructional Sequences

At this point in the systems approach the programmer designs and constructs procedures and materials that will be used for the actual teaching of the skills identified in the task analysis. The programmer begins this phase with the question: "What do I need to do to make certain that the students accurately and efficiently learn the behaviors evaluated by the criterion measures?" Since so many variables such as individual and subject matter differences influence learning, it is difficult to prescribe a rigid formula for establishing what "needs to be done" so that students will learn both accurately and efficiently. However, a few principles are available that can be used as guidelines for preparing instructional sequences. Those principles are presented in some detail in chapter 18. With practice the reader can learn to apply them in a variety of situations.

Once the programmer has developed a set of instructional sequences that conform as nearly as possible to recommended principles, then the *program* is complete and ready for testing. The package to be tested will include instructional sequences, criterion measures, and behavioral objectives if necessary. The task analysis was a working tool; that is, it was critical to the development of the final product, but it does not become a part of the final program.

In spite of the careful, systematic structuring of the program, its effectiveness as an instructional tool for remediating a specific learning disability must still be in doubt. It has not yet been shown to teach the behaviors that remove the deficit for which it was designed; therefore, it must be thoroughly tested and revised on the basis of student data.

Step 5: Implementation, Testing, and Revision

The implementation, testing, and revision aspect of the systems approach is often referred to as the "validation of the program." By implementing the program with subjects from the student target population, the teacher can establish empirically that the chosen instructional package is valid, that it does, in fact, teach the behaviors described in the objectives.

There are two methods by which the teacher will test the program: first, it will be implemented with individuals whose impressions, thoughts, behaviors, etc., will be monitored while completing the program; second, it will be given to a group of students whose correct and incorrect responses will be carefully tallied and analyzed. The analysis of the results of individual and group testing will lead to revisions of the program so that student errors are not duplicated by other students taking the same program. Following revision, the program is tested again to validate the changes that were made. Eventually, this testing-revision-retesting-revision procedure will generate a package that will produce predictable results with a given student population exhibiting a specific learning disability. Once the programmer is satisfied that the instructional program will achieve the desired results, then the systems programming process is complete and the package is ready to be used on a regular basis.

A Final Note

Experiential data have led the authors to believe that instructional programs can be developed for any type of behavior and by any instructor. This is not to say that all behaviors that instructors select as goals or objectives for students are appropriate, nor does it say that instruction for inappropriate goals should be programmed. For instance, the regurgitation of meaningless chains of words that many instructors call definitions is not any more appropriate or inappropriate as an objective for programmed instruction than for any other method of instruction. Regardless of whether or not the systems programming process is being used, the instructor is still primarily responsible for answering the question: "Why do you want them (the students) to be able to do (or know) that?" If the instructor can be certain that the behaviors to be learned do remove the specific disability, then he or she can just as readily apply the systems approach to the development of remediation procedures for learning disabilities as any other method (Bijou, 1965; Knight, 1964).

Part III

Techniques
for Solving Some
Common Problems

Though generally familiar with techniques and approaches to remedial work and having an awareness of overall administrative plans and options, the typical learning disability practitioner runs into some rather specific problem areas. Field workers frequently request supplementary help, consultants' ideas, workshops, and in-service training experiences to help them deal with these difficult areas.

Part III contains six chapters, each of which is directed at giving some direct help in one of these typical problem areas.

Chapter 9 presents practical information regarding the place and function of broad screening and diagnostic activities as opposed to specific individual diagnostic techniques. The emphasis is on information and techniques that are applicable to many different situations and that cover relatively large numbers of children.

Chapter 10 deals with the important task of communicating with other practitioners and professionals for the purpose of assembling or sharing relevant data about a particular case. Applying the principles contained in this chapter should facilitate interdisciplinary and team communication and improve the quality of the information and data assembled for working with a learning-disabled child.

Chapter 11 provides guidance on how to select and prepare remedial materials. The practitioner is provided with certain criteria against which to measure the adequacy and appropriateness of prepared materials. Some ideas on how to prepare efficient but inexpensive self-made materials are also presented.

Chapter 12 introduces the reader to various administrative and physical **153** organizations used to help bring remedial services to the deficit learner. The chapter also introduces examples of model programs and denotes purposes, objectives, and pros and cons of the major means of delivering services.

Chapter 13 is concerned with the problem of how to deal successfully with behavior problems that are frequently seen in the learning disabled child. Although there is no one-to-one relationship between learning disabilities and problem behaviors, these behaviors frequently appear together, and this chapter provides some guidance on how to work both areas at once.

Chapter 14 is directed toward the problem of counseling those who are affected by learning disabilities—the deficit learner, family, and the teacher. The emphasis is on how to handle problems of anxiety and functions other than specific remedial tasks.

9

Screening and Diagnosis

The organized attack on learning disabilities, a fairly young movement, has followed a pattern very similar to society's other attempts to alleviate major problems. A few isolated and independent groups were formed initially, each seeking to solve the problem and at the same time to draw attention to their plight in hopes of obtaining greater numbers and support. The next step always seems to be the organization of formal groups to assist in integrating and focusing the effort. The first major national organization for learning disabilities, The Association for Children with Learning Disabilities, is but a few years old.

As in the case of other social problems like alcoholism, drug abuse, and mental illness, a subsequent step to organizing remediation and treatment efforts has been the formulation of preventive measures with coordinating campaigns for disseminating important information about early symptom recognition.

In the past several years, more and more school districts have been moving to enrollment-wide screening programs that have as one major function the early recognition of children who are displaying signs of developing or impending learning disabilities. Although there are no universally accepted strategies for such screenings, there is nearly total agreement that screening does serve several functions in any organized attack on learning disabilities.

The most obvious and easily recognized function of screening is semi-prevention: problems diagnosed earlier are more likely to be less firmly entrenched and thus are more easily treated. Since many learning disabled children learn quite well, but, unfortunately, learn the wrong things (like learning incorrect phonic

Advantages
to a general
screening
approach

155

strategies in reading), identifying such misdirected learning early leads to easier extinction of bad habits and to the formulation of more productive behaviors. Other children who are not in a position to profit from typical developmental readiness periods due to some learning disability deficit are also frequently spotted in screening programs. Early diagnosis can lead to the removal of blocks to normally paced learning experiences for these children.

In addition to this easily defensible idea of getting an early start on problems, there are other advantages to a general screening procedure. Better placement is possible for children early in their school career. Such placement, or in more structured systems even some form of tracking, doesn't have to be thought of purely in terms of the stereotyped advanced, regular, and slow groupings. In today's better schools more sophisticated placement consists of matching pupils to teachers according to the pupil's peculiar needs (as identified in screening) and the teacher's peculiar attributes as identified by both teacher and administrator. Successful categorization of a pupil according to needs will consider the developmental level of the child and his or her particular approach to the learning situation, as well as general levels of abilities. It is possible, for example, to identify a young preschooler or a kindergartener who is developmentally young—small in size perhaps and socially shy—but who is also demonstrably bright and alert. This child should not be confused with or exposed to the same educational experience as a like-age child who shows developing problems based on lower ability or other problems. Even if it just consists of trying to place a child with a teacher who has a record of working "better" with such types, specialized placement helps prevent later problems in learning caused by failure to acquire important prerequisite learning behaviors at this early stage. Learning disabilities do not just happen. They are usually accidentally caused, and with little awareness of what's happening at the time. Unfortunately, the result is just as devastating as though deliberate damage and destruction were planned.

In this connection one frequently missed asset of an inclusive screening program is its identification of high and diverse levels and types of capabilities, not just problem children. The authors have experienced a screening situation where a district found that over half of the entering kindergartners in a particular urban school were found to have quite advanced reading and language readiness skills. Such knowledge helped the school officials revise their plans for these children, offer them more challenging and rewarding experiences, and thus take advantage of accelerated development during the first few months of the children's educational experience. Desirable as such actions are for their own sake, there is also a very important potential side benefit that might not be noted. The district may very well have headed off some future learning-disability problems by helping these eager and ready young students to avoid boredom, frustration, and similar behaviors that could lead to poor learning and uneven performance in later school experience.

There are also economic advantages to be gained from a well-organized screening program. It is almost always cheaper to treat problems in an early stage of development. Better placement is going to mean fewer problems of many different types later—problems that may be expensive to handle because of their advanced complexity. Frustrated pupils, for example, typically develop sporadic attendance records with a resulting loss of state matching funds, expenses for pupil attendance officers, and time-consuming parental interviews, as well as lost learning exposure. Early recognition of small problems may avoid the need for detailed individual assessment procedures at a later date, procedures that are always expensive in terms of the time consumed for involved professionals.

Another profitable aspect of screening is the acquisition of baseline data on the behavioral characteristics of entering students. Many times pupil personnel specialists and teachers will find that they have isolated a piece of student behavior that needs to be examined further for some reason. Without time-consuming effort, and sometimes even with such effort, it is not possible to determine when and to what extent the behavior has developed. A child experiencing perceptual problems for the first time in the third grade presents quite a different educational problem than a child who has developed such problems over several years and is simply observed for the first time in that grade level. Screening provides at least some simple baseline data information from which students' educational development can be measured in terms other than the traditional standardized achievement and performance batteries.

At least one more aspect of the screening process seems well worth noting for its positive effects. As we will see later in this chapter, well-planned screening programs have specific and carefully thought out objectives. Such planning almost invariably is the product of the work of many different people in and out of the classroom. Involving school personnel, and parents, too, in early organized and deliberate assaults on potential learning difficulties almost certainly guarantees better support and productive involvement in the other aspects of problem treatment and remediation that will take place at later dates in students' academic careers. Successfully attacking learning disabilities, or any social problem, involves an implicit philosophical dedication that helps encourage more active involvement. A screening program actively assists in the early shaping of such endorsement and expectations in staff and parents alike.

The Nature of Screening Activities

Some differentiation should be made between what screening is and what it is not. There are other activities that may easily be confused with screening. These include diagnostic or prescriptive assessment and behavioral analysis, all of which are activities used in this strategy for active intervention. The differences lie in at least three areas and discriminations between screening and the other activities can be on the basis of each.

Purpose

The purpose of screening is to identify or classify students successfully according to some predetermined taxonomic strategy. In the well-planned screening activity, the school is not trying to label or measure some suspected deficit area *specifically* or to achieve some type of individual psychological profile (as is the case in an assessment of activity). It might be argued that it would be profitable to obtain detailed assessment profiles of each pupil in a screening process, but the goal hardly seems realistic in terms of the time and cost involved. Also, proponents of this argument have failed to demonstrate any use for much of the data of pupils falling in average areas of a distribution ranging from problem to superior behavior.

Screening behavior usually has objectives closely correlated with the structural placement and educational capabilities of the school and its staff. Thus, if the screening decisions are predicated upon identifying advanced-reading-readiness individuals from the population, there should be some corresponding structure in the school that allows these students to be absorbed into the system in a normal way while making use of this identified characteristic. Perhaps the school has special reading readiness tracks, or teachers, classrooms, or materials so that post-screening action follows an already developed and typical flow of pupil placement and decision making. More specific assessment results are apt to require more atypical and idiosyncratic programs and placement.

Specificity

Most screening programs do not and probably should not involve any detailed or remediation or prescriptive planning assessment. The emphasis, instead, is on grouping and taxonification for the purpose of more efficient subsequent decision making. The successful screening program does not usually try to assess the specific behavior levels of individual children with problems or attempt to analyze their behavior in terms of what they are actually doing in a given educational task or situation. The former is the objective of prescriptive assessment while the latter is the main reason for individual behavior analysis as outlined in chapter 8.

A helpful way to conceptualize the output of screening procedures may be seen in Figures 9-1 and 9-2. Such a grid has cells that match the school's capacity to handle specially identified children. It is questionable to proceed with screening activities for any of the cells for which the school does not have the normal potential to act appropriately once such information is obtained. It should also be noted that the screening process and subsequent school action involves all cells and every level, not just problem cases and those in the lower or deficit cells. More involved assessment, analysis, and remediation activities will typically, on the other hand, be more concerned with cases falling in problem-related cells.

Since it is not feasible to do complete diagnostic and remediational analysis for every pupil, the general screening process, matched with the school's design for all pupils, is the first step in an active intervention program.

When screening indicates the need for additional data, it should not be automatically assumed that subsequent diagnostic examination will uncover negative data. The only safe assumption is that there is an area of behavior in a certain child (or group of children) that has yet to satisfactorily be described or assessed.

	Socialization	Reading Readiness	Physical Size or Health	Perceptual-Motor Development
Advanced Readiness Level				
No indication of any special problems or needs				
Potential problem identification uncertain				
Additional workup data warranted				

FIGURE 9-1

A Typical Identification Grid. Separate grids may be used for each child or, as is frequently done, a number of children are included on one grid by using code numbers for each child and inserting them in the proper cell.

It is frequently true, especially with younger children, that overt performance varies greatly from day to day. (It sometimes varies from moment to moment!) Screening personnel may check the "need for additional data" category for any of these reasons:

SOCIALIZATION

	Advanced Readiness	No Problem Indication	Potential Problem, Etc.	Additional Data Needed
Advanced Readiness	**1**			**2**
No Problem Indicated				
Potential Problem, etc.				
Additional Data, etc.				**3**

READING READINESS

FIGURE 9-2

A Two-Variable Identification Grid. Sometimes school personnel will wish to compare a child's or class's placement in two different areas. It is possible to combine areas and make such bivariate indentification visually easier. Children in cell one show advanced readiness on both variables; children in cell two show advanced readiness on reading, but need workups on socialization. Children in cell three need additional workups in both socialization and reading readiness, etc.

1. No behavior in this category was observed.
2. Observed behavior was so at variance with the behavior typical of this age or other behavior of this child (either too high or too low) as to suggest questionable validity or reliability.
3. Problems seem to be present.
4. Advanced skills of some undetermined nature seem to be present.
5. Separate observers (or separate observations) disagree.

Indications of a need for additional data

It is premature to conclude that requests for further data pinpoint a special child or a child with deficiencies.

Those concerned specifically with learning disabilities should make certain that screening activities include the appropriate cell to help discriminate those children needing more involved steps. At the same time the other side of the issue is equally important. It is tragic to successfully categorize children who need more specific intervention and not have the program, personnel, or time to follow through.

Instrumentation and Personnel

Screening differs from prescriptive assessment and behavioral analysis in both instrumentation and personnel. Generally speaking, assessment instruments and procedures for screening purposes are less refined, easier to administer, and less expensive (particularly in time) to use. Since the goal of screening is to make initial categorizations, not to measure or discriminate fine details of behavior, less sensitive instrumentation and less sophisticated techniques may be used. It should be categorically noted, however, that it is this precise difference in intent—broad categorization rather than individual behavior analysis—that permits use of less technical instruments and procedures. The user sacrifices some accuracy, reliability, and specificity. However, the loss is not damaging as long as the limitations are recognized and the assembled data are handled appropriately. The major pitfall to avoid at this stage of the strategy is any attempt to use this preliminary data as though it were the result of more detailed assessment and analysis.

Since the instruments themselves are less demanding in terms of the specialized administration and interpretation skills required, it is often possible and even advisable to involve more general school personnel in the screening activities than is possible in prescriptive assessment and other activities. Classroom teachers, administrative personnel, aides, and in some cases even interested parents can be used in screening without sacrificing accuracy or professionalism. Indeed, such a wide spectrum of involvement goes far in assuring broad support and continuing interest in follow-up procedures and activities.

Because screening seeks broad categorization rather than specific individual diagnosis and analysis, personnel using data obtained from a screening program should be fully cognizant of the limited conclusions that may be drawn from such data. Too often, pressure by parents or uninformed teachers is brought upon screening personnel to move from the categorization mode into individual behavior analysis or speculation about the possible implications for an individual pupil. Such highly motivated action does have a constructive side since it may provide solid backing for the subsequent steps of investigation of problems once the differences between assessment and screening are recognized. At the same time, though, pressure carries the threat of overgeneralization and the unwarranted predictive assumptions that frequently are found to be in error.

Planning a Screening Program

Once a decision has been made to establish and operate a screening program there are several identifiable questions that must be studied and answered in detail to assure any modicum of success. These are:

Questions
important to
a successful
screening
program

1. What are the identifiable purposes and objectives of the screening program?
2. How is it to be done in terms of organization, scope, and timing?
3. What techniques and procedures will be used?
4. Who is actually going to perform the necessary activities?
5. What follow-up activities will be involved?

Failure to answer any one of these questions adequately will certainly seriously limit the effectiveness of screening and will damage, if not destroy, any subsequent learning disabilities remediation program. Although we are concerned here primarily with learning disabilities, and examples and suggestions are limited to that area, it should be noted that screening programs most generally involve categorization of pupils for other areas in addition to L.D. and thus the question of the integration of different areas must be considered an important subpart of each of the questions above.

Purposes and Objectives

As we have already noted, the overall purpose of screening is to identify or classify students according to some predetermined taxonomy or structure. The decision-making process in the area of objectives consists of choosing and clearly defining the variables relevant to structure. A "successful" identification consists of a discrimination that allows or facilitates subsequent decisions to be made or events to occur at some desired rate of success. Choosing the level of discrimination that can be labelled successful depends upon several secondary decisions involving later aspects of the screening program.

Frequently the earliest stages of initiating a screening program stem from cries for help, such as "We've got to find children with reading problems earlier!" or "Pre-enrollment interviews are not good enough—we're missing too much valuable information!" The solid implication is that a screening program should discrimate *better, more effectively,* or perhaps *more quickly* or *more economically* than some

UTILIZING SCREENING GRIDS

Since screening is, in itself, a general rather than specific process, the groupings portrayed on grids should be considered coarse, preliminary groupings rather than as final diagnostic placements or guidelines for tracking.

However, the pictorial display of group characteristics as assembled in a screening program can be helpful. For example, the data displayed in Figures 9-1 and 9-2 might be used in this manner:

1. The school already has established programs or procedures for working with the special needs of children in *socialization, reading readiness, physical development and health, perceptual-motor development* or these would not be data categories in the screening program.
2. Knowing that there is a group of children with advanced reading readiness and advanced socialization skills too (Cell #1) alerts personnel (resource and classroom teachers, school psychologists, etc.) to the need for high-level materials and experiences to utilize the advanced skill levels and maintain motivation.
3. At the same time, the school has been alerted that not all the children with advanced reading readiness have definitely matched that skill with their social development. Confusing those who have with those who do not have advanced socialization skills could be disaster. Screening has helped avoid this difficulty by pointing to the need for a closer look at some children.
4. Finally, the displayed data prepares the school personnel for encountering a group of children who should be examined in more detail in both the reading readiness and socialization areas. Children found to be deficient in both may be displaying a broad developmental lag requiring some form of individualized educational planning.

existing discrimination process or system. If the pragmatic purpose is to spot children displaying patterns of problem-producing behavior more quickly, then early stages of planning should ascertain the present success rate in locating such children. Such success-failure data is often achieved after the fact and is difficult to ascertain ("Too many children are displaying problems in the third grade so we must have missed identifying them earlier.") Obviously, the ultimate evaluation of the screening program and comparison of success rates with other activities must involve some planned data-gathering for such a purpose.

Perhaps this is another way of saying that neither existing programs nor screening programs should be judged by a casual "seat-of-the-pants" evaluation. Such activity should be planned to achieve *something*, a clearly stated objective, at some desired rate or in some desirable manner, for a defined reason.

In working out clearly stated purposes and objectives, more than a success rate definition is involved. The planning must include firm decisions about what is meant by "identify" and "classify." The selection of tools and personnel will rest squarely upon such decisions; and the better planning is in these decisions, the easier and more effective later decisions and activities become.

The other major variable involved is the construction of a taxonomy or structure. We said earlier that categories of pupil identification must match the overall design of the school's ability to deal with pupils or there is a tragic waste of valuable information. This factor cannot be overemphasized in the initial planning phase. The identification and categorization structure that will be imposed upon the children processed through a screening program must make sense in terms of subsequent activities and the school personnel's capability to proceed meaningfully with data derived from such a structure. This initial step in building a screening program, the identification of purposes and objectives, is a vital one.

Organizational Decisions

Organizational decisions are largely dependent upon existing school system structure since any successful program must fit comfortably with other school activities and procedures. The major factors to be considered in organizational planning are probably scope, format, timing, and personnel (which will be dealt with here as a separate area). To a certain extent format or approach must also be considered, although a variety of approaches can be fitted to almost any organizational structure.

The scope of a screening program, like all other features, is related to its major objectives. Some school systems, suffering from a long history of not having identified children with certain types of problems, may choose to process an entire student body through the screening process regardless of age, grade, or any other factor. Such a massive program is rare, though, partly because of the time and expense involved, and partly because most systems establish objectives that are more relevant to certain selected subportions of the student body. A common target population is early elementary-age children, with the grades K through 3 being most commonly screened, although even teenagers are sometimes included and appropriate materials exist for most ages. Weiss and Weiss (1974), for example, have prepared a practical guide to test, identify, and remediate teenagers with learning disabilities.

Probably the most frequently selected program involves kindergarteners and/or first graders. Minor variations often include preschool nursery children and pupils enrolling in any of the first three grades for the first time within a school system. Programs of this type seem to work well since early identification is assured except for some pre-existing backlog of unidentified older children due to a previous lack of screening; normal screening follow-up tends to isolate those older children who have either been missed in earlier screening categorizations or who have developed problems at a later age.

The greater the age range in a screening program, the more difficult the process becomes since instrumentation and procedures and in most cases the taxonomy itself must all be adapted to fit different ages.

Planning the format of a screening program to a large extent involves selecting the degree of formal assessment versus informal assessment to be used. A screening program is really just an organized effort to gather information regarding certain behaviors and to display them in some meaningful way related to subsequent activities. The gathering of data and information may be either through formal instruments and procedures or by some consensual informal methods. Both approaches are used successfully in ongoing screening programs.

Any testing and assessment situation (even on the level of screening) includes some assumptions about the situation and the qualifications of personnel and instruments. As Smith (1969) has noted, these assumptions include five important points:

1. Examiner knowledge and skill must be adequate to the formal demands of the instrument and the situation.
2. Assessment techniques selected must be appropriate for the situation and for the objectives of screening.
3. Errors of measurement must be recognized, and results and conclusions must account for such error terms.
4. Comparable acculturation factors in assessed individuals is assumed if data is to be usable.
5. The behavior being sampled must be a good representative sample of the total behavior being assessed.

Assumptions about the situation for screening

In many cases it is easier to be sure that these assumptions are being met by using formal instruments and techniques. As we will see later, such more formal techniques do not necessarily mean including larger numbers of professionals with psychometric training. Many of the formal instruments that fit well in an elementary school screening program are suitable for use by classroom teachers and aides. On the other hand, informal techniques may be adopted by a system for a variety of reasons and often function quite well and provide much useful information.

The matter of timing screening activities, whether formal or informal, allows for a wide variety of choices. Some systems prefer to screen all children when they enter school. Others wish to take care of the screening before school entry either in the preceding semester or summer. Still others, particularly those selecting the informal approach, wait until sometime during the first school year—often in the early part of the second semester—so that pupils have had time to adjust to the school situation, and teachers and others have become better acquainted with the children they will be screening.

Time does seem to be a critical factor as far as successful identification is concerned. Its major importance is its relationship to the objectives of the screening. If the purpose is to identify children for tracking, remediation, special placement, or some similar activity, then early screening, even preschool-entry screening, seems preferable to waiting until a child is in an established routine that may have to be broken. Summer screening has the asset of more freedom of time and space for school personnel, but is also handicapped by frequent conflicts with parents' out-of-town vacation plans and the added difficulty of school-home communication during the summer.

Whatever timing decisions are made, it is wise to keep them uniform from year to year so that baseline and follow-up data may be compared and so that the results of one year's screening may be compared with those of another.

Techniques, Procedures, and Instruments for Screening

In choosing techniques, procedures, and instruments, decision makers should always keep in mind that the initial screening activity is only the first step in a sequential strategy aimed at the removal of those behaviors or behavior deficits that have caused children to be classified separately. This means, of course, that the format of data output should be easily converted into remedial planning and activities. This is of particular importance in the area of learning disabilities. Instruments that permit quick retesting without violating any reliability factor are preferred since constant evaluation of progress is an important part of any intervention strategy.

No instrument or activity should be selected solely for its own sake. No test battery, despite its reputation, should be used if it does not mesh well with purposes, objectives, and the general organizational structure. Too many file drawers are full of data that are useless to those trying to apply intervention strategies, but gathered anyway because "everyone seems to use that test" or "that procedure has a good reputation." Here, as in many other facets of the intervention strategy, the individual planners within the system should consciously assess their own ability to plan, choose, select, and organize meaningfully to fit available materials to their needs.

There are some guidelines to help in the selection of the necessary instruments or procedures. The repeated use of certain approaches by others suggests that they may serve at least some functional purpose as long as the various programs have common objectives. Although most screening programs are structured for the identification of more areas than those relating to learning disabilities, information contained here is limited to the learning disability area alone.

The authors have found that a common behavior to be found in children later diagnosed as learning disabled is a general aversion to learning activities. Such avoidance behavior is not limited to learning disabilities, for that is certainly not the case. But an initial step in discriminating children with and without learning disabilities might focus on the presence of such behaviors. Learning situations might be defined as any type of activity oriented toward new material and new experiences. They should also include activities inside and outside the classroom: the playground, home, and other locations may provide just as many behavior indicators as the regular classroom does. It is not necessary for a child to have formal school experience to demonstrate such aversions. Preschoolers also demonstrate avoidance behaviors due to aversion to learning situations.

We should reiterate that the purpose of screening is to discriminate broad groupings of behaviors and not to provide a thorough analysis of one individual's behavior in terms of either constructive or deficit aspects. Thus, those behaviors observed for hints of aversion to learning situations are not as precise and well defined as behaviors one would focus on in a thorough diagnosis and behavior analysis. As personnel make early choices about instruments and procedures in a screening program designed to pick out potential L.D. cases, some attention might be paid to providing means, formal instruments, or informal techniques for noting the presence of such behaviors and their relationship to a child's general aversion to learning as a result of the problems being present. It may be helpful to note several areas where observers repeatedly seem to find some preliminary evidence of such aversion. At least six broad areas seem to come to attention over and over:

1. *Auditory and visual attention.* Although described in various terms, the major symptom displayed is lack of attention to meaningful stimuli, often isolated to either the visual or auditory mode. The complaint is often voiced as "You might as well be talking to a wall...he simply doesn't listen!" Similar problems may be noted in the visual area or sometimes both. The child avoids learning by "turning off."
2. *Motor coordination.* "Clumsy," "His hands get in the way of everything he does." These and similar complaints seem to follow children with less than adequate motor coordination. When such complaints are coupled with a child's awareness of his or her own "stumble-bum" behavior, aversion is frequently a corollary behavior.
3. *Frustration tolerance.* Sticking with something that is difficult and sometimes slow in producing results is much easier when there is some positive reward or some reinforcement for doing so. The child who finds learning aversive has low frustration tolerance and often displays frustration openly and quickly.
4. *Behavior swings.* Moodiness and quick change of emotional tone can be symptomatic of a number of different problems. It is a frequently observed characteristic of learning disabled children as they work through the often disturbing and frustrating trial of trying to perform adequately at something they don't do well. This symptom often takes the form of school-oriented emotional or mood swings and sometimes may even correlate closely with different academic-type activities (e.g., reading).
5. *Performance levels.* The performance of a learning disabled child is often uneven and difficult to describe in terms of a particular level. As opposed to the retarded or very bright child who may demonstrate problems or a quick and high level accomplishment in many areas, the L.D. pupil will frequently perform adequately or above average in some areas while demonstrating strong deficits in others. This uneven performance is an area rather easily checked

General behaviors identified through screening

and quite productive in making early classification discriminations. Reaction to the learning situation will often parallel a child's performance record even to the point of the child showing wild enthusiasm for an achieving area apparently functioning as some sort of compensation factor while he or she completely avoids other less productive areas.

6. *Perceptual ability.* Learning disabled children suffer frequently from their inability to function adequately in the perceptual area. Because their behavior is not only less than average, but also often painfully visible, aversion to situations requiring perceptual ability is common. Fine coordination, form discrimination, body and space positioning, right-left discriminations are all common in learning activities. A child's aversion to these activities, activities usually highly rewarding to children and usually put in the "game" class by their own enthusiasm, is potentially significant and should be examined further.

Some concern for a definition of the scope of problem identification sought is important. Some school systems, making judgments based on their own immediate experience, choose to focus primarily on one or two major areas, such as reading readiness problems, for example. Others prefer broader inclusive screening program approaches and try, on paper, to fit them to existing facilities, personnel, and needs. Many models are available and most learning disability textbooks contain examples and suggestions. Hasty adoption of tools and techniques can be costly in several ways.

A common error of schools developing their first screening process is being too ambitious. Time, cost, and effort should be weighed against results. Often screening personnel will find that less specific data, gathered by a shorter and less demanding instrument, will suffice for gross discrimination—thus avoiding high budget cost, excessive fatigue for pupils, and the frustration of staff and personnel who might be overloaded with time-consuming demands involved in extensive testing procedures.

When examining existing programs, it is always wise to inquire why certain instruments were used, how well they worked out, and how the obtained information can be or is being used.

Instrument and procedure selection usually result in the decision to include both formal and informal approaches as a battery is developed. The blend is good since informal methods allow for fitting the program to individual needs and local structures while formal techniques help assure better reliability and validity, factors necessary for good measurement and prediction.

Informal Approaches

An approach might be labeled "informal" for several different reasons. In some cases this label applies simply because of the method or manner in which the procedure is handled. The viewing of everyday classroom behavior, although matched to some structured observational categories, is still an informal process requiring few unusual activities, equipment, or personnel. Checklists and rating scales also might be labeled informal for the same reason. In other cases, even a fairly highly structured testing procedure might be grouped with informal approaches due to the background and development of the instrument itself. If locally prepared, with little standardization or validity-reliability testing involved, such procedures must still be considered informal as a caution to overextending the use of the data they may produce. Although informal activities have many advantages, they also carry some inherent dangers, such as the possible lack of reliability, questionable validity, and less well-established information about the actual function of the instrument or approach in the broader screening-categorization process.

These dangers or weaknesses may be somewhat minimized by careful attention to their presence and alertness to the potential error factor they impose on screening decisions. The really unfortunate aspect of this potential error lies not in its lack of accuracy alone, but also in the difficulty in adequately ascertaining if and when it appears. It is truly an "unknown" quantity and thus especially dangerous if the data containing potential error are used in the same way as data where error is small and more clearly defined.

The development of informal, "do-it-yourself" techniques has, however, much to offer. Smith and Neisworth (1969) offer some guidelines for selecting activities to be used for collecting behavioral data from informal measures.

1. Every activity selected for the purpose of evaluation should be part of an ongoing program . . . should reflect all the many nuances of the real classroom situation.
2. Activities should be interesting to the student being evaluated.
3. Activities for diagnosis should be selected to measure specific educational dimensions.
4. Activities should be developed to measure directly a child's performance in each of these (specific dimensions) specific skills.
5. Every diagnostic activity should be chosen for objectivity.
6. Activities should be varied enough that the youngsters do not become too familiar with the tasks.
7. Activities selected to diagnose areas of educational relevance should provide valid measurement of the behavioral dimension.
8. Children should be tested on more than one occasion to gain a reliable evaluation.

Guidelines for informal testing activities

Informal techniques are often structured around areas. Myers and Hammill (1969) have suggested that in screening for learning disabilities seven specific areas should be assessed: (1) auditory functions, (2) visual functions, (3) tactual-kinesthetic functions, (4) vocal behavior, (5) motor behavior, (6) memory, and (7) sequencing ability.

Sometimes teachers, aides, parents, and others are asked to use behavioral checklists and inventories that help isolate behaviors that have demonstrated some relationship with the categorization strategy being used. Such checklists vary in style of operation. There are those that are used in a semiformal interview fashion but still have formal scoring standards, such as the *Vineland Social Maturity Scale* (Doll, 1953). Others are much less formal, simply listing behaviors that may be checked by individuals looking for potential problem situations. An example of this type is included here (Table 9-1). Developed in a study of over 3,000 second-grade children (Meier, 1971), this checklist of behaviors identified learning disability children who displayed each separate type of behavior. Such data helps in ascertaining the strength of an assumption that a child should be

TABLE 9-1

Behavioral Indices Identifying Different Proportions of Learning Disability Second Graders

BEHAVIORAL INDICES	PROPORTION OF ILD CHECKED BY TEACHERS		
	1/3	1/2	2/3
Avoids work requiring concentrated visual attention	X		
Unable to learn the sounds of letters (can't associate proper phoneme with its grapheme)	X		
Doesn't seem to listen to daily classroom instructions or directions (often asks to have them repeated whereas rest of class goes ahead)		X	
Can't correctly recall oral directions (e.g., item 11 above) when asked to repeat them		X	
Can't pronounce the sounds of certain letters	X		
Unable to correctly repeat a 7 to 10 word statement by the teacher (omits or transposes words)	X		
Is slow to finish work (doesn't apply self, daydreams a lot, falls asleep in school)		X	
Overactive (can't sit still in class—shakes or swings legs, fidgety).	X		
Tense or disturbed (bites lip, needs to go to the bathroom often, twists hair, high strung)	X		
Unusually short attention span for daily school work			X
Easily distracted from school work (can't concentrate even with the slightest disturbances from other students' moving around or talking quietly)			X
Mistakes own left from right (confuses left-hand with right-hand side of paper)	X		
Poor drawing of diamond compared with peers' drawing	X		
Poor drawing of crossing, wavy lines compared with peers' drawings	X		
Poor drawing of a man compared with peers' drawing		X	
Poor handwriting compared with peers' writing		X	

TABLE 9-1 *(continued)*
Behavioral Indices Identifying Different Proportions of Learning Disability Second Graders

BEHAVIORAL INDICES	PROPORTION OF ILD CHECKED BY TEACHERS		
	1/3	1/2	2/3
Reverses or rotates letters, numbers, and words (writes "p" for "q," "saw" for "was," "2" for "7," "16" for "91") far more frequently than peers		X	
Reverses and/or rotates letters and numbers (reads "b" for "d," "u" for "n," "6" for "9") far more frequently than peers	X		
Loses place more than once while reading aloud for one minute	X		
Omits words while reading grade-level material aloud (omits more than one out of every ten)	X		
Reads silently or aloud far more slowly than peers (word by word while reading aloud)			X
Points at words while reading silently or aloud		X	
Substitutes words which distort meaning ("when" for "where")			X
Can't sound out or "unlock" words		X	
Can read orally, but does not comprehend the meaning of written grade-level words (word-callers)	X		
Reading ability at least 3/4 of a year below most peers		X	
Has trouble telling time		X	
Can't follow written directions, which most peers can follow, when read orally or silently		X	
Difficulty with arithmetic (e.g., can't determine what number follows 8 or 16; may begin to add in the middle of a subtraction problem)	X		
Cannot apply the classroom or school regulations to own behavior whereas peers can	X		
Excessive inconsistency in quality of performance from day to day or even hour to hour	X		
Has trouble organizing written work (seems scatterbrained, confused)		X	
Seems bright in many ways, but still does poorly in school	X		
Repeats the same behavior over and over		X	
Demands unusual amount of attention during regular classroom activities	X		
Seems quite immature (doesn't act his/her age)	X		

From "Prevalence and Characteristics of Learning Disabilities Found in Second Grade Children" by J. H. Meier, *Journal of Learning Disabilities,* 1971, *4,* 1-16. Copyright by Professional Press. Reprinted by special permission of Professional Press, Inc.

placed in some specific category because he or she displays certain behaviors. Many school districts develop their own indices of this type based on previous experience with their own children.

Much of the basic information for simple informal techniques comes from studies done in the classroom such as that of Bryan and Wheeler (1972). They note that the amount of task-oriented behavior as opposed to nondirected, "fooling around" activity may be an observable difference between learning disability children and others.

In using teacher or parent observation as a major means of noting symptomatic behavior, it is very important to provide some observational categories if any reliable agreement is to be obtained. Raskin and Taylor (1973) feel that teachers and others in similar positions have developed a sensitivity to "incident clusters" or behavior patterns that make their observer's reports particularly useful. They suggest that there are several identifiable categories that are critical to the analysis and prediction of academic and other difficulties and that such categories should be used and perhaps added to by academic observers. They include: visual behavior, motor behavior, graphics, multisensory, physical, and socioemotional. Each of these categories is broken down into a short series of observable behaviors symptomatic of potential problems in that area. A behavior checklist that followed such a structure or some similar structure peculiar to a certain school district's needs could be a very useful part of any screening program. Careful planning and structuring to provide the type of data necessary for subsequent steps is still most important, however. Checklists or any other procedure must fit the program or their usefulness is questionable.

Sometimes a screening instrument may orient itself to a rather narrow problem area with other problems being identified in different ways. Shedd (1967), for example, has listed a number of behavioral characteristics of dyslexic children. He includes such items as poor performance on group tests that require reading and writing, poor spatial orientation, impaired reproduction of tonal patterns, frequent mild speech irregularities, nonspecific motor awkwardness, and a number of others.

TABLE 9-2
Performance Objectives in Reading for Kindergarteners

1. The ability to recognize and print his own name when given four name cards to choose from and the opportunity to select and write his own.
2. The ability to match pictures, shapes, and letters when given three items one of which is similar to the examiner's sample.
3. The ability to differentiate between colors when given specified pictures for which the learner is to select the appropriate crayon and color the picture.
4. The development of muscular coordination for cutting and marking with crayons or big pencils when given shapes over which to trace or around which the learner is to cut.

TABLE 9-2 (continued)

Performance Objectives in Reading for Kindergarteners

5. The knowledge of how to proceed from left to right so that the learner, when presented with a row of objects, can underline the first and last items in the row.
6. The ability to follow directions when given shapes to draw in specified places in a picture.
7. The ability to recognize proper grammatical language and complete sentence structure so that when the learner is presented with two sentences, one of which is complete and correctly spoken and one of which is incomplete and ungrammatical, he can identify the correct sentence.
8. The ability to study a picture and gain meaning from it so that the learner, when given a question about how the character in the picture feels, can select the appropriate face for the picture.
9. The ability to use careful listening skills to comprehend details so that when given three rather similar pictures, the learner can select the picture the examiner has described.
10. The ability to relate a familiar story to its proper sequence so that when given three pictures from one story, the learner can number them in sequential order.
11. An understanding of the meaning of the prepositions *on, under,* and *over* when given the picture of a line with specified objects to be located in the named places.
12. An understanding of the meanings of the prepositions *next to, behind,* and *in front of* when given pictures in which the learner is to circle the objects in the correct places.
13. An understanding of the pronouns *I, me, we,* and *you* when given pictures in which the learner is to circle the character representing the pronoun that has been given in a short sentence.
14. An understanding of pronouns *he, she, her* and *him* when given pictures in which the learner is to circle the character representing the pronoun that has been given in a short sentence.
15. An understanding of parts that make up a whole so that when given the picture of a whole object, the learner can select the parts called for by the examiner.
16. The ability to classify familiar objects such as food and animals so that when given four pictures, the learner can cross out the one that does not belong.
17. The ability to hear and select words with the same initial consonant when given pictures of four objects, three of which begin alike.
18. The ability to recognize and select the appropriate letter of the alphabet when given the name and sound simultaneously.
19. The ability to hear and select rhyming words when given pictures of three objects, two of which rhyme.
20. The ability to understand vocabulary related to the areas of literature, social studies, and science from experiences, association with materials, and stories throughout the year so that when given three pictures, the learner can select the appropriate picture to match the given word.

From "Performance Objectives and C-R Tests—We Wrote Our Own!" by Mildred Royal, *Reading Teacher*, April 1974, 701-703. Reprinted with the permission of Mildred Royal and the International Reading Association.

Such a list could serve as the basis for developing a simple screening instrument for children with reading problems. Criterion-oriented tests carry implicit behavioral objectives which are specifically spelled out and may easily serve as the basis for screening procedures. Royal (1974) has demonstrated how teachers may assemble such criterion-referenced objectives in reading, language arts, and arithmetic for children of kindergarten age. Table 9–2 contains the performance objectives she developed for these young preschoolers in the area of reading.

A careful perusal of the professional literature will uncover many aids toward the preparation of informal screening materials, selection of special screening instruments, or adaptation of existing instruments for screening purposes. These aids range from a selection of "dos" and "don'ts" for informal teacher testing (Bliesmer, 1972) to a detailed analysis of the content of existing reading readiness batteries (Rude, 1973). Even lists of words necessary for beginning readers are available (Harris and Jacobson, 1973). The more technical and detailed analysis of existing instruments, such as that presented by Rude (see Tables 9–3 and 9–4), can be very useful in decisions about what to include in any screening pattern. Researchers have directed their attention to the factor analysis of early learning behaviors, such as first-grade reading achievement, and have isolated those behaviors that appear to make the most substantive contribution. Lowell (1971) has pointed out, for example, that knowledge of alphabet letter names, general word learning ability, and the auditory discrimination of sounds in words seem to be the most important identifiable factors in early school reading ability. Armed with such research data, it is not too difficult to construct some preliminary screening procedures that check for varying levels of performance in these three areas by preschoolers. Further help comes from professional organizations such as the *International Reading Association*, which serves as publisher or distributor of much helpful literature.

Most of the examples noted here have been from the area of reading, which is no accident since this area certainly receives the preponderance of attention in any analysis of early school difficulties. However, much help is available in other areas. Some arithmetic has already been mentioned (Royal, 1974). Aids to the assessment of behavior or potential learning behavior can be found for such other areas as handwriting (Johnson and Myklebust, 1967), language (Trembley, 1969), spelling (Linn, 1968), and many other areas. Some existing informal rating scales may be covered in locally structured instruments and batteries (High, 1973).

Entire works dealing with sources and procedures for do-it-yourself inventories and with methods for integrating informal and formal screening and assessment are available. Typical of these are Mann and Suiter's (1979) *Handbook in Diagnostic Teaching* (a particularly good source for ideas about informal spelling and reading assessment) and Smith's (1969) *Teacher Diagnosis of Educational Difficulties*. The latter work consists of a collection of chapters by different authors and includes suggestions and important cautions relevant to the areas of perceptual-motor skills, reading, spelling, written expression, speech and language, arithmetic, and personal-emotional-social skills.

TABLE 9–3
Reading Readiness Batteries, Subtests, and Subtest Titles*

	METRO-POLITAN	MURPHY-DURRELL	CLYMER-BARRETT	GATES-MACGINITIE	HARRISON-STROUD
vocabulary develop.	word meaning				
listening	listening			listening comp. and following directions	using the context and using context and auditory clues
letter recognition	alphabet	letter names	recognition of letters	letter recognition	giving the names of the letters
numbers	numbers				
visual-motor coordination	copying		shape completion & copy-a-sentence	visual-motor coordination	
rhyming words			discrim. of ending sounds in words		
phonemes correspond.		phonemes	discrim. of beginning sounds in words	making auditory discrimi-nations	
learning rate		learning rate			
auditory discrim.				auditory discrim.	
auditory blending				auditory blending	
				word recognition	
matching	matching		matching words	visual discrim.	using symbols and making visual discriminations

* Subtest titles are given in the appropriate cells. From "Readiness Tests: Implications for Early Childhood Education" by Robert T. Rude, *Reading Teacher*, March 1973, 572. Reprinted with permission of Robert T. Rude and the International Reading Association.

TABLE 9-4
Prereading Skills as Measured by Five Reading Readiness Batteries*

	METRO-POLITAN	MURPHY-DURRELL	CLYMER-BARRETT	GATES-MACGINITIE	HARRISON-STROUD
grapheme perception	alphabet (matching)	letter names (learning)	recognition of letters (matching words) (copy-a-sentence)	letter recognition (visual discrimination) (visual-motor coordination) (word recognition)	giving the names of the letters (using symbols) (making visual discriminations)
left to right visual scan	(matching)	(learning rate)	copy-a-sentence (matching words)	(visual discrimination) (word recognition)	(using symbols) (making visual discriminations)
grapheme-phoneme relationships	phonemes	phonemes (learning rate)		(word recognition)	
phoneme blending		(learning rate)		auditory blending (word recognition)	

* Parentheses indicate subordinate subtests measuring skills in a limited manner. From "Readiness Tests: Implications for Early Childhood duration" by Robert T. Rude, *Reading Teacher*, March 1973, 577. Reprinted with permission of Robert T. Rude and the International Reading Association.

Formal Instruments and Batteries

A tremendous number of different instruments and batteries are used in screening and diagnostic programs across the country. Arriving at any consensual point where a specific instrument or set of instruments clustered as a battery can be universally recommended to all or even most school systems is virtually impossible. Validity, in a psychometric sense, should always be thought of as *validity for some purpose or objective*. Thus, again, the importance of carefully stating and defining objectives for a screening program is underlined. Instruments should be selected and batteries built along a line leading directly to the stated and intended objectives of the individual screening programs.

This is not to suggest that help is not available or that no precedence can be observed in the choice of others. Collections of notations of instruments currently in use are available along with some annotations and evaluations. The UCLA Graduate School of Education has prepared evaluations of preschool kindergarten tests (CSE-ECRC, 1971) and the Educational Testing Services (1971) publishes an annotated bibliography of school readiness measures contained in the Head Start Test Collections. The Mental Measurements Yearbook (Buros, 1949, 1953, 1959, 1965, 1972) is also a useful place to obtain evaluative and initial technical information regarding published instruments.

Some available material comes from school programs that have developed either their own instruments or a screening approach based on the use of parts of one or more standardized tests. The following tests are typical of the school-developed or based collections:

- *DIAL, Developmental Indicators for the Assessment of Learning.* This report covers the results of an attempt by the Illinois Office of Public Instruction (1972) to develop a preschool screening instrument.
- *Pre-Kindergarten Descriptive Inventory.* The Fairfield, Connecticut Public Schools (1972) have compiled a series of quick, individually administered items that are used to help identify needs of children before school entry.

Many systems have similar material, but often the information is obtainable only through personal knowledge and individual contact. The national convention of the Association for Children with Learning Disabilities is a convenient place to gather this information. Many individualized programs and techniques are reported at these annual meetings, and individual states have exhibits containing information and contact sources for many different programs.

Most textbooks focusing on learning disabilities carry some information about specific instruments, their format, use, and application.

A survey of the literature dealing with screening assessment and the notations about what instruments are being used most frequently by existing programs suggests that the following assessment procedures or instruments are highly rated and employed. There is severe disagreement in some cases about the appropriateness of certain approaches or specific instruments listed here and this listing does not necessarily imply blanket endorsement for all entries. Most instruments noted deal with the earlier childhood and school years, since screening and diagnostic activities are heaviest for that age group. Standard achievement tests, individually administered and interpreted, are often adapted for use with older children on an individual basis.

Table 9-5 notes which of the instruments seem to be most commonly used for screening and/or specific diagnostic workshops. Those instruments that are used primarily to obtain measures of intelligence have not been included in either the list or the accompanying table.

Anton Brenner Developmental Gestalt Test of School Readiness (Brenner, 1964).
Designed to assess school readiness in children five or six years of age, this individually administered instrument discriminates varying rates of maturation on a gifted to retarded continuum.

Basic School Skills Inventory (Valett, 1968). This instrument is used to identify a number of different academic areas where a child may be experiencing difficulty. This is primarily an achievement measure, prescriptive phases must be implied.

Bender Gestalt Test for Young Children (Koppitz, 1964) or *Bender Visual-Motor Gestalt Test* (Bender, 1938). An older instrument originally developed for clinical use with organic pathology, this test is used by many to check on or to predict academic achievement. There are severe disagreements about its efficacy for this purpose (Coy, 1974; Koppitz, 1970; Norfleet, 1973).

Boehm Test of Basic Concepts (Boehm, 1967). Administered to small groups, this instrument measures the mastery of concepts required for school achievement during the first few years.

Detroit Tests of Learning Aptitude (Baker and Leland, 1935). This test includes nineteen subtests measuring the basic elements of the learning process, such as visual and auditory attention span.

Developmental Test of Visual-Motor Integration (Beery and Buktenica, 1967). This instrument measures developmental status in the areas of visual perception and fine motor integration.

Developmental Test of Visual Perception (Frostig, Lefever, and Whittlesey, 1964). Frequently included in screening and diagnostic batteries, this instrument is designed to assess five different areas of visual perception. Like the *Bender*, this instrument has been the focus of considerable debate, and some doubt has been raised as to factor validity and the generalization of results from remedial programs based on DTVP data (Becker and Sabatino, 1973; Smith and Marx, 1972).

First Grade Screening Test (Pate and Webb, 1966). This instrument screens groups for potential early learning problems. Sometimes used for general "tracking" guidance.

Illinois Test of Psycholinguistic Abilities (Kirk, McCarthy, and Kirk, 1968). This instrument, probably the most frequently used evaluative instrument in learning disabilities, measures language skills in a variety of ways. Its stated age norms run from about 2½ years to about 10 years. In practice it is used most often with children in the 5- to 8-year-old range. The test is individually administered and quite time-consuming if administered in its entirety to a large number of children. Many screening programs have chosen to use selected subtests of the ITPA for screening purposes only, using the total instrument for more detailed individual behavior analysis. Some questions have been raised about this instrument's validity.

Kindergarten Teacher's Handbook (Meyers, Ball, and Crutchfield, 1973). This publication is actually a small booklet outlining a testing sequence for screening that includes a subportion of a number of different instruments, directions for interpretation, and some remedial recommendations. Of particular use may be the year-end evaluation form that allows quick and simplified rating of a wide variety of behaviors, including such items as body concept, expressive and receptive language, and math concepts. A number of individual behaviors are listed under each of the above and similar concept headings.

Lincoln-Oseretsky Motor Development Scale (Sloan, 1954). This instrument individually measures a number of different motor skill areas. Being somewhat time-consuming and complicated, this instrument is not typically used in large-group screening.

Meeting Street School Screening Test (Hainsworth and Siqueland, 1969). Individually administered, but relatively brief, this instrument is really a small battery of subtests yielding scores dealing primarily with reasoning ability, discrimination and motor response, and prior learning in academic areas (e.g., number concepts).

Peabody Picture Vocabulary Test (Dunn, 1965). Often used as a rough measure of intelligence in the young child, this older test also appraises receptive language vocabulary.

Preschool Inventory (Caldwell, 1970). Suitable for children three to six years old, this inventory measures achievement in areas prerequisite for school success.

Pupil Rating Scale (Myklebust, 1971). Printed as a small booklet and easily used by the classroom teacher, this scale rates young children in the areas of auditory comprehension, spoken language, orientation, motor coordination, and personal-social behavior. Some question has been raised as to whether or not these areas represent five independent factors (Bryan and McGrady, 1972), but the instrument's validity in rough screening seems to be fairly well demonstrated.

Purdue Perceptual-Motor Survey (Roach and Kephart, 1966). This survey (the authors carefully note that it is a survey and not a test) scores the children's performance in five general areas congruent with Kephart's general approach to evaluating and helping the slow learner (Kephart, 1971a). The areas include balance and posture, body image and differentiation, perceptual-motor match, ocular control, and form perception. The transfer of motor training to school-subject related behavior has recently become a controversial subject (Hammill, Goodman, and Wiederholt, 1974), but for those wishing to deal with the perceptual-motor area, this instrument probably is the most frequently used.

Screening Tests for Identifying Children with Specific Language Disability—Slingerland (Slingerland, 1964). Three sets of group screening tests for early primary ages. School personnel tend to feel comfortable with this instrument since its parts resemble typical schoolroom activities.

Spache Diagnostic Reading Scales (Spache, 1972). This individual test battery diagnoses reading difficulties in elementary-school-age children.

Stanford Diagnostic Reading Test (Karlsen, Madden, and Gardner, 1968). This group test measures a number of reading difficulty sub-areas for children in grades 2 to 8.

Test of Articulation (Goldman and Fristoe, 1969). Similar to the following instrument, this test focuses on speech problems. These two instruments are often used together in screening for speech and hearing problems.

Test of Auditory Discrimination (Goldman, Fristoe, Woodcock, 1970). Individually administered items check children's ability to discriminate important sounds relatively unconfounded by other factors. This test may be used for children as young as four years old.

Test of Language Development (Newcomer and Hammill, 1977). A prescriptive-diagnostic instrument incorporating measurement of a number of different spoken language sub-areas.

Test of Reading Comprehension (Brown, Hammill, and Wiederholt, 1978). This instrument appraises several different areas of reading comprehension with diagnostic supplements relative to the vocabulary of specific academic areas (e.g., mathematics).

Test of Written Language (Hammill and Larsen, 1978). A comprehensive measure of written expression in the elementary school child.

Valett Developmental Survey of Basic Learning Abilities (Valett, 1966b). This survey looks at skill development in the preschool and early elementary child in several different areas.

Vane Kindergarten Test (Vane, 1968). Administered in part to individuals and in part to small groups, this instrument assesses four- to six-year-old children's intellectual and academic behavior and potential.

Vineland Social Maturity Scale (Doll, 1953). A measurement of social development in the form of a social quotient is provided by this easily administered checklist of common behaviors for children up to age seven.

Wepman Test of Auditory Discrimination (Wepman, 1958). Using the task of discriminating like and unlike words in the auditory mode, this quick and very easily administered instrument screens (in a somewhat rougher fashion) for the same behaviors as the previously mentioned *Test of Auditory Discrimination* (Goldman et al., 1970). In many cases this simpler instrument is used for rough screening and the more sophisticated test for those cases needing more careful attention.

TABLE 9–5
Common Application of Listed Instruments

INSTRUMENT	PRIMARILY USED FOR SCREENING	MAY HAVE SUBPARTS APPLIED TO SCREENING	COMMONLY USED IN BOTH SCREENING AND DIAGNOSIS	PRIMARILY USED FOR DIAGNOSIS ALONE
Anton Brenner				X
Basic School Skills			X	
Bender Gestalt				X
Boehm Basic Concepts			X	
Detroit Learning Aptitude		X	X	
Developmental Visual-Motor Integration		X		X
Developmental Visual Perception			X	
First Grade Screening	X			
ITPA		X		X
Kindergarten Teacher's			X	
Lincoln-Oseretsky		X		X
Meeting Street School			X	
Peabody Picture Vocabulary			X	
Preschool Inventory			X	
Pupil Rating Scale	X			
Purdue Perceptual-Motor	X			
Slingerland Screening			X	
Spache Diagnostic Reading		X		X
Stanford Diagnostic Reading			X	
Test of Articulation		X		X
Test of Auditory Discrimination		X		X
Test of Language Development			X	
Test of Reading Comprehension			X	
Test of Written Language		X		X
Valett Developmental Survey	X			
Vane Kindergarten Test			X	
Vineland Social Maturity			X	
Wepman Auditory Discrimination	X			

Implementation and Follow-Up

Like an iceberg, much of the important mass of a screening program is hidden from easy view. As we can see from the many important decision areas already noted, the process is not one simply arrived at or nonchalantly undertaken. Good detailed planning along lines dictated by carefully selected and defined objectives seems to be a major key to ultimate success in any screening program.

The actual implementation and follow-up procedures may very well flow easily and logically if advance planning and careful sequencing of activities is included; but several specific areas do need attention in planning sessions concerning actual implementation and follow-up activities.

Publicity

Since the ultimate goal of any screening is to provide the best possible educational experience for individual pupils, it is obvious that wide and deep support is a valuable asset. Publicity programs should be sure to include attention to several specific target populations and the different problems and needs manifested by each.

Parental support is vital. Parents will want to know what is happening to their children, why it is happening, and when. Too many publicity programs merely give advance notice of times and places. But parents should also be informed and assured about the exact nature of the program and its activities. Objectives, clearly and simply stated, should be openly presented and explained to parents. Differences between screening and diagnosis should be clarified. Parents will frequently express concern about possible rigid tracking of their children as a result of screening; some will worry if inclusion in screening is the result of suspected problems. Other similar questions will arise. Questions should be anticipated whenever possible and freely accepted—indeed, solicited—wherever parents are involved. Such a procedure should be carried on openly, well in advance of the program if possible, so that necessary changes can be made in procedures and objectives to insure parental support. Media should be included both to spread the base of support throughout the community and to underline the openness and honesty of the program.

Teachers and other school personnel should also be the target of advance publicity and informational programs. Teachers need to be assured that the screening program is classroom-oriented and that teacher input is important. The relevancy of screening procedures and resulting data to educational activities should be made plain. The importance of a relevant and realistic set of objectives is again underlined when faced with this task. Teachers' questions are more easily answered when teachers' problems and ideas have been included in the input considered when establishing objectives. To some extent the children themselves need to be a target audience. Even very young children deserve to know what is happening to them and why. Fear of the unknown and of strange processes and perhaps unfamiliar people will attenuate the effectiveness of the program. This problem can be alleviated to some extent by careful contact and information sharing with the children. In some programs small groups of kindergarten children are allowed to tour the facilities and handle test equipment prior to their screening so that the strangeness may wear off and fear may be replaced with some degree of self-confidence and knowledge.

Procedures

Specific advice is difficult to give in this area since procedural questions are so closely related to instrument and technique choice, timing, and similar idiosyncratic factors. Some general points can be made, however. Perhaps a simple list will suffice:

1. Allow plenty of time. Procedures take longer than anticipated as a general rule, especially with young children. Long sessions are out with easily fatigued young children.
2. Be sure to plan for ample space and privacy. Young children are noisy. No amount of "shhh's" are going to keep them quiet and firm curtailment of noise may result in fear and shyness.
3. Plan for different kinds of usable space. Include assembling areas, small testing rooms, group testing rooms, play rooms, toilet and eating facilities, waiting rooms for parents (often these will need to be clearly separated from screening areas).
4. Anticipate "no-shows" and cancellations and children who stop unexpectedly in the middle of activities. Repeated testing procedures and replicated activities almost invariably are necessary.
5. Have some "minute-men" staff available who have no assigned responsibilities other than to be ready to fill in where needed. The need usually arises!
6. Plan for staff fatigue and comfort. A staff lounge, coffee and doughnuts, and similar niceties keep staff morale high and performance up.
7. Run a trial batch of a few students through the process to catch bugs before the mass of children is scheduled. If actual children cannot be used, at least walk through the process with the staff.
8. Use maps and diagrams and printed lists redundantly to emphasize processes, procedures, and objectives that are presented verbally. Do not rely on the memories of staff and pupils during times of stress and fatigue to remember routes, sequences of activities, etc.

Simple rules for administration of screening activities

Record Keeping

Early planning should include the design of a record-keeping format that is both easy to use and read. Attention should be given to the need for having forms that are easily understood, where data are easily entered, and where the actual process of record keeping follows the flow of activity in the program closely and logically. Thus, those individuals performing a screening activity should not have to leaf through a pile of forms to find the proper one for noting the results they gather. It should be in the right order, the logical place. Someone should be responsible for checking each individual record form while the child is still present so that omission, confusion, or error may be taken care of while memories are fresh and the pupil is still available. Quality control is the key in record keeping, and it can be accomplished quite easily with planning. Quality records will not come automatically, however, and data errors and omissions, unless caught immediately, may be virtually irreparable or irreplaceable.

Records are kept for several reasons, including (1) specific identification of the individual pupil and his or her characteristics as a single piece of a mass of data that will help identify group nature and trends; (2) as baseline data for future checks on pupil change; and (3) as basic information for starting the process of evaluating the effectiveness of screening procedures. In each case, slightly different data demands are inferred and planning should anticipate these demands and provide ways to meet them.

Updating and Improving the Program

Chapter 19 will outline activities and procedures that help revise a remedial program to fit the needs of an individual child better. To a certain extent the same general principles apply to screening itself. Any screening program will need some revisions. Evaluation should include the following:

Criteria for evaluating your screening program

1. Evaluation of the extent to which stated objectives have been met
2. Identification of those processes and procedures that have proven very useful or less functional than desired
3. Examination of the facilities and staffing and procedural activities for strengths and weaknesses
4. Consideration of input, actively sought if not proved spontaneously from all target populations involved: school, family, pupil, and community

Once information of this sort has been gathered and weighed and evaluated, the planning process can start again. Following a similar pathway as in the original model, planning, revisions, changes, and retention can occur as directed. No part of the process, from objectives to follow-up procedure, should be considered sacred or unassailable. Change where change seems warranted, but always provide the means for evaluating the results of such change.

Using Acquired Data

Since the objectives of screening are to provide general characterizations of a child's performance in certain specified areas, the last logical step in such a program is to make use of the data assembled. This process includes the identification of children for whom more information is necessary. This will be operational evidence of the effectiveness of a screening program. The process then goes to the acquisition of more detailed and specific information, a step covered in some detail in the next two chapters.

10

Communication of Diagnostic-Prescriptive Information

"Monday morning" discussions of factors that may have affected some recent events often give rise to a common cliché. Analysts are repeatedly heard to say, "It was really a matter of communication!" At this point the discussion ends, everyone nods agreement but, as Mark Twain reportedly said about the weather, "No one does anything about it."

Almost every remedial strategy calls for operating from a carefully assembled and analyzed baseline of information that defines the objective and directs the structure of remedial work. The ideal is to gather necessary data and information immediately at the scene of the problem. In many instances this is a reasonable objective that may be easily accomplished.

But there are frequent occasions when information is not available on the scene or where additional or different information is a necessary prerequisite to successful prescriptive planning. Such instances remind us of the importance of effective communication with others for the purpose of eliciting or transmitting important information about a learning deficit child. The necessity for communicating across disciplines is particularly critical in the field of learning disabilities.

There are easily demonstrable reasons for calling upon specialists from other disciplines. These range from those problems associated with learning crisis situations (Feder, 1967) to the anticipation of better research results through interdisciplinary efforts (Hallahan and Cruickshank, 1973). It has also been pointed out (Landreth, Jacquot, and Allen, 1969) that most professionals working with learning disability children agree that the problems these children face have a tendency to affect their total functioning, that they have potentially important and lasting effects on different behavior subsystems within the same person. The use of professionals from several disciplines (interdisciplinary teams) more nearly matches such an organistic theory of learning disabilities than the work of isolated specialists or specialists with a limited focus.

Perhaps some day the learning disability field will develop its own specialist whose training is similar to that of the old-time family doctor, a true general practitioner. Certainly such an individual would be very helpful to any program practicing diagnosis and remediation. In the meantime we need to avoid the problem of fragmentation and to facilitate better communication.

The individual practitioner must, to whatever extent practical, develop the skills to function as nearly as possible in the mode of the specialist. At this time we cannot reasonably expect most practitioners to have the tremendous depth and range of knowledge that such a specialist would need to possess if he or she were to function effectively. Our university training programs do not regularly provide such training even if one were to seek it. But the development of some rudimentary skills and techniques is possible and can be a helpful step in the right direction.

It is necessary to recognize now that students committed to a course of study and many individuals already on the job need help and need it quickly. Workers confronted with heavy caseloads or a variety of problem types must be able to turn to specialists of many disciplines for quick and effective actions. As Ullman (1971) has pointed out, "Each profession must not only be clear within its own frame of reference but be able to enter that of other disciplines and those who are responsible for the administration of benefits and services."

Because professionals are faced with such critical problems and heavy demands, criteria for successful programmatic remedial interaction between disciplines must be formed around practical and functional considerations. As Waugh (1970) has correctly emphasized, "The most appropriate criterion for a report is a practical one. To what extent does it clarify the current status of the child and suggest educational practices which ameliorate the existing problem?" The general criterion of functionality seems to be most important. Special attention to clarity of communication, behavioral descriptions, and similar tools of communication can go far to avoid dissonance and facilitate useful professional interaction. Even such simple techniques as avoiding discipline-related jargon and attention to the reader's special competencies and frame of reference pay high dividends in saving time and providing effective treatment.

Certainly, the heavy demands for individualized educational plans (IEP's) that have arisen out of the implementation of Public Law 94-142 focus attention on the need for more efficient and accurate communication skills. In teaching personnel who are assuming additional responsibility, prescriptive programmers are constantly faced with the two-edged questions:

• Where can I obtain the information I need?
• How can I meaningfully share that which I know?

It is easy to expand this problem to the entire process of learning disability identification, prescription, and treatment, therein identifying a number of major functional objectives that are dependent upon developing adequate inter- and intradisciplinary communication skills.

1. Maximizing the efficiency of diagnostic and remedial prescriptive work. The old adage that "two heads are better than one" is even more true when the two or more heads represent highly trained observers who have separate and frequently independent skills and talents. Efficiency is maximized in terms of the range and depth of examination and prescription. Additionally, the speed with which the full attack may be mounted is increased. Teachers are capable of assembling much of the diagnostic and prescriptive data vital to remediation. On the other hand well-timed involvement of other specialists may so speed up the notation of important variables and gathering necessary data that prescription and actual remediation activities can be initiated much sooner than would be possible if the teacher were to assemble and integrate all necessary data and information alone. Speed of information assembling by a team or by selected involved specialists means hours saved for the worker who has primary interface with the learning disability child, time that may be directed toward actual remediation or other activities. Since a common complaint of teachers is that it is difficult to find time to put appropriate remedial plans into operation, such time saving is important.

2. Substantiating a diagnostic or remedial hypothesis. Frequently specialist's advice and service will be sought for reasons parallel with the use of the specialized consultant in medicine. The teacher or "general practitioner" may, through observation and technical assessment, isolate what appears to be an area of significant difficulty. Since any resulting remedial activity is apt to involve not only the actual hours necessary for amelioration of the problem but also the time involved in the process of building an appropriate remedial program, some reaffirmation of the accuracy of the diagnosis and problem analysis may be warranted. The researcher calls this substantiating process "cross-validation." The procedure may be simply to recheck a diagnosis or some aspect of prescriptive programming. It may involve the somewhat more complicated steps of helping to choose from among several apparently equally viable hypotheses. In either event, whether the original position has been stated by a general practitioner or a specialist, calling upon others for validation is the most logical approach. The procedure may involve a carefully worded formal referral directed to some expert or clinic. Or the cross-checking may be only a casual request to "take a look at this and see if you see what I do?" It is the process and its efficiency that is important and the basis for determining relevant skills, not the actual procedures involved.

3. Obtaining missing pieces of information. There are times, perhaps more frequently than we would like, when we find we have done our best in observation, assessment, or prescription and still have not obtained a satisfactory result. Involving others and eliciting more or different information, the careful identification of what may be honest "gaps" in our ability to analyze or define the problem, becomes necessary to achieving ultimate treatment results. Such "gaps" may be due to unusual symptomatic behaviors in the observed learner, or they may represent areas of behavior that fall outside the province of the disciplinary training of the practitioner or specialist. They occur for many different reasons and do not necessarily reflect upon the worth or effectiveness of the individual experiencing them. A characteristic of the highly effective professional is an ability to quickly discriminate and admit his or her capabilities and limitations. In cases where help is needed it should be sought quickly. However, speed in soliciting assistance is an asset only when the appeal for help skillfully elicits the information that is needed.

4. Providing support and backing. One final major argument for developing effective cross-disciplinary information sharing centers around a problem that is more public-relations-oriented than prescriptive. Failure to consider this area may seriously attenuate remedial activities. Once the analytical phases of program building are completed, prescripted activities demand the involvement of personnel who must deliver the services. Such personnel may find it difficult to devote the necessary hours or may not have the high degree of involvement of those most intimately associated with the case. In some cases parents, teachers, or other involved individuals may even express reluctance to become involved, open skepticism about the efficacy of the prescribed approach, or frank antagonism to the activities suggested. Specialist interaction in such cases is often clearly helpful in lending weight and support to recommendations and plans. Sometimes the inertia or resistance centers around lack of clarity about the issue or confusion over the goals or steps in the program. The fresh approach of someone else, who is knowledgeable, a recognized expert, or perhaps only less emotionally involved, can often help clarify such issues and reduce opposition. The appeal to the expert in such a situation is clearly one of asking for support, advice, or recommendations for facilitating services, or for some alternative approach which may be more successful. Again the ultimate criterion is whether or not the activities lead to fewer deficit behaviors in the learner. The supportive weight of an expert can help accomplish this. Developing the communication skills to elicit such support where appropriate is important.

In suggesting that learning disability practioners develop sound communication skills for the purpose of providing and eliciting better information, there is an implicit assumption that problems or less-than-effective behaviors do exist. Practical experiences and reports from others in the field seem to support such an assumption.

Specifically, what are the problems?

Problems in communication

In general, a survey of people in the field and the professional literature suggests that the problems may cluster into three broad categories: (1) problems relevant to interpersonal relationships and role definitions; (2) problems related to clarity, form, and structure; and (3) problems involving objective or purpose.

Noting such categories, an approach to avoiding such problems can be directed toward three sets of criterion behaviors, goals, or standards. One might say that if the communication between professionals of varying disciplines is to be effective, such communication must accomplish the following:

- Facilitate mutual understanding and respect for the varying viewpoints held and services offered by specialists of different fields
- Be of a form or structure that is clear and unambiguous
- Provide goals and objectives that aid rather than inhibit effective information transmission

Goals
for effective
communication

Let's briefly examine some problems that arise when these criteria for effective communication are not achieved.

1. *Problems relevant to interpersonal relationships and role definitions.* Even with those whom we know best—our wife or husband, brother or sister, parent or child—we find ourselves investing a significant amount of time and effort in interpreting and clarifying each other's positions, ideas, and intents. Such clarifications seem to be prerequisite to effective interaction.

In 1955 the American Psychological Association convened a special conference to study the role of school psychologists in an attempt to improve their functioning in the schools. In the course of that conference, attention was directed to major criticisms of school psychologists as perceived by other school personnel. Each of the five major criticisms that were noted involved an indictment that school psychologists failed to interact successfully with someone in a different role. The problems that were noted are listed below:

1. Unfortunate personal characteristics that antagonize teachers
2. Failure to understand the practical problems of the classroom
3. Failure to adequately communicate recommendations
4. Failure to recognize their own limitations; too inclusive or too specialized
5. Poor general community relations (Cutts, 1955).

These problems all indicate the presence of unsuccessful interpersonal adaptation—failures not characteristic, we are sure, of school psychologists alone. Communication is a primary medium through which the necessary cues for successful interpersonal adaptations flow. In each of these isolated problem areas there seems to be the underlying theme that communication is insufficiently explicit and that roles or role concepts may be both confused and confusing. One practical answer seems to be to direct communication efforts along a programmatic line with the need for providing or receiving explicit information being the constant, most important objective. Only then can such requests be shaped to meet both the needs of the inquirer and the role capabilities of the specialist.

The need for explicit objective-oriented communication has been noted by others, such as Rosner (1968) who stressed the problems of understanding the functioning of related, though separate, disciplines (ophthalmology and optometry) unless one thoroughly understood their differing treatment objectives and goals. Waugh and Bush (1971) underlined the role of similar dynamics between teacher and consultant in the field of learning disabilities.

Many requests for information go unanswered or are answered ineffectively because they are directed to the wrong people or sent through inappropriate channels. Although some problems arise out of a lack of respect for those of other disciplines, the major obstacle is more often one of ignorance. Misdirected questions, questions unrelated to the discipline of the specialist to whom they have been referred, questions that require the specialist to call upon still another specialist—all such inquiries waste time at best. At worst they short-circuit or completely break down the communication system: Learning disability practitioners need to know what other specialists can and cannot do in conformity with professional role expectations. They need to convey respect for the type of information that such specialists can provide. And, in demonstrating a deliberate interest in another field, they shape at the same time a mutual respect for themselves in the eyes of other specialists. Such mutual respect eases the mechanics of communication and greatly facilitates passing worthwhile and relevant information.

2. *Problems related to clarity, form, and structure.* The authors recently asked a group of school personnel of varying specialities what they, in their own positions, most frequently observed as weaknesses in requests for information or in the reports of information gathered by others. The replies were succinct, quickly presented, and remarkably uniform across specialities. They declared that too many such communications contained jargon meaningless to the uninitiated, misued terms, and lack of definition regarding the behavior observed or the information needed. "Of what use," they asked, "is a phrase such as 'Beth reads poorly'?" They almost unanimously asked for behavioral explanations, explicit questions, listing of basis for assumptions and similar aspects related to the actual syntax and logic of a request or report.

The criterion behavior that avoids these problems obviously involves such attributes as clarity, lack of ambiguity, and preciseness.

3. *Problems related to objective or purpose.* The same school personnel quickly addressed themselves to this problem as well. Too often, they pointed out, a professional receives a request for information that he or she may be able to supply in several different forms or at several different levels and the request in no way specifies how the information is to be used, what the purpose is in asking, or for whom it is being collected. "I'm not the least bit interested in prying into who is going to read my report," a reading specialist told us. "I simply want to know if I am talking to a parent or a teacher or some other type person so I can provide the form of information most meaningful to them. Numbers and names of books may have meaning to a teacher in my

system and have no value at all to a parent. I wish to be of the most help possible."

Other complaints related to this problem area seem to center around queries that are too global—"Tell me all about his language skills!"—or queries that are perhaps too highly specific to be helpful to the specialist—"How many words can she read?" The more carefully defined the questions, the more meaningful the answer may be. In asking a psychologist about the intelligence of a pupil, questions may range from "How bright is he?" to "Is his memory good enough for him to use abstract ideas a week or two after he has learned them?" It is obvious that the latter type of question is more apt to elicit meaningful information than the former.

If practitioners can achieve two simple goals, cross-discipline inquiry will be much more functional and effective:

1. Shorten the period of time it takes to obtain requested information.
2. Improve the explicit relevancy and usefulness of elicited information.

A useful framework for achieving these two goals exists. It consists of five sequential steps designed to help the questioner improve the quality and directness of his or her questions. This increased quality and explicitness hastens the specialist's reply because the question is easier to answer, and less time is spent decoding the inquiry to figure out just what really is sought. The usefulness of the elicited information is incremented through deliberately directing the question toward those exact pieces of information most important to the inquirer.

Step 1: Sharpening the syntax of the original question or statement

As every practitioner knows, a substantial amount of question-and-answer interview time (with parents new to the concept of L.D., for example) is spent in educating the discussants about the meaning of unfamiliar technical terms (e.g., *abstract verbal intelligence*) and in determining what certain "catchall" terms mean in the context of the current discussion (e.g., the child is *nervous*).

As an initial step, the inquirer should look at original statements or questions with an eye toward removing ambiguity, lack of preciseness, meaningless or misinterpretable technical jargon, and ineffectual, catchall phrases. Let's look at an example or two.

In a teacher-parent interview regarding a child transferring from another school, the parent says, "When it comes to reading, Mary is simply out of it. I'm afraid she'll never catch up. Her last teacher called her a retarded reader."

Presuming in this case that the teacher is anticipating having to use the services of a reading specialist, what can be done with this parent's statement? Simply asking the reading specialist if Mary is a retarded reader is not sufficiently precise. The statement contains obscurities and other problems. What does "simply out of it" really mean? Is the parent speaking of academic achievement, daydreaming, emotional reaction to failure, or some other undefined phenomena? What is the implication of "never catch up"? And just what did that other teacher mean by retarded reader? Eliminating these ambiguous statements and replacing them with more behavioral information puts the inquirer in a better position to ask the right questions. Further inquiry might permit this parent's original statement to be reworded to say, "Mary's reading is poorer than her class. I worry if she can improve enough even with help to catch up with them. Her last teacher says that her reading is simply not improving as fast as her other work."

The statement is still not in the final form one should strive to achieve before calling upon the specialist, but it's moving in the right direction: it's clearer and more precise.

One more example may help. A teacher reported, "Fred sees the word but it just doesn't register. Anything that requires him to use language or listen is out of the question." As a school personnel staff member, you are being asked to carry this information to some appropriate specialist to ascertain "what's wrong with Fred." What words and phrases need to be clarified or perhaps changed? The following words, at least, are open to more than one interpretation: "sees," "register," "anything," "requires," "use," "language," "listen," and "out of the question." Not a very encouraging analysis is it? A little work, some appropriate observation or questions, and more careful attention to word selection can greatly improve the situation. With the removal of some of the ambiguity, the result can be startling.

Suppose we have been able to clarify some of these things to the point where we can make these statements. "See" means literally that Fred can perceive, which he demonstrates by discriminative pointing. "Register" was just a careless word selection, since there are no connotations or indications of any differential reaction to authority or demand as apart from a casual request. "Use" means to couple memory with production by recalling a word previously read and using it now in another sentence. "Language" means vocabulary use in a creative sentence construction form. "Listen" was again a sloppy choice, since no inference of auditory involvement was intended. The word refers simply to the memory-language problem regardless of whether the stimulus is visual or auditory. "Out of the question" means he doesn't like to try and when he does try his performance is below that of the other boys in his class to the point of causing reading problems. Now, the statement could be rewritten as an initial step toward getting important information from a specialist.

As part of this "syntax-cleaning" procedure it may be helpful to follow these specific guidelines until the process becomes a familiar and almost habitual one.

Guidelines for syntax-cleaning

1. Redefine sloppy or loose words.
2. Avoid colloquialisms that may have different meanings for different people (e.g., "out of the question").

3. Translate technical or possibly technical terms into behavioral phrases (gross-vision deficit becomes overall trouble in seeing well).
4. Avoid misinterpretable comparison terms (e.g., slow, doing great, out-of-it).

Finally, in looking over the statement with the fine eye of an editor, the seeds of effective strategy may be sown by asking yourself a question (the answer to which will direct statement revision and clarification): "What piece(s) of information about behavior must I know to start removing this child's learning deficit?" Looking for the answer to this question will demand sharp attention to clean and useful syntax.

After a statement has been generally cleansed of ambiguities and obscure statements, the inquirer is ready for the next step, which involves the deliberate building of a focused, prescriptive inquiry.

Step 2: Selecting a point of reference for explaining behavior

When someone asks the psychologist, "How bright is that boy?"it is entirely appropriate for the psychologist to inquire in reply, "In reference to what?" Once we become involved in this type of "clarify-reclarify-further clarify" communication exchange, it becomes obvious that somewhere along the line someone isn't communicating efficiently. Replies become bogged down in memos requesting clarification or the reply comes through and the specialist's inference about the appropriate frame of reference may be incorrect and the received information is useless, inappropriate, or subject to misinterpretation.

There are any number of ways in which orientations or frames of reference might be categorized. And the exact framework selected by one attempting to improve cross-disciplinary communication is not as important as recognizing the need for clearly communicating what reference point is being used. One useful set of references can be examined here as an example of how such frameworks can be used to elicit better information.

In this framework, a reference area is intended to mean a way of looking at behavior in terms of a specific context of the behavior itself or with a certain purpose in mind.

Seven key words discriminatively identify different frames of reference: *normative, contextual, internal, external, predictive, potential* and *educational*. In shaping a question, the effective inquirer will indicate the frame of reference being used and the one he or she prefers the responder to use. By specifically referring to a defined point of reference, one assures that both the writer and the reader are operating in the same conceptual framework.

A *normative* reference area refers to typical behaviors of some identifiable group or standard. Given such a reference a question might follow: "At what elementary grade level is Mary now reading?" Although not in the form we would recommend as a final product, such a question begins to have meaning to a specialist who now can perceive exactly what is sought and attempt to provide it. If this is what the teacher really wants to know, then such a question *will* yield a *normative* answer, such as "Mary reads at the 7.5 level based upon such-and-such a test."

A *contextual* reference area refers to a certain identifiable environment or situation and asks the one who is explaining behaviors to do so in regard to a given situation. The same problem with Mary, considered in a *contextual* frame of reference, might yield this question, "How well does Mary read in relation to other girls in her class?" A question might be posed or information sought using both the *normative* and *contextual* reference points: "What is the overall reading ability of the girls in Mary's grade and how does Mary read in comparison with them?" This is a better question because it elicits better information.

An *internal* reference area refers to how an individual's behavior affects his or her other behaviors and is particularly useful in dealing with motivational aspects and symptomatic problems of learning disabilities. Mary's case might yield an *internal* reference question, such as "Has Mary's reading difficulty affected her academic performance in arithmetic?" Even more direct and behavioral might be the question: "Can Mary read suffiently well enough to handle her arithmetic assignments?" Often the problems noted initially will only be symptomatic of actual behavioral deficits, and then inquiries with *internal* frame of reference become appropriate. Mary's problem might first have been noticed in her failing marks in arithmetic and *internally* referenced questions could have elicited information regarding deficits in reading as a central cause of the arithmetic failures.

An *external* frame of reference refers to the effect an individual's behavior has on the behavior of others and carries ramifications for both the individual and others. When a child acts atypically, he or she presents stimuli to others that are not of the usual pattern. Other children then respond to these unusual stimuli, and the behavior of the individual and his or her associates are both affected. One might ask in Mary's case, "Is there any indication that Mary's girl friends reject her in any way because of her reading problems?" Such an *externally* referenced question yields pertinent interaction data.

A *predictive* frame of reference refers to explaining an individual's behavior in terms of outcomes, future events, and effects. The teacher might ask a reading specialist, "If Mary is a half-grade behind her class now and her general rate of improvement continues, how will she be performing by junior high?" It can be seen that good *predictive*-referenced questions really carry other frames of reference with them by inference. To answer the above question satisfactorily, the expert really should know whether the inquirer is asking him or her to predict in a *normative, contextual, internal*, or some other sense.

A *potential* frame of reference refers to the capability and behavioral capacity of the individual. In a sense it carries connotations of the *predictive* frame of reference too, since it deals with the future. In this case, however, the thrust is toward what *could* be or what it is possible to do rather than what *will be* the effects of some certain behavior or program. It would be reasonable to be concerned about Mary's potential and to ask, "Are there any indications that she might read up to her grade level with the proper tutoring and efforts?"

A final frame of reference, and one suprisingly often overlooked, is the *educational*. The most frequent locus of learning-problem behavior, particularly for young children, is in the school. Very often one must face the possibility that learning-deficit behaviors have different ramifications in the school than elsewhere. The educational frame of reference refers to the individual's behavior and its educational-learning relevance. Since most remedial prescriptions are written with school-type behaviors in mind, answers to questions with this frame of reference are vital. One might ask about Mary, "The mother reports that Mary does not like to read and this seems to be accurate. Is this dislike sufficiently strong to cause educational difficulties for Mary?"

There are some problems that fit most of the diagnostic stereotypes for a specific learning disability that, upon appropriate educational questioning (sometimes coupled with other types of questions), will be seen to be relatively unimportant to the child's educational status or future. The typical letter-reversals seen in the very young child are certainly genuinely perceived behavior. In most cases, however, that problem has little carry-over to school work and disappears spontaneously. An educationally relevant question might go far to alleviate the worry of some preschooler's mother and father, thus saving the child from the negative effect of anxiety about school performance that could generalize from overly concerned parents.

Step 3: Choosing an approach to make evaluative judgments

By far the most common reason for going to a specialist is to obtain some type of evaluative judgment. When asked to provide such judgmental information, each professional will have a variety of ways to obtain the information, draw conclusions, and express evaluations. It is not the province of the inquirer to direct the specialist in making decisions about what instrument or technique to use. However, it is very helpful to the specialist to know something about what the questioner has in mind and just what type of evaluative information will be most helpful.

A number of different technical procedures exist for making evaluative judgments. As Glaser (1963) has noted, there are several different factors to consider when facing the problems of assessing levels of competence and achievement. The technical problems are many, and some of the basic questions should be answered by trained specialists who must decide between criterion-referenced and norm-referenced measures. These and similar decisions are not typically the function of the questioning practitioner, but awareness of optional approaches to evaluation will help practitioners ask more meaningful questions.

In requesting any evaluative judgment, the inquirer should clearly communicate his or her preference for one of the four most common categories or approaches to evaluation. Further technical selection then rests with the specialist who must make the judgment. Again using the example of Mary, let's examine how an evaluative query might be formulated within the framework of each of these four approaches.

Evaluation by Level. This approach assumes that there is some acceptable or definable reference point from which to work. The individual's behavior will be evaluated, given other defined frames of reference, in respect to a particular reference point. Two major types of reference points are frequently used. In the first instance, the reference point is some normative standard and the question is asked much in the same fashion as was described under the first point of reference covered earlier, "Is Mary's work acceptable based upon the national norms (state, local, etc.) for a person her age?"

It is also quite possible to evaluate from a reference point that represents a level of acceptable behavior but which is not the expression of any group norm. In such cases, the standard is some defined behavior and the evaluation is said to be criterion referenced. Given this approach, judgments are most frequently binary, that is simply yes or no, although the introduction of subcriterion task levels may cause a type of scaling to result rather than a yes-no evaluation. A questioner using this approach might ask, "Can Mary read this printed page?" Deficits are handled differently in each approach (Ullman, 1971). A deficit in the normative approach is defined as a difference between what is expected and what is actually observed or performed. A deficit in the criterion-referenced approach is defined as a difference between what is required and what is actually observed or performed.

Evaluation by Pace. A completely different type of evaluation judgment is necessary if the question is one of rate or pace. In such instances the concern is not about the level in reference to either norm or criterion but about the rate itself.

"Pace" questions frequently focus on whether or not there are changes occurring in a person's behavior without being concerned with whether a certain level of improvement has been reached. In Mary's situation we might ask, "Is her reading improving at the rate we would expect for a person receiving this type of instruction?" Pace helps one evaluate program effectiveness, individual potential (to some extent), and such otherwise behavioral intangibles as motivation and interest.

Evaluation by Trend. This approach asks the evaluator to make a judgment about the predictable positive-negative indications of behavior. It is, of course, somewhat related to questions of pace. It is most useful in getting an overview from a large sample of individual behaviors, some of which are positive and some of which are negative. Thus, one might be concerned with a question such as "Mary's reading performance last year was stronger in silent reading than in oral reading. This year the two are about the same although her vocabulary is weak. Would you please evaluate her reading behaviors in terms of what trend seems to exist and give me an idea of whether or not my remedial program is resulting in general improvement?" It should be apparent that trend questions are not generally easily answered. As is the case when generalizing from any sample of behaviors, the more information made available to the evaluator and the more good samples he or she sees, the more accurate the prediction is likely to be.

Evaluation by Ratio. This approach might just as easily be labeled evaluation by specific comparison. Generally, questions of this type are asked within an internal frame of reference as explained previously. The following questions might be included: "How does Mary's reading compare with her other language skills?" or "It appears to me that Mary reads silently only about 75 percent as well as she does aloud. Would you please check this for me?" Ratio evaluations help one obtain a general picture of the individual's potential or overall ability. They also help sharpen contrasts between behaviors one can and cannot perform, thus helping with behavioral analysis procedures.

Step 4: Establishing a hierarchy of need-to-know

When consulting a specialist one may be tempted to ask, "Tell me all you know about everything." While such a question may be flattering in a sense, it is also frustrating to the busy specialist who must then take time to determine just what is important enough to tell and what can be omitted. Before finally wording an inquiry to an expert in another discipline, it is good to establish some type of hierarchy about what you really wish to know. It is always true, of course, that you wish to know as much as possible. Although total information transmittal is seldom, if ever, possible, a clearly indicated hierarchy communicates important information to the specialist. It says, in essence, "If you must limit yourself to one set of questions, please direct them to this particular problem."

Every practitioner can develop his or her own particular format for establishing a hierarchy of need-to-know, but the results of such decision making should clearly provide at least these four pieces of important, guiding input to the individual who is going to receive the inquiry:

1. The order of importance of the separate questions
2. The area of focus if some areas are to be treated in less depth
3. Relative urgency for receipt of information in each of the separate areas queried
4. Uses to which the information is to be put

Guide for choosing a hierarchy

The final category subdivides into separate areas that help convey to the specialist how he or she should make decisions on the inclusion and exclusion of information. In asking for information, the inquirer should always discriminate between the separate uses of the data being elicited and should identify how each piece of information is to be used. Uses might include the following:

Uses for data

1. Use for determining entering behaviors in a program
2. Use for cross-validating already obtained information
3. Use as information to fill current data gaps
4. Use as a basis for prescripting specific remedial procedures
5. Use as an outline for reporting to others (the *others* should be clearly identified)

Step 5: Formulation of the actual inquiry

The first four steps are actually only the preparatory procedures for arriving at the focus point of this whole process—elicting information that you need from others. Without reiterating the entire procedure step-by-step it is possible to reemphasize the main points. The process is simply one of speaking to someone clearly, precisely, with directness of purpose and intent. The final query, whether it is written formally or conveyed casually in a personal conversation, should contain each of these important specifications.

"What I want to know is this: _____. I am asking from this particular frame of reference and with this general evaluative approach in mind. My need to know this information rests upon these factors of preference, focus, and urgency. I intend to use this information as follows." Such an inquiry, carefully worded, would go far toward improving the quality of information elicited from those of other disciplines and professions.

One final aspect may be helpful to the practitioner in working toward building better communication lines with other disciplines. A conscientious program of self-improvement along the lines of nomenclature and areas of relevancy will help the practitioner become more easily conversant with fellow professionals. Knowing their language and areas of special focus should facilitate both communication and understanding. An informal survey of some professional journals is a step in the right direction. Many college textbooks carry helpful glossaries.

Another approach is to become conversant with the subcategories of information that specialists can provide. Most professionals are usually only too happy to make such information available upon request. National organizations of many professional disciplines provide explanatory literature through individual members.

Some idea of how general information can be further broken down into more meaningful and more easily handled bits of data can be seen from examination of the lists in Table 10-1. In this case, the broad areas of intelligence, arithmetic, reading, perceptual-motor behavior, and language-speech have been further subdivided. Such subdivisions frequently form the conceptual logic for the construction of assessment instruments. Thus, the arithmetic area as listed here coincides

TABLE 10-1
Major Topic Areas Subdivided into More Meaningful Behavior Bits.

INTELLIGENCE
1. Abstract idea capability
2. Speed of working
3. Memory power
4. Attention span
5. Information pool
6. Social sensitivity
7. Language usage
8. Nervousness or anxiety
9. Arithmetic ability
10. Fine motor skills

ARITHMETIC
1. Ability to handle different basic content areas, example-numeration
2. Ability to do specific operations, example-addition
3. Applications

READING
1. Frustration level
2. Potential learning level
3. Present functioning level
4. Oral reading ability
5. Silent reading ability
6. Listening comprehension ability
7. Word recognition
8. Visual memory
9. Spelling
10. Auditory analysis
11. Readiness
12. Vocabulary
13. Syllabication
14. Beginning and ending sounds
15. Sound blending
16. Sound discrimination

PERCEPTUAL MOTOR
1. Balance and postural flexibility
2. Perceptual-motor match
3. Ocular control
4. Form perception

LANGUAGE-SPEECH
1. Auditory reception
2. Visual reception
3. Visual and auditory sequential memory
4. Auditory association
5. Visual and auditory closure
6. Verbal expression
7. Grammatic closure
8. Sound blending
9. Speech problems with
    a. Plosives
    b. Continuants
    c. Nasals
    d. Articulation

with the *Keymath* assessment instrument (Connolly, Nachtman and Pritchett, 1971); the reading area has some parallel in the *Durrell Analysis of Reading Difficulty* tests (Durrell, 1955); the perceptual-motor list deals with the same general areas as the *Purdue Perceptual-Motor Survey;* and, the language-speech list largely coincides with the *Goldman-Fristoe-Woodcock Test of Auditory Discrimination.* Further lists and breakdowns could be compiled by talking to other specialists or by noting areas surveyed on other popular assessment instruments.

11

Preparing
and Selecting
Remedial Materials

For the practitioner, the whole focus of studying learning disability approaches, techniques, systems, models, and theories finally centers upon working with a specific child who needs help overcoming a specific learning deficit. A richness of background information and theoretical understanding is useful only if the knowledge and insight can be put to use in a practical way.

The selection or preparation of functional remedial materials is a vital part of any attack on a learning disability problem and the selection-preparation process is not as simple as it might seem at first. Good remedial materials must meet definite criteria, and every worker in the field knows that satisfying these criteria can be both a time consuming and difficult procedure. Failure to recognize the important criteria or to select materials that meet the criteria can lead to frustration, disappointment, and remedial failures that can and should be avoided.

Basic Criteria for Remedial Materials

Without getting into specific points about different theoretical approaches—standards that will vary according to the theoretical orientation of the user—we can identify several basic criteria that all remedial materials should meet, regardless of the theory being applied. While it is difficult to establish any absolute hierarchy in the importance of these criteria, there does seem to be a general consensus among practitioners that all are important and that some semblance of their ranking of importance may be present in the order in which they are presented here.

Goodness of Fit

This term, often used in a statistical sense by psychometricians and statisticians to indicate the degree to which the shape of one curve is the same as another, has a similar meaning here. Any remedial device or material must fit at least three different aspects of the situation in which it is applied.

The most obvious qualification is that the remedial material must be behaviorally relevant to the problem being attacked. As Gilbert and Sullivan sought to have the "punishment fit the crime," so must remedial activities fit the learning dysfunction under remediation or correction. There are two ways in which this criterion may be applied.

Face Validity

First, materials may have apparent "face validity." The materials can be obviously related to the problem by involving the same items, objects, processes, or actions. Thus a child having trouble discriminating letter shapes may be working with sample letters learning to discriminate their shapes. Something is said to have "face validity" when it *appears* to be related or to be doing what it says it is doing. The advantage of such "face validity" is that it may help maintain the motivation of workers and children involved by being directly problem oriented and by maintaining the individual's focus on the problem behaviors themselves. Improvement observed during use of such remedial materials has obvious relevancy to the problem and is usually quickly and strongly reinforcing. In such cases there is no need to explain how accomplishing a remedial goal will help with the basic learning problem. Using materials that have such ease of fit is something like "learning by doing" and has many advantages. Interestingly, the major disadvantage may stem from some of the same features. If the relationship between remedial materials or activities and the problem situation is so apparent, anxiety from the problem may generalize to the remedial steps and present difficulties. Failure to improve quickly in remedial work may be doubly discouraging since it can remind all concerned of the major problem involved and sub-criterion performance. These disadvantages can be severe but usually can be prevented or alleviated by carefully programming such activities or material use so that each step is sufficiently small to ensure success and avoid failure and frustrations.

Using Proven Materials

The criterion of goodness of fit may not always result in materials or activities that have face validity. This criterion may be applied in a second way by selecting materials that have demonstrated theoretical or sequential relevance to the problem. Thus, the practitioner may use materials that have behavioral relevance to the deficit; successful performance with these remedial materials has been demonstrated to lead to incremented performance in the deficit area. Obvious and apparent "face validity" relevancy may not be easily perceived in such circumstances. This type of material is often found in models that attack basic processes or strategies as the source of a deficit learning performance. In such a case, the child's failure to discriminate letter shapes successsfully might be thought of as a failure to learn a discrimination strategy. Remedial materials that assist the individual in learning such a strategy will have behavioral relevance even though they may not involve making exactly the same letter discriminations or require letter discrimination in any form.

Obviously, this second approach to assuring goodness of fit requires a great deal of skill and some thorough knowledge of the component behavior parts of the learning process. Using the psychometrician's language once again, such an approach needs to be based at least upon some "construct validity" and should involve some "predictive" or "criterion" validity. That is to say, the very least information upon which material selection should proceed is an awareness that identical theoretical and conceptual components are involved in remedial and ultimate criterion performance behaviors. The approach is strengthened if the user has some baseline data about how such materials lend to improvements in specific areas or relate to some other measure of improvement. This information usually cannot be gathered haphazardly or incidentally. It comes, almost always, only as a result of careful planning, precise measurement and observation, and through deliberate efforts to identify, quantify, and conceptualize interrelationships between the component parts of any learning task.

When used well, this second approach offers a sound basis for remediation. When used poorly, it is extremely dangerous for it may carry the implication of accuracy and insight with no way to check on such claims. Even when done well some problems are inherent in this second approach to assuring goodness of fit. Probably the most common problem encountered is maintaining motivation in the subject or even in the remediator if he or she is not totally versed on the less-than-obvious relationships involved. Everyone likes to experience and observe positive results. If the results are not easily perceived or if accomplishments with remedial materials are not apparently related to the removal of the problem disability, then motivational difficulties may arise. Providing plenty of information about the relationship may help. But in some cases, peripheral activities or materials (possibly brief excursions back into the actual deficit learning task area) may be necessary to maintain involvement by providing more apparent rewards and reinforcement.

Matching Materials

Total goodness of fit does not rest only upon materials matching the problem area. Materials and activities must also match the user of the materials, thoroughly meshing with his or her skills and approach. They must also suit the subject, the child for whom they are being applied. Any selection of materials must take into consideration all three of these aspects of goodness of fit. The materials and activities must fit the problem, the user, and the subject. Failing to do so may seriously limit or destroy the usefulness of any remedial approach.

Immediacy

This criterion is often overlooked in building general programs ready to meet a range of learning disabilities, but it is important. Practitioners all agree that materials should be on hand or quickly and easily accessible. While it is true that a search through catalogues and flyers will usually turn up a sample of almost any remedial material one could possibly want, such procedures take too long— especially when they must be followed by tedious ordering procedures and awaiting shipment. Opportunities for remediation frequently arise in an *ad hoc* form, unexpected, unplanned, yet potentially highly effective due to fortuitous circumstances, personnel availability, motivational readiness in the child, or similar circumstances. If a program or treatment center wishes to limit itself to a narrow range of disabilities, it can often assure relative immediacy by stocking formal programs and material-activity sets that closely relate to the treatment area being undertaken. When dealing with the full spectrum of learning disabilities, such preplanning and stocking is costly, difficult to accomplish thoroughly, and lacking in the kind of spontaneity that is frequently desirable. It seems obvious that any plan that allows for immediacy based on an on-site evaluation of what is needed at the moment is going to be a real advantage for the practitioner. If it is to function best, immediacy should be defined not only as ready accessibility, but readily related to the immediate situation and personnel. In this way, this criterion interrelates with flexibility.

Problems that may be encountered when immediacy is lacking are obvious. Such maxims as "strike while the iron is hot" certainly apply here. As we have noted in previous chapters, learning-disabled children suffer from all the negative features of severe frustration and are joined by their parents, friends, and sometimes even their teachers. There seems to be no excuse for adding to such frustration by being unable to move quickly when a demonstrated need for help is present and when the child and those around him are ready to become therapeutically involved.

Flexibility and Adaptability

In a sense, this criterion is also involved with the first criterion of goodness of fit. Preconceived programs and materials, though well thought out and carefully constructed, are based upon some stereotyped categorization of disability. The problem of stereotyped programs that don't exactly match any child (rather like the awkward saying that the average family has 2.5 children) can be minimized by dealing with small bits and pieces of behavior in program planning so that different module parts can be joined in different situations. Yet the problem still is not completely eliminated. Effective practitioners almost invariably demonstrate their effectiveness at modifying existing programs and materials by changing parts and activities so that they fit an individual child better.

While this flexibility and adaptability seem to be part of the skill pattern of successful learning disability workers, these elements aren't completely dependent upon the practitioner. Materials can be collected, built, and assembled in a fashion that meets this important criterion more easily. Some techniques for doing this successfully are described later in the chapter.

Failure to meet this criterion in selecting remedial materials results in a correlated lack of success in remediation. When remedial activities don't quite "hit the mark" because they are rigid and incapable of being made to fit a specific situation, any subsequent success may be limited to the amount of correlation present between the problem area, the child, the user and the materials being applied. Like other problems we have seen, lack of flexibility is a problem that is rather easily avoidable.

Economy

As the saying goes, "last but not least" is the simple but very important criterion of economy. Remedial materials and activities should be as economical as possible both in terms of money and time. To a large extent all three of the criteria already noted relate to economy of time. Goodness of fit, immediacy, and flexibility all suggest that time should not be wasted trying to use materials that don't really satisfy the need. There seems to be no good reason why such problems are encountered frequently. Although everyone occasionally expects to face an unusual case where the peculiarities involved may take more time than usual, that situation shouldn't be a regular occurence. As we will note later, there are useful approaches that limit the frequency of such experiences.

It is equally important to stress that good remedial materials and activities do not need to be expensive either. Too often, commercially prepared materials, which incidentally do not always meet some of the first three criteria, include charges for overhead costs like advertising, limited production runs, sales promotion, packaging, and other aspects which really add nothing to the program material. While some commercially prepared materials are virtually impossible to emulate in do-it-yourself form and others involve equipment and special aspects one would not wish to even try to replace, many learning disability problems respond to materials and equipment quickly and inexpensively prepared by local practitioners.

It is not the intent of the authors in any of the ideas and procedures outlined here to suggest that practitioners should violate copyrights either actually or de facto by reproducing commercial materials or literally copying such items. Rather it seems to be a viable stratgey to arrive at some workable proportions of commercially prepared and individually constructed materials that maximize the probability that all four of the above criteria can be met. To the extent that self-constructed or locally assembled materials and items best or equally meet the above criteria they should be used. In those cases where it is impossible to best meet the criteria except by resorting to commercial materials, then the appropriate materials should be purchased. Individual practitioners, provided with an awareness of their own capabilities and limitations, can soon develop the necessary discriminations for such choices.

The following steps and techniques are designed to facilitate the development of such awareness.

User Preparation

As Durkin (1974) has pointed out, teachers and others who frequently use commercially prepared academic materials often waste time on instruments that are erroneously directed at problem situations. The fault may be in an instrument that is poorly constructed, hastily validated or inadequately explained in literature describing its appropriate uses. However, it seems to be as often true that the locus of the problem lies as much with the user as the instrument or technique. This is probably due to a generally uncritical, unquestioning blanket application of anything commercially produced on the assumption that such materials must be useful or they would not be made available. The first step toward achieving a consistently functional strategy in the selection and application of remedial materials lies in some preparation on the part of the user.

Guidelines for Choosing Materials

We would like to outline some specific steps the practitioner should take when reviewing materials for adoption.

1. Practitioners Should Become More Knowledgeable. There is no reason why the user of remedial materials should not develop as much consumer awareness in the selection and application of remediation materials as in the choice of clothing or the purchase of food. Comparative shopping by checking the competing prices of different manufacturers, careful analysis of material content, and the application of advertised materials to the user's own situation is important. Some simple but all-important technical knowledge about the basic psychometric characteristics present in any remedial material and a general sensitivity to what characteristics typify a product designed primarily for effective use rather than heavy sales is also valuable. As with any sales program, the producers of consumer goods must bend to the will of the consumer if the user forces the point by refusing to purchase anything that is not all that it claims to be. One need not assume that questionable materials are deliberately fraudulent, because that is not usually the case. The fact is, however, that much of the material marketed for obstensible use in learning disabilities and other special education areas leaves a great deal to be desired in the four criterion areas mentioned above. Even when the mistakes are honest ones, due to ignorance or overenthusiasm rather than fraudulent intent, the end result is the same. The user is left with materials that fall short of expectations because of failure to meet one of the four criterion areas. "Let the buyer beware" is still good advice. The best way to demonstrate being *beware* is to be obviously *aware* as a result of acquiring knowledge about remedial materials and their uses.

2. Practitioners Should Always Have a Specific Goal Orientation. The label currently hung on the problem we're dealing with in this whole book is *specific learning disabilities*. In selecting remedial materials and activities, the user should keep in mind the specificity of the goals he or she has in mind. With such an orientation one is not so easily overwhelmed with sharp sales pitches or by attractive packaging. If the user, when faced with a materials choice, always asks four basic and simple questions, goal orientation will generally be assured.

Basic questions to assure goal orientation

1. What am I trying to do with this material? Do not ask, "What is the material meant to accomplish?" for, as effective as it may be in meeting an advertised goal, if that goal is not congruent with the user's goal, efficiency is forfeited.
2. How do I intend to apply the materials? It is the application dimensions including the general context, the immediate situation, and the assets and limitations in users that are all-important. A ship is useful only where there is water. Remedial materials should be approached in the same way. If the user is sure that the capabilities of the instrument or materials fit the mode of use in mind, the purchase is more defensible.
3. When must I use the materials? This is a simple but often overlooked question related to the criterion of immediacy. If the materials are for an immediate problem then not only shipping times but user preparation times must be considered. Some very good remedial reading programs are available if one has time to train someone to present them. Such advance preparation is desirable but not always practical or even possible. The Minute Man might like a supporting artillery barrage but to remain a Minute Man he may have to settle for a quickly available musket.
4. Who is going to be using the materials? Some materials require not only immediate preparation in the user but long-range professional preparation and training. Others are based upon assumptions of basic knowledge about various curriculum related matters, such as phonics or arithmetical constructs. In the hands of those possessing the necessary background, the materials may be most useful. In the hands of an aide or an uninitiated parent or the dysfunctioning child himself such materials may be less effective or totally inadequate.

3. Practitioners Should Always Clarify Instructional Roles Related to Remedial Materials. The principles involved in this step are simple. The same questions of what, how, when, and who should be asked but should be related specifically to the instructional relationship. What relationship between user and subject is sought? Is it to be a one-to-one relationship? Is it to be one of increasing independence so that the pupil finally becomes self-instructional? The "how" and "who" questions should be oriented in part around the location of instruction, the degree to which untrained volunteer help (such as parents, peers, siblings) will be used, and the effect such selections may have on remedial material choice. "When" questions should consider time demand both in terms of the amount of time available per lesson or for an entire remedial improvement sequence, and also in terms of proportions of supervisional time available, necessary, or desirable under different case situations. The nature of the instructional scene shifts from problem to problem and these variables interact differently leading to different remedial material choices.

In working through these first three steps it often becomes obvious that no catalogue or manufacturer's list contains exactly what is needed. At this point the practitioner should be sensitive to two final steps toward effective material selection.

4. Practitioners Should Develop Self-Confidence in Their Own Ability to Create and Produce Effective Remedial Materials. By combining their own practical experience in the learning situation with an adaptability enforced by ever-changing problem situations, and with a sensitive, evaluative critique of existing materials, most practitioners have all the tools necessary to be effectively creative. It has been the authors' experience that in dealing with learning disability workers who have developed even a modicum of these three attributes, all that is needed to set off a creative deluge is some schematic design or plan of action. Some ideas about how to set up such a plan will be outlined in following pages.

5. Practitioners Should Learn to Enlist the Remedial Attributes of Everyday Situations and On-Site Personnel. If people have some creative ideas about designing their own materials or adapting other materials to meet a certain need, one final step lends effectiveness to the choice and selection strategy. Often the very best tools and people to involve are naturally present in the situation. One or two brief examples should demonstrate this point. If a child's deficit is made obvious due to contrasts between his performance and the performance of his classmates, a ready-made modeling and built-in instructional situation is already present. His classmates provide both the model and often the unobtrusive instructional help he needs. Pairing him with a child who does perform adequately assures a criterion level peer-mate. Add to this a ready-made remedial activity that can be used by the two children together and the chance for instructional progress is greatly increased over any highly individualized, teacher-with-pupil-in-a-special-room situation. Efficient practitioners can be found using all types of people and both professional and nonprofessional personnel in remedial programs. A child falling back on pointing to avoid a deficit in verbal expression can be unobtrusively forced into practicing correct behaviors by a cafeteria server who requires in a friendly manner that the child verbalize food choices in the lunch lines. Janitors, crossing guards, school bus drivers, parents, friends, peers—all of these people are potential helpers when they are carefully involved in a well thought out and original remedial strategy.

Having followed these recommendations, what faces the practitioner who would make wise selections or who would create effective remedial materials? Actually, given this kind of conceptual preparation, only two main processes are left: first, the identification of specific remedial areas for which to prepare materials; and second, the choice or preparation of the materials themselves.

Identification of Remedial Material Areas

The identification of an area for which to prepare materials depends upon two main variables: the nature of the diagnostic input data with which the practitioner is working and the specific therapeutic goals or objectives desired.

As with instrument and procedure selection in screening activities, diagnostic data should be assembled under some conceptual or pragmatic basis that makes it useful and readily accessible for decisions such as the selection and preparation of materials. Amassing a large amount of descriptive diagnostic data wastes time and money if the data serve no useful purpose. One of the criteria for choosing particular diagnostic techniques over others should be that they fit the expected remedial activity range and fall within the capability of the practitioners who must apply such data. Such capabilities should be defined not only in terms of what a learning disability practitioner can do, but also by what the worker can reasonably be expected to do considering realistic time and money contingencies. A most important part of this consideration is the availability of already prepared or easily accessible remedial materials and the possibility of easily creating materials for indentified needs when such materials may not be at hand.

The process of building successful remedial programs often requires the identification or establishment of several important pieces of behavioral information (as will be described in some details in the final section of this text). Two very important pieces of information are concerned with the identification of the behaviors the disabled person must eventually be able to perform (to remove the disabled or deficient label) and the behavior the disabled person is presenting at the moment (behavior that apparently is insufficiently satisfactory so that he or she is labeled as having a learning disability). The former, final goal behaviors, technically called *criterion performance behaviors*, are obtained as the final step in task analysis. Present, inadequate behaviors, the latter piece of data, are called the *behavioral repertoire* and are obtained through a procedure known as *behavior analysis*. Both procedures are discussed at some length in later chapters. In preparing diagnostic strategies, however, it is useful to remember that such behaviors are going to be used in program building and that advance consideration of the eventual need for such data will facilitate the selection of remedial materials.

The steps to ensure this early consideration of data needs are fairly brief and easily achieved. Following through with the steps has a nice spin-off bonus, since it usually provides the practitioner with additional insight and awareness into the nature of the diagnostic procedure itself and relates to everyday behaviors. As we will see later, a close relationship between measurements activities and actual behavioral situations facilitates accurate assessment and is highly desirable whenever possible.

1. Study the diagnostic instrument(s) typically used in your everyday situation for the behaviors they require.
2. Break the instruments down into their designated subparts (often individual subtests, though in some cases this may include small groups of subtests) according to some meaningful conceptualization related to problems you are dealing with.
3. For each classification, briefly list examples of the type of behavior an individual must be able to do to score satisfactorily in that area.
4. Note simple examples of behaviors frequently seen in individuals who are not scoring satisfactorily in these areas. Do not make these opposites of the satisfactory (e.g., satisfactory is counting from 1 to 10, unsatisfactory is not being able to count 1 to 10). Rather, note behaviors that frequently indicate deficits being present (e.g., cannot tell how many balls are in a basket by counting them).
5. Both the criterion-type performances and the evidences of subcriterion behavior should be listed in chart form according to each subarea.

Sample pieces of such charts for the *Illinois Test of Psycholinguistic Abilities, Key-Math,* the *Durrell Analysis of Reading Difficulty,* and for the *Purdue Perceptual-Motor Survey* can be found in Tables 11-1 through 11-4.

Obviously, if discrete behavioral deficits have not been observed and identified, the procedure described here cannot be successfully applied. Too heavy dependence upon such a method may involve the user in two different types of problems:

1. In those cases where deficit may be the product of a highly generalized nonproductive behavior form (such as the "passive learner" syndrome, which cognitists are currently investigating), the remedial "bits" must be relevant to the general behavior as well as to the immediate deficiencies. Without conscious attention to the former, the prescriber may overlook it.
2. Sequential "bits" can be misappropriated as evidence of a developmental basic process. Since many of these have yet to be empirically substantiated, the users of the technique described here should avoid slipping into that mode which gives rise to invalid or unsupported assumptions.

Once these five steps are accomplished, the worker is ready to do an inventory of existing remedial materials. This may include formal and informal materials as well as general compilations of diagnostic remedial materials that are available

Five steps for determining remedial areas

TABLE 11-1

Excerpts from the Remedial Materials Selection Chart for the Illinois Test of Psycholinguistic Abilities*

SUBTEST AREA	CRITERION EXAMPLE	DEFICIT EXAMPLE	PUBLISHED SOURCES	LOCAL MATERIALS
Auditory Reception	S responds appropriately to an orally presented question (e.g., "Do trains swim?").	Failure to follow a simple auditory cue, such as "Run when I say go!"	Kirk & Kirk, 1971 Ashlock & Grant, 1972 Bush & Giles, 1969	Program cards Nos. 17, 21, 42, 43, 50, 61
Visual Association	S can choose the correct alternative to complete a visually presented analogy.	S fails to identify visual relationships, such as the "go to jail" square on the monopoly game.	Frostig, 1967 Mann & Suiter, 1974 Kirk & Kirk, 1971 Bush & Giles, 1969	Program cards Nos. 3, 4, 5, 19, 37, 38, 51
Visual Closure	S can identify an object when only part of it is visible.	S needs to see an entire polysyllabic word before recognizing the word.	Blanco, 1972 Kirk & Kirk, 1971 Bush & Giles, 1969	Program cards Nos. 1, 9, 27, 41, 44
Verbal Expression	S can adequately describe an object shown to him.	S has difficulty in describing an object S brings to "show and tell."	Glens Falls, N.Y., program material Kirk & Kirk, 1971 Bush & Giles, 1969	Program cards Nos. 7, 12, 22, 32

* Not all subtest areas are included in this abbreviated form and the list of published sources is considerably shortened by using only one or two examples. It should also be noted that the listed deficit behaviors should not be considered as stemming only from process-related disorders. Other causes may also produce these problems.

TABLE 11-2

Excerpts from the Remedial Materials Selection Chart for the Key-Math*

SUBTEST AREA	CRITERION EXAMPLE	DEFICIT EXAMPLE	PUBLISHED SOURCES	LOCAL MATERIALS
Numeration	Given a set of objects, S correctly tells the total.	S has playground and gym problems in following directions, such as "Hit three balls and then give someone else a turn."	Mann & Suiter, 1974	Program cards Nos. 13, 14
Subtraction	Given two numbers, S can find the difference.	S has problems in following distribution-of-materials directions, such as "Give this group two less crayons than the other group."	Commercial flash cards	Program cards Nos. 6, 23, 24, 25
Word Problems	Given an addition problem with addends of "once" and "twice," S solves the sum.	S shows substandard problem solving when operations are described rather than listed (e.g., S can solve for $3 - 2$ but has problems with "What is three less two?").	Mann & Suiter, 1974	None prepared
Time	Given a clock set at an "hour" time (e.g., 4 o'clock), S can state what time it is.	S fails to be on time or follow activity time schedules.	None on hand	Program cards Nos. 2, 60, 62, 63

* Not all subtest areas are included in this abbreviated form and the list of published sources is considerably shortened by using only one or two examples.

211

TABLE 11-3

Exerpts from the Remedial Materials Selection Chart for the Durrell Analysis of Reading Difficulty*

SUBTEST AREA	CRITERION EXAMPLE	DEFICIT EXAMPLE	PUBLISHED SOURCES	LOCAL MATERIALS
Visual Perception of Word Elements	S can recognize a word when shown it for very short time (e.g., ½ second).	S's problems are similar to problems in ITPA visual closure areas.	Ashlock & Grant, 1972 Mann & Suiter, 1974 See also Peabody sets.	Program cards Nos. 8, 15
Phonic Abilities	S can spell a word by sounding it out.	S mispronounces words (e.g., pronoun-ciate instead of pro-nun-ciate). S has spelling problems.	See sets of reading curriculum materials in clinic library.	Program cards Nos. 10, 26, 39, 40
Learning Rate	A nonreading S can identify a word 30 seconds after having seen it for the first time.	S fails to remember new written instructions.	Mann & Suiter, 1974	Program cards Nos. 71, 72, 73
Reading Speed	S can read at the norm rate of his or her age/class peers.	S produces late assignments when reading is required.	Kaluger & Kolson, 1969	Program cards Nos. 11, 16

* Not all subtest areas are included in this abbreviated form and the list of published sources is considerably shortened by using only one or two examples.

TABLE 11-4

Exerpts from the Remedial Materials Selection Chart for the Purdue Perceptual Motor Survey*

SUBTEST AREA	CRITERION EXAMPLE	DEFICIT EXAMPLE	PUBLISHED SOURCES	LOCAL MATERIALS
Balance and Posture	S is able to maintain balance while hopping in place.	S is generally awkward. S is shunned by other children in choosing sides for games demanding coordination.	Check Merrill "Slow-Learner" series for help in all PPMS subareas. Kephart, 1971a Blanco, 1972	Program cards Nos. 20, 28, 29, 30
Perceptual-Motor Match	When asked to do so, S can draw a circle in correct size, shape, and direction.	S produces sloppy paperwork. S shows deficit art performance.	Mann & Suiter, 1974	Program cards Nos. 45, 47, 52, 53, 54
Occular Control	S is able to establish eye contact and then follow a moving object with his eyes.	S loses the place in reading. S gives poor gym performance (e.g., in batting a ball).	None on hand	Program cards Nos. 18, 36, 46
Form Perception	When shown a design, S can reproduce it.	S reverses letters and has visual letter discrimination problems.	Frostig, 1967	Program cards Nos. 55, 56, 57

* Not all subtest areas are included in this abbreviated form and the list of published sources is considerably shortened by using only one or two examples.

213

on the market (Ashlock and Grant, 1972; Blanco, 1972; Bush and Giles, 1977: Mann and Suiter, 1979).

Using the same chart one should reference the specific materials on hand relevant to each area. Thus, when a child's diagnostic profile shows a deficit-level score on a ITPA subtest, the practitioner should be able to gauge by looking at the chart what type of behaviors are to be expected on this subtest by the nondeficit child, typical problem behaviors presented by a deficit child, and the availability of prepared materials for achieving a criterion level of behavior.

Choosing and Preparing Materials

It soon becomes obvious that a facility or program is rarely supplied well enough to have formal materials relevant to every subarea which their diagnostic instruments are capable of identifying. Sometimes it is necessary to ad lib in preparing materials because no formal method is available or because the needs of the situation are so idiosyncratic that they call for specialized materials to fit the subjects.

Workers in the field have long been aware of such needs and almost every facility has its own supply of individualized, homemade, or "cannibalized" materials that the local workers have found to be useful. While it is true that not every need can always be anticipated, it is equally true that there are some fairly simple procedures that will decrease the number of times one is faced with unforseen gaps in needed materials. Some individual groups, and in some cases even state-wide organizations like the Michigan Association for Children with Learning Disabilities, have developed useful supply procedures. These consist pimarily of assembling some easily prepared, accessible, and relatively inexpensive materials that can be either used over and over or can be replaced easily after use. The Michigan association calls its fairly well-organized program of assembling materials the "Bucket Brigade." They use the analogy of being ready to put out spot fires through speedy application of simple remedial procedures before big fires and problems develop. Such "homemade" preparations are well worth considering.

For several years the authors have used a set of homemade materials for such purposes and have seen many local workers copy the technique successfully for their own programs. The steps are quick and easy and provide a set of materials that are not only very functional but also inexpensive, readily replicated, and widely useful with a variety of volunteer workers, including parents, aides, friends, peers, etc.

The place to start is with charts, prepared as we described above (Tables 11-1, 2, 3, 4), identifying individual subareas and specifying criterion and typical deficit behaviors. At this point the individual worker may wish to identify areas for which no formal materials are on hand or may instead wish to have some remedial redundancy capability by preparing "local" materials even for those areas where formal procedures are available. The former process is faster and easier. However, we favor preparing original materials for we have found that they are not only functionally effective, but they are also more likely to be related to activities and procedures that local users and subjects find familiar, easy to use, and self-motivating.

At this point individual creativity comes into play as the worker begins to create materials that provide the user with the opportunity to move from deficit behavior (can't count the number of balls in a basket) to criterion behaviors (being able to count from one to ten). First the workers assemble a store of source materials. In numerous workshops we have taken groups of workers on trips to the local variety store with directions to spend no more than a total of $5.00 to provide the raw materials they need to build remedial activities. The shoppers are aiming to fit all the subareas for the four assessment instruments noted in Tables 11-1 to 4, a total of forty-one subtest areas!

Here is a list of "raw materials" assembled by one worker on such an excursion.

- Scotch tape
- 3" × 5" cards
- Paper clips
- Small package paper cups
- Colored paper
- Play money
- Poker chips
- Rubber bands
- Marbles
- Package of plastic cowboys
- Envelopes
- Colored Crayons
- Straws
- Paper tablet
- Child's card game (Letter Lotto)
- Rubber stamp of a star and stamp pad
- Paper lunch bags

Easily obtainable and inexpensive materials

In addition, the worker brought from home the following:

- Six small empty juice cans
- An 8" square board with 36 finishing nails pounded in at regular intervals
- Blocks obtained from sawing 1" pieces off a 2' section of 1" × 2" board
- A net bag salvaged from the supermarket
- Three small cardboard boxes of different sizes
- ½ lb. dried beans, peas, rice, and elbow macaroni

Using these materials, the worker began to assemble a number of separate devices or activities that could be applied in different ways to many problems.

For example, poker chips can be used for counting, color discrimination, fine-motor skills, etc. Once a "device" or activity is prepared, it is given a number for future reference and is packaged in some convenient way. Refrigerator-size plastic bags are frequently used to hold separate sets of materials since they are light, easily replaceable, and transparent. The real secret lies in seeing how many different ways an individual device or activity can be used. A brief direction card is prepared for each use telling the user exactly what to do with the materials. Many sets of materials can be used over and over for different purposes. To facilitate storage and referencing we have found it useful to use boxes from liquor stores that already have subdivisions creating six to twelve compartments that can be easily numbered. The height of the box can be cut to fit the materials at hand (see Figure 11-1).

The 3" × 5" cards are then filed according to the subareas on the diagnostic activity chart, and when a deficit area is noted the practitioner can refer to the card file for ideas on how to use the materials. The card should contain several pieces of information. Cards we use in our workshops follow a format that includes diagnostic subarea involved, materials location [referenced according to cubbyhole numbers in which the material(s) can be found], directions for users, and sometimes additional information. Figure 11-2 is an example of such a card.

Once a workable set of materials is assembled (and some trial and error may be involved in finding just what works in a particular situation) additional sets may be prepared simply by duplicating materials and cards and storing them in the subdivided boxes. In some locales where we have worked, high school community involvement clubs have volunteered to replicate such kits. In others, interested parents, service clubs, and local chapters of the ACLD have helped with the reproduction. If the program develops some volunteer resource person-

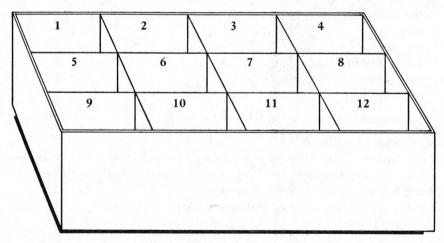

FIGURE 11-1
Materials Storage Box

nel who prove to be particularly adept at using such materials, these volunteers may wish to create sets for themselves. All sets are cross-referenced against the diagnostic areas typically discriminated in the local program, greatly facilitating material selection and personal involvement.

The following list provides a few examples of what workers prepared from the materials they brought and areas for which they were used. Other possibilities are limited only by the creator/user's imagination and resourcefulness.

Examples

1. The six juice cans were filled with different dry objects such as beans, peas, rice, macaroni, etc., and were then sealed with tape and painted. The cans were used for several different purposes including auditory discrimination (see Figure 11-2 for the corresponding program card), auditory sequential memory, sound matching, etc.
2. Rubber bands were packaged with the nail board (see Figure 11-2) and the two were used for form discrimination, visual memory, fine motor coordination, etc.
3. Marbles were used for counting exercises and when combined with paper

---

Activity No. 43 Area: Auditory Discrimination

Related Subtest Areas: ITPA Subtests 1, 4
                       Durrell Subtest 3

Materials: 6 juice cans with objects inside	In Compartment 2

Directions:
  Use #1 T picks can at random, shakes it. Replaces it among other cans. Asks S to shake various cans until S can pick out correct can.

  Use #2 T asks S to place cans in order of loudest sounding can when all are listened to in order.

  Use #3 T asks S to find which can is out of order in loud to soft order.

FIGURE 11-2
Remedial Materials Card

cups were used for sorting and simple addition and subtraction drills.

4. Straws were cut into proportional lengths and used in exercises similar to those employing Cuisenaire rods. They were also used in varying lengths for size discrimination and visual sequential memory activities.

5. Letter cards were extracted from the card game and used in form discrimination, reversal training, sound discrimination, and sound blending activities.

6. Paper lunch bags were used to make hand puppets for use in verbal expression practice, for sorting bags, and for memory drills with different objects being hidden inside and then recalled on demand.

7. Play money was used for memory drills, counting and simple arithmetical activities, visual closure exercises as well as "money" exercises related to *Key-Math* subtests.

8. The rubber stamp was used for discrimination, counting, spacial orientation, and memory work.

9. Envelopes were used to hold letter and number and form cards drawn on and in some cases cut from the 3" × 5" cards. These were used in drills obviously related to these symbols, such as letter and form discrimination, sound recognition and discrimination, form discrimination, memory, and matching exercises.

10. The plastic cowboys were used in both manual and verbal expression games, in memory exercises, in counting and visual association drills.

11. Blocks were used in counting and various number- and letter-related activities. Letters, numbers, and forms were drawn on the sides with the colored crayons and all were stored in the net bag.

12. Leftover beans were placed in one of the small boxes and were available for counting, sorting, and memory work.

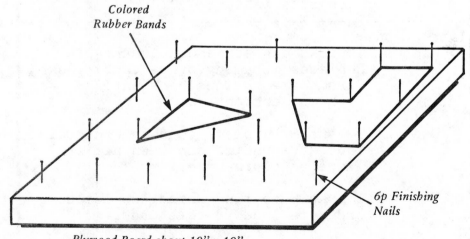

Colored Rubber Bands

6p Finishing Nails

Plywood Board about 10" x 10"

FIGURE 11-3
A Homemade Form Discrimination Board

A considerable number of additional activities created spontaneously by workshop participants could be listed using these materials in different ways and in different combinations with each other. A typical twelve-compartment source box, filled during a one-day workshop using these procedures, usually yielded somewhere around fifty separate activities spread over almost all of the nearly four dozen subtest areas discriminated in the assessment instruments being used. Subsequent reports indicated that most workers tended to expand their number of activities without much change in the basic source materials and that remedial results were generally quite as good as when using commercially prepared materials.

SUMMARY

Material choice, selection, and creation is not a particularly difficult procedure. It does require attention to some important criteria and some sensitivity to how and why materials are going to be required. Most workers with only a little training will find themselves capable of making good selections and being productively creative in filling material and activity gaps not provided for by commercial materials. Such homemade substitution does not seem to result in less effective or less useful remedial materials and may even result in more motivating activities.

12

Delivery of Service Alternatives

Perhaps nowhere else in education can one find as wide a diversity of models and practices for delivery of services as in special education. Although a few basic models seem to predominate, close inspection of how a model is actually operated discloses such a variety of ideas, arrangements, organizational structures, and practices as almost to defy succinct classification. And, as Willower (1970) has indicated, since the majority of those involved in special education have been predominantly interested in remedial practices, applied techniques, and similarly more visible components of the system, educational administration of special education is largely untouched and unaided by such potentially helpful analytical disciplines as organizational theory and social system analysis.

The field badly needs a thorough social analysis along some specialized lines of inquiry that might lead to valuable information about the relative effectiveness of different delivery of services models and practices. Among such inquiries should be a systematic analysis of the organizational nature of schools as they exist in the culture they serve. Special education as a definable subculture within the public school should also be examined. And of particular interest to those concerned with learning disabled children, who by definition possess normal potentialities, should be the study of the process of the adoption and assimilation of the special education child into the everyday education milieu, the process popularly labeled *mainstreaming*.

Current practices and trends are lending themselves to such examination and analysis perhaps more than in the past. Educational trends, such as the contemporary emphasis on mainstreaming, are leading to increasingly thorough organizational study with an eye toward developing a more effective delivery model.

Various sources have contributed to the refining process by identifying specific areas of emphasis and characteristics necessary for effective service in the area of learning disabilities as distinguished from the special education field in general. More and more programs, such as one initiated by the Santa Cruz County Office of Education, are emphasizing behavorial characteristics typical of children progressing successfully through a remedial experience. Such information provides a baseline against which to measure the effectiveness of other delivery models. More substantial data of this nature are badly needed. However, identification and evaluation of organizational models are very complex. As McIntosh and Dunn (1973) note, special education services involve not one but at least four separate delivery models including ancillary referral services, assessment services, placement services, and intervention services. Such diverse service systems also involve different loci of function, including the home, the regular classroom, the environmental milieu, and a number of specialized locations (see Figure 12-1).

In the past, and unfortunately to a large extent in the present, resolution of the delivery of services decision has too often been based upon an arbitrary categorization of children that may have little if any relationship to their actual behavioral deficits or capabilities. Such categorizing has tended to establish stereotypes leading to grouping and treatment practices based upon an unfounded assumption of the homogeneity of behaviors among the children involved. Labeling has become fixed and stigma-ridden and has led to negative expectations among those working with children displaying special problems.

The individuality of such children, long recognized by sensitive workers in the field, is getting increasing attention however and the effect on delivery models is predictable. As Reynolds and Balow (1972) have explained, source or surface variables—behaviors that tend to result in stereotyped grouping labels—are being seen as less important. Instead, delivery systems are being established that depend upon the interaction of an individual child's aptitude with specific treatment techniques for information leading to remedial activities. Such a trend moves away from descriptive labels and toward specific interaction effects. It encourages better descriptions of children's needs as opposed to stereotyped descriptions of groups of children. Delivery systems also lead to the training and development of practitioners who specialize in working with special need categories rather than with generalized types of children. All of these positive developments provide increased flexibility in the delivery of services, which is necessary if organizational structures are to be responsive to individualized needs.

The assumption of homogeneous grouping has persisted since public day-school programs for educably mentally retarded were first established in Rhode Island in 1896. Such an assumption embodies the idea that these groups of children exhibit similar needs, that such placement leads to a unique and better curriculum, and that specially trained personnel (special education teachers) pos-

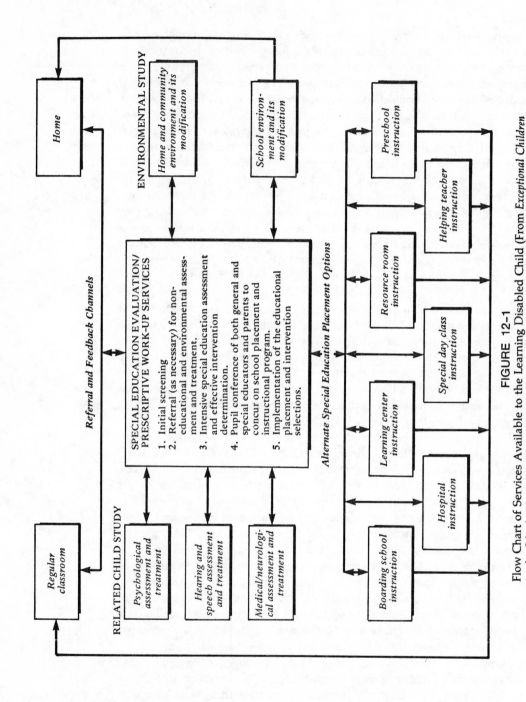

FIGURE 12-1

Flow Chart of Services Available to the Learning Disabled Child (From *Exceptional Children in the Schools: Special Education in Transition*, Second Edition, by Lloyd M. Dunn, Editor. Copyright © 1963, 1973 by Holt, Rinehart and Winston, Inc. Reprinted by permission of Holt, Rinehart and Winston.)

sess better or distinctive skills for working with these children. As Bruininks and Rynders (1975) report, there seems to be little if any evidence to support these assumptions consistently.

Present organizational development appears to be replacing some of these poorly substantiated ideas with individually prescribed instruction based on the normalization principle that was first developed formally in Scandinavia. This principle firmly states that special children profit most from integration into normal school routines through maximizing their abilities and developing an array of service systems designed to meet their individual needs and problems. Organizationally, the normalization principle has resulted in the establishment of a number of different administrative plans that permit segregation of the individual child as much as really necessary but that also encourage normal-child/special-child integration whenever possible. Dunn (1973) has identified eleven major administrative plans that allow for such progressive segregation or integration (see Figure 12-2). These eleven plans serve four broad types of exceptional children grouped on the basis of the amount and type of integration they experience rather than upon some assumed but undemonstrated behavioral homogeneity.

Such trends in support of a normalization principle involve more than purely organizational structure. As the array of segregated-to-integrated school services develops, parallels of differentiated personnel roles and instructional resources must also develop (see Table 12-1). Indeed, any explanation of delivery of service models must include the interaction of all three aspects of the model's functions: personnel roles involved, instructional resources required, and possible administrative placements.

There is also another shift in emphasis and practice increasingly visible in contemporary delivery services. This is the tendency to think of the extension of services designed to meet an individual child's special needs as something in the nature of a personal contract with the child and his family. Such a contractual arrangement may be a deliberately formalized special education contract as described by Gallagher (1972), where certain specific objectives and time-lines are developed and agreed upon by all parties. Or it may consist of less formal arrangements where contractual-like responsibilities are inferred by the remediator as he or she attempts to respond to an individual's personal needs and response to remediation.

This change in focus from broadly based stereotypes to more highly individualized programing has not done much to shift the responsibility for working with special children away from the schools. Although ancillary services have developed, the major focus and attention on the problem still remain the province of the school through a variety of special facilities and formats. The expensive nature of special programs, staffing, and physical plants seems to be more readily handled by institutions relying upon a tax-based support (Edgington, 1967). As programs have moved away from labeling and into more flexible support services some special needs, peripheral to the delivery of service model but vital to its successful function, have been recognized. These include the need for training educational teams as well as for specialized individuals; developing specialized programs and techniques for effecting mainstream objectives; and, finally, developing training models logically and pragmatically related to service models so that effective practices can be generated across a wider population of developing practitioners at all levels (Hafner, 1972).

Grosenick (1971) has called attention to the fact that special placement should be considered only a temporary intervention. The syndrome of institutionalization and the manner in which it tends to perpetuate special placement; the diffi-

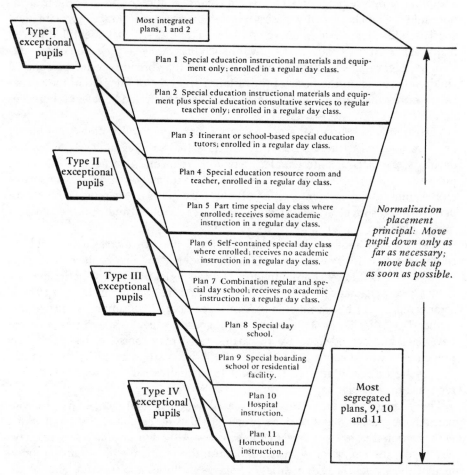

FIGURE 12–2

A Model of Administrative Plans for Special Education (From *Exceptional Children in the Schools: Special Education in Transition*, Second Edition, by Lloyd M. Dunn, Editor. Copyright © 1963, 1973 by Holt, Rinehart and Winston, Inc. Reprinted by permission of Holt, Rinehart and Winston.)

culty in providing "normal" experiences within the confines of even the best of special placements; and the importance of the personality, cooperation, and special skills of the regular classroom teacher have all drawn attention to the need for work on the concept of mainstreaming as more than a philosophical principle.

TABLE 12-1
Parallel Educational Services for Special Education (EMR) Children

PERSONAL ROLES	INSTRUCTIONAL RESOURCES	ADMINISTRATIVE PLACEMENTS
1. Paraprofessionals—support and extend the capability of classroom teachers. 2. Case managers—assume child advocacy roles, coordination of services, etc. 3. Child development specialists—expand the capability of classroom teachers to accommodate a wider range of individual differences. 4. Instructional specialists— serve regular and special education teachers in consultative roles. 5. Resource learning specialists—serve children directly and consult with classroom teachers; specialize in particular developmental areas (language development, mathematics, etc.). 6. Diagnostic specialists— diagnose educational problems; prescribe appropriate materials. 7. Special education tutorial personnel—provide short-term assistance to children. 8. Special class teachers— serve very small groups of children with severe educational handicaps.	1. Programmed learning materials and other self-instructional programs. 2. Instructional technologies— a. teaching machines b. computer assisted instruction c. closed circuit TV d. listening centers e. language laboratories f. etc. 3. Instructional materials centers. 4. Diagnostic and prescriptive instruction centers. 5. Specialized curriculum materials and remedial education systems.	1. Nongraded, open school arrangements—self-directed learning, individually prescribed instruction, etc. 2. Regular class—special education support to classroom teacher. 3. Regular class—special education assistance to classroom teacher; short-term ancillary services to child (tutoring, diagnosis, etc.). 4. Regular class—intensive special education assistance to children and classroom teachers. 5. Special class—some academic and non-academic instruction in regular classes. 6. Special class—only non-academic contact in regular classes. 7. Special class—little significant contact with children in regular classes. 8. Special day school for retarded pupils—no significant contact with children in regular school settings. 9. Homebound instruction— individual instruction for children who are unable to attend school. 10. Residential school—contact with pupils in nearby community programs. 11. Residential school—no significant amount of contact with pupils in community programs.

From R. H. Bruininks and J. E. Rynders, "Alternatives to Special Class Placement for Educable Mentally Retarded Children," in E. Meyen, G. Vergason, R. Whelan (Eds.) *Alternatives for Teaching Exceptional Children.* Copyright 1975 by Love Publishing Company. Reprinted by permission of the publisher.

Here, in an area where the field has achieved a better recognition of the importance and worth of the individual, specific attention to developing effective techniques, skills that contribute to successful remediation, and therapeutic personality variables is almost desperately needed. It seems increasingly important that practitioners seeking to develop and apply any delivery of service model realize that, as Taylor et al. (1972) say, "One scale or dimension that is common to all children, regardless of possible handicaps, is their *readiness for regular classroom functioning.*"

In some respects, the approach of those focusing on learning disabilities—in contrast to those dealing with special education problems in general—differs somewhat both in terms of general philosophy and specific techniques. As Wiseman (1970) has emphasized, the "learning disability approach" differs from the more global approach to remedial education in that the learning process itself has been introduced as a significant and relevant variable; individual evaluation and program planning are strongly emphasized; and, finally, considerable attention is paid to revising strategies and techniques of educational methods.

Mainstreaming and delivery systems

The general concept of *mainstreaming* permeates almost all present-day learning disability delivery systems as practitioners attempt to discriminate and facilitate clearly the development of such readiness. Since diagnosis of "learning disability" carries with it the intended implication of normal potential, the whole idea of keeping the deficit performing child as close as possible to the normal classroom situation and demands has long been functional in the learning disability portion of the special education field. The current emphasis on *mainstreaming,* the strategy wherein the special child is kept in as close touch with the everyday flow of normal classroom activities as his handicap will possibly allow, fits quite easily with many current and common learning disability remedial practices. Though the concept of mainstreaming ranges from a transitional modified resource room or resource-teaching approach (Hammill and Wiederholt, 1972; Sabatino, 1971) to almost complete integration of the majority of handicapped children (Berry, 1973), it seems to be a most logical choice as a fundamental guide in establishing more detailed characteristics of individual delivery of service models.

Some of the more popular approaches, such as the use of resource rooms, seem to have gained a major proportion of their popularity because of their links to the concepts and principles of mainstreaming.

The major principles of mainstreaming are quite clear and their relationship to popular approaches to remediation for the learning disabled child are easy to perceive. The general tenets leading to espousing some form of mainstream delivery model include these important points:

The major principles of mainstreaming

1. Categorization of children by gross-diagnostic category labels is counter-productive.
2. Evaluation of children's strengths and weaknesses should be more related to specific instructional objectives than to academic skills as characterized in the three Rs.

3. Children should be grouped according to defined needs, not according to diagnostic taxonomies.
4. Diagnostic, perscriptive, and remedial activities should involve common personnel whenever possible. When specialists or consultants are necessary they should demonstrate direct student-need, classroom application.
5. If part-time or partial segregation of severly handicapped children is necessary, it should be based upon performance ability criteria, not handicap classifications.

These principles obviously support a strong humanistic approach to recognizing the potential worth of individual children. Those who support or reject mainstreaming emphases, however, tend to do so not primarily on humanistic terms but for pragmatic reasons.

There seems to be no question that mainstreaming is currently rising to the forefront with most attention being directed to *how* rather than *whether* to use the technique successfully. Some, such as Gickling and Theobald (1975), suggest that the philosophical commitment to mainstreaming may have outraced its research support. They point out that children may suffer in mainstreaming situations due to teacher biases and the lack of a sufficient service-delivery model. According to this more wary adoption of mainstreaming principles, "a needs-assessment relative to teacher attitude and program viability of the involved organization appears appropriate. . . ." Gickling and Theobald suggest examination of such factors as the degree of communication that exists between special and regular education personnel, the perception of mainstreaming held by both groups, past organizational patterns and procedures controlling educational services, and the attitudes and biases of involved personnel.

Similar cautions have been raised by others. Yates (1973) feels that the major problem of mainstreaming lies in teacher education, and he points out, "Most preservice education programs within universities do not require special education preparation for regular classroom personnel." Therefore, continuing and in-service training is necessary. Some laboratory and experiential approach may be needed to change teachers' attitudes toward successful integration of handicapped students into the mainstream of educational experience. Certainly, teacher concerns are an important variable in any delivery of service model, and planning for successful organizational function must include means for eliciting favorable and constructive responses from the personnel most involved. This seems to be particularly vital when dealing with the learning disabled child where a return to normal performance and acceptance by peers and teachers is a basic objective of all remedial work.

Some of the concerns of the regular classroom teacher about the integration of the special child into the regular classroom have been identified by Birch (1974). These concerns include: potential inappropriate classroom behaviors by special children; how to accomplish necessary curriculum adjustments; negative reaction of regular classroom pupils toward special children; lack of teacher preparation and experience; inadequate support services; difficulties encoutered in assessing achievement in heterogeneous groups; teacher liability for insufficient improvement; and other similar questions.

Birch has also outlined the teacher attitudes apparently conducive to success in mainstreaming. These include such things as belief in the right of equal educational experience for all children; a willingness to cooperate with other teachers (specialists or otherwise); willingness to share competencies in a team approach; openness to including parents as well as other professional colleagues in planning and working for children; flexibility with respect to class size and teaching assignments; and recognition that social and personal adjustment can be taught and are equally as important as academic achievement.

Although current trends are obviously in the direction of integration of the special child, learning disabled children included, even a casual survey discloses a large number of different types of programs, models, organizations, and systems for delivering services. Dunn (1973) and Bruininks and Rynders (1975) have listed many programs that are displayed in Figures 12-1 and 12-2. The many terms, catch phrases, and labels used to describe the basic different administrative plans are interesting evidence of the variety, and to some extent the uncertainty, present in the field about what delivery of service model really is most functional. Commonly encountered labels include such terms as resource rooms, self-contained classrooms, resource schools, special early learning centers, community remedial programs, recuperative teachers, private-public centers, diagnostic teachers and diagnostic teaching, itinerant teachers, special boarding schools, consultative remediation, home instruction, helping teachers, diagnostic-remedial specialists, child guidance clinics, master teachers, placement specialists, area learning centers, summer catch-up programs, boards of cooperative educational services, and interdisciplinary attack teams. The list is almost endless.

There is, of course, a great deal of redundancy in the different labels and more similarity of both intent and practice than the uninitiated might believe when first confronted with the long list.

The authors of this work have found that practically all of the important delivery models may be accounted for under five major headings:

Types of delivery models

1. Models oriented toward specially trained personnel
2. Models focusing on restructuring of the school program and/or setting
3. Models depending primarily upon internal support services
4. Models depending primarily upon external support services
5. Models conceived for dealing with specially identified populations or groups

Examination of some sample programs or ideas representing each of these five major models may be useful to a more thorough understanding of what possibilities exist in choosing among the possible delivery of service models available.

Specially Trained Personnel
Models

Some school systems, especially those with budgets sufficiently large to handle specialized staff, devote much attention to achieving the services of specially trained personnel who may or may not be used in connection with one of the other models. As we mentioned in chapter 5, sometime ago Kirk suggested the need for a learning disability remedial specialist. This kind of individual, sometimes trained across a broad spectrum of deficit areas but more often specializing in one or two areas, such as reading, arithmetic, or motor problems, is beginning to appear in the field. Often the individual involved already has basic training in a related field such as remedial reading, school psychology, or perhaps general education, as a classroom teacher. Special training in diagnostic work is usually added to this background, along with programming, utilization, preparation and use of materials, and similar areas.

The role of the learning disability specialist is broad and varied as pointed out by Lerner (1976), who outlines the responsibilities of such a professional as including setting up diagnostic programs, instructing learning disabled children, finding and screening the handicapped, consulting and interpreting reports of other professionals, testing, prescribing, implementing educational remediation. These goals are accomplished both through teaching and through either locating or creating appropriate materials and methods, interviewing and counseling, consulting with school staff about understanding children, and helping the learning disabled child to understand himself or herself better.

If the individual functions independently of a regular classroom assignment, his or her title may be *learning disability specialist* or *diagnostic-remedial specialist*. If on the other hand this trained individual is expected to display specially honed skills within a classroom (which may be either self-contained or integrated), then the term *diagnostic-clinical teacher* is more frequently used. Sometimes this specialist is used to direct in-service training and to provide on-hand, on-site help to other teachers on an on-call basis and may then be called *a helping, recuperative,* or *master teacher*. These teachers frequently head the staff of a special resource center or room under one of the basic models. If the school district's organization calls for these specialists to be available to several different school buildings, either on an irregular or rotating basis, they are frequently called *itinerant teachers* or *itinerant specialists*.

In some instances, the specially trained specialist works in a more limited area and may deal only with that portion of the decision process which handles the placement of the child in the proper remedial situation or at the most advantageous level in a program. Operating in this sense, the specialist may be called a *placement* or *remedial diagnosis specialist* and may or may not be working with the day-by-day activities of a remedial program. Finally, some schools are beginning to develop teams of specialists who may sit in consultation on individual cases as needed or as a regular part of the placement-prescriptive process.

In those cases where systems are unable for one reason or another to develop their own specially trained personnel (fortunately the incidence of this is decreasing), only consultant use may be employed. The trend today is to require consultants to be primarily pragmatically rather than theoretically oriented. These consultants are expected to provide much the same type and range of services as any of the above specialists, although usually on a less regular and therefore probably less productive basis.

A frequent chain of events seems to be that a school system will, upon recognizing the high incidence of learning disability problems among its children, set out to obtain or prepare some specialist help. Once such individuals are working in the schools, the effectiveness of special attention to these children is easily demonstrated and observed. So it seems natural to develop a more thorough program along the lines of one of the models we will discuss, a program involving more than a few isolated and often overworked specialists.

Models That Restructure the School

Many have realized that integration of the child with special problems into the mainstream of normal school experience is not accomplished easily or effectively without making some changes in those everyday experiences. As we have already noted, sometimes changes in attitudes and philosophy are needed. But it is equally true that sometimes physical settings need to be changed as well and the flow of curriculum experience may also require alteration.

Some models of delivery of services have focused on such physical and programmatic change more than, or in addition to, personnel training. Valett (1969b) has been very vocal about the need to restructure the everyday school experience to accomodate the learning disabled child. He has suggested that after two or three months in kindergarten (typically after the Christmas break) the typical kindergarten class should be subdivided into three levels or groups representing the levels of childrens' functioning at immature, average, or mature. Nongraded groupings would then follow. The class day would contain built-in early-dismissal tutorial options for those children needing some special programming. The school would contain a special learning disability class, a total segregated experience for some but for most essentially a resource room. Children involved in this room would not vary in age range by more than three years and would be subjected to a very carefully planned physical setting (see Figure 12-3 for his proposed room layout). A detailed daily schedule would assure programmed exposure to those remedial activities deemed most likely to provide the growth necessary to return the child to the regular classroom setting.

Establishing special physical settings doesn't have to perpetuate the segregation of individual children. Taylor et al. (1972) describe certain basic behaviors or
abilities that seem to define readiness for regular classroom functioning. They
list:

1. The ability to pay attention, respond, and follow directions as formulated by
   developmental sequence
2. The academic abilities of being neat, correct, and able to read, spell, write, and
   do arithemetic
3. The ability to function in the instructional settings that occur in a regular
   classroom

Specially designed physical settings may serve the purpose of helping to shape

*Readiness
behaviors for
classroom
learning*

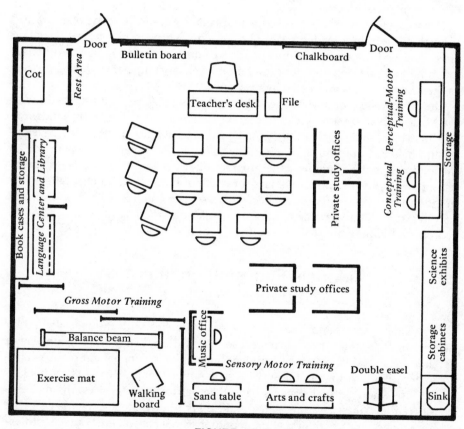

FIGURE 12-3
Model Room Layout for Learning Disability Classes (From *Programming Learning Disabilities*
by Robert E. Valett. Copyright © 1969 by Fearon Publishers. Reprinted by permission of
the publisher.)

these readiness behaviors as well as working on specific deficits. When this readiness is established, then remedial work may proceed within the mainstream definition of integrated, regular classroom experience. The Santa Monica Madison plan for merging the regular and special classroom is a product of such planning.

The Madison plan attempts to help deficit children proceed through four levels of competence ending in the achievement of regular class readiness through curriculum and physical facilities. These four levels include: (1) preacademic competence: the ability to function at the readiness or process level of learning; (2) academic competence (those points made under the second item on Taylor's listing as noted previously); (3) setting competence or the ability to function physically in a regular classroom setting; and (4) reward competence or the child's ability and willingness to perform for the typical incentives and rewards of the regular classroom.

The students involved in this sequential-competence-developing plan proceed through a carefully designed series of daily experiences in physical settings that are established to provide the most effective context for shaping desired behaviors. Children phase in and out of different levels of competency during the day as their own abilities and behaviors warrant.

The effectiveness of such a specially planned school day is maximized under the Madison plan by use of learning center classrooms that permit the student to face demands and opportunities commensurate with his or her own development. The physical layout of the learning center is a vital part of the plan and an integral part of the attempt of the program directors to face a number of problems: how to provide support service for children not able to function effectively in the regular classroom; how to best assign staff to children with special needs; how to assess children's progress toward regular classroom readiness; and how to coordinate the program with the entire school and its staff.

Models Focusing on Internal Support Services

Many school systems approach the problem of dealing with the special child by attempting to establish special support services within their own program. These services are available to staff and student body alike to supplement regular classroom experience. Although the services may not be literally "within" a school, as in the case where several systems band together for joint services, the model is considered an "internal" one since it depends upon school personnel serving their own needs rather than relying upon nonschool consultants, outside professionals, or nonschool-connected clinics or centers.

Although there are a number of separate models, often differing only in minor detail, three major types of internal support services predominate: those involving in-house resource rooms, more centralized resource centers, and cooperative efforts of several systems working together to provide facilities and staff for special efforts.

There are of course many differences in staffing and facilities among the variety of internal support models in the field today. Such differences are often small and relatively unimportant. There seem to be three major dimensions along which noticeable differences may be seen to exist [also identified by Jenkins and Mayholl (1973)]: (1) whether or not the resource personnel offer direct or indirect service to the student in need; (2) whether the emphasis is upon specific skills (such as the three Rs) using task analysis approaches or upon general ability with more focus on central mechanisms (such as motor or psycholinguistic abilities); and (3) whether the resource center is literally in-house, centrally located, or itinerant-traveling in nature.

Almost all resource programs share some common factors as identified by Jenkins and Mayholl. These include some individualized instruction, management of individual programs that may take place partly outside the center, regular (often daily) instruction and assessment, and frequent use of identified criterion performance levels. Even when some of these functions may be lacking, they usually represent the target aspirations of such models.

Resource Rooms and Centers

There are several excellent examples of this type of delivery of service focus. The Des Moines Public School system operates a center for learning problems that is staffed by a director, a psychologist, two learning specialists, four demonstration classroom teachers, a teacher associate, secretarial help, and a bus driver to provide transportation for the involved children. This center attempts to provide early identification of learning disabled children, to educate regular classroom teachers regarding specific characteristics of children with identifiable needs, and to educate parents regading children's deficits, remedial needs, and expectations.

The Harrison School Center operating in Minneapolis provides a learning center of a different type. In this model the pupil is placed in the resource center for testing and evaluation periods during an initial two or three weeks. Subsequent planning and conference sessions are designed to yield a remedial program individualized for the pupil and based upon a brief thirty to ninety minute daily stay in the supportive atmosphere of the center. The resource teacher provides the regular teacher with support, consultation, and specific help during behavior episodes when the center may be needed as a type of crisis center using behavior modification techniques to reshape nonproductive behaviors. Continuous evaluation, preparation of daily records, and constant reevaluation of instructional objectives are carried out by resource center staff in cooperation with classroom personnel.

The El Dorado, Arkansas, learning disabilities model program offers a combination of several strategically located resource rooms in the schools and a mobile van unit, furnished and equipped as a small classroom. Along with a certified learning disability teacher, the van's staff provides services to schools that do not have resource rooms. This program handles the typical diagnostic and remedial programming activities and also is involved with regular parental conferences, sponsoring a parent group that meets regularly. It is also integrated with a physical education program designed to help children diagnosed as having motor skill needs.

In San Francisco, the Unified School District Program operates an "Intensive Service" model that coordinates with the regular program through the use of master teachers who serve as consultants at all stages of remediation. The program provides full day classes where necessary to handle individualized needs. This system is somewhat novel since it provides separate service centers for different ages, as well as different techniques and scheduling at various levels. The intensive service centers also serve as training laboratories for specialist interns. Students may be referred to the center for help for periods ranging from a single contact up to eight weeks in length.

Cooperative Effort

Since providing special services can be an expensive proposition, many schools band together to share facilities. This seems to work in a variety of situations. In a widely scattered rural district a centrally shared service, perhaps county-wide, helps defray the expense that would be prohibitive if accepted independently by each centralized school district. In more heavily populated areas, large numbers of students in need can frequently be handled better when districts seek to avoid staff proliferation and redundant efforts by centralizing and sharing a particularly well-staffed and planned facility.

The Orleans-Niagara Board of Cooperative Educational Services in New York State is an excellent example of this type of delivery of services model. Serving several thousands of pupils in the district it represents, this program provides a multitude of services: self-contained classrooms and comprehensive support services for children in regular classrooms; diagnostic and prescriptive consultation to teachers; in-service training for teachers; individualized programming and specialized instruction and consultation by comprehensive support teachers; teachers of the multihandicapped; teachers and aides for educable and trainable retarded and for the learning disabled; occupational teachers, social workers, psychologists, speech, and hearing personnel, as well as many noninstructional support services aides such as a secretarial staff, library staff, and bus drivers. The range of services obtainable through such a facility as well as the depth of treatment of specific problems is greatly increased because of the size—a size that would be impossible to duplicate if each district were to attempt to provide its own facility.

The success of such programs, whether funded jointly by individual districts or through state or federal funds, depends a great deal upon the level of communication between the central facility and the individual schools and their staffs. In the Orleans-Niagara program, communication is an important part of the operation. Procedures required for communication and consultation between supervisors from the center and individual classroom teachers and administrators are part of the standard operating procedures of the organization.

External Support Models

External support models are decidedly in the minority in most locations. In general such programs are of four broad types: community-sponsored programs apart from the school systems themselves; private clinics or programs; hospital-related services; and university- or college-related programs.

Czerniejewski and Tillotson (1973) describe a community sponsored program that operated on Saturdays and during the summer as a supplement for public school education. Such a service provides remedial sessions for those who may be awaiting placement in other services or for whom classes or services may be unavailable. It also provides supporative service for the child who needs supplemental resources and/or instruction. A spinoff asset of such a center is that it may, as in the case reported by these authors, also provide a center for interesting and training professionals and paraprofessionals in the community who may not otherwise have come in contact with such a remedial effort. In several locations, organizations such as the Association for Children with Learning Disabilities help sponsor and fund these operations.

Although some private clinics do exist they are relatively few and far between. Where such individual operations can be found, they are more likely to operate in some narrow area of learning disabilities rather than across the whole spectrum of deficits which one might expect to face in a school-age population. Perhaps the most frequently encountered special areas are those of remedial reading and perceptual-motor problems. The effectiveness of such training in a private remedial-reading clinic has been reported by Pearlman and Pearlman (1970). They found that severe reading disability is often correctable by relatively short term and consistent treatment and that youngsters who have received treatment in private clinics can continue to improve if they have also been taught the necessary skills for independence relative to their grade level in the schools. The Pearlmans seem to be saying that the clinic, private or public, needs to provide the type of regular classroom readiness already noted as a necessary prerequisite by Taylor et al. (1972).

Where hospitals are involved in the treatment of learning disabilities, it is usually in connection with a teaching-hospital paradigm involving the training of new physicians and other medical staff, or it may be offered as an extra service in association with treatment facilities generally considered ancillary to learning disability remediation, such as physical therapy, visual problems, or similar areas.

A number of college-related programs or models are available. The Psychological Services Clinic of the State University of New York at Plattsburgh provides diagnostic, prescriptive remediation and short-term treatment of learning disability children in cooperation with its program for training school psychologists. There is a university-affiliated treatment center connected with Georgetown University in Washington, D. C. that combines the services of a number of different specialists and involves blending diagnostic service, preschool-cooperative nurseries, local school systems, day care programs, and the special education programs of local school systems. Almost invariably such programs are run in connection with a training paradigm where interning specialists are used extensively in the work of the center. Often a high level of remediation is available through such facilities due to the abundance of full-time specialists available, an up-to-date inventory of materials and tools, and the ready availability of special and individualized consultation on hand.

Models Conceived for Working with Special Groups

Apart from different geographical locations and those variations which occur as a result of being predominantly rural or urban in nature, some school systems have developed distinctive programs because of the groups the programs are designed to serve. Several different examples can be noted here by way of suggestion that any learning disability delivery of services model can be shaped to meet the distinctive needs of special groups.

In today's social milieu, with increasing awareness of the need to prevent social unhappiness and ineffectiveness wherever possible, considerable attention is paid to programs and activities that help prevent as well as remediate learning problems. Many workers in the learning disability field feel that there is a need to attack such disabilities earlier when remediation may consist more of preventing problems from developing than having to worry about removing those that have already surfaced. Adkins and Walker (1972), for example, call for "early learning centers." These centers would be specially designed to allow children who may be beginning to display learning disability symptoms to begin at an earlier age than usual to acquire those skills that make them reasonably ready to compete successfully in the first few years of public school. The centers would provide these children with something of a head start in a protected and sympathetic environment, so that the initial years of school experience have a better chance of reinforcing enthusiasm for learning rather than feelings of frustration because of demands too severe for the developmentally lagging child to cope with easily. Such centers are not common, and problems of successful early screening and diagnosing of learning disability problems still prevail. But we are beginning to draw attention to such early start programs.

Two other age group levels warrant special attention because of the unusual problems they present. These are junior high and senior high students, many of whom display learning disabilities. These older age groups are difficult to work with because of motivational problems, the length of time their deficits have existed, and a greater lack of trained personnel to handle special learning problems than exists at the elementary level.

The Mercer Island School District in Washington State is one example of a school program developed to handle junior high pupils (Haring and Miller, 1973). This program focuses on those variables that seem to influence performance most (labeled VIPs in the program) and seeks to isolate and increment or decrement these variables according to their usefulness in helping junior high youth attack their learning problems. Using highly individualized instruction and designated VIP teachers, the program seeks to rearrange instructional materials, establish systematic procedures to reinforce a youth's correct responses, and to tell teachers about more precise ways of assessing pupil's progress regularly. Realizing that motivation is an important problem, a major emphasis of the program is on obtaining growth in unresponsive students. Intervention strategies, behavioral objectives, and precision teaching are all used extensively by the VIP teachers, volunteers, and half-time aides.

Secondary students present similar motivational problems and in many cases are often overlooked in favor of the younger disabled yet more flexible child. When the less frequent secondary programs are encountered they are apt to be more subject-skill oriented and necessary flexible curriculum accomodations are seen to be more difficult to work out in the school system. Secondary learning disability pupils have typically experienced long-term frustration and have developed strong, although frequently nonproductive, compensation habits. They have stronger peer group identifications and are more susceptible to criticism and pressure when faced with specialized instructional routines. They certainly seem to be even less homogeneous as a group than the younger learning disabled children, and therefore group programs are difficult to organize for this age level. Outside referrals are more common with the teenagers and though some internal resources can be found, along with some interdisciplinary team intervention, dependence on outside referral sources is apt to be high—a procedure that tends to increase even more the teenagers' problems of frustration, low self-esteem, and peer group alienation.

Some attempts at secondary model programs have been established. As part of a larger learning disability program under the supervision of the Ohio Division of Special Education, a model program has operated attempting to design and implement a functional instructional program to aid secondary school youth with severe learning and/or behavior problems (Bonham, 1975). Making heavy use of criterion-referenced measuring devices in addition to standardized instruments, the program provides interview and program planning for the individual high school student from the time he is identified as a learning disability pupil until he finishes secondary school. It also helps plan and carry out remedial activities with emphasis on basic reading and arithmetic. Additionally, recommendations for specially selected core courses are made and help with the development of productive social concepts, through both individual and group concepts, are provided.

Alternative service delivery tracks are sought for the comprehensive learning center. These include a diagnostic track involving interviews and daily assessment activities over several weeks ending in recommendations for the most productive prescription and placement for the individual child. A second possibility is the moderate instructional services track that may involve some daily tutoring, teaching intervention with adjusted content outlines in specifically assigned core courses, and small classes taught by specially trained teachers. A third track involves extended instructional services with teaching intervention at a more intense level than in the moderate track.

The ultimate objective of such activities is the development of skills permitting the secondary student to take part in regular class placement, work study or occupational work experience programs, vocational or technical programs, college preparatory or college bound programs, or to be placed directly in the job market. Careful record keeping, considerable attention to teacher and aide training, and the preparation of special tools for assessment are all part of this ambitious model program.

In a slightly different approach, the Cushing, Oklahoma, public schools have developed a model demonstration center for secondary-level learning disabled students (Browne, 1974). Of particular note in this district's approach is a conscious awareness of the need to recognize the social and emotional pressures so characteristic of the secondary student. Using an intervention team of a school psychologist and two teachers with particular abilities in developing educational prescriptions for learning disabled secondary students, the program approaches the individual student with extra sensitivity to the teenager's need for being part of the group and to be accepted by his peers. An attempt is first made, with the help of special instructional materials, modern media, and individualized approaches, to break the persistent frustration cycle so commonly experienced by a child of this age. Attention is paid to developing behaviors more conducive to learning so that the child can experience more success and achievement and therefore find prescriptive activities intrinsically rewarding as he or she works on individual deficit behaviors. Separate courses of study are highly individualistic and cover a wide range of both directly and peripherally academic activities.

Many other special groups can and have been served by distinctively designed programs. The Cherokee program in North Carolina (Neff, 1974) is administered by the Bureau of Indian Affairs and strongly supported by the Tribal Council of the Eastern Band of Cherokee Indians. Although not greatly different from many other model programs, it was planned and operated predominantly for the purpose of working with the learning deficits of native Americans. Another model program has been functioning in Puerto Rico and has faced the atypical problem of bilingual parents, pupils, and teachers (Nieves, 1974). The program has demonstrated success to the extent that other school districts on the island have adopted component parts of the model for use with their children.

Summary

Since learning disabled children themselves are not a homogeneous group and since they come from many different situations, locales, and geographical-ecological contexts, it is not suprising that a large variety of delivery of service models can be seen to be operating at varying levels of success.

We would like to make two or three summary points. First, although a number of different models can be demonstrated as being successful by a number of different criteria, we really know relatively little as of this date about which model is really the most productive, the most efficient, or the easiest to operate. A great deal of organized research along this line is still needed. Second, and perhaps more encouraging, there seems to be no situation or context in which it is completely impossible to deliver some type of service of use to the learning disabled individual. Even in those cases where a school must depend upon a relatively poorly trained individual as opposed to a large, well-organized, and strongly staffed resource center, individual children may be helped. The ideal is to service as many people as possible. But even modest attempts seem worthwhile and often bear fruit by attracting stronger support, broader interest, and eventually more productive delivery of service activities.

13

Handling Behavior Problems

It is a rare instance when the remediation of a diagnosed specific learning disability is uncomplicated by other factors. Children's handicaps do not typically remain confined to isolated areas of their lives. Instead, most children who experience a handicap, whether it is a learning disability or some other type, are faced with other kinds of problems.

When working with a child experiencing deficit learning problems, one of the most common complications that the teacher encounters is the presence of additional problem behaviors. These behaviors are specifically academic in nature and cause difficulty in and of themselves. These added problems often seem to be more the product or results of the poor learning experience of the child rather than a cause. Such behaviors might easily be confused with symptoms of a more fundamental emotional disturbance but very often the problem is found to stem instead from the learning disability situation. Debilitating as these problems may be because of the stress experienced by both the child and those working with him, these added behavior problems seem to be resolved and to respond rather quickly to traditional treatment approaches as the learning disability itself is decreased. The prognosis for such difficulties may be better than for similar behaviors rising out of deeper emotional disturbances. But they can nevertheless be serious barriers to remediation programs for the basic learning disability. In some instances such behaviors complicate matters by making the child difficult to control and resulting in additional situational and programming problems.

240 Effective communication is often decreased as teacher and child are forced to cope with more than a simple learning problem. In other cases difficulties come from excessively rigid emotional responses on the part of those who must work with the learning disabled child—the parent, the teacher, siblings, and even peers. And too often such problem behaviors represent detrimental changes or shifts in the child's own motivational pattern, in the interest he or she has in learning new skills, and in his or her self-concept. Such changes and shifts must be reversed or handled carefully if successful involvement in a remediation program is to be achieved. Indeed, with some age groups, such as the junior and senior high ages, changes in the individual's motivational pattern, shifts of learning interests, and self-concepts (consisting of viewing one's self as incapable, unworthy, or unlikely to learn) may be the greatest problem encountered in attempting to build and implement remedial activities.

It is not difficult to see how a child suffering from the discouragement and frustration that frequently go hand-in-hand with learning disability might develop behaviors and patterns of adjustment that reflect his or her disordered and nonrewarding world. Though the professional learning disability worker realizes that remedial prognosis is good for such children, this positive insight is not so easily available to the child. These children are frequently misunderstood by those around them, and often they do not understand themselves very well. They have experienced rejection through comparison with more able peers or siblings. They may have been publicly labeled as "retarded" or "nonreaders" or "slow learners." Even the term "learning disability" carries frightening and uncertain derogatory connotations to the uninformed or inexperienced.

Despite the prevalence of special behavior problems appearing in connection with learning disabilties, the debilitating effect such problems have, and the frustration experienced by both the child and those around him, it is important to point out that both clinical and research evidence seems to indicate that (1) these behavior problems are not of any peculiar, especially involved type, and (2) that such behaviors seem to yield (often with better than average prognosis) to a range of treatment strategies.

The emotional problems and negative behaviors evidenced by handicapped children, including learning disability cases, are no different than those found in other children of similar ages. A diagnostic model that would categorize such behaviors as exclusively learning-disability-related behavior problems is not functional. Instead, examination of these children's behaviors, the situations and circumstances in which they appear, and events that seem to have an antecedent effect upon them all seem to point to the interaction of several definable variables that frequently appear in the experiences of most children, with and without handicaps.

The major variable categories that seem to be functioning in such interactions are the following:

1. The observable behaviors
2. The situations or circumstances in which the behaviors appear

Interaction variables

3. The response of others to these behaviors
4. The effect upon the child of other's responses to the behaviors

Each of these categories interacts with the others to produce the entire range of problem behaviors encountered in learning disability children. What is involved in each of the categories?

Observable Behaviors

The specific behaviors encountered are common ones. As Shepherd, Oppenheim, and Mitchell (1966) found with "problem" children treated in a child guidance clinic, such children seem to experience and display the same fears, the same tantrum and disruptive activities, and the same hyperactivity as nonclinic children. These findings could easily be generalized to learning-disabled children. In a well-known study McCarthy and Paraskevopoulos (1969) used factor analytic techniques to examine the behavior patterns of learning disabled, emotionally disturbed, and average children. Three major factors were isolated: unsocialized aggression, immaturity-inadequacy, and a neurotic-type personality problem. It was found that teachers do differentiate between the behaviors of the emotionally disturbed, the learning disabled, and the average child. However the differences tended to be displayed more in terms of severity and amounts of behavior than in clear-cut differentiated types. It was found that both problem types (emotionally disturbed and learning disabled), when compared to normal children, displayed more conduct problem behaviors (disruptive, fighting, attention seeking, etc.) than those with immaturity or neurotic-type personality problems. Emotionally disturbed children showed more immaturity than those with neurotic-type behavior. These two other problem areas appeared about equally as often in learning disabled children. The greater the severity of the conduct problem behaviors, the greater seemed to be the likelihood of some emotional disturbance rather than a learning disability being present. Identification was based on a continuum of amount of problem; however, no special types or absolute all-or-none-categorizations were found.

The high prevalence of conduct disorders in learning disabled children has been further noted in work by Wright (1974) who found that over half of a group of boys referred for conduct disorder problems also could have been identified as learning disabled with a high prevalence of reading ability deficits being present.

A number of different attempts have been made at establishing some type of meaningful category system for problem behaviors. Quay (1969) has suggested a four-point differentiation of such problems.

Quay's categories of problem behavior

1. *Conduct disorders*, including attention seeking, boisterousness, rudeness, hyperactivity, physical and verbal aggressiveness
2. *Anxious withdrawn*, including active retreating and noninteracting types of behavior

3. *Inadequate-immature*, including sluggishness, daydreaming, reticence to respond
4. *Social-delinquent*, including group or gang activities

The first three seem more relevant to learning disabilities and were the general categories used in a checklist from which the McCarthy and Paraskevopoulos data were drawn. As with any firm categorization scheme, the main problem seems to be that individuals do not easily fit into any clear categories. It would be difficult to determine accurately whether shy behavior, for example, should be considered as anxious-withdrawn or inadequate-immature under Quay's categorization. Neither is the usefulness of such a listing easily demonstrated once a categorization decision has been made.

Espousing a behavior management approach to handling such problems, Gardner (1974) has suggested a more comprehensive as well as more behavioral listing

TABLE 13-1
Learning-Related Areas in which Problem Behaviors Occur*

1. *Attention*
   Problems related to focus of attention, distractibility and hyperactivity
2. *Curiosity*
   Problems of undeveloped, reduced, restricted, or limited exploratory and investigative behavior
3. *Motivation*
   Problems of disinterest, lack of persistence, low enthusiasm
4. *Memory*
   Problems of retention, recall, and learning of memory strategies
5. *Imitation*
   Problems of poor mimicking, identification relationships, basic imitating behaviors
6. *Transfer*
   Problems of generalization and extension of learning
7. *Incidental learning*
   Problems of failure to profit from nonstructured or unplanned experiences
8. *Learning facilitation*
   Problems relating to behaviors which compete with or disrupt the learning task through avoidance behavior or competing responses
9. *Frustration tolerance*
   Problems related to inability to tolerate failure or delay gratification
10. *Independence*
    Problems of restricting dependency upon others
11. *Activity level*
    Problems of apathy, inactivity, and limited emotional reactions
12. *Rate of learning*
    Problems related to the pace at which new behaviors are acquired and become part of the behavior repertoire

* From *Children with Learning and Behavior Problems* by W. I. Gardner. Copyright 1974 by Allyn and Bacon, Inc.

of areas of difficulty (see Table 13-1). It is his intent (one that we would strongly endorse) that such a listing should be only a preliminary step to a precise definition of the difficulties a child is experiencing and the problem behaviors he is evidencing.

In working with actual problems it is sometimes helpful to start the description with a more casual definition and then work to the necessary and required precision prerequisite to effective remediation. A simple way to begin is to note that most problem behavior is a case of "too little, too much, or inappropriate." Obviously some children display combinations of these tendencies. Thus an initial assumption is that the child's behaviors are not in and of themselves "wrong" or "sick" or even "problems" but rather represent an ineffective, inappropriate, or misinterpreted application of what, under other circumstances or better control might be reasonably effective behavior.

Under the "too little" heading one should consider that some problem behaviors are simply a manifestation of residual behaviors that remain when some other important behavior is absent or removed. Rude verbal behavior or interrupting another's speech is a problem only in that it may indicate a lack of sensitivity to other activity or lack of control to delay speech, to suppress, or to lower the rate of such behavior. Other behavior-deficit, "too little," problems are those which occur when a required behavior is within the capability and response repertoire of a child but appears only irregularly or sporadically. Such behavior is a problem largely through its unpredictable inconsistency. Still other "too little" problems are represented by behaviors that are absent under certain defined, important circumstances. This is the type of "problem" every parent has experienced when trying to show off a child's newly acquired skills while visiting friends. The comment, "Well, he does it perfectly at home," matches exactly the problem behavior situation where a child's behavioral control is lacking only in a certain learning environment or situation. A final example under the general category of behavior deficits is behavior that can and is called forth under the appropriate circumstances but only with an unusual amount of demand, coercion, or subsequent reinforcement.

On the other hand, some behaviors are simply problems of excess: the behavior is present more than desired, there is "too much." As with the "too little" category, the behavior becomes a problem not so much by virtue of the specific behavioral activities involved but because control and management seem to be lacking. In general, there are four broad types of problem behaviors that fall easily under this heading: *Some behavior simply appears too often.* Examples may range from too much handwaving in response to a teacher's question to more compulsive activities such as repeated questions or trips to the pencil sharpener. *Other "too much" behaviors are problems only because they are too intense, too loud, too forceful, too uninhibited.* A simple change in voice level can sometimes shift behavior from the disruptive to the contributing classification. *Behavior can be "too much" if it has insufficient latency.* Children sometimes respond too quickly or fail to wait for their turn or for certain important cueing stimuli. This failure to temporarily inhibit a response (rather than permanently suppress as in the case of other types of grossly undesirable behaviors) can be a major difficulty. *Finally, some "too much" behaviors are problems because they are overgeneralized.* Overgeneralization may occur in two ways. The child may react with what he or she feels is desired behavior to a situation that in reality does not really call for or elicit such behavior. In this instance the overgeneralization is really a case of "inappropriate" behavior, the general category mentioned above. Often, however, a child's overgeneralization comes not through failure to discriminate eliciting cues in the situation or environment but simply through an overgeneralization of the desirability of the behavior as he or she thinks it is perceived by others in his world. Thus the child may be able to tell you that speaking out loud in an assembly is not typical or generally desirable behavior but may have difficulty resolving that conception with the encouragement he or she has consistently received from parents and teachers to "speak up more—don't mumble and talk so others can't hear you." Children showing excessive behavior that generalizes too much may be demonstrating a conflict rather than a discrimination problem where they see themselves trapped between "the devil and the deep blue sea."

Simple inappropriate behavior (third category), where the level or intensity or rate is not excessive or unusual, is more apt to be a discrimination problem where learning appropriate cues may result in better behavior choices. Failure to make good discriminations almost always produces inappropriate responses that can easily turn into highly visible problem behaviors.

Any first-order categorization of behavior, such as the one demonstrated above with the "too little, too much, inappropriate" categories, must of course be followed with a more specific behavioral analysis. Such analysis leads logically into consideration of the context in which such behaviors appear.

Situations in which Problem Behaviors Appear

Several researchers (Baldwin and Baldwin, 1974, Shepherd, Oppenheim, and Mitchell, 1966) have noted that individual annoyance at the problem behaviors of children with handicaps and conduct disorders seems to be as important as the behaviors themselves in determining which behavior becomes a problem and which does not. The importance of this factor is compounded by the circumstances in which these behaviors occur.

Practically no segment of our society is uncompromisingly tolerant of behaviors such as rude interruption and disruptive aggression. But there are certain contexts and situations in which such behaviors can be particularly labeled as aberrant. Under certain circumstances the annoyance generated by problem behaviors is likely to be maximized, thus increasing the range of effects suffered by all involved. Any time an individual is functioning in a situation that has rather highly structured activities, generally clear models of ideal behavior, and fairly well-established goals and methods for achieving such goals, behavior out of synchronization with the activities, models, methods, and goals is made more obvious. Since most schoolrooms have such structured and defined activities and procedures, problem behavior in the schoolroom is particularly visible. Since the atypical behavior is apt to be disruptive to others as well, thus causing even further deterioration in the ideal model, the negative reaction to problem behaviors is increased and contributed to by authority figures and schoolmate peers as well. The effect is something akin to speaking loudly in a library or church as contrasted to loud speech in a supermarket. Loud speech is inappropriate under each of these circumstances but is more easily tolerated, less obvious, and probably less disruptive and less apt to elicit punitive responses if it occurs in the marketplace. Schools, even of the more liberal model, still carry a heritage of the strict disciplinarian mood of the colonial one-room school with the rigidly authoritarian, unchallenged schoolmaster in charge. Corporal punishment and the tall dunce's hat may not be so quickly imposed today; but the fact remains that no one really expects to hear a loud disruptive shout in a schoolroom, and the reaction is immediate, highly focused, and generally consensually negative. It is true that such behaviors are more often expected in certain special education facilities and in those portions of the regular school set aside for such classes. However, learning disabled children do not look like a special problem case; their disabilities are not visually apparent. Learning disabled children are by definition essentially normal, healthy children and abnormal or "sick" behavior is not readily linked with them—certainly not by their appearance. Since the principle of disparity operates so clearly with learning disabled children, much of their behavior is normal by almost every comparison that is to be expected of children of their general age and status. Learning disabled children do not "look" like problem children. They fit no visual stereotype. Thus problem behavior presented by such a child quickly becomes classified along the same lines as a felony committed by a respected member of the community. The crime may not be so bad, but "it certainly is not what one would expect from someone like him." The community, in the case of the child it is likely to be the school and sometimes the parents, is apt to overact, condemn, and grossly misunderstand.

If the individuals involved in the problem situation are themselves hypersensitive to structural authoritarian demands, perhaps undertrained and a little uncertain about how to handle such behaviors effectively, the magnitude of the problem is increased. In some situations, people simply overreact.

Any behavioral analysis of problem behaviors must consider the context in which they occur. The context must be examined for indications of either manifest or latent structure and social interactions that might tend to influence the occurrence of such problems initially or to perpetuate the behavior or increase the negative effects of such behavior once it has occured. As we will see later in this chapter, some remedial strategies are directed primarily at environmental and situational changes that will help elicit more positive behavior and assist in extinguishing the behaviors that cause problems.

Responses to Problem Behaviors

The interaction effect between major variable categories is nowhere more apparent than in the response of others. When normal appearing children, sitting in ideally modeled classrooms, present disruptive problem behaviors, the effects are quick, strong, and rather highly predictable. An immediate response by authority figures, even those with the best of intentions, is usually one of suppression. Upon hearing loud talking in the library the almost universal, virtually automatic response in our culture is to say,"Shhhhh!" Parents may not rationally believe in lending credence to their child's temper tantrum by giving it attention, but if the tantrum occurs in the middle of the restaurant floor the most immediate response may be anything that will "get the kid to shut up!"

When negative behaviors pour forth from a normal appearing child, less patience, sympathy, and understanding are apt to result. As Baldwin and Baldwin (1974) point out, children with handicaps do have trouble interacting socially with others but the quality of interaction is likely to reflect the general pattern of social adaptation more than the pattern of handicap. In an earlier publication (1970) the same authors point out that control over parent-child relationships functions to a large part as a result of what has been called "naive" psychology. Individuals are apt to have implicit common-sense assumptions about behavior and hold expectations of behavior that are based upon preconceived ideas more than empirical evidence and upon hearsay more than evidence. Their resulting behaviors, the ways in which they give and request information of others, the manner in which they "feel" about some emotional aspects of behavior, and the expectations they have about others' "feelings" all serve to influence, direct, and sometimes rigidly channel their behaviors in directions that are not necessarily helpful.

The "halo" effect of preconceived notions about learning disability children and responses set by parents and teachers alike is a major part of the problem of handling problem behaviors in learning disability children. Anyone who has ever faced parents with the fact that their child has a diagnosed, or even suspected, specific learning disability has seen this factor at work. To some the diagnosis is like a sentence of death which, without supplementary support by the professional, would foreclose any subsequent positive remedial activities. For others it is a challenge for setting aside goals in favor of a total attack on the deficit area. Some parents actively battle against inclinations to reject their children under such circumstances while others experience waves of guilt. Shepherd, Oppenheim, and Mitchell (1966) have noted that "problem" children seem to have mothers who have generated more anxiety than others. The possibility that the cause and effect relationship is reciprocal is high.

✓ Receiving a diagnosis of learning disabilities in a child is a time of stress for any parent. To a lesser extent or perhaps occurring less often, it also produces stress in the teacher of such a child. The presence of such stress, even when well

The "halo" effect

handled, increases the probability of anxiety and stress in the child which in turn increases the likelihood of behavior problems occurring (through modeling on stress reactions if for no other reason) and sometimes decreases the ease with which such problems may be relieved.

The parents of a learning disabled child face a whole gamut of potential problems and worries. Many of these parents have never heard of learning disabilities and the diagnosis label can be as frightening as something that is much more serious. Once the definition of the problem area is clarified for the frightened and confused parent the specter of possible basic cause arises. Even though the professional worker may not orient in the least toward the establishment of some specific etiology, a question parents almost invariably ask is "What could we have done to have prevented this?" Implicit in such a question is the double factor of unexpressed guilt or hostility and worry over potential problems of a similar nature for other children in the family. "Will his little brother have the same problem?" is another very common question provoked by an overflowing reservoir of worry and concern.

Parents faced with such concerns often overreact and complicate problems by fostering dependency through overprotection perhaps as a reaction to some inner feeling of guilt and urge to reject the child.

Nonbehavioral labels can maximize such parental overreactions. Gross labels like *dyslexia* or the even more frightening *minimal brain dysfunction* have nothing to offer in terms of alleviating parental concerns and avoiding strong emotional reactions that may lead to behavioral problems in the child. Simple, educational, task-related behavioral terms are handled much more easily by the anxious parent or teacher.

When a learning disabled child also presents behavioral problems, all of these concerns and potential problems are magnified. The lack of a clear relationship between the learning deficit and the problem behaviors, the similarity of the problem behaviors to those shown by children with different problems than learning disabilities, the frequently encountered general ignorance of parents about learning disabilities and problem behaviors, and the need to deal remedially with two apparently unrelated problem areas—all of these problems contribute to parental anxiety. The importance of the need for careful examination of the response of others to the presented problem behaviors of these children cannot be overemphasized. The interaction of individuals' responses with the other major variable areas is an extremely important factor to consider.

Effects of Others' Responses
upon the Child

As Gardner (1974) emphasizes, learning problems are especially important to the developing effectiveness of a child's behavior since they are so closely involved with important accomplishments at critical stages and because the effects of poor learning are cumulative over an entire lifetime. The normal child with no particular handicaps or learning deficits is for the most part a happy child. Despite the constant challenge of new material and a seemingly unending flow of input, learning seems to be at least in part intrinsically rewarding and reinforcing for the average child. There is enough research evidence about general curiosity behavior to suggest that learning has some value just in itself.

As the learning disabled child experiences the constriction and frustration that can accompany such a deficit, he or she also begins to sacrifice some of this intrinsic reward of learning. Learning becomes frightening, harder work, less fun. When demands for adequate behavior keep flowing, facing a new learning task can become a repelling, adversive experience to be avoided. Staying away from learning and avoiding new experiences can become rewarding tactics as they help the child avoid obvious failure. When simple retreat from new learning experiences and repeated failures to perform adequately are responded to with still more demands, greater structure, increased explicit expectations, special attention, and individual recognition of failure, the result can be overwhelming. It is no wonder that a learning disabled child—sacrificing the joy of successful learning, experiencing the pain and worry of failure and the absence of any but the most threatening of attention and social reinforcement—begins to show signs of deteriorating behavior in other, nonlearning behavior areas. The pressure in some cases becomes unavoidable. The force of society's demands meets the apparently unmoveable deficit skills and something has to give way. The emotional reserves and normal control aspects of the child's behavior often sag under this pressure.

Having faced repeated failure and increasing concern from parents, teachers, peers, friends—and when the diagnostic stage is reached, even from strangers—the child begins to show the compound effects of his or her own sense of failure and others' responses to those failures. Sometimes suffering from either too much protection or too much pushing accompanied by insufficient understanding, the child's general rate of response begins to drop or become erratic and unpredictable. Erratic and unpredictable reinforcement contingencies do not tend to lead to regular, orderly, scheduled behaviors. The drop in efficiency is inevitable. Hesitancy and uncertainty of response also develop. Reactions to failure and threat of failure may begin to take the form of withdrawal and noninvolvement. Or, when retreat is impossible, panic may spill over into an attack-mode of excessive emotionality and negative, disruptive reactions. As the hesitant, extra-cautious behavior becomes coupled with nonacademic goal-oriented emotional responses, the failure rate increases and the problem becomes circular with failure inducing failure.

As Richardson, Hastorf, and Dornbusch (1964) report, handicapped children, perhaps seeing themselves as less whole, less functional, and less flexible than average children, begin to think of and describe themselves differently. Active behaviors, physical abilities, locomotion, interpersonal relationships with other than his own parent (usually the mother) are less often referred to in these children's self-descriptions. They tend to overgeneralize their own lack of ability. They have lower than average self-esteem. They show a greater than average need for group attention and social approval. Such behaviors and feelings often find temporary reinforcement in overt, socially disruptive problem behaviors. As Wright (1974) has noted, when behavior disorders and learning disabilities occur together, the resulting environmental stress, the negative reactions of others, the failure to meet group role expectations, and the feeling of social failure tend to contribute to the problem.

Recognizing the complexity of these problems, it becomes particularly important to carefully prepare strategies that are capable of meeting such complexities. It is especially important that activities aimed at relieving problem behaviors that accompany learning disabilities and at remediating the learning disability itself be carefully programmed to avoid adding to the problem. These children already experience enough frustration and failure. It is important, as Valett (1969) says, that "children with learning disabilities . . . be carefully programmed to ensure success experiences."

General Strategies for Alleviating Problem Behaviors

Several different strategies that can be found in use today are described in this section. All are widely applied and frequently are used together in combinations as learning disability workers combine two or more approaches for maximum effectiveness.

The classic approach to behavior problems, the approach with the longest history and perhaps the most publicity for the layman, has probably been the psychodynamic approach derived from the application of principles of Freudian psychology to behavior problems. Much of the past appeal of this approach has been due to its novel and interesting theoretical assumptions about the structure of personality and its ready adoption by psychiatric personnel, particularly during the early years of work in that field. The heavy child-centered emphasis of the psychodynamic orientation has also been appealing to teachers and parents. Unfortunately, the success record of traditional psychotherapeutic approaches, including psychodynamic, for dealing with behavior problem children has not been good. Many studies, such as those by O'Neal and Robins (1958a, 1958b), have reported results that are ambiguous at best. Greater interest has begun to be shown to approaches that are less concerned with personality structure and oriented more towards overt behavior. These approaches appear to demonstrate more functional effectiveness.

The Educational-Strategy Approach

One of these approaches has received widespread interest and adoption under a variety of titles and labels. This general orientation has been variously called a *behavioral deficit* approach (Graubard, 1973); a *psychoeducational strategy* (Morse, 1965); and in application of the general principles to a specific problem area, a *learning disability* approach (Kirk, 1972). In some ways it represents a blend of the older psychodynamic orientation with current behavioral emphasis. It is strongly centered on the individual child and involves greater emphasis on the child's feelings and affective nature than a pure behavior modification program. It also tends to stress etiology with the emphasis much more upon demonstrable behavioral cause-and-effect relationships than relatively nondeterminable personality structure, such as is suggested in a Freudian approach.

Fitting what might be described as a classical remedial-education paradigm, the educational-strategy approach follows three major steps, often repeated over and over again until success is achieved. The three steps are based on the common assumption that a child's maladaptive behavior (problem behavior) is a function, directly or indirectly, of experiencing frustration and failure in school. The three steps are listed below:

1. Test, observe, evaluate, and analyze behavior for the purpose of locating and defining academic and/or social deficit areas.
2. Prepare a remedial program directed at removal of the specific deficit areas.
3. Using the remedial program, provide for opportunities of success and accomplishment in learning to build the necessary basis for positive adaptive behavior—a good self-concept and feelings of self-esteem.

Remediation steps for the educational-strategy approach

From the standpoint of this approach, the relationship between frustration-failure experiences and problem behaviors is a repetitive cycle that results in increased deterioration of effective behavior. The child, suffering from the absence of skills or the presence of a well-learned but ineffective strategy, is faced with demands for adequate academic-social performance. As the child's own behaviors fail to measure up to some standard, he or she is forced to face failure and a realization of obvious inadequacy. The child's view of himself or herself as a capable, adequate, effective individual begins to fade and is replaced by lowered self-esteem; the child is hesitant and unsure. Awareness of his or her own inability to achieve what others request (often reasonable requests even in the eyes of the child) and the failure to measure up to even his or her own aspirations causes frustration—both real and anticipated. Frustration further limits effectiveness. More demands are made, more failures follow, and the cycle goes on sometimes at a quickening pace to the point where effective behavior of a "normal" nature seems virtually impossible. Bizarre alternatives or simple irrational escape or attack behaviors sometimes are substituted. These behaviors are labeled *problem behaviors* by parents and teacher. The goal of the educational strategy approach is to break the cycle and substitute a sequence of behaviors that lead instead to the inverse of these negative steps. Success leads to praise, which leads to feelings of self-worth and an increased desire to try, which leads to further accomplishment and a self-concept of capability and effectiveness.

The specific substrategies applied by proponents of this approach vary considerably. Some principles are held in common. All subvarieties of the approach seem to depend upon the use of precise and usually formal diagnostic testing and evaluation to define deficit areas. All make use of some integrative procedures to help the child correlate new academic success with the development of a more positive self-image. This aspect of the approach is very much like the principle of conjunctive therapy with any patient where minor problem areas are given help or support while major complaints are under more direct attack. All who adopt this strategy seem to agree that remediation attempts should be directed at helping the individual get closer to criterion competencies in his or her deficit areas and should not become involved with activities that promote compensation mechanisms by developing either dependency upon or overfacility with areas of strength.

Some have emphasized the direct role of the teacher in using the educational-strategy approach and have offered a variety of alternative teacher behaviors under different circumstances. For example, Long and Newman (1965) suggest that a teacher may draw from several different approaches in using this general strategy as an attempt is made to handle the day-by-day problems that arise from disruptive behavior problems. They indicate that the teacher may use a *preventative planning* approach so that the actual physical and emotional situation is structured to ward off problem behaviors, while more academic remedial strategies are applied to the educational deficit. Or the teacher may use a *sanctioning* or *permitting* mode where problem behaviors are allowed to occur but under controlled circumstances and in environments where the loss of individual control by the child will be less disruptive. Another suggestion is that the teacher at times adopt a *tolerating* stance, allowing the behavior to happen without either acceptance or punitive measures. Such a choice would be based upon an awareness that the child does not always have the necessary control and that punitive measures will not be effective in stopping the behavior and might instead increase the problem. Finally, strategists suggest that the teacher may use an *interruption* mode in which behavioral sequences that seem to lead to ultimate problem behavior displays are broken or interrupted before they reach a critical stage. Interruption can be accomplished by imposing controls, lessening demand, or by introducing competing behavior cycles that dilute or change the direction of the developing behavior. We will see later that the same techniques are used in intervention tactics.

Morse (1965), a major proponent of the psychoeducational approach, suggests that the diagnostic testing procedure should include a analysis of the life-space of the child. He proposes that a program should be built around "crisis" teams that, when alerted to developing problem behaviors, can apply ameliorative procedures and use careful analysis to help formulate hypotheses that may lead to effective remediation programs. Educational intervention, under Morse's system, offers several options. These include: (1) the reduction of pressure on the child, (2) development of teacher coping strategies, (3) working on pupil-teacher interpersonal relationships, (4) working on pupil-peer group interpersonal relationships, (5) attempts to change the child's motivational pattern or level, and (6) specific attempts to enhance the child's self-concept thus reducing a basic cause for the development of maladaptive behaviors.

In many respects the actual application of an educational-strategy approach has great overlap with a behavior modification approach. Both approaches tend to plan programs for an individual child posited upon baseline and criterion-level behaviors. Both tend to make use of preplanned and fairly inflexible strategies to assure structured predictability in the child's experience. Both approaches are competency- rather than structure-based. However the educational-strategy approach is more etiologically oriented than behavior modification; makes much heavier use of formal psychometric approaches and instruments; is more explanation oriented; and has more sequential-behaviors orientation rather than the final goal emphasis that is found in behavior modification strategies.

A major characteristic of this approach, which tends to emphasize its conscious blend of behaviorism and humanism, is its constant reference to and dependence upon the importance of a healthy and well functioning set of interpersonal relationships. As Kirk (1972) emphasized, acceptance of the child as a potentially worthwhile individual despite his adverse behaviors and the development of positive adult-child relationships are vital to effective treatment under this model.

The Behavior Modification Approach

This approach to handling behavior problems is based on the work of learning theories dating as far back as the early writings of John Watson immediately following the first world war. It is currently exemplified in the theoretical writings of B. F. Skinner (1953), and in explicit applied contributions by Bryen (1975), Gardner (1974), Ayllon and Azrin (1968), and many others.

Essentially, the assumption of this approach is that any behavior deviance is the definable consequence of either mislearning or restricted learning (Szasz, 1960) and that normal, healthy, or desirable behaviors may be acquired to replace or supplement undesireable behaviors by consistently applying established principles of learning. The approach is not concerned with etiology or the historical development of problem behavior but focuses entirely on changing overt behavior to meet some established criterion or standard. Neither is behavior modification concerned with psychometric assessment. The approach is almost entirely methodological and in theory can be applied to elicit practically any behavior of which an organism is physically capable. The only limiting question posed is whether or not the desired behavior is within the range of the subject's present or potential response repertoire.

It is always necessary to precede a behavior modification method-clinical approach with some basic decision making about what behaviors are and are not desirable. The process by which such decisions are made, any taxonomy of behaviors, labels, or diagnostic categories which are so established, are outside the focus of this approach and accordingly are not considered a meaningful part of the educational treatment phase. Due to its largely methodological orientation, this approach may contribute to treatment planning under a number of different philosophical or descriptive schemes.

Although behavior modification offers no input about a diagnostic or evaluative approach, some such knowledge is obviously necessary as an initial step. The starting point of the method requires that an adequate description of existing behavior be available and that a program of educational behavior shaping be relevant to the final desired behaviors.

The methodology involves five discrete steps.

Behavior modification approach methods

1. *The collection of behavior data regarding target behaviors*
   At this point the manager of the program must choose which behaviors will be the goals or targets, how they are to be measured, at what levels criterion performances will be established, and finally obtain "baseline" data (level of target behaviors before application of treatment).

2. *The analysis of contingencies and application of reinforcement to establish what functional relationships exist*
   During this step the manager determines what behaviors he or she shall choose to reward under what circumstances and also establishes what consequent events or states are so meaningful to the subject that incrementing or decrementing them will result in correlative changes in behavior.

3. *The treatment or management phase*
   Consistency is the key word in this step. A detailed plan eliciting even small approximations of desired behavior to be followed by reinforcement is established. The plan may be highly formal as in the case of *contingency contracting* or may follow a much more casual deliberate reinforcing of desired behaviors as they occur in situations structured to make their appearance likely.

4. *Evaluation and revision*
   It is vital to this approach that even small changes in behavior be noted so that appropriate changes in planning, reinforcement schedules, etc., can be made. Record keeping is usually emphasized since it encourages consistent treatment and also tends to have intrinsic reinforcement properties for both manager and subject.

5. *Generalizing and stabilizing the behavior*
   The final step is often the most difficult. Subjects frequently perform well under a management scheme but not as well in real or perhaps less well-structured situations. To insure that the behavioral changes noted are not merely treatment artifacts, every good program seeks to establish a clearly functional generalization of results to a selected range of situations or contexts.

This approach, more than some others, has developed its own technical terminology which is used extensively. Here are some terms and phrases that occur repeatedly.

Reinforcement	Any consequence following behavior that increases the probability of the recurrence of that behavior.
Positive Reinforcement	A consequence that *when present* tends to increase the likelihood the antecedent behavior will be repeated.
Negative Reinforcement	A consequence (not to be confused with punishment) that *when removed* tends to increase the probability that the antecedent behavior will be repeated.
Punishment	A consequence that tends to suppress temporarily the recurrence of an antecedent behavior.
Shaping	The process of developing final behaviors through learning sequential, approximated steps in the direction of the final target.
Social or Activity or Material Reinforcer	Different kinds of events or situations that have reinforcer properties (e.g., approval by one's group is a social reinforcer while money may be a material reinforcer).
Extinction	The elimination of behavior due to the removal of reinforcing consequences.
Contingency	The basis or criteria upon which reinforcement will be presented.
Contingency Contracting	An agreement between a behavior manager and a subject about which behaviors will earn reinforcement at what rates and/or levels.
Token Economy Programs	A contingency contract arrangement where the subject earns points (tokens) that may subsequently be exchanged for more basic, primary, or back-up reinforcers.

Behavior modification programs may range from very highly structured "token economy" systems (Ayllon and Azrin, 1968) to a much softer, "social interaction with appropriate consequences" approach as suggested by Ogburn (1974). In the latter approach, the manager combines a more humanistic touch with behaviorism by trying to create an interpersonal situation that facilitates "catching the child at being good." Such behavior is followed by some material type of reinforcement that offers immediate gratification coupled with social reinforcement gained from the enhanced social relationships. This, in turn may be complemented by the presence of some academic success as well as with its inherent social and activity reinforcers. Ogburn's approach also puts considerable emphasis on making sure that operating contingencies carry a cognitive as well as a behavioral message that can be decoded to help strengthen the desired behavior. Thus the manager deliberately includes a reinforcing message coupled with a behavior description and a notation of potential consequences at the same time as presenting material reinforcers.

The child who presents a desirable behavior may receive a token or material reinforcer but would also be told, "I like it when you are quiet while others work because it helps them get their job done." Too often, according to Ogburn, the child incorrectly decodes negative or nonreinforcing consequences. Thus when the child is shown that the teacher dislikes his or her noisy behavior by being told, "Be quiet!" he or she may interpret or decode such a message as meaning, "You are a bother and annoying." The message becomes more meaningful and is more accurately decoded when behavioral consequences to others are included. Therefore a teacher should say instead, "Be quiet, because when you are noisy other people cannot work, and they become angry." This can be correctly decoded to show behavioral consequences and thus help the child establish his or her own reinforcement contingencies. The child can literally say to himself or herself, "If I only do what I want then certain things happen to others and their reaction will not be something I like." No question of personal evaluation ("I am a pest") enters in, but instead there is an awareness of different consequences for different behaviors.

Such an approach offers real possibilities for many who have felt that pure behaviorism was too uninvolved and coldly manipulative. It is quite possible, following Ogburn's approach, to establish a well-defined behavioral management program within an interpersonal context that fosters cognitive and affective interpersonal factors as well.

There are a number of different reasons to support teachers' use of behavior modification techniques in the classroom. Bryen (1975) lists five which are frequently noted by other behavioral advocates as well:

Support for modification techniques in the classroom

1. Behavior problems occur with too great frequency for special referral services and more traditional therapeutic services to handle them adequately. The problem must be attacked in the classroom.
2. The efficacy of traditional psychotherapeutic approaches is not supported by empirical evidence.
3. Behavior problems, many of which are face-to-face social or emotional problems, cannot successfully or meaningfully be compartmentalized apart from the classroom and academic failure experiences. They should be dealt with in the classroom.
4. The majority of problem behaviors encountered are of the mild to moderate nature and do not call for ancillary services even when they are present and are demonstrably effective.

5. Teachers have demonstrated that they can be effective management personnel and can adequately cope with these problems under a behavior management paradigm.

The effective application of behavior modification to behavior problems has been demonstrated in a number of different types of problems and a variety of situations.

Lahey (1976, 1977) and Hasazi (1972) have demonstrated the successful use of behavior modification techniques with children diagnosed as learning disabled. Valett (1969a, 1969b) offers a number of guidelines for general use of the principles with children. Graubard (1969) lists several successfully demonstrated strategies for using contingency management with both groups and individuals involved in disruptive behavior. Hall, Fox, Willard, Goldsmith, Emerson, Owen, Davis, and Porcia (1971) have reported on teachers' roles in working with disruptive and talking-out children. Hopkins, Schutte, and Garton (1971) list successful results in dealing with the failure to complete school work in academic subjects.

Behavior modification as an alternative to pharmacological intervention for the treatment of hyperkinesis has been investigated by Ayllon, Layman, and Kandel (1975) and Shafto and Sulzbacher (1977). Other applications run from small detailed programs for working on a single discrete piece of behavior to conceptual organization for an entire academic program or classroom based upon such principles. Writing about a behavior modification classroom for Headstart pupils, Allen, Turner, and Everett (1970) delineate a number of specific principles and techniques for using behavior modification at the preschool level. These items, listed below, are easily applied to this approach in academic surroundings at any age level and are finding increasing favor with those who must deal with behavior problems in school children.

1. Vital management behaviors include objective behavior assessment, careful record keeping, and precise selection and definition of target behaviors.
2. Only one or two small target behaviors should be worked on at any one time.
3. Use every interacting adult as a potential social reinforcer.
4. Make heavy use of natural environmental reinforcers.
5. Remember that extinction of an undesirable response does not necessarily automatically provide alternative replacement behaviors. They must be learned.
6. Be willing to note and reinforce progress in terms of small, sequential successive approximations.
7. Plan for careful, stepwise reduction of artificial reinforcers if behavior is to be maintained past the treatment phase.
8. Keep in mind that a potential strong reinforcer exists in the fact that extinction of maladjustive behavior frequently generalizes in a positive sense to increment desirable behaviors because the subject is working in a more favorably responsive context.

Techniques for using behavior modification for preschoolers

The Environmental-Ecological Approach

Although both the *behavioral deficit* and *behavior modification* approaches attract advocates because of their heavy focus on the individual child, not everyone adopts such a viewpoint without reservations. To some the traditional psychotherapeutic activities and the more behaviorally directed activities appear to overlook an important segment of the child's world, the culture in which he or she operates. Emphasis on the environment (conceived more in a social interaction than physical sense), on the cultural context of the child, and on his whole social ecosystem is for many the most important target of any remediation program designed to alleviate "problem" or socially unadaptive behaviors. Based primarily on the work of Rhodes (1967, 1970), this approach seeks to examine and possibly restructure the transactional interaction that occurs between the child and his culture. As Rhodes (1967) writes,

> In this alternative view of disturbance it is suggested that the nucleus of the problem lies in the content of behavioral prohibitions and sanctions in the culture. Any behavior which departs significantly from this lore upsets those who have carefully patterned their behavior according to cultural specifications. The subsequent agitated exchange between culture violator and culture bearer creates a disturbance in the environment. It is this reciprocal product which engages attention and leads to subsequent action.

Functionally, such an approach calls for the teacher and school to be engaged in two separate though related endeavors. One calls for the teacher to develop cognitive and academic skills and behaviors. The other forces the school to be involved in the child's "world," including helping the child shape and adjust the demands of culture to fit and also helping the community that receives the child make some adjustment for individual differences. In a sense remedial activities involve a type of moderating behavior as effective behavioral compromises are sought between the individual who is responsible for a cultural standard (the culture bearer) and the individual who is displaying problem behavior (the culture violator). The premise is that when problems exist there is a lack of goodness-of-fit between the individual and his or her culture and that such incongruency or dissonance must be resolved in some way if problem behavior is to disappear and "normal" or "healthy" behavior is to replace it. A great deal of attention is paid to identifying the presence and function of social sanctions and inhibitions, cultural ideals, and the operation of small "ecological units" which in the smallest example may be a dyadic interaction between a child and one other person.

The approach has been tried at some length in different settings. The state of Tennessee sponsored a demonstration project in the 1960s (Tennessee State Department of Mental Health, 1963), and others have followed. In general the approach has been effective (Weinstein, 1969). In implementing this method, teachers use a variety of specific techniques including behavior management programs, group activities, and a great deal of individual goal-setting behavior. Emphasis is placed upon making the daily activities interesting and exciting for the child as he progresses toward such goals. Some of the basic principles involved in such an approach have been outlined by Hobbs (1969), who has been involved with the establishment and operation of schools following this orientation. Hobbs lists the following important principles:

1. Life is to be lived now and children should be involved in purposeful activities with high success probabilities.
2. Children tend to improve with time which often proves to be an ally but the child should not be separated from the family unit for more than about six months.
3. Since social and personal interaction is the keynote of this approach mutual trust is a vital aspect.
4. The child must be managed and the environment manipulated so that the child gains competence and general self-confidence and respect.
5. Symptoms themselves should be controlled and handled rather than oriented toward the treatment of causes or underlying etiologies.
6. The child is capable of learning cognitive control and such behavior should be taught.
7. Children should be encouraged to show feelings and emotions.
8. Group relationships are an important aspect of culture and educational practices should be organized around group structures.
9. Ceremony and ritual lend stability and order and structure to an environment and so are used as a normal part of the educational approach.
10. Physical activities are encouraged since the body is considered to be the "armature" of the self.
11. The child must become involved with his community through planned activities.
12. Happiness and joy are so important to the child's well-being that the child's day must be structured to assure the experiencing of some of this emotion.

Hobbs' principles for the environmental-ecological approach

Major differences between the environmental-ecological approach and the prior two are not really in specific methodology or treatment techniques since there is frequent overlap and use of a number of common principles. Differences are centered around the use of heavy social interaction and the group structure emphasis which seeks to shape the child into being a successful and obvious contributor to and participant in his formal culture. The major reinforcement principles applied are therefore apt to be of the social type with less dependency upon material or highly individualistic personal reinforcers.

The Therapeutic Teaching Approach

Some of the research directed at better defining possible differential behavior patterns in learning disabled children has produced an interesting and important by-product: information regarding the differential interaction of teachers with such children. One such study (Bryan, 1974b) has yielded several important findings. Bryan noted that when compared to the normal child, the learning disabled child in the classroom generally displays less task-oriented behavior, less attending behavior to teachers, and somewhat less attending behavior to classwork. It also was determined that, though the learning disabled child tries to gain the attention of both his or her peers and teacher as does the normal child, he or she is less apt to succeed in each case. The study determined that teachers were three times as likely to respond to the verbal initiations of non-learning-disabled children. This occurred despite the fact that at the same time teachers were devoting a larger proportion of the time spent with learning disabled children on problems requiring help (50 percent as opposed to 25 percent with normal children) rather than on other types of interactions. Finally, it was established that learning disabled children do not seem to have any habitual "nonattending" syndrome as may be present with brain-damaged cases (Schulman, Kaspar, and Throne, 1965). Any nonattending behaviors seem to be specific to a task rather than generalized. The work of Ross (1976) would seem to suggest, however, that attention problems may be more widely present in learning disabled children than Schulman and his colleagues indicated. Most importantly in this respect it was noted that the quality and amount of the attending behavior of the learning disabled child increased when the interacting teacher was a learning disability specialist.

Such findings as these, similar to findings reported of behavior problem children, have encouraged a movement oriented toward the planned preparation of special teaching methods and attitudes that are in themselves potentially therapeutic. The underlying principle advocated by such an approach is that behavior problems respond to specifically differential teacher interactions and that usual or typical teaching methods and approaches are not in and of themselves adequate for such therapeutic interaction. This approach is similar to what others have called "clinical teaching."

Swift and Spivack (1974) have reviewed the therapeutic teaching methods used in working with behaviorally troubled children. They note that most of the techniques seem to center around problems of inattentiveness, anxiety, and classroom disturbance or defiant-hyperactivity behaviors. Many therapeutic teaching techniques for dealing with these problem areas have evolved from dozens of practitioners and theorists but may be categorized into some generally consensual suggestions such as these:

Therapeutic teaching methods

- *In working with attentiveness problems,* use pre-alerting strategies, clear and simple instructions, shared responsibility activities, and visible positive response to attending behaviors.
- *In working with anxiety problems,* use slower pacing, decreased demand pressure, increased involvement without performance demands; allay fearfulness through careful and thorough instructions.
- *In working with classroom disturbance, defiance-hyperactivity problems,* use unqualified praise for adequate behaviors, personalized mild punishment, self-recorded be-

havior, self-reward choices, planned time-outs, and good behavior games involving classroom help.

Although evaluation of the effectiveness of such activities indicates some ambiguous results, some generally effective principles seem to emerge as pointed out in the Swift and Spivack review. A program seeking to make use of therapeutic teaching as part of its remedial approach might well adopt these principles as basic guidelines:

1. Remember that appropriate, desirable behavior should always call for a recognizable positive teacher response.
2. All rules and contingencies should be made very clear.
3. Nonrewarding teacher behavior in response to inappropriate behavior should always be informational rather than punitive.
4. Use immediate feedback to help a child become alert to his or her own behaviors.
5. Make frequent use of teamwork and outside support.
6. Keep demanding task periods and structured activities short.
7. Use gaming techniques to reduce anxiety and fear.
8. Obstreperous, active, aggressive behavior is most responsive to a positive teacher tone.
9. Contingencies and consequences must be kept and followed consistently.

Principles for a
therapeutic
teaching
program

Of particular concern to those who would adopt such an approach is the problem created by the fact that a number of significant behavior problems exist for which no demonstrated effective therapeutic teaching techniques have been reported. The six major deficit areas identified by Swift and Spivack follow:

1. Overreliance and dependency problems
2. Inadequate student participation involvement
3. Child-teacher personal relationship difficulties
4. Differentiation between single and multiple behavior problems
5. Inadequate generalization of therapeutic results
6. Guidelines for differential teaching for particular problems or combinations of problems

Until such areas are covered and really definitive research results can be obtained for the whole process, the possibility of a general placebo-like effect being present remains a viable hypothesis. Nevertheless, sufficient inferential evidence is present to stimulate further research and foster continuance of programs of this type to provide more information about the therapeutic role such as teaching attitudes and techniques play.

The Developmental Teaching Approach

This approach is really a more precisely structured and theoretically based type of therapeutic teaching. The developmental teaching approach is based somewhat on a classic developmental orientation (Gesell and Ilg, 1943), although it uses different terminology and somewhat different conceptualizations of progressive stages. This approach is best exemplified in the work of Hewett (1964, 1967, 1968). The approach operates on the basis of an assumed sequence of educational goals through which the child must progress in an orderly and meaningful fashion. The dependence upon such sequential development is not of the same degree or type as would be true in a strict "ages and stages" approach, such as that proposed by Gesell and Ilg. The chronological age at which a child should proceed through a sequence is not at issue, perhaps not even determinable in a meaningful sense. And each step of the sequence is not assumed to operate in any way completely independent of the others.

As described by Hewett (1968), learning can be exemplified by a triangle (see Figure 13-1) bounded by a task description, reward contingencies and nature, and a structure that is comprised of conditions or situations in which the learning is to take place. Hewett points out that both teacher and learner have separately conceived learning triangles for the same educational task and that therapeutic teaching consists of making the triangles cofunctional although not necessarily identical.

According to Hewett, the child proceeds through the educational sequences of attention, response, order, exploration, socialization, mastery, and achievement as he or she works toward an educational goal. Each educational sequence oper-

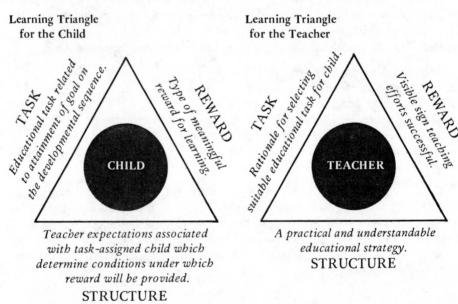

FIGURE 13-1

The Learning Triangle for Child and Teacher. (From *The Emotionally Disturbed Child in the Classroom* by F. Hewett. Copyright 1968 by Allyn and Bacon, Inc.)

ates on several levels, which include the child's problem, the educational task itself, the learner's reward, and the teacher's structure (see Figure 13-1). The teacher's task is to help the problem learner (or the average learner) "learn to be a student." The teacher uses an engineered classroom which contains three parts: (1) a mastery center, (2) an order center, and (3) an exploratory center. The teacher guides the student's participation into the appropriate area; giving the student the tasks he or she needs to learn, the tasks he or she is ready to learn, and the tasks for which some success is assured. Stricter behaviorists fault Hewett's directions that a child be reinforced for demonstrating "student behaviors" as opposed to specific goal achievement on the basis that such reinforcement is at best unproductive since it is noncontingent reinforcement or at worst is the reinforcement of undesirable behaviors. Hewett's response is that the appropriately trained teacher anticipates developing undesirable behavior and, by reguiding the student's level or type of task, steers him or her into areas where appropriate behaviors follow, thus avoiding the situations to which the behaviorists object.

This approach, like most sequential stages approaches, involves a great deal of attention to just what goes on at different levels and different sequences. Ability to complete a matrix like the one outlined in Figure 13-2 is a necessity for the teacher who would function effectively under this paradigm. Hewett has devoted an entire book to the development of such a strategy, and this work would be the handbook of the teacher using his approach (Hewett, 1968).

The Crisis Intervention Approach

In some cases, school personnel are seeking a technique or strategy that allows them to handle an immediate problem successfully so that a longer range remedial program and strategy may evolve. Some guidelines may be found for successful intervention techniques although no well-formed program or strategy exists for such an approach. Intervention strategies are useful to help combat the effects of negative self-image that may result from unchecked behavior disruptions and others' responses to them. In general, all crisis techniques tend to stress acceptance, openness on the part of the teacher, informality, maximizing success probability, and similar relaxing-cathartic interactions. However, as Roth (1970) has pointed out, the teacher's faculty for relating warmly to the child seems to be the most relevant variable and almost certainly is more relevant than the specific technique used.

Lovitt (1973) has shown that some self-pacing activities with children experiencing behavioral difficulties help them both to ride out crisis situations and to avoid them in part. Cohen and Douglas (1972) have emphasized that hyperactive children seem more dependent upon feedback and visible external reinforcement and so stress the use of these techniques in helping resolve disruptive behavior outbursts. Since these children also seem to find failure more disruptive than normal children, careful programming to assure success seems especially important for them. Teaching a child to regress deliberately to a point previous to experiencing failure so that he or she may once more try to approximate success may be a healthful shaping technique.

Dykman, Ackerman, Clements, and Peters (1971) point out that by only slowing down the pace and encouraging the child to give self-directed verbal commands, the teacher may be helpful in interrupting a mounting failure-crisis cycle evolving from poor attention behaviors.

Douglas (1974) noted that a simple reduction of stimuli doesn't necessarily improve behavior or meet a crisis. Even the reinforcing of alternative desirable behaviors frequently fails, with the reinforced behavior rather quickly extinguishing once reinforcement is withdrawn. He does point out that use of attractive materials and stimuli helps along with attention to part rather than whole learning. Small task demands and goals are more easily fulfilled and feelings of success thereby are experienced.

A set of temporary influence intervention techniques has been suggested for teachers by Redl and Wineman (1957). To manage the surface behavior of school children better they suggest the following optional techniques:

Redl and Wineman's temporary influence techniques

1. *Planned ignoring,* where disruptive behavior is ignored but disruptive effects are softened through environmental manipulation
2. *Signal interference,* through cutting off in advance the stimuli that seem to elicit the negative behaviors
3. *Proximity control,* using physical closeness to suppress or dampen undesired behaviors
4. *Interest boosting,* use of alternative activities to divert attention
5. *Tension decontamination through humor,* a type of "laughing it off" approach
6. *Hurdle lessons,* the avoiding of tension-producing academic demands by going over or past them
7. *Program restructuring,* actual curriculum changes to avoid problem materials or situations
8. *Support from routine,* used to reduce anxiety by providing a dependable, predictable structure
9. *Direct appeal to value areas,* use of personal relationship or social reinforcers to elicit desirable responses
10. *Removal of seductive object,* an "out of sight, out of mind" technique where negative behavior eliciting stimuli are removed
11. *Antiseptic bouncing,* temporarily removing a child from a situation that cannot improve while he or she is there
12. *Physical restraint,* used in severely hyperkinetic, acting-out cases to temporarily break an incrementing self-reinforcing cycle of negative behavior

Examination of the large variety of techniques suggested by these and other writers stresses the range of applied behaviors available to the teacher wishing to intervene in a crisis situation. In almost every case, advocates of a particular technique point out that intervention is simply that and does not represent a positive step toward active remediation. Most people who employ intervention techniques use them as the psychotherapist often uses a tranquilizer: to place the subject in a position of less stress and less active, disruptive behavior so that he or she may be more amenable to protracted and more complex remedial procedures.

Those involved in such intervention activities are often subsequently asked for information regarding the behavior they have observed or shared with the problem child. It is difficult to be objective and to provide meaningful data without some forethought. And since crises are crises largely because they are so sudden and unexpected, some general preparation rather than specific anticipation is helpful. One technique that is useful in searching out repeated patterns of behavior interaction and in reporting behaviors that have occurred is the use of an observer-subject matrix form. Such a form, easily reproduced on a 6′ × 8′ card or dittoed on a regular 8½′ × 11′ sheet of paper can be prepared in advance. On one axis it usually lists a range of student behaviors and on the other a range of teaching behaviors (see Figure 13-2 for an example). Checks in the appropriate cells where the two behaviors interact serve to describe what behaviors are happening by noting what each participant was doing at the time. The specific behaviors listed in each margin will vary from situation to situation as the range of behaviors available to the participants may change and the type of behaviors

CHILD'S NAME: _____ OBSERVER: _____ INCLUSIVE DATES: _____					
	Aggressive Response	Aggressive Initiation	Distress	Positive Affect	Withdrawal
Group Work in Class					
Individual Work Situation					
Free Time Situation					
Playground					
Gym or Art Class					
Cafeteria					

FIGURE 13-2
A Sample Behavior Interaction Form

needed to be recorded may vary. Workers in different situations usually can select appropriate terms by asking themselves and those to whom they must describe behaviors just what types of activities and interactions they may wish to communicate.

Summary

We want to reiterate that learning disabled children do not suddenly sprout horns or display unusual or bizarre behaviors. They display the usual range of aberrant behaviors that might follow repeated frustration and failure in any child or adult. Individual differences are no greater or no less with these children than with other children. A wide range of approaches and techniques is available to the practitioner. Although research evidence tends to support some approaches more than others, results gained from any single approach remain somewhat ambiguous as the multivariable complexity of the situation limits definitive statements. The single most important operating factor seems to be the consistency of the individual applying a technique. Effective treatment personnel almost invariably know their chosen technique well, understand the range of childhood behaviors and misbehaviors thoroughly, and are predictably consistent to both observer and participants as they apply their technique. There seems to be no substitute for the thorough learning of a technique and the professional, responsible administration of the methodology a technique requires. No technique or methodology is so efficient in itself that it will work without the user being a well-trained and efficient practitioner.

14

Counseling Those
Affected by
Learning Disabilities

Any type of prolonged interruption of the regular flow of academic progress is apt to have emotional implications for all involved. An extended illness that keeps a child out of school for several weeks, delay of school activities due to interference with regular school performance by natural disasters, strikes, or other factors, present special problems; and people, as a result, display extraordinary reactions. Concerned parents are even inclined to hesitate over a temporary absence caused by an extended vacation though the activities of the child on that vacation may themselves be educationally oriented.

When such interruptions are the result of a child's failure to adequately perform within the regularly scheduled context of school activities, the negative results may be compounded. Anxiety over immediate as well as potential consequences, concern over the tendency of school-related problems to generalize to other areas of life, apprehension about the response of others to the child's performance are all common effects of the debilitating influence of a specific learning disability.

Of particular note is the fact that such anxiety, concern, and apprehension may present itself across an extended variety of individuals, each of whom is in some way affected by the presence of the disability. The effects are not always centered upon nor even necessarily directly involved with the learning disabled child. Certainly the disabled pupil is likely to suffer from such disturbing feelings, but others, too, feel the debilitating effects. Parents, siblings, peers—each of these must make special individual emotional as well as educationally adaptive responses to the presence of a learning disability in a child, brother or sister, or friend. Still another group of involved individuals is strongly affected, a group often overlooked when consideration over the emotional effect of learning disabilities is expressed. This group is comprised of the educational personnel, teachers and staff, who must evaluate and weigh their own performance, adapting as necessary to meet the special needs of special children within contexts that are often both atypical and trying.

While there is no reason to suppose that any peculiarly different approach to counseling is warranted by the counselee needing help because of a learning disability involvement, it is worthwhile to note the variety of circumstances that may call for the initiation of a therapeutic relationship. Such relationships need to supply assistance in developing better emotional coping behaviors; and therefore, their objectives are different from the assistance rendered to help in the achievement of successful remedial educational activities.

Trained counselors might legitimately be expected to apply any one of the generally practiced theories or approaches to counseling in such circumstances. The one common consensual factor is that help, guidance, and support are often needed. It is also true that the inexperienced counselor, the professional whose skills and experience are more commonly directed toward educational goals, should seek out professional guidance and assistance rather than trying to undertake any type of depth-relationship role demanding special therapeutic knowledge, sensitivity, and skills. Such specialized guidance and direction is not attempted here. Rather, the objective of this chapter is to note some of the special circumstances and problems that may call for help of either common or specialized nature. This is done because the individual who is sensitive to the probable presence of an emotional component in the learning disability situation is in a better position to respond appropriately when calls for help are heard.

Counseling the Learning Disabled Person

One of the most unfortunate aspects of having a learning disability is that the pupil involved, even when quite young, is almost always painfully aware of his or her own personal academic inadequacies though the exact nature of them may not always be clearly recognized or conceptualized. Since, by definition, a learning disability signifies the presence of an area or portion of behavior clearly disparate from the individual's own personal norm, the contrast between what can be done in most areas and what cannot be adequately done in a deficit area is often discouragingly obvious.

Anyone working with the learning disabled knows that these individuals are often susceptible to lowered self-confidence, loss of self-esteem, high frustration, anxiety, depression, and despair—all the emotional effects that follow an awareness of inadequacy in the face of inevitable demand for public performance. The most successful practitioners seem to be those who can adequately blend effective remediation activities with a thorough understanding and presentation of empathetic responses to accompanying emotional overtones. The draining off of the inhibiting anxiety and frustration that block constructive effort is often a most important prerequisite and concomitant of functionally effective remediation.

An initial step toward providing the understanding, empathy, and appropriate supportive reactions to disturbing emotional effects is to recognize what the typical concerns of the learning disabled individual are likely to be.

Sources of Concern

Since learning disabilities may affect the learning behavior of individuals of any age, the range of concerns is wide. A cataloguing of specific worries and anxieties could be as comprehensive as any list of potential worries might be. However, the most obvious point upon which to initially focus is the need for awareness of the basic issues facing the afflicted individual. These issues fall generally within three broad categories, though they will be expressed differently by those of different ages.

1. What is really wrong with me that I cannot perform as well in some areas as others?
2. Can I really get rid of this problem? Is all the work and effort involved in remediation worth it?
3. How does this problem affect other aspects of my life, my relationships with my family, friends, authority figures, etc.?

Worries of the learning disabled

Effective counseling with the learning disabled requires taking a close look at the ramifications of each of these major concerns.

What's Wrong with Me?

How well this concern is conceptualized depends primarily upon two factors. The first factor is the age of the person involved. Obviously, older children are in a better position to clearly recognize the presence of sharply defined inadequacies and therefore may be more likely to react with anxieties directly tied to these deficits. In the older pupil, particularly the adolescent, this query is also apt to be concerned with comparisons of individual worth between the disabled student and age or situational peers. Adolescents, though overtly demanding individuality and independence, are very group-status-oriented individuals. Assuming substantial individual poses requires far more ego strength and self-confidence than the average adolescent possesses. Any factor or event that forces an adolescent to stand out from or be separated from the masses is at least potentially threatening. It may even be devastating to the emotional security of the individual so spotlighted.

When the discriminating factor is a negative one, such as a physical handicap or lowered skill capability level, the adverse effects usually are magnified. When the additional factors of high visibility, unavoidability are present and effective compensation or avoidant behaviors are absent or ineffective, the reaction will probably be even stronger. For the older child, a learning disability is often accompanied by each of these complicating factors. To have a learning disability means to be unable to perform as well as one's peers or even as well as is expected by one's self. The deficit behavior is often in an area where compensation or avoidance is difficult to achieve. To be unable to read, for example, is a handicap almost impossible to ignore or overlook in today's world. To make matters worse, the problem often occurs in behavior that is subject to day-by-day evaluation and constant monitoring. The older learning disabled student lives in a world of poor grades, incomplete assignments, and report cards and evaluations that focus on his or her failure on a regular basis.

The second factor that affects the conceptualization of personal inadequacy is the individual's sensitivity to himself or herself as an individual with capabilities relevant to and responsibilities and interactions with others, in other words, his or her social sensitivity. Unfortunately this places the learning disabled individual squarely in the middle of a potentially destructive dilemma. To be saddled with an untreated, uncorrected, or unhelped disability promises a future of frustration and lowered accomplishment, which in itself attacks emotional stability. But, to squarely face the reality of the presence of inadequacies, deficits, or inabilities, which place the individual apart at a lower level from peers, clearly emphasizes the aspect of individuality, negatively considered, into higher relief. To remedy a learning disability, simply stated, is to correctly diagnose and treat it. To diagnose and introduce treatment, however, requires identifying and approaching the learning disabled individual as somewhat different than others. To pointedly recognize such discriminated differences is to invite stronger and more clearly defined questions of concern about how and why one is different, less capable than other individuals of similar age and circumstance.

Obviously, the dilemma must be faced. Equally obvious though, since many individuals do satisfactorily progress through diagnosis and treatment activities without deep emotional trauma, the situation is not hopeless.

What guidelines assist the practitioner in undertaking successful counseling related to this type problem? Several suggestions seem to have been helpful in similar situations encountered in the authors' clinical work with the learning disabled.

Right of the learning disabled to know the truth

It would be very helpful to most learning disabled persons if every practitioner would endorse what would amount to a personal "Sunshine Law." Nothing seems to increase the probability of disruptive anxiety mounting in the deficit performing individual than to be kept in the dark about the nature, extent, and prognosis of problems that are obviously present and causing difficulty. This is an area where almost invariably "honesty is the best policy." Even very young children experience concern about the nature of their own disability. And, these same youngsters profit emotionally from a matter-of-fact, honest explanation of the nature and extent of their problem and what can be done about it. Such explanations should be geared to appropriate age and conceptualization levels, of course, but should strive at the same time for a conciseness which in essence underlines the *specific* nature of a learning disability, clearly delineating deficit from adequate areas of performance. Much of the fear and anxiety experienced by the learning disabled comes from a lack of understanding about the nature or extent of the problem they face. Overgeneralization and magnification of importance are very common errors of misconception.

Of course, this policy of direct and concise explanation is easier to follow and put in effect if the practitioner is "objective-oriented" rather than "developmentally" or "process oriented," but the approach is possible under any theoretical aegis.

Since remedial objectives should always be behavioral in nature, it is helpful to explain the steps whereby a specific learning disability is to be overcome in the same way. As a component of such explanations, use of jargon and professional or technical labels should be assiduously avoided. Introduction of explanations of what is often speculative theory in defense of remedial decisions is a waste of time. In view of the tendency of the layman to confuse theory with fact, it is probably unethical as well.

Since remedial activities almost always involve sequential steps pointing toward normal behavior, it also takes some of the mystery—and therefore the anxiety—out of the situation if the activities' sequential nature is explained to the pupil. It is helpful for the pupil to know that, "the reason we are working on this series of tasks is because, by doing so, it will help you notice the difference between the shapes of different letters so you can then learn to recognize different words." There is no reason to be covert about remedial activities; and there are very good reasons, including the reinforcement value, for the pupil to know why the activities are being used. Such conceptual awareness provides a type of backup redundancy which is helpful in maintaining the strength of learner response throughout the whole process. Such explanations lead as well to effective answers to the second major question that occurs to those suffering from a specific learning disability.

Am I Going to Get Better?

In the vast majority of cases the answer can be an unequivocable "Yes." Fortunately, the reality of the situation is usually in harmony with the answer most helpful in alleviating anxiety over eventual prognosis. The only real qualification placed upon such a positive response is one that, if thoroughly explained, also benefits rather than attacks the emotional health of the pupil. This qualification is primarily a motivational one encouraging increased focus and participation by the pupil, "Yes, if you will work hard on the activities and tasks we'll plan together, you will get better."

It is not surprising, given the repeated experience with failure that the learning disabled individual encounters, that they may consider their condition hopeless. The pupil sometimes begins to adopt a self-concept based upon an assumption of genuine inferiority and permanent substandard capability.

If those counseling with the learning disabled are sensitive to the possibility that such a personal self-judgment has occurred to the pupil and in many cases may be already firmly established, some very effective steps toward better emotional help may be taken.

Initially, the establishment of an open and honest relationship based upon frank communication will help. However, since the building of such rapport will take time, it is always best to supplement it as quickly as possible with behavioral consequences that in themselves are immediately reinforcing of the contradicting assumption, that is, that improvement is a likelihood, a consequence to be anticipated and expected based upon effective use of the individual's adequate personal resources. This is one of the main reasons for building instructional sequences that march toward the ultimate criterion level performance in very small incremental steps. Small steps can be taken easier than large ones. Progress comes more quickly in small steps than in large ones. Particularly in the early stages of remediation, but also later on at times when plateaus in improvement have been temporarily reached, perceiving some improvement, even quite small acquisition of better skills, is very important.

Ideally the remediator should be able to direct the pupil's attention to obvious evidences of improvement and emphasize how such increments represent a paradigm for eventual major changes to the good. But, it is very important that when such examples are noted they be genuine. There is no place for dishonesty, even with the best of intentions, when dealing with the student struggling for self-control in the face of academic failure. If even minute improvements are not present, the remediator and others concerned should take two important steps, probably simultaneously.

Steps to take when a remedial technique fails

• *First:* Use whatever approach or method will work with the individual pupil to convince him or her that removal of a specific learning disability consists of finding and using a yet-to-be-found certain method of learning, an approach to learning that works for that particular child. Failure, with the child who is trying, is a matter of having not yet discovered the right approach; and it is important to emphasize that the search is not hopeless. Failure is not resident within the inability of the child to learn. Rather, pupil and teacher-remediator* together must search out an appropriate method or technique. Given ample motivation and perseverance, these workable approaches can and will be found.

• *Second:* While such reassurance of the pupil's ability to improve is being given,

---

* Since individuals with many different responsibilities and titles are often involved in remedial programs, the title *instructional-manager*, one who has the responsibility for managing an instructional phase or program, is beginning to receive popular acceptance. It implies stewardship over efforts and activities rather than overall authoritarian control.

a re-examination of remedial instructional sequences should be underway. It is not necessary, at least upon a first brush with failure or temporary impasse, to place the total program, its prescriptive diagnostic goals and objectives under total suspicion. One of the first places to search for trouble is in the size and nature of the instructional sequences being used at the moment. The most common source of failure to improve lies in steps that are too large and that make assumptions about improvement based on prerequisite behaviors that have not yet been acquired. This is more than a technical aspect of the improvement of a remedial program. It also demonstrates the underlying philosophy that the loci of functional effectiveness in such cases lies more in the educational methodology applied than in the learner. In simple terms, such philosophy should be conveyed to the pupil. (A later chapter in this text explains in detail how to proceed through the technical steps of trouble-shooting an ineffective program.)

Either the initial established presence of a specific learning disability or an impasse of the type mentioned above is apt to precipitate the third question that may be causing emotional concern to the affected pupil.

What Do Others Think about Me?

Young elementary school children are heavily involved with a desire to learn. To learn to read, to compute, to communicate through spelling and writing are for most young children important tools that they wish to possess. Older children and young adults carry these same desires but are also encompassed with a very strong need to be accepted, liked, included in group activities and patterns of life.

The presence of a specific learning disability is a serious threat to the successful fulfillment of these goals.

To be set apart as one who is different from, not as good as, less capable than one's peers is a heavy load to carry. Strong emotional reactions are common. The young child may withdraw or conversely act-out to try and cope with real or imagined rejection. The older pupil may do the same but often devotes much energy toward developing compensation behaviors designed to alleviate the supposed alienation. Neither withdrawing nor acting-out behaviors are in harmony with the type of involvement necessary for effective learning. And, unfortunately, the types of compensation behaviors applied by the older individual, the adolescent secondary student for example, do not tend to be any more effective.

The best prevention of severe problems as a result of this concern over the reactions of others is early recognition. However, if the problem is thoroughly developed before alleviation is attempted, then several things will help. Since the principle of disparity can usually be easily demonstrated in the learning disabled, its realities can be used to reinforce concepts of self-adequacy if carefully applied. Honesty again helps. Depending upon the age of the child, awareness of the exact nature of the problem and its defined scope is a valuable conceptual asset to have in hand.

In an everyday sense, the younger child needs to be given subtle reassurance through regular opportunities to express himself or herself in areas where the learning disability is not displayed. Although use of resource teachers and resource room activities, tutoring, and part-time specialized remediation all have their obvious, helpful place in treating learning disabilities, it is seldom that the difficulty is such that a decision to totally isolate the individual into a special room, a special school, or similar restrictive environments can be justified. To do so merely invites the development of emotional concern about the reactions of others. The learning disabled individual needs to be strongly reinforced in forming a self-concept of one who is able to cope alongside peers. Any type of personal relationship that strengthens this will help prevent or alleviate self-destructive emotional responses. Normal rather than isolated, atypical situations should be sought.

With younger children, peer coupling with non-L.D. pupils not only helps in the modeling of desired learning behaviors, but also assures the type of nondiscriminatory relationships that are vital.

With secondary students, more and more schools are becoming aware of the value of relating remedial work to vocational training and the development of life-coping skills (Wiederholt, 1978; Touzel, 1978).

The overall goal should be to establish a context of normalcy wherever possible, emphasizing similarities rather than differences, capabilities rather than inadequacies, potentiality rather than substandard contemporary performance. Finally, it seems worthwhile to reaffirm, for the benefit of the developing learning disability worker, the reality of probable recovery from a specific learning disability. Individuals who are experiencing inadequate learning behaviors can improve, can be helped to remove debilitating behaviors and increment deficit performance. Clear, firm, and obvious belief in this, consistently conveyed to the pupil, is powerful emotional medicine that should be prescribed in every case.

Counseling Family and Friends of the Learning Disabled

With some problems, not of the learning disability type, there is very little real interaction between family and friends and those responsible for treatment. Except for peripheral support and postoperative recovery assistance, the family of the appendicitis victim, for example, is relatively little involved.

Such is not the case with learning disabilities. Since learning does not compartmentalize so as to involve the child only at school, all those with whom the child experiences learning may legitimately and desirably be involved.

As has been mentioned elsewhere in this text, parents and friends may often be used to assist with remedial activities, and practice activities, or be called upon to help build and sustain motivation. It is only reasonable therefore that these same individuals should sometimes also develop real concern over the presence of learning disability problems in their children and friends, and be subject themselves to attacks of worry, anxiety, and apprehension as are the pupils.

Sources of Concern

While the treatment of emotional problems of those affected indirectly by the presence of a learning disability is not the main province of learning disability workers, it is of major concern. These emotional involvements are often projections of those being experienced by the child. In other instances they may be transmitted to the child, reversing the flow of anxiety. Since these related individuals are often used in instructional programs, their degree of mental health is of substantive importance in building an effective remedial program.

The exact nature of the concern these individuals may feel and the degree to which it may develop problem characteristics or levels depends a great deal upon the individual personality makeup of those involved and to this extent is not predictable in any generalized way. However, practical experience with many cases involving such problems has led to an expectancy of certain types of concerns developing as a common occurrence. Four broad examples of these concerns are noted here:

1. Concerns about the general nature of the learning disabilities themselves
2. Personal concerns: guilt, other children in the family, and similar problems
3. Concerns over the nature or progress of treatment
4. Crisis situations, usually occurring at initial identification states or during times the pupil is not progressing satisfactorily in treatment.

Concerns of parents and friends

The Nature of Learning Disabilities

It is a pretty safe generalization to say, despite the extensive campaigns designed to improve general public knowledge, that the average parent of a newly identified learning disabled child does not have much understanding of the nature or extent of learning disabilities.

Counseling in this problem area really consists, to a large part, of the draining off of anxiety that stems from misinformation and establishing a feeling of security through learning the truth. Though it is seldom that a firmly authoritarian role is necessary in any type of school-parent or counselor-counselee relationship, this instance may warrant a very firm, professional, and self-confident role that clearly conveys the message, "I know that what I am telling you is correct and you may without doubt depend upon it being both factual and accurate."

Individuals floundering in a morass of half-truths, exaggerated fears, and unclear assumptions need the security such a stance provides. If the practitioner does not feel that he or she possesses such information about the nature of the field, then a clear responsibility exists for obtaining it. Although there are many "soft" areas where debate is high, and many other areas where our information is only speculative, there are also some well-defined areas of information where consensus is virtually 100%. This information can and should be conveyed to the confused and frightened parents and friends.

While an extensive list of what might be noted could be compiled, certain areas seem to arise over and over again. Some of the most common of these are noted here. Practitioners should be ready to explain the facts involved in each.

Areas where helpful information can be easily provided

1. A clear and concise definition, in plain terms, of what a learning disability is and how it affects learning behavior
2. Differentiation between learning disabilities and mental retardation
3. Differentiation between learning disabilities and emotional problems, including such categories as emotionally disturbed, neurotic, and psychotic
4. Cause and effect relationships between learning experiences and deficit behaviors as a general rather than specific fault finding relationship
5. Familial and genetic relationships to learning disabilities
6. Prognosis once remediation is underway, including the low probability of relapses once criterion behavior is established
7. Where to get help and more detailed explanatory information (the practitioner should know of both personnel and written resources that may be offered)
8. Possibility of the problem generalizing (being "contagious") to other children in the family

Within the framework of such questions, the practitioner will also often encounter worry over what may be described as more personal concerns.

Personal Concerns

Once parents and or family become clearly aware that a learning disability problem exists in their midst, it is only natural that they be expected to develop individual concerns that, though precipitated by the learning disability, have their immediate focus upon family or personal concerns. These problems may only be extensions and projections of already existing difficulties inherent within the life space of those involved. In such cases the problems cannot be or should not be handled by those whose responsibilities are primarily concerned with and whose training is directed toward the remediation of deficit learning behavior. However, it is often true that specific questions and worries may arise that have more immediate relationship to learning disabilities. Though it may be true that the frequency of such problems appearing and their severity may have some relationship with the general mental health of the family, the learning disability practitioner can often help alleviate the high negative valence that such problems produce.

Some of these concerns will be negated by the presentation of accurate general information as noted in the preceding section. However, others will require specific attention. The approach should still be largely one of presenting information rather than taking a therapeutic stance. However, solid factual material, presented with empathy for the anxiety present, does carry therapeutic effect in many cases and will help reduce anxiety to levels where the usual coping reactions and adaptive behaviors of the family can handle it.

Those working regularly in learning disabilities should expect to encounter and deal with problems such as these:

1. Personal guilt by parents who feel that somehow their parenting behaviors have precipitated the learning disability

2. Concern by parents who feel that the situation has forced them into an unresolvable conflict between giving enough time to the afflicted child while not neglecting other children in the family

3. "Reaction formations" to worry and guilt where normal structure and demands usually placed upon the child are lifted for the learning disabled pupil—a response that often evokes undesirable behaviors in both the L.D. child and siblings and/or feelings of insecurity in the child due to the lost security which previous habits and structure afforded

4. Problems of cumulative fatigue in parents who have focused so much attention on the problem situation that they run short of reserve, patience, and tolerance

5. Concern over the effect on siblings, including the possibility that younger children may eventually develop similar problems

6. Doubt over the authenticity of the problem, complete with suspicions of malingering by the involved pupil or technical errors by professionals

Problems parents of L.D. children experience

The list could be extended, but the examples noted present an overview of the type of family concerns that may be encounterd. The difficulty is essentially one of realizing that the introduction of atypical learning patterns (a specific learning disability) may very well cause the development of concerns about the efficacy of established parenting behaviors and normal everyday family routines. Doubt and concern need to be faced, and in many cases the learning disability worker can help reduce them in a very tangible way.

At the same time, these workers should be aware that these very same problems can grow to serious proportions. When positive responses and healthier behaviors fail to follow the simple informative approaches suggested here, referral to more clinically trained sources of help and advice is warranted. The average learning disability worker is professionally equipped to counsel only on a very basic, undemanding level, when there is little if any involvement in serious personality and emotional difficulties.

Concerns over the Nature and Progress of Remediation

Concerns falling within this category may be the easiest to handle since the learning disability practitioner may be more able to fall back upon training and experience more related to this type of problem than others.

The problems encountered fall into two general categories: those relating to the nature of treatment, and those centering on treatment results.

In the first instance, parents and family should always be informed as to what is taking place in remediation and the reasons why. In the best of all situations, family members may be actively engaged in working with remedial activities. The professional worker should stress the sequential nature of learning behaviors and the importance and meaning of a good task analysis, as well as the remedial activities developed as a result of such analyses. Both final criterion and subcriterion tasks and measures (as explained in detail in later chapters) should be thoroughly explained. The relative importance of vital and essential entering

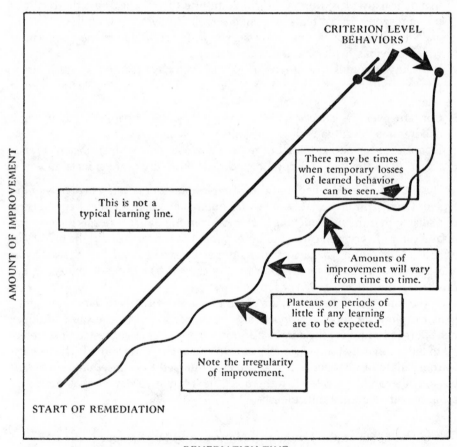

FIGURE 14-1

Learning characteristics do not typically follow a straight-line path of incremented steps leading directly to a goal.

behaviors and subsequently acquired behaviors, which become prerequisites to still more complex behaviors yet to be learned, should be explained.

Concern over the progress of remediation usually centers about the validity of what is being done—"Are you sure this is the right treatment?"—or the rate or consistency of progress.

Careful explanation of the task analyis involved in choosing instructional sequences and the obvious face validity of the smaller tasks that build to the major objective should serve to help alleviate worry over validity. It is well to prepare all concerned, in advance, for the likely need to alter, update, realign, or make constructive changes in a remedial program as the student progresses through it. It should be pointed out that there is considerably more reason for worry over a suggested program that is so rigidly conceived and constructed that it is not susceptible or amenable to change as needs arise. This idea can be explained to even very educationally naive individuals, but explanations are more easily made in advance of the development of worry and doubt.

Worry over rate of progress or temporary slowdowns in improvement is easy to understand. Those connected with a learning disability problem have typically experienced or witnessed much frustration and failure. Even when effective remediation is underway, emotionally involved individuals may spend anxious moments waiting for "the other shoe to drop"—for even worse problems and diagnoses to arise. Prevention is much simpler than cure. The nature of learning and the incrementing of acquired behaviors should be explained in advance. All concerned should be prepared for plateaus of little or no progress, for slowdowns and temporary setbacks. Calling early attention to the characteristics of learning as displayed in Figure 14-1 may go a long way toward preventing the later development of such problems.

Crisis Situations

In genuine crisis situations there is one rule of therapeutic intervention that always should be followed: crisis intervention should seek only to maintain the individuals through the immediate crisis, not to undertake long-range or substantive behavior changes.

It is rare that the learning disability worker will ever be involved with a real "crisis" situation as the term is used in a clinical sense. Some situations will be encountered that, because of their momentary nature, their arising out of a quickly accelerating concern generated by immediate events, and because of the amount of emotional energy generated in comparison to average response patterns, may be labeled as "crisis situations."

Experience indicates that these situations are most apt to arise in connection with any one of four common contexts: (1) the need to solve a problem related to immediate diagnostic or remediation activities, (2) culmination of a steadily increasing amount of anxiety that results in feelings of panic about being able to "weather the storm" until improved learning is a reality, (3) the need for support in the face of opposition or disagreement by other family members or friends, or (4) difficulties that are the result of communication breakdowns or the failure to convey or understand ideas and concepts essential to effective coping in the remedial situation.

In each case, "crisis" interaction follows about the same basic steps:

1. Basic acceptance of the reality of the concerns
2. Empathy for the debilitating effect of such concern
3. Personal support for the moment until more effective coping behaviors can be established
4. Low-keyed presentation of alternative response patterns and sources for more substantial assistance
5. Clear-cut termination of the crisis-induced relationship to avoid the shaping of dependency habits

In almost every clinical discipline, developing professionals in training worry about the incidence of crises they will be called upon to face and the ability to handle them once they are encountered. It may be comforting to know that serious crises are rarely encountered in working with the learning disabled. When they are, they are not typically of long duration or of especially severe consequences. It is also helpful to realize that previously established credibility as one who knows the field well, who is capable of making effective diagnostic and remedial decisions, and who is aware of and sensitive to the needs of the learner involved is probably the most effective characteristic a worker can possess to deal effectively with crisis situations.

Specific Roles for Counselors and Parents

Sometimes major sources of anxiety in learning disability situations arise out of concern for the roles different individuals should or could be taking. Teachers want understanding, cooperation, and responsiveness from parents, and these expectations are justified in terms of the positive effect they have on the eventual outcomes of remediation. When these parental roles are not forthcoming, the instructional manager can function in a counseling role to assist in achieving a match between expectation and performance of the people involved in the remedial work. The outlining of role functions accompanied by explanations of why such expectations arise and the effects that various role fulfillments and failures may have, can often prove helpful in resolving dissonance.

Parents, on the other hand, often have serious questions about their roles. They want to know how to better manage their time, for instance, when faced with demanding remedial activities while having to care for several other children. They will often ask for help and direction on other related problems. The activities demanded of the parent functioning in a remedial aide's capacity are sometimes overwhelming and frequently frightening. The experienced worker can offer very calming and helpful counsel on how to carry out these responsibilities in the most effective manner.

Parents will frequently ask questions about the management of normal discipline and the maintenance of regular family routines in the face of lowered frustration tolerance and raised emotional levels of those who are tired, frustrated, or frightened. Cruickshank (1977) offers considerable practical advice about such mundane but important questions as whether "sparing the rod" will truly "spoil the child" when dealing with an individual struggling with learning disability problems. There are probably no universally applicable answers to such questions, but often any idea will help provide support and reassurance. It is in such contributions that learning disability workers can substantively influence pupil and family mental health through personal interaction and counsel.

As Reynolds and Birch (1977) have pointed out, parents possess a number of clear expectations of teachers and school personnel when the special needs of pupils call for individualized educational plans. Among the expectations most commonly voiced are for an adequate assessment of the pupil's needs, a realistic management plan which matches the resources of home and school, a knowledge of community resources other than the school, clear and understandable reports, parental access to reports with school interpretation, careful explanations of diagnostic findings, some problem-solving help in child-rearing problems as they may interact with the handicap, an understanding and application of the pupil's assets as well as deficits, help with coping with inadequacies in the delivery of needed services, a positive outlook on the whole diagnostic-remedial-planning-implementation situation, and the inclusion of the parent in the ongoing process.

Anytime one or more of these common expectations are not met or appear to be receiving less than sufficient attention, one can expect emotional reactions to increase, and anxiety and apprehension may quickly follow. The practitioner in the field should be prepared to deliver help in the fulfillment of these roles wherever possible and in the unavoidable explanations of deficits. Such counseling interaction, seemingly only peripheral to first-hand remediation activities, can be an essential component of a successful attack on a child's learning difficulties.

Special Sources of Help

It is sometimes impossible for individual remediators or even a school system to provide all the personal attention, help, information, and guidance desirable. It is well to have at one's fingertips a variety of sources where dependable supplementary help is available. There are several ways in which this supplementary support can be provided.

1. *Assembling an informational library of materials suitable for dissemination can benefit those seeking additional help and guidance.* There are a variety of pamphlets and informal explantory materials, much of which are often found to have been produced

locally to meet the special limitations of a specific community, which can be of great help. Effective pracitioners will have such literature, references, and hand-outs readily available for dispensing when the need arises. Familiarity with the learning disability literature should be expanded to include an awareness of material suitable for the nonprofessional layman to use.

2. *Professional organizations can be very helpful through providing literature and factual information* ranging from addresses of other resources to sample sets of remedial materials; and in many communities they will be able to put interested people in touch with local community chapters or groups that hold regularly scheduled meetings helpful in providing support. While many organizations may be able to help in one way or another, in the United States and Canada two are outstanding for both their willingness to be of assistance and the scope of their activity as related to learning disabilities. Information about state or regional chapters of either country may be obtained by writing to their national headquarters. Inquiries should be addressed to:

The Division for Children with Learning Disabilities of the Council for Exceptional Children, 1920 Association Drive, Reston, Virginia 22091
or
The Association for Learning Disabilities, 5225 Grace Street, Pittsburgh, Pennsylvania 15236.

In some localities other organizations such as the *YMCA* or the *Association for Retarded Children* will be able to provide direction to more specific sources. Departments of Special Education, Educational Psychology, and Speech Pathology in nearby colleges and universities may be able to either provide first-hand assistance or be willing to serve as a referral agent to other sources. Regular involvement in such organizations and groups should be part of the ongoing professional activity of the learning disability practitioner. Through such personal involvement, it becomes easier to find extra assistance for the dispairing parent.

3. *Some learning disability workers develop an interest in becoming especially proficient in some particular phase of interaction with those affected by learning disabilities.* These special interests should be encouraged and those involved should be aided in their attempts to build skills in harmony with their increased interest. Whenever such specially skilled individuals are available in the community, other workers should depend upon them for help and guidance. Perhaps the most effective type of in-service training occurs when an individual already functioning within the system, having already achieved recognition and acceptance, is able to assist others in building the same skills that set him or her apart as a specially capable practitioner. Workers interested in such individual personal improvement will not have to look far for helpful materials. There is a wealth of supportive instructional literature available for the professional who seeks to improve specific skills. By way of example, if a worker were interested in the problem of achiev-

ing better communication between parent and teacher, an initial step might be to read and practice the suggestions of Kroth (1975) in a small paperback published for precisely this purpose. Other areas have equally ready sources available to help the interested teacher.

Counseling the Teacher of the Learning Disabled

Probably because of their high level of professional involvement, one is apt to take for granted the teacher when considering the various components of the remedial equation. However, just as teachers and their aides represent a fundamentally important aspect of the remedial process, so too are they subjected to special strains, unusual demands, and atypical situations when confronted with the learning disabled child. Anxiety, worry, and even fear may ensue. The special areas of concern that these teachers express are equally worthy of attention when considering the emotional overlay that surrounds the learning disability problem.

Sources of Concern

There is no reason to suppose that teaching personnel are immune to any of the apprehensions or strains that elicit heightened emotional reponses in others. Certainly one could expect to find replicated in teachers' problems the same type of anxieties, insecurities, frustrations, and emotional problems encountered in any other group facing similarly difficult situations. It is probable though that, in day-by-day interaction with teachers involved in working with the learning disabled, the average practitioner is going to encounter teacher concerns centered to a large degree around three principal topics. Teachers are concerned about cause-and-effect relationships in learning disabilities, about unusual time and method demands placed upon them as a result of their involvement with this disabled population, and about problems related to the need to interact effectively with other individuals involved in the diagnostic-prescriptive-implementation process.

Cause and Effect Relationships

To some degree, especially among new teachers or those inexperienced in working with the learning disabled, this type of question arises in relation to whether or not the teacher has done or is doing something in the classroom to cause or maintain a learning disability. Seldom, of course, is the answer ever in the affirmative. The roots of a specific learning disability are rarely ever that easily pinpointed and in almost all cases will be found to have a more complex history than merely episodic interactions with a particular teacher in a given classroom situation. Still, when concerns are voiced, reassurance is called for and probably is most helpful when it is presented in the informational format as previously suggested. Helping concerned teachers understand the true nature of a learning disability goes far to dispel this particular type of concern as it may relate to any growing assumptions of personal guilt or responsibility.

For the most part though, teachers' concerns over cause and effect are centered instead upon worries about what can be done within their sphere of operation to help alleviate problems. The most common emotional reaction seems to be one of frustration and feelings of helplessness. The key phrase most often heard from teachers experiencing these feelings is something like "I've done everything I can think of and still that child doesn't learn. I don't know where to turn next."

Importance of "Supportive Interaction"

Counseling need not be concerned with dispensing detailed information about the nature and availability of alternative teaching methods and materials, of course. But supportive interaction can render valuable assistance in providing the concerned teacher with accurate information about the probability of eventual favorable outcomes within the scope of normal remedial effort once key instructional sequences are established and applied. When teachers are expressing this "helplessness" reaction, it is usually an indication of high motivation and involvement. Highly motivated individuals are especially susceptible to the introduction of any positive steps toward achieving better classroom results, and they make good learners.

As has already been noted, classroom personnel, rather than being looked upon as an elite cadre of specialists, are viewed as the most effective personnel for achieving long-range remedial effectiveness. This suggestion in itself carries the implicit assumption that despair is probably not warranted. But looking elsewhere for assistance and guidance, for new ideas or more effective methodology, is called for. To be most effective in working with teachers experiencing this type of difficulty, learning disability workers should be ready to initially provide this type of positive philosophical support. But, for the support to have a lasting effect, it should be quickly followed with suggestions on how to acquire or apply skills and methods that maximize personal effectiveness, thus obviating the major cause of the helplessness-hopelessness reaction.

Such suggestions should be explicit and concrete. Teachers may be introduced to self-help programs (such as found in the last section of this book), collections of ideas and materials (many are available targeted toward use of resource rooms, special approaches in reading, etc.), and sources of accurate information about specific problems.

Despite the temptation to be of ready assistance, it is probably generally a mistake for the learning disability worker to step in and say, in essence, "Here, let me do that for you." While this may remove the immediate source of concern, it probably makes the individual teacher even more open to future feelings of inadequacy and accomplishes nothing toward the goal of broadening the resource base for dealing with the learning disabled in our schools. Some personal crisis intervention may be justified, but it should be accompanied by steps deliberately designed to help the worried teacher build or acquire the necessary skills and knowledge to function more effectively in the future.

Special Demands

Even when the involved teacher has a wide repertoire of skills and materials available, reactions of inadequacy and helplessness may be encountered. When this occurs under such circumstances, it usually stems from chronic fatigue and worry over how to fit still more activities and effort into an already busy schedule and demanding day. The teacher is not stating, "I can't help the child!" Instead, the teacher is probably saying, "I can't find time to help the child."

There is no way of course that anyone can stretch the day without adding increased demands upon the already fatigued teacher. It is also very true that the presence of special children with special needs inevitably requires some special effort and often increased time. Obviously, the success of any special program, such as *mainstreaming* under P.L. 94–142, rests in part upon the capability of the system to provide not only the skills and materials necessary, but the time as well.

What the learning disability professional *can* do is help the teacher make the most effective use possible of whatever time is available. This includes the application of several principles basic to the approach suggested in this book. Unnecessary labor and the resulting fatigue may result if the principles are ignored. Apart from direct emotional support, the learning disability practitioner can help create a general school environment conducive to mental health by advocating the establishment and use of a system that avoids unnecesary effort or duplicated work. Following these principles will help:

1. Identification of learning disabled children should always take place as early as possible in their school life so that problems are not allowed to become unnecessarily ingrained, disguised, and well-established.
2. Screening and diagnostic approaches should be designed to provide data that is immediately relevant to existing or available methods and materials, thus not requiring subsequent interpretation and adjustment by staff.
3. Diagnosis should always be prescriptive in nature so that established information provides guidance for the next sequential steps rather than mere labels or obtuse categorizations hinting at what steps might follow.
4. Schools should establish files of task analyses of common academic tasks within their curriculum so that these will not have to be prepared anew each time problems in these areas are encountered.
5. Remedial programs related to these identified and analyzed tasks should also be saved and filed for easy, quick access and reuse.
6. Criterion levels and measures should be clearly established and also filed for ready use.
7. Development of specific skills and abilities among individual staff should be

Principles for the establishment of an effective, remedial system in the schools

rewarded and then well publicized so that teachers may utilize specialists among their peers rather than trying to do everything themselves.

8. Participation by nonteaching staff (aides, parents, volunteers, high school students, cafeteria help) should be utilized wherever available in a systematic way. This corps of help may be called upon when time demands of a particular case become overwhelming.

There will also be occasions when individual teachers will correctly perceive the need for individualized instruction or prescriptive skills that they do not themselves possess. Although the teacher is considered to be the front line of attack on learning disabilities, it is unreasonable to expect that each teacher should be able to produce every skill and methodology called for in any possible program. There do exist areas of high specialization, categorized by content— reading, arithmetic, physical education; by approach—psychological evaluation and therapy, speech therapy; or by virtue of their store of information—resource teachers, curriculum specialists, etc. Overloaded teachers should be encouraged to make use of these special resources with no sense of guilt over being unable to do everything themselves. The effective school system will even be ready for such "emergencies" by having established a simple procedure for asking for and receiving help.

When a time-crisis or special skill demand does arise, helping the teacher quickly find and utilize special resources is probably the best supportive "therapy" that can be provided.

Dealing with Individuals

Today's well-trained teachers should be viewed as something more than classroom staff members, particularly as they are involved in working with a pupil presenting special needs. Most teachers find themselves involved in a variety of tasks ranging from the obtaining and/or providing of highly specialized information to and from other professionals to counseling with parents, to serving in a public relations position with media and community groups.

As such diverse tasks present themselves, teachers often express concern over the efficacy of their efforts. Their worries are usually expressed in terms of concern about having adequate knowledge and sufficient skill in communicating with different professional specializations; or they may be apprehensive about practical considerations relating to their personal capability to do certain things such as public speaking, handling emotionally upset individuals, or being persuasive or soothing with those whom they must confront in an adversary role.

Once again, the presentation of good information and exposure to effective methodology seems to be the most positive answer that the experienced worker can provide.

An earlier chapter in this book offers many practical suggestions for sharing information with other professionals. Practice in applying these principles will do much for raising the self-confidence of the average teacher. The material covered within this present chapter should also be of assistance to the teacher who must interact with parents and friends of the learning disabled.

It is beyond the province of the learning disability worker to try to help the individual teacher achieve public speaking or similarly unrelated skills. However, the well-trained worker can assist the teacher in compiling important and relevant information useful for presentations to media, clubs, PTA groups, and other organizations. The same can be done toward providing resources for working with individual parents, or others who may confront the teacher with demands for explanations, information, interpretation, or advice.

Working from an adequate base of knowledge and information can do much to alleviate the rise of unhealthy worry and anxiety. Familiarity with both the problem area and a wide range of solutions is a very strong protection against insecurity. The learning disability worker can help provide this protection for others as well as acquire it for personal use.

Summary

A few words of summary are necessary. First, a note of caution. Despite the title of this chapter, learning disability workers should not consider themselves to be in a counseling profession. Working with the personality and emotional problems of others requires highly specialized skills that come as a result of much supervised practice and training.

What is described here as "counseling" is in reality a two-fold personal interaction that attempts to provide some emotional support and empathy accompanied by a heavy reliance upon an established body of accurate information.

However, this two-fold approach can go a long way towards helping alleviate the nonpathological concerns and worries of those facing the often disturbing reality of deficit learning behaviors. Personal interactions should be directed to such an end, and the practitioner should keep in mind that the underlying objective in all relationships and activities is the improving of the learning efficiency of the individual suffering from a specific learning disability.

Part IV

A Systematic Strategy for Remediation

If the reader were to view this book as a set of maps leading through a strange land of new concepts, questions, and philosophies, then Part IV would signal a major change in direction. At this point, the text takes a right angle turn and proceeds into an area of a specific methodology. That methodology has been variously called a "systems approach," "behavioral approach," or "systematic instructional design." Because we are taking a specific direction, the methods or procedures lying in other areas are not going to be explored. Rest assured that they are there, and one can go to them for applicable techniques, but we have found the systems approach to be highly functional for the classroom teacher (Morasky, 1971; Johnson, Morasky, and Plumeau, 1974).

Chapter 15 discusses in some detail the step called "task analysis." It is a critical first step and the reader should come away from this chapter with the necessary knowledge to analyze behavior according to any one of three different methods, each suited to particular behaviors and problems. Chapter 16 deals with the development of measures that can be used to evaluate behavioral performance. The products described in this chapter are directly related to the analyses explained in the previous chapter. In a like manner the behavioral objectives described in chapter 17 flow from the analyses and measures prepared in the previous steps. Chapter 17 carries the reader through the characteristics of adequate behavioral objectives as well as identifying the functional aspects of such objectives. Chapter 18 presents a series of instructional principles that permit the development of exercises specifically tailored for the individual child. **289**

Chapter 19 outlines a means for evaluating and revising a remedial program. With the attainment of a revised and validated program, the process is complete and, hopefully, the reader will have a sufficient grasp of the systems approach to enjoy following a teacher working with a specific problem in the detailed example given in Chapter. 20.

15

Analysis of the Educational Task

Task analysis or analysis of the educational task is the part of the systems approach to instruction in which the practitioner identifies the component or prerequisite tasks a learning disabled student must ultimately be able to do in order to perform the final desired behavior (Gallegos and Phelan, 1974; Markle, 1973). In other words they are the normal, necessary sequential tasks a nondisabled person performs to complete the final criterion behavior. Note that no mention is made of analyzing "how to teach the student." Task analysis has very little to do with instructional methodology. It has everything to do with figuring out how people go about doing certain tasks.

Why is it necessary for the instructor to analyze the final task? First, it must be done in order to establish a sequential behavior pattern against which the student may be compared to determine whether or not he or she actually does have a definite behavior deficit. Second, a task analysis must be done so that the proper skills, decisions, discriminations, etc., are identified and taught once a deficit or discrepancy is identified (Resnick, Wang, and Kaplan, 1973). Superficially, tasks often appear to be very simple (especially when an expert is doing them), but upon further examination they can turn out to be quite involved and complex. Third, a task analysis is done in order to identify what knowledge or behavior a student must have in order even to begin learning the new task (Resnick et al., 1973). Fourth, the task analysis will often indicate the most obvious instructional sequence if a particular one is necessary (Bellamy, Greiner, and Buttars, 1974).

Reasons for doing a task analysis

291

Let us consider some example situations for each of the four analysis reasons stated above. First, a task analysis will identify the behaviors that *should* be performed by the student under normal circumstances. These can then be compared to what *actually is being performed.* The difference between these two sets of behaviors is indicative of the deficits in the child's behavioral repertoire. The former set of behaviors, that is, those which should be performed, is called in this book the analysis of the educational task. The latter, or what actually is being performed, is called an analysis of the student's behavior or his behavioral repertoire. If one expects that a child ought to be able to recognize that a "3" and "8" are different, but actual performance indicates that he cannot, then a specific behavior deficit has been identified. The steps performed in discriminating a "3" from an "8" would be identified through a task analysis. What the child does instead would be noted in a behavior analysis.

In addition to aiding in the identification of specific deficits, the task analysis also helps the practitioner itemize the proper skills, decisions, and discriminations that must be identified before they can be taught. A task like "open a door" is certainly one which is simple and, obviously, *anyone* can *teach* it without doing an elaborate analysis of the task . . . or can they? Reflect for a moment on what you do when you approach and open a door. Do you ever have difficulty recognizing a door? That seems to be a good place to start the task. What signals or cues do you use to identify doors? Then, what indicates to you that you should lift your right instead of your left hand? or vice versa? What stimuli do you recognize that signal that your palm should be down to grasp a knob, or out to come in contact with a push-plate? How do you know whether to push or pull? Do you look for hinges? Do they tell you whether the door will come at you or move away? How in the world *do* we perform the simple task of opening a door? An old puzzle asks which way a door knob must be turned to open a door. Many are surprised to find that turning the knob either way works just fine.

As you can see, simple tasks often require a great many actions and decisions that we take for granted *if we can already do the tasks.* If we cannot do them, however, then each little item in the task becomes an important aspect that must be learned in order to achieve adequate performance and to avoid failure, frustration, and continued ignorance. A task analysis helps the teacher identify each aspect involved in performing a task.

The third stated reason for a task analysis was that it helps the instructor identify what knowledge or behavior a student must have in order even to *begin* learning the new task. For elaboration let us assume that an instructor plans to begin instruction on Task E at Point D. The instructor will quite probably tell students that in order to begin work on Task E they must be able to do Tasks A, B, and C before even coming to Point D. How does the instructor determine that Tasks A, B, and C must be done *before* D? Well, one way is to do a thorough task analysis. As a task is being analyzed, the analyst will often come across a behavior that is critical to the task, but which should be learned prior to learning this task. For example, in the analysis of the task of dividing two-digit numbers by a one-digit number, the task of subtracting a lesser number from a greater number is critical and must be learned before division can be learned. Task analysis is a tool that instructors can use to identify prerequisite tasks, behaviors that, though vital, are often subtle and overlooked without analysis (Llorens, 1973).

We stated that the final reason for employing task analysis was that it "will often indicate the most obvious instructional sequence. . . ." An example of the use of task analysis for identifying instructional sequence can be seen in the task of "pointing to a triangle, rectangle, square, pentagon, hexagon, or circle when instructed to do so." This is a task that preschool children might have to learn to perform in reading readiness activities; therefore, a teacher should analyze it before attempting to teach it. The analysis will probably lead the teacher to decide that each of the geometric figures will have to be discriminated from each other figure. But which ones do you begin with? What two figures should the child see first? The teacher should make a list of the figures to be discriminated as follows:

A. Two lines intersecting to form an angle
B. Any three-sided figure
C. Figure with three equal sides
D. Any four-sided figure
E. Figure with four equal sides
F. Any five-sided figure
G. Figure with five equal sides
H. Any six-sided figure
I. Figure with six equal sides
J. Irregular shapes like circles

Then a possible sequence in which they should be presented becomes a little clearer. For example, if the teacher wishes to move from less complex to more complex figures, then "two lines intersecting to form an angle" and "any three-sided figure" would be presented first. "Two lines intersecting" and a "figure" with "three equal sides" would be discriminated second and so on. From this point it would not be difficult for the teacher to prepare a matrix like the one in Figure 15-1. The columns marked A–K identify the figure to be discriminated. The row figures are what the column figures will be discriminated from, that is, the cell where column C and row B intersect is the C-B cell or the cell designating that the C figure should be discriminated from the B figure. The numbers in the cells on the matrix designate the discriminations that must be made and the order of the discriminations. It must be noted that *all* figures must be discriminated from *all* other figures by the student. But the order that the instruction will follow is indicated by the numbers on the matrix. And this order arose from the task analysis.

Now that you have seen some examples of what a task analysis can do and how it can be used, it is time to consider the actual process of performing a task

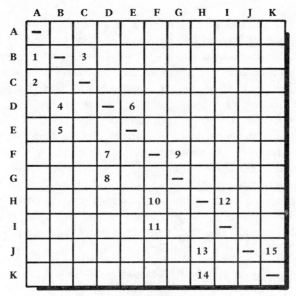

FIGURE 15-1
Teacher Prepared Matrix

analysis. There are three major analysis techniques or approaches: discrimination analysis, flowchart analysis, and generalization analysis. Although these three techniques differ in significant ways, they have two aspects in common that must be discussed before attention is given to their differences. All three techniques require a *final task description* and a list of *assumptions*.

Final Task Description

One of the important things to do when you begin a task analysis is to prepare a clear, succinct *final task description*. Obviously, you are going to analyze some task that a student will learn to do by going through programmed materials. You must write a brief description of that final task before you begin to analyze it.

The major characteristic of a final task description is that it should be concrete rather than general, vague, or abstract. For example, a final task description such as "understanding the nature of sets" is too vague because there are several ways to show that someone "understands" set theory. Each of the ways of showing understanding is itself a task that should be specified.

Listed below are some inadequate final task descriptions and some corresponding ones that are more detailed and adequate:

(Inadequate)   To know numbers

(Adequate)   To point to the appropriate numerals from 1 to 10 when the corresponding numeral is orally named by the teacher

(Inadequate)	To be able to tell time
(Adequate)	To state the time when given "on-the-hour" arrangements of clock hands
(Inadequate)	To know vowel sounds
(Adequate)	To point to the appropriate vowel when its name is orally presented by the teacher
(Inadequate)	To have no perceptual-motor problems
(Adequate)	To walk a ten-foot balance beam without falling

Note that the adequate final task descriptions above are specific and detailed, not vague general statements of performance. Once you have a final task description that sufficiently describes the terminal behavior you desire, then you can begin to consider entering behaviors or assumptions that you will make about the behavioral repertoires of students before instruction begins.

Assumptions Regarding Entering Behavior

Sometimes it is useful to list assumptions regarding the entering behavior of the person who might be doing the task (Corey, 1967). Theoretically, every task we perform can be analyzed down to the very early discriminations that we made as neonates. In order to avoid this lengthy and, perhaps, unnecessary procedure, you can list assumptions about already established behavior and then analyze the task from that point forward. It is important to note here that we are not describing the actual skill level of individual students *you* work with, but rather the skills or behaviors *anyone* must have in order to start learning the task you are analyzing. Assumptions are sometimes called the "necessary entering behavior" of the student. For example, in the analysis of the task of "arranging blocks from left to right in decreasing order of size," you might wish to state the following assumptions:

1. Given two blocks of different sizes, the student can recognize the difference in size.
2. When asked, "Which is larger?" the student can point to the larger of two blocks.

The two statements above describe the behaviors a student will have to have in order to work with the task of "arranging blocks from left to right in decreasing order of size." The assumptions do not say that all your students *will* have these skills, but that they *should* have them before starting on the new task. Of course, if all your students cannot meet the assumptions, then the skill described in the assumption will have to be taught before teaching the task that you are analyzing.

Suppose, for instance, that a particular child, who you suspect might be a learning disabilities case, cannot use personal pronouns properly. You are going to analyze that task, and the final task description will be: *To use the pronouns "I" and "me" correctly in conversation.*

Here is an assumption that is appropriate for that task: The student can say "I." An assumption like "The student can write his name" is not appropriate because it is not a skill related to the final task or even to learning the final task. Another assumption you might wish to make is this: The student can say "me." It is entirely possible that you would not wish to state any other assumptions. The two stated above could be the only entering behaviors you will assume the student can already perform.

The practitioner should be careful not to state assumptions that are unwarranted for the student population or for the task being analyzed. For example, in the task above, the assumption that the student can say "I" is unwarranted if you *know* that the specific population of students is autistic and might need to be taught this task. Here is another example of an assumption that is unwarranted for the task: *The student can recognize that "I" and "me" refer to the self and are not interchangeable in sentences.* Such an assumption is unwarranted because it is probably one of the subtasks you will be teaching the student. It is reasonable to expect that a student who could meet this unwarranted assumption could also perform the final task. A similar situation exists in the case where a teacher assumes that a child can count ten items correctly when the task to be analyzed is to "place equal numbers of items from one to ten in groups to form sets." If you assume the person can do the task (count ten items correctly), then he or she can probably also do the task you are analyzing. Therefore, it is an unwarranted assumption. If you determine later that the student actually can count ten items correctly, but cannot make equal sets, then you have support for your assumption, and it should be stated.

Once you have a final task description and a list of assumptions, you are ready to begin the heart of the task analysis: breaking the behavior down into component parts.

Flowchart Task Analysis

Most learning tasks and, therefore, many tasks related to learning disability problems involve chains or sequences of behaviors (Mechner, 1965). The behaviors coming later in a chain are sometimes dependent on earlier behaviors, and it is often the case that certain behaviors must follow other behaviors. Analysis of such a sequence of behaviors can be aided through the use of a flowchart. The job of the analyst in a flowchart analysis is to identify the parts of the chain that are critical to the correct performance of the total chain of behaviors. The flowchart approach is used when the task to be learned has a sequential set of actions and/or there are decisions to be made between actions. (The reader should consult Brien and Laguna [1977], Page et al. [1976] and Neef, Iwata, and Page [1978] for excellent examples of the application of flow charting analysis techniques.)

The Parts of a Flowchart*

In its simplest form, flowcharting consists of the use of *action boxes or rectangles* and *decision diamonds*. Boxes are used to represent graphically the *actions* performed by the person doing the task while diamonds are used to illustrate decisions made by the same person. For example, a person using a telephone is performing a sequential set of actions and decisions. An *action* performed is to *lift the receiver and listen*. That action is placed in a rectangular box like this:

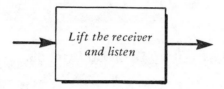

A decision has to be made next: "Is there a dial tone?" This question is placed in a diamond like this:

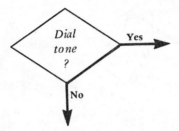

Note that lines and arrows are used to connect the boxes and diamonds. By combining a series of appropriate actions and decisions one can show the flow of a specific behavior chain regardless of how complex or lengthy the sequence might be.

Where to Start

What is the first thing you do when flowcharting an analysis of a task? Often it is beneficial to look at the last action or behavior in the task and work backwards from there. For example, suppose a learning disabilities specialist is preparing an instructional program to aid children with sequential memory deficits, and, furthermore, one of the sequences to be learned is the quite practical one of check-

* The major examples given under the flow charting analysis techniques section do not appear to readily relate to learning disabilities. However, the reader is cautioned to keep in mind that a disability is inferred from an inability to perform specific tasks such as those in these examples. In the systems approach these are the specific tasks central to remedial programming, so they must be identified and analyzed. Inability to perform correct telephone operating behavior or correct check-out procedures could be diagnosed as an auditory or sequential memory problem but, regardless of the label, the deficit behavior remains the focus of the instructional program.

ing a book out of the library. The librarian who is assisting in analyzing the task of checking out a book may decide that the last action taken by the book-borrower would be to get the book back from the checkout desk. That action would be illustrated this way:

> *Get book back from check-out desk*

Using Decision Symbols

The example task obviously involves decisions as well as steps. For example, the librarian felt that before giving the book and library card to the desk librarian, the student must decide if the book should be checked out. That was illustrated in the following manner:

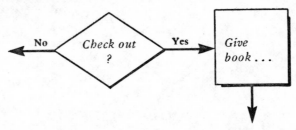

When the answer to a decision is "yes" the sequence goes on to the next action. If the answer is "no," the sequence might go off on a separate track that often will wind its way back to the main flow.

For example, suppose the library procedure was analyzed this way:

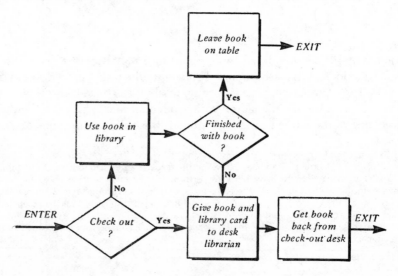

You can see how the decision whether or not to check out the book could lead to other actions and decisions that could eventually arrive back in the linear flow.

Once the last action in the sequence is identified, the analysis simply works backwards to the first step. For instance, the librarian decided that the action just before getting the book back from the checkout desk was to give the desk librarian the book and a library card. She illustrated it this way:

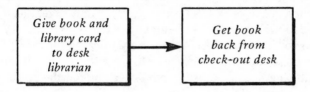

Described below is a task similar to checking out a library book with which a child with a specific learning disability in the area of sequential memory might have trouble. Figure 15-2 is an example of how this task can be analyzed using the flowchart approach.

Example

Students must sign out equipment that is available in the science corner of a classroom. The procedure for signing out this equipment must be followed in order to have an orderly room. First, the student selects the piece of equipment he or she needs, then the student takes the tag from the equipment and carries it to the teacher while leaving the piece in the science corner. Next, the student presents the tag to the teacher, who will check to see if there are other tags hanging by the student's name. If there are no other tags the teacher will have the student hang the new tag by his or her name and go back to the science corner to get the piece of equipment. If there are other tags the student may not take a new piece of equipment. After using the equipment the student returns the equipment with the tag to the science corner.

Decisions, Decisions, Decisions

If you look closely at a sequence of human behaviors, you will quickly note that an evaluation and correction process is almost constantly in process. This means that the analyst is making a multitude of decisions that guide his or her current and subsequent actions. Is it necessary to put each and every one of these decisions in a flowchart analysis? No, it is not. During the analysis you attempt to identify those decisions that are critical points in the sequence and those that are so unusual that the person will probably have to be taught how to make the decision. For example, in the earlier example of securing a book from the library two actions were placed in sequence.

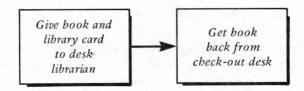

Isn't there a decision to be made between these two actions? Shouldn't one decide first whether the book has been properly stamped, registered, or in some way processed by the librarian before getting the book back? Well, yes, that decision is part of the sequence, but it is not critical to the task *from the point of view* of the person performing the task. It is critical to the librarian's task of registering outgoing books, but the person checking out the books simply waits until the book is available. It is noteworthy here that some implicit assumptions have been made regarding the speed of the registering process, that is, it takes only a few minutes. If it took several hours or days, the analyst might wish to

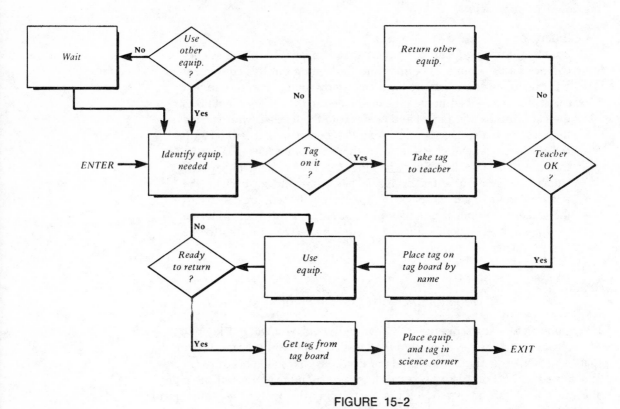

FIGURE 15-2
Sample Flowchart Analysis
Here is one example of how the task of signing out scientific equipment might be analyzed by the flowchart method.

build in a set of actions and decisions for inquiring whether or not the book was ready yet. Since it is assumed that the process takes only a few moments and the person simply waits to get the book back, it is not necessary to place a decision between the two actions.

Two Simple Rules

There are two rules that you can apply to a flowchart analysis in order to evaluate its accuracy and completeness.

> **1. All decision diamonds must have two paths leading away—one labeled "Yes," the other labeled "No."**

The decision
rule

The following decision diamond is incomplete

It must have a "No" choice or path that leads to a subsequent action or decision in the event that the switch is not in the "on" position.

> **2. All paths must lead to a subsequent action, decision, or termination point.**

The dead end
rule

The second rule eliminates the possibility of "dead end" paths that leave you wondering about what to do next. For example, the following portion of a flowchart from an analysis of the task of using a tape recorder contains a dead end:

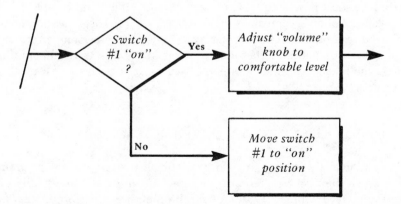

What happens after you move Switch #1 to "on"? As the flowchart exists now, this is a dead end. The arrows indicate that you should not go back to the previous decision, but there is no indication of where to go from this point. The analyst has not completed the job. If the task is finished after Switch #1 is on, then an arrow should lead to an "EXIT" box.

 EXIT

The term *exit* is used to indicate that a sequence is finished. If a subsequent action is necessary, then a line with an arrow should show where to go. In the tape recorder operation flowchart, for example, a line should go from the *Move switch #1 to "on" position* box to the *Adjust volume* box.

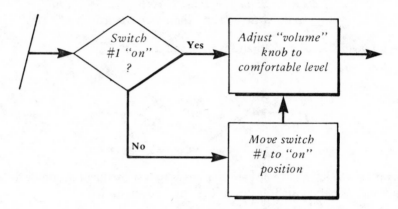

Finishing a Flowchart Analysis

You will recall that earlier in this chapter we stated that a final task description and a list of assumptions were necessary parts of all of the analysis techniques. A flowchart analysis is finished when (1) each of the critical actions and decisions in a behavior chain has been identified, (2) the actions and decisions have been placed in a logical flow with all alternate paths identified and complete, (3) the final task description accompanies the flowchart, and (4) a list of assumptions has been stated regarding the critical entering behavior of the person performing the task and the condition of certain critical items in the task environment. In Appendix 1 the reader will find examples of several task analyses that meet these four criteria.

Discrimination Task Analysis

Discrimination analysis is a particular type of task analysis that the programmer can use when the final task requires that the student be able to identify differences (Evans, 1961; Gilbert, 1962a). Often the analyst will perform a discrimination analysis after he or she has completed a flowchart analysis, because many of the actions or decisions in the flowchart will be based on discriminations that the student must make. On the other hand some tasks do not require a chain or sequence of behaviors, so the analyst will skip the flowchart analysis and go immediately to a discrimination analysis.

The basic aspects of discrimination analysis are the identification of subtasks and attributes that allow for discrimination. In order to perform the task of adding two-digit numbers, the student must be able to—

1. Recognize the value of the written numbers 0 to 9;
2. Recognize the combined values of any two single-digit numbers;
3. Recognize the "place" location of decimal sets.

There are other subtasks that a student must be able to perform in order to add two-digit numbers, but the three subtasks listed above are part of the prerequisite set of tasks and serve as an example of a partial discrimination task analysis. Table 15-1 contains examples of two reasonably complete discrimination task analyses. The analyses given are in some cases adaptations of those done by other programmers, and in other cases they represent the initial attempt to analyze a problem.

Subtasks as Discriminations

Once the final task description and assumptions have been stated, you can begin to break the task down into its component parts. This simply means that the task must be reduced to a series of discriminations that the student must make in order to do the final task. For example, suppose the final task is *to recognize your own name when it is placed with the names of other members of the class.* If we start with the assumption that the student can recognize points in space and discriminate between lines of varying length and slope, then in order to do the task he or she will need to also discriminate between the letters of the alphabet used in his or her name and the names of classmates. In addition the student will need to discriminate the letters that make up his or her name and the letters that are in the other names. Finally, he or she would need to discriminate the order of the letters in his or her name.

An analysis like this is called a "discrimination analysis" because the tasks the students must do involve the process of seeing or recognizing differences between things. A discrimination task analysis is based on the notion that if there are a variety of "things" that are different, the naive student has not yet perceived the differences. Another way of saying this is that the variety of "things" all "look" alike to him or her ("look" does not imply that this is limited to visual differences). During the learning process the naive student will discriminate the differences, hence the terminology of a discrimination task analysis tends toward words like "recognize," "identify," or "discriminate." There are other acts or behaviors that students must be able to perform, but discrimination analysis is primarily concerned with the perception of differences. For example, the letter "a" is different in shape from the letter "d," and the student must recognize or

TABLE 15-1
Examples of Discrimination Task Analysis

TASK ANALYSIS #1
An analysis of the task of blending letter sounds to form two syllable words (auditory blending)
A. Final Task Description: To blend letter sounds to form two syllable words
B. Assumptions about entering behavior (it is assumed that the subject can do the following):
    1. Attend to and discriminate individual letters in a word
    2. Discriminate letter groupings as words
    3. Discriminate the sequential order of the letters
C. In order to perform this task the student must learn to do the following:
    1. Recognize and say the phoneme (sound) for each grapheme (letter)
    2. Recognize and say the phonemes (sounds) in sequence as presented
    3. Recognize and say (blend) the groupings of phonemes (syllables) as is done in familiar language to form two separate syllables with an interval between the syllables
    The analysis can easily be expanded to include the specification of each phoneme and grapheme and the regular or high and low frequency syllabic structures. The analysis presented is a basic, general structure that can be applied to specific situations.

TASK ANALYSIS #2
An analysis of the task of naming the secondary color resulting from the combination of two primary colors
A. Final Task Description: To identify the two primary colors which produce a given secondary color
B. It is assumed the subject can do the following:
    1. Recognize and name cards of the following colors: red, blue, yellow, purple, green, orange
C. In order to perform this task the student must learn to do these things:
    1. Recognize the colors red, blue, and yellow as primary
    2. Recognize that the combination of any two primary colors produces a third, different color
    3. Recognize that purple is the color resulting from the combination of red with blue
    4. Recognize that orange is the color resulting from the combination of red with yellow
    5. Recognize that green is the color resulting from the combination of blue with yellow

see that difference. The letters in the name "Tom" must be in a certain arrangement in order to be correct, and the student must see or recognize the correct order as opposed to the incorrect.

Suppose we wanted to develop a visual perception nature study program on the task of naming oaks, birches, poplars, maples, and elms when shown either the tree shape, the bark, or a leaf. Listed below are discriminations that would be a part of doing that task and behaviors that would not be a part of the discrimination analysis.

In order to do the final task, the student must be able to do these things:

(Appropriate to the task)	Identify the difference between the shape of an oak leaf and a maple leaf
(Not appropriate to the task)	Draw an oak leaf
(Appropriate to the task)	Recognize the difference in the texture of birch and poplar trees
(Not appropriate to the task)	Recognize the difference between the root structure of trees and house plants
(Appropriate to the task)	Recognize the difference in limb structure between a birch and an elm
(Not appropriate to the task)	Be able to spell the words, "oak," "birch," "maple," and "elm"

You can see from the choices given above that in order to do the final task of "naming oaks, birches, poplars, maples, and elms when shown either the tree shape, bark, or leaf," the student must be able to do at least three subtasks:

1. Recognize the difference between the shape of an oak leaf and a maple leaf
2. Recognize the difference in the texture of birch and poplar trees
3. Recognize the difference in limb structure between a birch and an elm

But if the student could do these three subtasks (and no other) could he or she successfully do the final task? The answer to the question above would have to be "no" because there are many more than three subtasks that must be performed in order to be able to do the final task as specified. For instance, it would be necessary to discriminate the oak leaf from the birch, the oak from the poplar, the oak from the maple, and so on. It is sufficient to say in the task analysis that the student must be able to discriminate each tree leaf from each other tree leaf. But all we have in the three subtasks stated above is that the student must be able to discriminate the oak from the maple, which is not enough to complete the final task.

The following example is the start of a discrimination analysis of the task of *stating the time when given clocks showing only "on-the-hour" arrangements of the hands.* (The clocks only point to one o'clock, two o'clock, etc.) Again, correct and incorrect analysis statements are given.

A. Assumptions about entering behavior: It is assumed that the student can do the following:
1. Recognize the numbers 1–12 and say them when displayed
2. Recognize the one-to-one relationship between the numbers 1–12 and one to twelve items
3. Discriminate between the relative temporal relationships of "before" and "after"

B. Task analysis: In order to perform the final task the student must be able to do the following:

(Correct)   Recognize the difference in size between the two hands on the clock

(Incorrect)   Understand that "time goes by"

(Correct)   Recognize the relationship between the "big" hand and the term "o'clock"

(Incorrect)   Be able to adjust a clock to indicate proper time

(Correct)   Recognize the relationship between the "little" hand and the time designation

(Incorrect)   Recognize the difference in rate of movement between "big and little" hands

Identifying Differences

Sometimes it is a major job for the instructor to identify the differences between the items that the student must learn to recognize. It is often difficult to identify why two things are different. Why is a triangle different from a square? What clues or "attributes" do we use to tell them apart? The angles? The sides?

As an example of the difficulty involved in identifying how things are different, consider the letters of the alphabet. How can you systematically identify differences in order to analyze the task of recognizing each of the twenty-six figures? Several researchers have attempted to identify (and help students identify) the differences between letters by placing the letters on a 5" × 7" matrix and noting the differences in the spaces taken up by the letters.

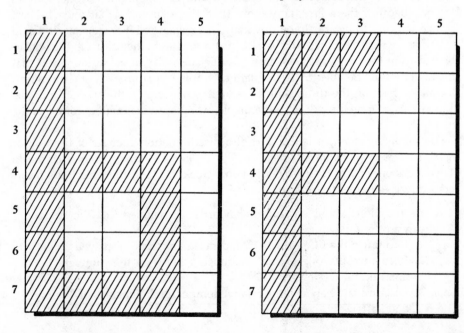

There are other tools besides matrices that can be used to help you identify the differences between items. A chart can be used that names the units to be discriminated and the features or characteristics of the unit that make it different from other units. For example, on the chart below, the programmer is trying to identify the differences between three common traffic signs in order to use them in a visual perception program. We know even before we begin that the signs are different because they serve different functions. But just how does the perceiver tell them apart? By location? By the words on them? By the lighting? Look at the chart:

UNIT	DISCRIMINATIVE ATTRIBUTE
"Stop" sign	8 sides, red, S-T-O-P printed on it.
"Yield" sign	3 sides, yellow, Y-I-E-L-D printed on it.
"Speed Limit" sign	4 sides (rectangle), white, S-P-E-E-D L-I-M-I-T and numerals printed on it.

From the chart you can see that the programmer thinks a driver could identify the three signs by looking at shape, color, or words printed on it.

Suppose that you have several children with deficient abstract organizational skills, as reflected in their inability to identify family-tree relationships, school administration/teaching personnel relationships, etc. Assume that you are going to prepare a sequence on city government to illustrate functional organization and that you are going to do a discrimination analysis. On the following chart the positions of city officials to be discriminated are listed on the left and on the right the attributes that will be used for discrimination are described briefly. Attributes are those specific parts of the item that allow you to tell it from other items. Can you finish this chart?

UNITS	DISCRIMINATIVE ATTRIBUTE
Mayor	Plans budget, selects department heads, presides over legislative meetings
City Chamberlain	Accountant for the city, responsible for all city finances
City Attorney	
Director of Public Works	

You can see that the chart will be complete when the analyst has identified those characteristics or attributes that differentiate a City Attorney and the Director of Public Works from other city officials.

Finishing a Discrimination Analysis

Once you have identified the parts or attributes of a "thing" which make it different from other "things," then you can complete the discrimination task analysis that involves that thing. For example, if you finished the chart on government officials above, you identified the attributes that made the mayor different from the city chamberlain, from the city attorney, and from the director of public works. The task analysis that would develop out of that item might look like this:

Final Task Description:

The final task that the student is to perform is to "describe orally the differences between city officials."

Assumptions:

It is assumed that students can do the following

A. Identify the city as a governmental entity
B. Recognize the city officials as part of a governmental entity
C. Recognize that the words, "mayor," "city chamberlain," etc., designate different city officials

Task Analysis (Partial):

In order to perform the final task, students must learn to perform these tasks:

A. Recognize the differences in job or function between the mayor and the city chamberlain (e.g., the mayor plans the use of city finances while the city chamberlain keeps track of the finances.)
B. Recognize the differences in function between the mayor and the city attorney (e.g., the mayor presides over legislative meetings while the city attorney advises the mayor and the legislative body on the legality of their actions.)
C. Recognize the difference between the city attorney and the city chamberlain (e.g., the city attorney advises on legal matters while the city chamberlain keeps track of the finances.)

An example of discrimination task analysis

The following is another example of a task analysis for a spatial perception problem involving the recognition of geometric forms.

Final Behavior Description:

The final or terminal behavior the student should perform can be described as follows: *When given a geometric form model of two intersecting lines, triangle, square, rectangle, pentagon, hexagon (both equal and unequal sided), the student will identify other items like the model on the basis of shape.* An example of this behavior would be a situation in which the student was shown a triangle and asked to identify other triangles in a group of mixed geometric shapes like squares, rectangles, circles, etc., choices differing in size, side length, and position. It is basically a simple matching task with geometric shapes.

Assumptions:

It is assumed that students will be able to do the following as entering behavior:

A. Identify a point in space or a series of points forming a straight line

B. Discriminate a curved line from a straight line

C. Discriminate a straight line from two lines intersecting to form an angle

Task Analysis:

In order to perform the final behaviors, students must be able to do the following subtasks:

A. Discriminate a figure with three equal sides from two lines intersecting to form an angle and from any three-sided figures

B. Discriminate any four-sided figure from two lines intersecting to form an angle, any three-sided figures, and figures with four equal sides

(Several more statements like A and B are necessary in order to detail the entire list of discriminations that need to be made before the student can perform the final task.)

In order to begin analyzing the given task, the teacher tried to identify the various geometric forms encountered in the task and to determine what characteristics they possess that would allow discriminations between them. The following chart was used to identify the attributes involved in the items (geometric forms):

An example of discrimination task analysis

ITEMS	ATTRIBUTES
Two intersecting lines	Two straight (as opposed to curved) lines intersect to form one angle
Triangle	Three-sided figure, three angles, closed figure
Equilateral triangle	Three equal sides, three equal angles, closed figure
Rectangle	Four-sided figure, four angles, closed figure
Square	Four equal sides, four equal angles, closed figure
Five-sided figure	Five sides, five angles, closed figure
Pentagon	Five equal sides, five equal angles, closed figure
Six-sided figure	Six sides, six angles, closed figure
Hexagon	Six equal sides, six equal angles, closed figure
Circle	Closed figure, no discernible sides, no discernible angles (Without drafting tools student will probably not use other attributes.)

Given these attributes, the analyst decided which discriminations the student must make and what attributes will be used for discrimination. This resulted in the subtasks listed previously.

You will note from the examples of discrimination task analyses that the most prominent act or behavior to be learned is that of "recognizing" or "identifying" something. The act of discriminating one object from another involves seeing, hearing, feeling, or in some way perceiving differences between things. A discrimination task analysis is the tool a practitioner or teacher would use to identify what differences exist and which ones the student will have to recognize.

As we mentioned previously, the discriminations to be made can be part of a chain of behaviors and decisions or they can be discrete behaviors that are not sequenced with other behaviors.

When the task involves something more than just recognizing differences, programmers can utilize yet another analysis technique called *generalization analysis.*

Generalization Task Analysis

Another method for completing a task analysis necessitates identifying the generalizations that are used when the task is performed (Glaser, 1961). Generalizations are sometimes called *rules,* or *rul* in the short form. In addition, a number of concrete examples of the generalizations must also be identified. These examples are sometimes referred to as *eg's* and together with the *ruls* they make up what is often referred to as a *Ruleg* analysis.

An instance of a generalization that is used to define complete sentences follows:

A complete sentence must have a subject and a predicate.

You can see that generalizations can apply to many different situations, but do not specify any particular situation: examples work with specific situations. It is the job of the task analyst to investigate the task and determine the generalizations and examples that may apply and that are critical to the completion of the task. Listed below are some instances of generalizations and examples:

Generalization:	When converting decimals to percents, the decimal point is always moved two places to the right.
Example:	.65 becomes 65%, .04 becomes 4%.
Generalization:	An apostrophe should be placed before the "s" when the singular possessive is being used.
Example:	In the phrase "Charlie's horse," the apostrophe should be placed between the "e" and the "s" in "Charlie's."
Generalization:	Non-deciduous trees do not lose their leaves.

Example:	Norway pines, white pines, and ponderosa pines are types of non-deciduous trees that do not lose their leaves.
Generalization:	Nouns are persons, places, or things.
Example:	Car, Abraham Lincoln, and Australia are nouns.

Assume that you are going to prepare an instructional sequence on the use of commas in punctuation. Listed below are some of the generalizations and examples that govern the use of commas and would be part of a generalization analysis.

Generalization:	When more than two items are named in a sentence, the words naming the items are separated by a comma.
Example:	Boats, cars, trains, planes, dog sleds, and rockets were pictured in the exhibit on transportation.
Generalization:	When writing the name of a city and state, the city name is separated from the state name by a comma.
Example:	Detroit, Michigan Buffalo, New York Yuma, Arizona
Generalization:	When writing a date, the day of the month and the year are separated by a comma.
Example:	June 15, 1956 April 2, 1802 December 15, 1586
Generalization:	A comma always follows the closing in a letter.
Example:	Best regards, Yours truly, Sincerely,

Selecting Enough Examples

When identifying examples you should select a sufficient number so that the rule is well illustrated, and so that the range of possible applications of the rule is covered. For instance, the example of the rule above on the use of commas to separate successive items in a sentence does not include all possible applications of that rule: items could appear as objects or verbs or prepositions in a sentence, more than six items could be named, items need not be single words, etc.

Here are some examples of the generalization: "When writing the name of a city and state, the city name is separated from the state name by a comma":

• Chicago, Illinois
• Denver, Colorado

There are other examples that are necessary to cover the range of application of the generalization:

- West Falls, Washington
- Little Sun, New Mexico
- West Willow Beach, West Virginia

When the situation being analyzed is very complex, a number of different examples may be necessary. Journalists compile such examples into a collection called a "style book." Athletic officials such as basketball referees compile theirs into a collection called a "case book." Both serve the same purpose of identifying the generalizations to be used in adequately performing a task. Grammar, spelling, and arithmetic are all academic areas that rely heavily on generalizations or rules.

Identifying Unstated Generalizations

An instructor or task analyst who is using the generalization task analysis technique to deal with a learning disabilities problem will be looking at a certain task in order to determine if any particular practice is followed over and over again and, if so, how that particular practice can be described in a general way. If the task analyst talks to someone who can do the task in an expert manner, he will often be told the rules that must be applied. However, this is not always the case. Often people follow routines as if rigid rules existed, yet they will not be able to express those rules in the form of generalizations. Nevertheless, the task analyst will view rigidly followed practices as rules or generalizations and attempt to convert them into generalization or rule statements.

Completing a Generalization Analysis

Like the other types of analyses discussed previously, generalization task analyses should include a final task description and a list of assumptions as well as all the generalizations that apply to the task and sufficient examples to illustrate the range of the generalizations. In Appendix 1 the reader will find a number of complete generalization task analyses that illustrate the necessary components.

Combining Discrimination, Flowchart, and Generalization Analyses

Often a programmer will encounter a task that can be analyzed according to more than one of the analysis techniques. For example, the task might initially appear to be a simple chain of behaviors and decisions that require a flowchart analysis. But after completing the flowchart, it might be decided that the student will have to be able to make some discriminations in order to do the task, so a discrimination analysis would also have to be done.

Let us consider a concrete example of this situation: suppose an instructor was attempting to help a child with a general perceptual-motor disability coupled with a minor sequential memory problem, and it had been decided that manipulation of a calculator would be a possible mode for remediating the difficulties. Suppose, further, that the instructor was analyzing the task of multiplying two-digit numbers on a calculator and started with the following flowchart analysis:

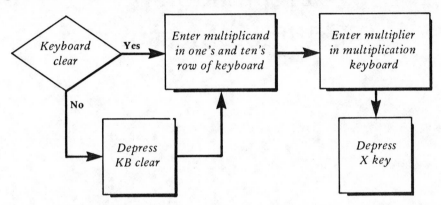

The programmer might quickly realize that the student will also have to be able to do the following subtasks that are part of a discrimination analysis:

1. Recognize when keyboard is clear
2. Recognize keyboard clear key
3. Recognize one's row on keyboard
4. Recognize ten's row on keyboard
5. Recognize multiplication keyboard
6. Recognize X key

Thus, the programmer has used both the discrimination and the flowchart analysis techniques when looking at a task. You should not hesitate to experiment with each of these techniques when confronted with an analysis problem.

16

Preparation of Criterion Measures

Criterion measures are the tests the practitioner uses to determine if the learning disabled student can do the task that is to be (or was) taught (Glaser and Klaus, 1962; Hammock, 1960; Morasky, 1971). For example, if the task in question is to "find a book in the school library and then check it out," a criterion measure might require that the student actually go to the library, find a book on a particular subject, and then check it out. This particular criterion measure would be a means for evaluating the student's ability to do the task.

There are at least two times when an instructor might want to use a criterion measure like the one above; the first is prior to instruction in order to determine whether or not instruction is necessary; the second is after instruction in order to determine whether or not the behavior was learned.

Although criterion measures evaluate a student's performance much like ordinary tests, they are usually quite different from standard quizzes and tests commonly seen in a classroom. One of the reasons for the difference is the careful, systematic way criterion measures are developed. The rather rigid characteristics criterion measures must exhibit also make them different from most teacher-made measurement tools. This chapter is devoted to an explanation of the systematic manner in which criterion measures are developed and the characteristics that are evident in a good measure.

314

The Source of Criterion Measures

Criterion measures are the logical extension of a good task analysis (Gallegos and Phelan, 1974). You will recall that a completed analysis includes a *final task description*, a listing of the discriminations to be made, and/or a flowchart of the steps to be followed, and/or a listing of the generalizations and examples that apply to the task. A well-stated final task description can be quite easily converted into a *final criterion measure*. For instance, if the final task description was this: "to write complete sentences," then the criterion measure designed to evaluate whether or not the student could perform the final task would have to be one in which the student was actually required to write complete sentences.

If, as a final task, the teacher wanted students to "name the vowels—A, E, I, O, and U," then as a final criterion measure it would be appropriate to ask the student, "Name all of the vowels." On the other hand, it would not be adequate to simply ask, "Is 'T' a vowel?" Even if the teacher questioned the student about each and every consonant it would not be an adequate final criterion measure because the behavior of "naming the vowels" had not been done. Such a question would involve neither naming nor vowels, both necessary in a final criterion measure matching this example of a final criterion measure.

Subcriterion Measures

Whenever the task analysis results in a set of sequential subtasks, each subtask must be evaluated by means of a criterion or *subcriterion measure*. For example, suppose the final task was "to give the correct name for each farm animal when the sound it makes is heard (cow, sheep, chicken, pig)." The final criterion measure for this task could involve a teacher playing a record of the "moo" sound, and the child being required to say "cow." And the same for the rest of the animals. During the task analysis, however, the teacher would probably decide that a subtask of the final task would be to "discriminate the animals from each other." Therefore, a subcriterion measure would be necessary in which a cow would have to be identified as different from a pig, sheep, or chicken; the sheep identified as different from the cow, pig, or chicken; and so on. *Subcriterion measures should be prepared for each task that has been identified as leading up to or part of the final task.*

Below is a partial analysis of the task of "identifying objects in pictures of farms."

In order to do the task the student must learn to do the following:

1. Identify by name the cow, horse, pig, sheep, goat, chicken, and goose when presented singly and all together in pictures
2. Identify by name the farmhouse, milkhouse, chickenhouse, barn, and garage when presented singly and all together in pictures

3. Identify by name the tractor, plow, hay rake, combine, trailer, and baler when presented singly and all together in pictures

You can see that a criterion measure (or subcriterion measure) will be necessary for each aspect of this task; that is, the first criterion measure would involve showing the student a picture of a cow and asking him to give its name, the second criterion measure would require the same thing with a horse, a third with a pig, and so on.

Here is partial analysis of another task: identifying the two primary colors that produce a particular secondary color. In order to perform this task the student must learn (1) orange is the result of mixing red with yellow; (2) purple is the result of mixing red with blue; and (3) green is the result of mixing blue with yellow.

Listed below are some appropriate and inappropriate subcriterion measures for the secondary colors task:

> *(Appropriate)*   Teacher points to a purple card and asks, "What colors are combined to produce this color?"
>
> *(Inappropriate)*   Teacher asks, "Why are red, yellow, and blue called primary colors?"
>
> *(Appropriate)*   Teacher points to an orange card and asks, "What colors are combined to produce this color?"
>
> *(Inappropriate)*   Teacher asks, "Which color do we add to orange to make it darker?"
>
> *(Appropriate)*   Teacher points to a green card and asks, "What colors are combined to produce this color?"

The three appropriate subcriterion measures above would evaluate a student's ability to perform the subtasks associated with the final task, but a further measure is also necessary in order to evaluate the student's skill with the final task itself. That final measure might look like this:

> Given a large card with purple, orange, and green paint patches, pieces of cloth, pieces of cellophane and paper on it, the student is asked to name the colors that are combined to form each color in the item on the card.

The final criterion measure and the three subcriterion measures identified above make up the complete set of measures associated with the analysis of the task of identifying primary color combinations that produce certain secondary colors.

Most analyses will require sets of subcriterion measures that evaluate performance on the individual parts of an overall task.

The Need for Direct Measurement

You can see from the examples above that criterion measures must directly evaluate a person's ability to perform a task (Glaser and Klaus, 1962). For instance, simply asking a child, "Can you tell your right hand from your left?" and accepting a "yes" answer is not an adequate criterion measure for the task of "identifying one's own right and left hands and feet."

If the task a student is to perform is "give his address," then as shown below some measures can be more direct than others.

(More direct)	The teacher asks the student, "What is your address?"
(Less direct)	The teacher asks the student, "Is your address 17 Maple Rd., Saranac, New York?"
(More direct)	The teacher says to the student, "Tell me your address."
(Less direct)	The teacher asks the student, "Which of these addresses is yours?" (She holds up four addresses, one of which is correct.)

This direct measurement characteristic is often referred to as "having a criterion measure that is as close a simulation of the actual task as possible" (Morasky, 1967). If a task is to be performed adequately, then there are responses the performer must make in the presence of certain stimuli. Those responses should be as much like the responses required in the real-world or real-life task as possible. Likewise, the stimuli should be as close as possible to those in real life.

Over the years, since the advent of formal instructional programming procedures, programmers have employed a variety of stimulus-and-response combinations in criterion measures. Some combinations are very close to real-life situations; that is, the stimuli are those encountered in a noneducational or actual living situation and the response of the student is similarly close to a real-life behavior. For example, in a self-instructional program called "Teach Yourself to Use the Tape Recorder," the student must go to a machine in the audiovisual room and operate it correctly while a supervising teacher watches. This criterion measure is real-life in its stimulus presentation; that is, the stimuli in the audiovisual room are precisely like those encountered by anyone performing the task of operating a tape recorder, and the responses of the student are real-life—the student must do what anyone performing that task must do.

Less direct criterion measures involve stimulus-response combinations which are only "simulations" of the real-life situation. A common "simulated real-life" criterion measure is used by airlines to evaluate a pilot's ability to perform various flying tasks while in a computer-controlled simulator that can provide nearly all of the stimuli encountered in real life. The simulator requires nearly all the responses of real-life performance, yet it can only provide an approximation

Real-life measures

Simulated real-life measures

or simulation of the real-life situation. The teacher who has the class operate an in-the-room grocery store where goodies are purchased with play money has developed a simulated real-life situation. You can see that in this example both stimuli and responses are equally removed from real life. Even in this case, however, every effort is made to cause the situation to appear realistic to the subject even though he or she is aware of being in a simulated real-life situation.

Recorded and simulated measures

Moving a little further from "real-life," one might encounter a criterion measure in which the stimuli are presented through some recording media and the response is a simulation of real life. For example, a criterion measure from a program called "Learning Directions" would require that students take four step directions from a tape recorder and, then, carry out the required four tasks. The response of taking directions is like that required in a real-life situation, but because the recorded message is used only for training, the response is simulated; and real life is only pretended or imagined. The stimuli are like those encountered in a real-life situation, but they are recorded, rather than actually occurring at that moment.

Written description measures

Another form of recorded presentation in a criterion measure involves the use of the written description of real life. Often programmers will describe in writing the stimuli that should be present and the student will respond in a similar manner, that is, he will make a written response. Other examples of this type of criterion measure in a classroom involve such things as arithmetic story problems being presented on cassette tapes and carried out as if they were real problems or problem-solving situations being given on slide projectors and pursued by students as if the problems were real. An example of this form of criterion measure comes from a learning disabilities program titled "Sequencing Events" in which the student reads the following:

> Imagine that you are walking through an alley and come upon a gun,
> a box of money, a bag of jewels, a torn shirt, and a little boy crying.
> Write a description of what you think happened.

Because of the relative cost of various modes of programming, the "written description of real life with a written response" criterion measure is popular and commonly used. In the above example the situation could have been presented in a slide or a movie or even role-played—at greater expense.

A common combination of stimulus and response in a criterion measure is a written description of real life with a "rule statement" response. The rule statement is simply a written or spoken description of the rule or generalization that is appropriate to the situation. For example, the following criterion measure was taken from a remedial program titled "Reversal Problems":

Rule statement measures

> Here is a note you receive from a friend:
> Meet me dehind the dank.

> Your friend would know that "dehind" and "dank" are misspelled
> if he knew what rule about the shape of two particular letters?

The stimulus in the criterion measure above is a written description of a real-life situation. The response, however, does not involve a written description of what would actually be done or said, but rather, a statement of a rule that should be followed. Note that the ability to state a rule does not insure the ability to perform the behavior to which the rule applies and a criterion measure with a rule response is ordinarily a very poor measurement tool unless the student was actually only supposed to learn the *rule statement.*

The criterion measure furthest from real life and probably the least accurate measurement tool (if something other than memory is being measured) is the one that has as a stimulus the command to "state the rule . . ." and a statement of the rule as the response. "Rule request with rule statement" criterion measures only evaluate the student's ability to recite, perhaps as a result of memorization, a statement which he might not be able to comprehend or translate into behavior in a real-life situation. Thus a child may be able, upon request, to recite certain spelling rules yet have poor spelling skills.

The stimulus-response combinations in the criterion measures illustrated above range from what may be called "real-life" to "non-real-life" and with some manipulating can be fitted onto a continuum like the one below.

Real Life
|——Real-life stimulus/Real-life response
|——Simulated stimulus/Simulated response
|——Recorded stimulus/Simulated response
|——Written description stimulus/Written description response
|——Rule request/Rule response
Non-real Life

It would seem apparent that systematic manipulation of a multidimensional item such as a criterion measure would result in many more than just six variations. This is entirely true. The six variations listed above are representative of the most commonly produced criterion measures, and, as such, become the framework for the continuum shown above. At certain places on the continuum one could locate a "simulated stimulus/written response" or a "recorded stimulus/written response" or any other combination of stimulus and response. The variations presented above are simply six main points on the continuum which a practitioner can use to locate other combinations. For the practitioner who is specifically concerned with learning disabilities programs, the continuum can be used by first locating where a particular criterion measure falls on the continuum and, second, asking the question, "Can I redesign the measure so that it can be located higher on the continuum, thereby increasing the directness of the measure?"

Note that as a criterion measure moves up the continuum, it comes closer to directly measuring the student's ability to do the task given realistic conditions, and, more importantly, the higher level measures subsume the lower levels. For instance, if a student can write a description of her behavior given a written description of the situation, then there is evidence to show whether or not she has followed the rules that apply to that behavior. Even though she has not written out or recited the rules, she has performed behavior that subsumes the rules and, as such, is an illustration of the application or comprehension of the rules. On the other hand, if a student can write out the rules that apply to a given situation, there is no evidence to show that he can write out a description of his behavior or actually perform the behavior according to the rules he can recite. Consider the child who successfully reduces fractions to their lowest common denominator. Must he tell you what rules he uses? Conversely, a child's ability to define syllables is not an indication of his ability to divide words into syllables.

More simply stated, if a student demonstrates his or her ability to perform a response at one point on the continuum, then it is quite likely that all the responses lower on the continuum are accounted for, but the responses higher on the continuum require more measurement. When developing a criterion measure for evaluation in a learning disabilities program, the practitioner should make as direct a measure as possible and this will usually mean locating it as high as possible on the continuum.

There are constraints, however, that prohibit the simple restructuring of criterion measures for optimal height on the continuum. You should consider the following:

Constraints to restructuring criterion measures

1. *The practicality of a more direct measure:* At which level is it most practical to measure a student's ability to perform the task of terracing a farm field? The most practical measure in this case might be a less direct one.
2. *The cost of a more direct measure:* For example, can fire departments afford to burn down actual twenty-story buildings to provide real-life stimuli for measuring the responses of student firemen? A less costly situation such as a recorded set of stimuli or a simulated building might be more feasible than destroying real buildings.
3. *The sufficiency of the measure:* Within the educational operation where the criterion measure will be used, is a less direct measure adequate for the needs and demands of management and consumer?

Within the limits set by the constraints listed above, the programmer should produce a set of criterion measures that are as direct as possible and that adequately tell whether or not the student can "do what you want him or her to do."

Multiple-Choice and Production-Type Criterion Measures

You might have noticed from the previous examples that some criterion measures evaluate a student's ability to do something or perform some behavior that is directly evaluated, while other criterion measures simply ask the student to choose the correct item from several alternatives. Both types of criterion measures are legitimate if they measure exactly what you want the student to be able to do. For example, if you want the student to identify an oak leaf from among other leaves, then a *multiple-choice* criterion measure is appropriate. A multiple-choice measure would not be appropriate, however, if you wanted the student to "draw an oak leaf." The ability to choose something from among alternatives is not the same behavior as producing that thing (by drawing or building or whatever) (Cutler, Hirshoren, and Cecirelli, 1973).

Listed below are some sample task descriptions that necessitate multiple-choice and some that call for production-type criterion measures.

Production:	The student should be able to draw a circle on the blackboard.
Multiple-choice:	The student should be able to point to a circle drawn on the blackboard.
Production:	The student should be able to spell house.
Multiple-choice:	The student should be able to place a check by the correct spelling of the word "house."

Covering the Range of Possible Situations

A criterion measure should cover the range of possible situations in order to be considered an adequate measure (Brethower, Markle, Rummler, Schrader, and Smith, 1964; Gagnè, 1970; Glaser and Klaus, 1962). For example, consider the task of "identifying the right and left hands of people in pictures." The criterion measure for such a task would have to show humans in a variety of views in order to cover the range of people positions in pictures.

The range of possible positions is limited in the example above just as in the earlier task of identifying secondary colors. Often the tasks will offer an unlimited range of possibilities. For example, the task of "identifying nouns" requires a criterion measure that has examples of all the different classes of nouns (i.e., persons and places), but it would be practically impossible to present anything more than just samples of the full range. The criterion measure can be designed to evaluate the student's ability to identify some examples within each class, but certainly not all nouns in all classes. The practitioner should attempt to cover the range of possibilities as much as possible in a criterion measure.

A Criterion Measure Does Not Teach

In addition to covering the range of possibilities, a criterion measure should also, in fact, measure whether or not the subject (or student) can do the task without additional or outside aid (Brethower et al., 1964; Glaser and Klaus, 1962). Often instructors inadvertently prepare criterion measures that teach the student how to perform the task, or they give information that permits correct performance without the knowledge desired. For example, the following situation was supposed to measure whether or not a child could discriminate rectangles from triangles and circles:

> The teacher shows the student a card with a rectangle, a circle, and a triangle on it and says, "Remember, a rectangle has four sides and a triangle has only three sides. Now, count the sides on these figures and tell me which one is the rectangle."

A student *would not need to know* that a rectangle has four sides *before* taking this criterion measure nor would he or she need to know that counting the sides is a way of identifying rectangles *before* taking the measure. Why not? Because the teacher is going to give that information in the beginning of the measure anyway. Therefore, if the student did the task correctly, the teacher would *not* know if he or she could do it without prompting. Criterion measures should *not give* any information that you expect the student to possess.

Below are further examples of criterion measures that measure and those that teach part or all of what is to be measured:

From material entitled "Grouping into Classes."

Teaches and Measures: The teacher gives the following directions: "I will name some things and you raise your hand if they are in the group or class of things with a ball, an orange, or a circle. Remember, for something to be in a class of things it must be like other things in that class."

Only Measures: The teacher gives the following directions: "I will name some things and you raise your hand if they are in the group or class of things with a ball, an orange, or a circle."

From material entitled "Drawing a Diagonal through a Square."

Teaches and Measures: Instructions: Use a ruler to draw a diagonal line in the square below:

Only Measures: Instructions: Use a ruler to draw a diagonal line in the square below:

Criterion Measures Must Be
Relevant to the Task

You must be careful to make certain that the responses in the criterion measure are all relevant to the task you are trying to measure. For example, the task of "naming triangles, squares, and circles when shown individual geometric figures on a series of cards," requires the following skill: The student must be able to discriminate triangles from squares.

The criterion measure below appears to measure that skill:

Cut out the triangles with scissors.

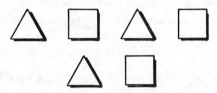

But in fact there is an added set of responses in the criterion measure that is irrelevant to the task—can you see it? It is the use of the scissors. The child might be able to recognize squares and triangles, but not use the scissors. So this criterion measure actually evaluates something you aren't concerned with: the child's ability to use scissors.

Instructional programmers often build irrelevant responses into criterion measures by requiring that a student state the rule or generalization associated with a task when the performance of the task is actually desired. There are a great many tasks performed correctly each day by people who cannot state the generalizations that apply to the task; moreover, being able to state the applicable generalization would not help improve or maintain their performance on these tasks. For instance, if a program were being developed for nursery school children that had as a final task the recognition and naming of squares, triangles, and circles, would it be advantageous to require the children to say that "squares are enclosed figures having four equal sides and angles?" Being able to make such a statement is irrelevant to the task of recognizing and naming the figures.

A Final Note on Criterion Measures

Even though all the criterion measures for a program should be prepared at one time prior to the preparation of any instructional material, they eventually wind up scattered throughout a program. That is, in a program the student will confront some instructional material and then be tested in a subcriterion measure, then will confront more instructional material and another criterion measure, and so on. This has been described as the "give a little—ask a little" technique. Remember, however, that all criterion measures for a program are prepared before any instructional materials.

The following is a reasonably complete analysis of the task of identifying whether or not groups have the same number of things in them. It is intended to serve as a comprehensive example of the process of attacking a learning disability from the task analysis to criterion measure preparation.

Final Task Description:
Identifying whether the Same or Different Amounts of Items are Present in Sets of Items

Assumptions:
A. Student can do match-to-sample tasks.
B. Student can recognize when nonquantitative (noncountable) things are the same or different, that is, colors, shapes, etc.
C. Student can group or formulate sets of items.

Task Analysis (In order to do the final task, the student must learn to do the following):
A. Match a given number with a quantity of items, for example, one item with the numeral "1" and the numeral "5" with five items.
B. Recognize that when two unequal sets of items are present, the one with the *greater* number has "more" than the set with the lower number.
C. Recognize that when two unequal sets of items are present, the one with the *lower* number has "less" than the set with the greater number.
D. Given objects of like nature, describe differences in terms of more or less, for example, Set One with two marbles is "more" than Set Two with one marble.
E. Recognize that when the number of items in two sets is equal, the two sets are the "same."
F. Given equal sets, be able to say "same."
G. Identify sets as "same" when the number in each set is equal and the item nature is different.

H. Identify sets as "different" when the number in one set is more or less than the number in the other set and the item nature is different.

Criterion Measures (a partial set):

#**1.** (Instructor reads directions.) "Draw a line from the number here (instructor points) to the group over here which has that number of things in it."

XXX	2
XX	1
XXXX	3
X	5
XXXXX	4

#**2.** (Instructor reads directions.) "I will hold up two cards with pictures of things on them. You point to the card that has *more* things on it than the other card."

#**3.** (Instructor reads directions.) "I will hold up two cards with pictures of things on them. You point to the card that has *fewer* things on it than the other card."

17

Preparation of Objectives

Behavioral or instructional objectives traditionally have been statements that describe what the student will be able to do as a result of completing an instructional program (Bloom, 1956; Mager, 1962; Popham and Baker, 1970). As such, objectives serve a communication function; they convey a picture of the behaviors the teacher can expect from a student after instruction is completed. This communicative function is the primary reason for having objectives. Is there a need for such information in specific learning disabilities instructional programs? In many cases there is no such need; the classroom teacher is cognizant of the criterion behaviors required of the child, and there is no one else to whom they need be communicated. On the other hand a variety of people might wish to have the information that objectives provide: parents might want to know what their child will learn; the child might benefit from knowing what he or she is supposed to learn; teachers receiving a child in a classroom might wish to know what he learned previously. Objectives provide information for all of these people.

The functions of objectives

In addition to providing information about instruction, objectives have traditionally played an analytic role. This is particularly true of instructional programming procedures that do not call for a task analysis phase (Gronlund, 1970; Popham and Baker, 1970; Vargas, 1972). During the process of preparing an objective, the programmer must look closely at the student response and the conditions under which he or she is required to respond. This requires that the instructor consider much of what is explained and demonstrated in the chapter

326

on Task Analysis. If a task analysis has not been attempted or adequately completed, then writing objectives can help clarify the goal of the instruction in relation to the task and the student responses. Obviously, the systematic approach to the development of remediation for learning disabilities described herein includes the task analysis phase; therefore, objectives would serve primarily a communication function in programs produced under this method.

However, if objectives are to function even in a minor way as a tool for aiding the programmer in analyzing the task, then an attempt should be made to prepare a set of objectives before criterion measures are prepared (Ammerman and Melching, 1966). Criterion measures are then prepared from the statements of objectives rather than the other way around. If the task is well analyzed and criterion measures can be developed quite easily directly from the analysis, then objectives can be prepared after the criterion measures. More will be said about when objectives should be prepared later in this chapter, but keep in mind that the job of writing objectives can be accomplished either before criterion measures are prepared if objectives serve an analytic function, and after criterion measures if they serve a communicative function.

Student Behavior in Objectives

Regardless of when objectives are prepared for a remedial program, they must conform to certain characteristics or criteria. The first characteristic that should be evident in a good objective is that *it must be stated in terms of student behavior.* Teachers are often taught to state objectives in terms of their (the teacher's) behavior, but for instructional programming purposes this is an incorrect practice. For example, the objective

> The student will point to his street and block when shown a map of the area where he lives.

is correctly stated in terms of student behavior. The objective:

> The teacher will expose the students to alternative methods for solving problems.

is stated in terms of the teacher's behavior and therefore, is incorrect for our purposes. Note that with the latter, incorrect objective, we know pretty much what the teacher will do, but we have no idea what the desired student response is. Here are some contrasting, correct and incorrect examples of objectives from learning disabilities programs:

(Incorrect)	Show them a film about geometric shapes.
(Correct)	The student will name the square, triangle, and circle.
(Incorrect)	The teacher should help them understand numbers.
(Correct)	The student will correctly add one-digit numbers.

Objectives that do not state the behavior expected from the student can often be revised easily so that the student behavior is clearly stated.

Here are some examples of objectives that do not state student behavior:

1. I will teach them to multiply by 2.
2. A film on listening will be shown.

Here are those same objectives rewritten so as to state student behavior:

1. The students will correctly multiply by 2 all the numbers from 1 to 9.
2. The students will listen and correctly respond to a set of filmed instructions containing three sequential actions.

Measurable Objectives

In addition to being stated in terms of student behavior, objectives in learning disabilities remediation must specify a behavior that is observable and measurable. For example, if the objective is "the student will print his given name," the behavior of printing one's name is observable and measurable. *Several different people could watch* the student perform the task, and they would probably *all agree* about whether or not the task was performed correctly.

On the other hand, if the objective is "the student will understand the difference between b—p, t—d, k—h initial sounds," the behavior specified would not be measurable; therefore, the objective would be incorrectly stated. Several different people might not be able to agree about what behavior actually shows that a student "understands" something such as voiced and unvoiced initial sounds.

There are a number of commonly used words that need extensive definition (and can be replaced by more concrete, descriptive terms) if they are to be used in objectives. Such terms as "understands," "knows," "think," "think about," "observe," "appreciate," "comprehend," and "use" are all words that should be avoided when objectives are being prepared for a learning disabled child. Use terms like "point to," "touch," "draw a circle around," "say," "write," "draw," "print," and "cut" when preparing objectives. Terms such as "discriminate, recognize, or identify" mean to "point to," "circle," "place a check by," or in some other way choose the correct alternative when multiple choices are given. Similarly, "produce" means to "write," "draw," or do something without multiple-choices available.

Here are some examples of correct and incorrect objectives from learning disabilities programs:

(Incorrect)   The student will know the ten new words in his weekly paper.

(Correct)   The student will spell aloud the ten new words in his weekly paper.

(Incorrect)   The student will know how to proceed from left to right given rows of objects.

(Correct)   The student will name familiar objects in a left to right sequence when given a row of eight objects.

(Incorrect)   The student will learn to see triangles that are part of a larger, composite figure.

(Correct)   The student will point to triangles that are part of a larger, composite figure.

It is not unusual for a teacher to adopt an established program for a learning disabled child rather than develop one independently. But even commercial programs or programs developed by colleagues will often include objectives that are vague, incomplete, or of a different style from those presented here. Often such objectives do not specify a measurable behavior, but these objectives can be revised. For example, here are two objectives that do not specify measurable behaviors:

1. The student will understand what rhyming words are.
2. The student will know how to follow objects with his eyes.

Here are the same two objectives rewritten to provide measurable behaviors:

1. The student will say "yes" when given rhyming pairs of words and "no" when given pairs that do not rhyme.
2. The student will maintain eye contact with a moving light (flashlight) for twenty seconds.

When you want to rewrite an objective that is not measurable, look at the verb or action word that appears in the sentence. In the incorrect examples of objectives above, look at the words "understand" and "know." Then ask yourself what people do who "understand" and "know"? They list, report, recite, write, etc. If "listing" or "reporting" or "writing" is what they do when they "understand," then you should say so in your objective. If they do none of these measurable behaviors, then you cannot assume they "know" or "understand." Once you have decided what it is that is performed by people who "know" or "understand," then use the observable performance in your objective. You will see in a later part of this chapter that incorrectly stated objectives can and should be revised to describe what is actually happening in the criterion measures, so the task of rewriting them does not typically depend on your definitions of vague terms like "know" and "understand," but on the content of the criterion measure.

Describing the Conditions for Performance

There is another characteristic that objectives should possess if they are going to be correctly stated and optimally functional for a learning disabilities program: the objective must describe the constraints or conditions under which the student will operate. This characteristic can best be understood if you remember that the objective simply describes what the student will do in the criterion measure. The criterion measure presents certain conditions and gives the student directions to respond. The constraints or conditions to be included in the objective are those that will (or do) appear in the criterion measure. For instance, the objective, "the student will point to her first name," meets the requirements of being stated in terms of student behavior and being measurable, but suppose the criterion measure actually had all the students' names (in a classroom) on a sheet and each student had to point to his or her own name? Does the stated objective describe the conditions under which the student will operate? No. You need to add the phrase, "given a sheet of paper with all the students' names from a classroom printed on it . . . ." This phrase can be added either to the beginning or the end of the objective, "The student will point to her own name." The additional phrase provides needed information about the actual nature of the task.

(Stated in terms of student behavior)	The student will
(Observable, measurable behavior)	point to his street and block
(Conditions or constraints on the performance of the task)	when shown a map of the area where he lives.

The statement describing the conditions under which the performance of the task will be made can be very detailed if the programmer so chooses. However, it is not necessary to give a detailed accounting of *all* the conditions. You only need to give a general description of the conditions.

Below are examples of objectives that in some cases include conditions and are correct while in other cases are incorrect because conditions do not appear:

(Incorrect)   The student will point to triangles of different sizes and in different positions.

(Correct)   The student will point to triangles of different sizes and in different positions when given a sheet with squares, rectangles, and triangles on it.

If in a criterion measure a student is presented with a plastic bag, a piece of cardboard, a wooden spoon, a scrap of wool, and an aluminum can and asked to point to the hard items, then the objective would include the following:

(Incorrect)   The student will point to hard items when asked to do so.

(Correct)   The student will point to hard items when given three hard and two soft items.

(An incorrect objective)   The student will draw a matrix when asked to do so.

(A correct objective)   The student will draw a 5 x 5 matrix and label the rows 1 through 5 and the columns A through E.

Complete objectives for learning disabilities program: (1) are stated in terms of student behavior; (2) are measurable; and (3) include a description of the conditions for performance. If all three characteristics appear in an objective, then it will communicate to the reader what the student is expected to be able to do. Now that you *can identify* what objectives should include, it is time to return to the question of when to begin writing them.

Preparing Objectives from the Task Analysis

If you prepare statements of objectives *before* preparing criterion measures, then you will have only the *task analysis* to refer to for direction. For example, if a task analysis resulted in the following:

> In order to do some particular task the student must learn to—
> 1. discriminate one stimulus item from two, three, or four items;
> 2. discriminate two stimulus times from three or four items; and
> 3. discriminate three stimulus items from four items.

then you might prepare the following objectives:

1. Given a picture of three sets of single stimulus items (a car, boat, airplane), one set of two stimulus items (bicycles), two sets of three stimulus items (boats and wagons) and three sets of four stimulus items (horses, cars, airplanes, bicycles), the student will point to the single stimulus set when given the directions, "point to the groups that are like this (the model)."
2. Given a picture of three sets of two stimulus items, three sets of three stimulus items and five sets of four stimulus items, the student will point to the sets of two stimulus items after being shown a two stimulus items set and given the directions, "point to the groups that are like this (the model)."
3. Given a picture of four sets of three stimulus items and five sets of four stimulus items, the student will point to the sets of three stimulus items after being shown the model and given the directions as in 1 and 2 above.

As you can see, the objectives above simply describe the criterion measures that *will be developed* from the task analysis.

Here is a partial analysis of the task of "naming place values in numerals":

> In order to do this task the student must learn to—
> A. identify the first digit on the right end of a numeral; and
> B. name the first digit on the right end of a numeral as the "ones" place value.

Here are four examples of correct and incorrect objectives that would come from the partial task analysis above.

(Correct)   The student will point to the digit on the right end of a given numeral.

(Incorrect)   The student will say how many digits are in a given numeral.

(Correct)   The student will say "ones" as the place value for the digit on the right end of a given numeral.

(Incorrect)   The student will say the complete place value for a four-digit numeral.

This is a partial analysis of the task of "telling time":

The student must learn to—
1. identify the numbers on the face of a clock; and
2. recognize the sixty different minute positions on a clock.

Here are four examples of correct and incorrect objectives that would come from the partial task analysis above.

(Incorrect)   When asked to do so the student will write the numbers that would appear on a clock face.

(Correct)   Given a picture of a clock face with only the numerals 3, 6, 9, and 12 appearing, the student will point to the location of 1, 3, 4, 8, 9, and 11.

(Incorrect)   The student will know where 10-, 25-, 30-, 42-, 45-, and 58-minute locations are on a clock face.

(Correct)   The student will say "yes" when the teacher points to a minute number and says the correct number using the 10-, 25-, 30-, 42-, 45-, and 58-minute locations on a picture of a clock face.

Preparing Objectives from Criterion Measures

If you prepare objectives *after* you have prepared the criterion measures, then the objectives are simply a description of those criterion measures. (This is sometimes a much easier procedure than writing them before the criterion measures.) The criterion measures, of course, are prepared directly from the task analysis.

For example, the following criterion measure might appear in a program on "Visual Discrimination":

Circle the bridges over the river in this map.

The objective associated with that criterion measure would be the following:

The student will draw circles around all the river bridges when given a small portion of a map.

The objective describes the behavior of the student; it includes behavior that is measurable; and it describes the conditions that exist given the associated criterion measure. In short, it is a statement designed to communicate to the reader what is being evaluated in the criterion measure, therefore, also describing what the actual goal of the instruction is.

Here are a couple more examples of objectives derived from criterion measures.

> The item below is a criterion measure from a program for the task of "arranging things according to size."
>
> The student is shown a picture like this:

—given a set of blocks like this:

—and instructed to arrange them like the picture.

This objective is stated incorrectly for the criterion measure described above:

> The student will point to an arrangement of blocks that is like a given picture.

This objective is stated correctly:

> Given a picture of four blocks arranged according to size, the student will place four actual blocks in a similar arrangement.

Consider another example from a program designed for a learning disabilities problem:

Here is the criterion measure:

> The teacher shows test card X to a student and says, "Point to the triangles."

This objective is correct:

> The student will point to the triangles when shown a card with triangles, circles, squares, and other four-sided figures on it.

This one is not:

The student will point to triangles when instructed to do so.

A Final Note about Objectives

Objectives and criterion measures for a learning disabilities problem are obviously related. The criterion measure is a means of evaluating the behavior of a student, and an objective is a statement that describes that behavior. It is important to note that when a student has successfully completed a criterion measure, he or she has also achieved one of the objectives of the instruction. As the student continues to pass or complete criterion measures, he or she continues to achieve objectives.

Because they have different functions, criterion measures and objectives appear in different places in a program. The criterion measures are used to tell the instructor whether or not the student has learned what was wanted, so they generally appear scattered throughout the program. Objectives are used to describe what behavior will be learned by someone going through a program, so they generally appear in a list at the beginning or end of a program. In order to help you see how a list of objectives might be presented in a learning disabilities program and, also to let you see the progressive nature of objectives, two sets of objectives from programs are presented below.

Example 1:
Objectives from the program "Arithmetic Factoring"
1. The student will recognize (place a check by) the factors of a given product when given five alternatives from which to choose.
2. The student will write the factors of a given product.
3. The student will recognize the common factors of two given products when given five alternatives from which to choose.
4. The student will write the common factors of two given products.
5. The student will recognize the greatest common factor of two products given five alternatives from which to choose.
6. The student will write the greatest common factor of two given products.
7. The student will recognize the correct use of the greatest common factor to reduce a fraction to its lowest terms when given four alternatives from which to choose.
8. The student will reduce a given fraction to its lowest terms by using the greatest common factor.

Example 2:
Objectives from the program "Recognizing Shapes"
1. The student will point to the triangles in a picture with other geometric shapes when verbally instructed to do so.

2. The student will point to the equilateral triangle in a picture with other geometric shapes when verbally instructed to do so.

3. The student will point to the rectangle in a picture with other geometric shapes when verbally instructed to do so.

4. The student will point to the square in a picture with other geometric shapes when verbally instructed to do so.

5. The student will point to the five-sided figure in a picture with other geometric shapes when verbally instructed to do so.

6. The student will point to the pentagon in a picture with other geometric shapes when verbally instructed to do so.

7. The student will point to the circle in a picture with other geometric shapes when verbally instructed to do so.

If you would like to see additional examples of sequentially arranged behavioral objectives, an excellent set can be found in Gross, Carr, Dornseif, and Rouse (1974).

18

Preparation of Instructional Sequences

This particular chapter could have had a number of equally descriptive and appropriate titles. "Learning Principles in Programs" or "Learning and Instructional Procedures" would have adequately indicated what the chapter contains. Indeed, this chapter is concerned with "the teaching process," "the learning process," "instruction," or call it what you will when the phenomenon of learning occurs. At this point in the procedure of systematically preparing materials for learning disabled children, the instructor begins to consider the actual methods and materials that will be used to help the student move from a position or condition of not being able to complete a criterion measure (deficit behaviors) to a learned state where he or she can respond correctly to the criterion measures.

It is important for the practitioner to keep in mind the implicit definition of learning which appears above. Generally stated, learning occurs when a student moves from a condition of not responding correctly in a criterion measure to a condition of being able to consistently respond correctly to a given criterion measure. It is the job of the instructor to design, build, revise, and rebuild a sequence of instruction that optimally moves a student from the unlearned state or condition to a learned state or condition.

The programmer has a number of tools at his or her disposal by the time he or she reaches the job of designing and building an instructional sequence. The task analysis provided a sequential set of behaviors that the student must learn in order to perform the final task. A succinct description of the final task itself came from the task analysis, so the instructor has a clear picture of the goal of the

336

instruction. Associated with each part of the task analysis are criterion measures that the programmer knows can be used to evaluate the student's progress, and *at the same time evaluate the effectiveness of the instruction.* So the programmer knows where he or she wants the student to go, and he or she knows how to tell if the student is there yet, or at least if the student is on the right track. Now it is time for the programmer to develop a way for the student to get to where the programmer wants him or her to be.

But what should go into an instructional sequence? Do we know that much about learning that we can say, "If you do X, then the student will learn Y?" The answer is no, the *science* of teaching is not yet that sophisticated (Skinner, 1968). All is not completely lost, however, because a good bit has been gleaned from basic and applied research on human learning. It is possible to state some principles which, if followed, will increase the probability that learning will occur—and most importantly, if learning does not occur, then the programmer will have the evaluative tools, criterion measures, to tell him or her where and when the instruction or remediation went wrong. With this information the programmer can evaluate the use of the known principles for instructional sequences and, subsequently, revise the instruction *until it does work.*

The remainder of this chapter is devoted to an explanation of several principles and their related corollaries that can be applied when preparing an instructional sequence.* In some cases the principles have stood the test of research and have come through unchanged from their original form; others are still somewhat conditional and apply only to specific instances or with specific populations. Nevertheless, the programmer who is prepared to use any or all of the principles when designing an instructional sequence is in the best position to produce an efficient, effective program of instruction to deal with a specific learning disabilities problem.

> *Principle 1: In any instructional sequence the student must be called upon to make regularly scheduled, active responses relating to the task to be learned.*

The "Active Response" principle

Active responding on the part of the student has been one of the unchanging characteristics of programmed instruction since its beginning (Brethower et al., 1964; Markle, 1969; Skinner, 1968). The notion expressed in this principle is that a passive student is not necessarily making responses to the instruction or making the appropriate responses to meet objectives. Another way of viewing this principle is that the student will learn those things to which he or she is actively responding. For example, if a student actively completes one part of an arithmetic problem, but not other parts, then the learning taking place will relate closely to the response or part of the problem to which he or she actively responded.

In the early formats for programmed instruction with "normal" populations, each active response made by a student was part of a "teaching frame." The

* These principles also appear in Unit Nine of *Learning Experiences in Educational Psychology* by Robert L. Morasky, published by Wm. C. Brown Company Publishers, 1973.

concept of frames probably arose from teaching machines where small bits of information were presented along with a provision for a student response. The information and the provision for a student response usually appeared in a window or "framed-in" area; hence the term "teaching frame." In the system of programming for learning disabilities presented in this book, the frame is not an important concept; but the characteristic of regular, active student responding is. A programmer who uses the principles and corollaries presented herein will quite likely produce units that could be called "frames," but there is no need to restrict oneself to "frames" simply on the basis of tradition.

Here is an example of how a simple task associated with a handwriting problem can be broken down into a series of active responses:

> Billy is learning to print his name. The teacher has already found that Billy can recognize the difference between "B," "i," "l," and "y," but he cannot print his name. Here are the responses he is called upon to make in the *instructional program* for printing his name:
>
> 1. Given an incomplete letter* "B," he must complete the letter.
> 2. Given a model of the letter "B," he must print the letter on a separate line.
> 3. Given an incomplete letter "i," he must complete the letter.
> 4. Given a model of the letter "i," he must print the letter on a separate line.
> 5. Given an incomplete letter "l," he must complete the letter.
> 6. Given a model of the letter "l," he must print the letter on a separate line.
> 7. Given an incomplete letter "y," he must complete the letter.
> 8. Given a model of the letter "y," he must print the letter on a separate line.
> 9. Given an incomplete set of letters "Bi," he must complete both letters.
> 10. Given a model of the letters "Bi," he must print the letters on a separate line.
> 11. Given an incomplete set of letters "ll," he must complete the letters.
> 12. Given a model of the set of letters "ll," he must print the letters on a separate line.

*An incomplete letter is one that is formed with dotted lines which the student must connect to form the letter. A student will often need more than one example of this type and often it is necessary to make only part of the letter incomplete. For example, in the letter "B" the vertical shaft could be solid and the loops dotted for his first example. The second example would have the loops solid lines with the vertical shaft dotted. Finally, the complete letter could be dotted.

13. Given an incomplete set of letters "lly," he must complete the letters. (Note: It is usually not necessary for the programmer to list a description of the responses called for from the student. It was done in this case to illustrate the breakdown of the learning of a task.)

14. Given a model of the set of letters "lly," he must print the letters on a separate line.

15. Given an incomplete set of the letters "Billy," he must complete the letters.

16. Given a model of the set of letters "Billy," he must print the letters in order on a separate line.

Note that the responses Billy is called upon to make during this program are regularly spaced with small bits of information presented between responses. "Smallness" is, of course, relative to the task and the person learning the task, and a standard for "small" bits of information is not available. However, a rule of thumb to remember is that it is desirable to have the student progress as rapidly as possible and experience as much success as possible, so the program should initially make steps forward that are as large as possible. If at a later time data indicates that the steps are too large, then smaller steps can be built into the program.

In order to help the reader comprehend this principle of active student responding better, the following contrasting examples are provided. Suppose a certain child had a specific learning disability that involved auditory discrimination, and the teacher wished to use nonphonemic sounds for discrimination training. The teacher would be violating the principle of active responding if the student were to listen to a thirty-minute tape of different bird sounds, and afterwards be tested on his ability to identify each one.

It is easy to see in this example that the student plays a passive role for thirty minutes and, then, actively responds for a block of time. On the other hand if the student listened to an example of a bird call and was asked to identify which of two given calls was like the example, and this was done with several different bird calls, then the student would be actively responding in accordance with the principle.

Here are two more examples of the principle of active responding being properly and inproperly used with a visual perception problem:

1. Given a line painted on the floor, the student is instructed to place the right foot on the line (teacher demonstrates).

2. Given a line the student is instructed to place both feet lengthwise on the line.

3. Given a line, the student is instructed to stand with both feet lengthwise on the line and look up to right and left hands extended outward at shoulder height.

4. Given a line, the student is instructed to move forward, always placing the left foot on the line and the right foot beside the line.

Proper use of the principle

Improper use of the principle:

1. The teacher walks on the line demonstrating placing one foot in front of the other.
2. The teacher shows the student the importance of moving slowly and placing the feet carefully.
3. The teacher demonstrates the proper carriage of the arms while balancing.
4. The teacher reviews orally the parts of the act of walking on the line.

The necessity for "active" responses called for in *Principle 1* should not be confused with the question of whether the student must respond overtly or covertly. A substantial number of studies have shown that covert responding is as advantageous as overt responding; the difference being, of course, that the instructor cannot observe a covert response (Anderson and Faust, 1967; Goldbeck and Briggs, 1962). It is desirable for the instructor to be able to witness the student response in order to evaluate the correctness of the behavior, while at the same time being able to evaluate the effectiveness of the instruction (Markle, 1969). "Active" in the sense it is used here signifies an involvement on the part of the student because he is presented with uncertainties or called upon to respond to instructional stimuli. The student who is actually listening to a lecture, for example, is responding, but only in a passive sense. His or her auditory sensory system is being activated by vibrations set up by the instructor's vocal system, but the student is not presented with uncertainties to which he or she must respond, nor is the student called upon to respond to any particular instructional stimuli. The instructor could remedy this situation by having student response sheets and requiring that the students write answers to questions at regular intervals during the lecture. In this way the students are not only responding in the passive sense of listening, but also, regularly responding in an active sense to presented uncertainties.

Principle 1 requires that regular active student responses occur in a sequence of instruction. A secondary aspect of that principle is stated below as *Corollary 1.1*.

The Relevancy Corollary

Corollary 1.1 The responses the student is required to make must be relevant to the final task or performance as exemplified by the criterion measure.

Relevant responses are those that are like the responses called for in the criterion measure. For example, if the criterion measure requires the student to point to the circles in an array of figures, then a relevant response in the instructional material would be one that was like the identification of circles. *Writing* the word "circle" is *not* a response that is related closely to the task of pointing to a circle.

The most common violation of Corollary 1.1 is an instructional sequence in which the student is required to name or "talk about" something which he or she must later "point to," "draw," or in some other way manipulate in a criterion measure. For instance, writing the word "vowel" in the following instructional sequence is irrelevant to the subsequent criterion measure.

(Irrelevant instructional sequence)	Vowels are the letters A,E,I,O, and U. The letter Y is also a vowel sometimes. You would call the letter "I" a ———.
(The criterion measure)	Underline the vowels in these words:

HIT	LET
CAT	ROT
RUT	NOT

The active, observable response in the instructional sequence above is writing the letters v-o-w-e-l in that order. The active, observable response in the criterion measure is drawing lines under the vowels. These two responses have different topographies and the former is irrelevant to the latter. One might argue that the student must learn to associate the word "vowel" with the letters, A, E, I, O, and U; therefore, the instructional sequence response is relevant to the criterion measure response. In fact, it is the case that the student must associate the written word "vowel" with the letters, but it is not the case that he or she must learn to write the word, "vowel." What the student must learn to do is point to the A, E, I, O, or U when given the written stimulus word "vowel." Relevant instructional sequences would have the student doing just that.

Imagine that a teacher is working with a child who has a visual perceptual disability, and the intent is to combine natural science with visual discrimination training. In the pairs of response descriptions below, the first description is relevant to the criterion measure of "naming oak, maple, birch, elm, and poplar leaves when pictures of the leaves are displayed." The second is not.

(Relevant)	Drawing lines from the word "maple" to a picture of a maple leaf; from the word "oak" to an oak leaf; and so on.
(Irrelevant)	Drawing a picture of a maple leaf.
(Relevant)	When given a picture of an oak leaf, the student circles the word "oak."
(Irrelevant)	When given pictures of tree bark, the student is to identify the oak, maple, and birch.

If the criterion measure from another program for the same child requires that the student draw a triangle upon command, there are many responses that could be relevant to that task. Note the differences between the relevant and irrelevant response descriptions below:

(Irrelevant)	The student writes "triangle" in a prescribed space when the teacher says "triangle."
(Relevant)	The student traces over a dotted form of a triangle.

(Irrelevant)	The student says "triangles are geometric shapes" when the teacher asks, "What is a triangle?"
(Relevant)	The student draws in the third side of a triangle when given the first two sides and one angle.
(Irrelevant)	The student selects the squares from an assortment of geometric forms.

Active, relevant responding is necessary in a program for learning disabled children, but other characteristics are important also. *Principle 2* specifies the type and order of responses that should occur.

The "Produce Versus Identify" principle and corollary

Principle 2:   Before learning to "produce" the correct response for a given task, the student must learn to "identify" the correct response.

Corollary 2.1:   The difference between a "production" and an "identification" response is that in the former the student recalls or generates the response from memory, whereas in the latter the student chooses the correct response from given alternatives (Fry, 1959; Markle, 1969).

Here are two examples:

Example 1

Billy's criterion measure is to print his name. Before being called upon to print "B," he should be given the task of identifying (pointing to or circling) the "B" when it is paired with such other letters as the "I," "E," "F," etc. Printing or writing the letter "B" is a production task; that is, he must produce the letter from memory. Pointing to or circling the letter "B" is a recognition task; that is, he must identify the letter when given alternatives. ("Recognition" and "identification" are used interchangeably here although in much research literature they have different meanings.)

Example 2

Ellen's criterion measure is to draw triangles and rectangles. The criterion measure requires a production-type task. First, however, Ellen must learn to identify a rectangle from among other geometric forms. After we are sure she can recognize a triangle or a rectangle when she sees one, then we can begin to teach her to produce (draw) them.

If *Corollary 1.1* were applied rigorously, then a recognition response would appear to be irrelevant in any instructional sequence where a production response was required in the criterion measure. In fact, however, *Principle 2* states that a recognition response is a necessary prerequisite to production; therefore, in any sequence where a production response is required, it is relevant to have recognition tasks in which the thing to be produced is identified (Cutler, Hirshoren, and Cecirelli, 1973).

Regular, active, relevant responses with recognition preceding production will be the basis for a well-designed program, but to aid student learning a few more principles should be observed.

Principle 3:   In any instructional sequence, that is, any sequence of responses where the student is supposed to learn something, a model of the response the student is to identify or produce should be available (Gagnè, 1965; Hively, 1962; Morasky, 1968).

Here, again, are two examples:

Example 1

Betty is learning to print her name. If the first response called for is to identify the "B" when given the "B" and "X" together, she should have a model of the "B" available. Here is one way this can be done:

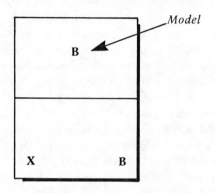

Teacher says, "This is the first letter in your name." "Circle the one down here which is like the one above."

Example 2

Often the concept to be learned has a nearly infinite number of examples or instances within it, so different models are appropriate. For example, in a program on "Rhyming Words" the concept of final letters being alike might be represented by three models as follows:

Teacher says, "We want to make pairs of words in which the last letters are the same, like these:"

DOG and LOG

"and another would be:"

BAT and HAT

"and another would be:"

BOY and TOY

"Dog, log, bat, hat, boy, and toy" are all models of the response the student will have to recognize or produce when he or she rhymes words according to the final letters. The teacher should leave the six words as models for the student to use when he or she is required to identify or say pairs of words like the models.

It should be observed that visual models are currently technologically easier to make constantly available than auditory models. Imagine the difficulty encountered in a "bird call" program in which the response required is to identify the Cardinal call when given two bird calls. How do you keep the model, a Cardinal call, available? You could say to the student, "Here is a Cardinal call," and present the proper call. Then say, "Which of these two is a Cardinal call?" In that sequence the student must keep the model call in memory or be allowed to ask for a repetition of the model whenever necessary. On the other hand, visual items like the triangle can be constantly displayed for the student.

The
"Alternatives"
Principle

Principle 4:   In any instructional sequence where an identification response is called for, there should be two alternative responses.

Principle 4 (if followed) makes it highly probable that the student will choose the correct alternative of the two given, and that he or she will see the point(s) of difference between the two choices given (Gagnè, 1965; Gibson, 1940; Resnick, 1963; Underwood, 1953). Remember, you are trying to help the student learn and make learning as efficient and nonstressful as possible. Keep in mind that learning should occur *during* the time the student is completing this sequence of instruction. It is implicit, then, that before processing the information and making a response the student *has not yet* learned what the programmer wishes him or her to know. However, after responding, the student should have learned some part of the final task. The structure of the situation to which the student must respond plays a part in his or her learning. In addition, you are trying to program the situation so that he or she will learn what you want. With more than one *incorrect* alternative, you can't be certain that the student saw the critical points of difference that exist between the correct and the incorrect alternatives. This principle is used very well in the highly successful program, *Child Management* (Smith and Smith, 1966).

An example of the proper use of two alternatives would be an instructional sequence for a specific learning disability in which the student was told to listen to the musical note "C" on a piano and then asked to choose which of two notes played was the "C."

Another example would be a situation in which the student was shown the numeral "6," then asked to circle the 6 when shown a "3" and a "6" together. It would be incorrect to have the student circle the "6" when shown the "3," "7," "5," and "6" all together.

Below are some examples of correct and incorrect applications of *Principle 4*:

(Incorrect)   Here is a triangle:

Circle the triangle:

(Correct)   Here is a triangle:

Circle the triangle:

Here is an instructional sequence that is incorrect according to *Principle 4:* The nursery school teacher says, "This is the numeral '4' (and she points to the 4). Which of these is a '4'?" She displays a card with numerals on it like this:

4   2   6   8   3   4   5   1

This sequence should be broken down into several smaller two-choice sequences to conform to *Principle 4.*

Note that *instructional sequences* should have two alternatives. Criterion measures can (and in most cases should) have more than two alternatives from which to choose.

> *Corollary 4.1:   In preparing an instructional sequence, the incorrect alternative of the pair given in an identification response task should initially be a choice that is least like the model and later as close to the model as necessary.*

The "Difficulty Transition" principle

Billy still can't print his name because the teacher gave him a model for the "B," but asked him to identify the "B," with letters that are very much like the "B"; that is, "P," "E," and "H." The teacher should have made a model "B" available while asking Billy to choose the correct letter when given a pair like the "B" and the "M," the "B" and the "S" and so forth—eventually working closer to letters (P, E, H) that are like the "B."

If the purpose of an identification or recognition sequence is to help the student see points of difference between alternatives, then *Corollary 4.1* suggests that learning will be more efficient if initially the differences in alternatives are more obvious than later when the student will learn less obvious differences. This is a rather basic tenet of experimental work with discriminations (Hively, 1962; Resnick, 1963; Terrace, 1960). In addition, this procedure provides for controlled, minimal stimulus change (Atkinson and Seunath, 1974).

Suppose a student with auditory perception difficulties needed to discriminate sounds of varying pitch and an instructional program was to conform to *Principle 4* and *Corollary 4.1*. Regardless of the instrument used to produce the sounds, it would be essential to make the incorrect and correct alternatives initially as far apart as necessary to permit easy discrimination. The two alternatives would become more similar as the student correctly identified the differences in sounds. One can readily see the folly in ignoring the other principles in a case like this. For example, if the student could not reliably identify the correct alternative given a model and two choices, there would be no point in having him attempt to produce the correct sound on his own. "The correct sound" for this child would be a wide range of sounds among which he could not discriminate.

A Checklist for Instructional Sequences

The four principles and corollaries on the preceding pages of this chapter will provide a basis for designing instructional sequences, but they are only a basic structure and not necessarily the complete blueprint for all instruction with learning disabilities. In order to help you remember and apply the principles and corollaries, a checklist is provided in Table 18-1. This checklist can be used to evaluate instructional sequences that you prepare, or to evaluate programs already available to you.

TABLE 18-1
Instructional Sequence Checklist

A "no" answer to any of the questions below suggests a revision to the instructional sequence.

1. *Principle 1:*
   Is the student required to respond at regular intervals?
2. *Principle 1:*
   Are all the responses active, that is, can they be observed?
3. *Principle 1:*
   Does the student actively respond to everything you want him or her to learn from the program?
4. *Corollary 1:1*
   Are all responses relevant to the final task?
5. *Principle 2*
   Are identification responses always before production responses?
6. *Corollary 2:1*
   Are you certain that the student can identify the thing to be learned before he or she is required to produce it?
7. *Principle 3:*
   Are models of the correct response always available in all instructional sequences?
8. *Corollary 3:1*
   Do all criterion measures require responses without a model available?
9. *Principle 4*
   When an identification response is to be learned, is the number of alternatives to choose from always two?
10. *Corollary 4:1*
    Do the choices in an identification task become more difficult; that is, do they move from those things least like the model to those things most like the model?

The program below was prepared by a novice learning disabilities specialist who did not use the instructional sequence checklist to evaluate and revise the materials. As a short test of your ability to apply the principles and corollaries, use the checklist in Table 18-1 to identify where mistakes have been made in the program. If you have difficulty, you should consult Table 18-2 which follows the original version of the program and notes the correct answers.

TABLE 18-2
An evaluation of the "Drawing Triangles" program according to the Instructional Sequences Checklist

INSTRUCTION SEQUENCE CHECKLIST QUESTIONS

INSTRUC-TION SEQUENCE	1	2	3	4	5	6	7	8	9	10
1	No	No	Yes	NA*	NA	NA	NA	NA	NA	NA
2	Yes	Yes	Yes	No	No	No	Yes	NA	NA	NA
3	Yes	Yes	Yes	Yes	No	No	?	NA	NA	NA
4	Yes	Yes	Yes	Yes	No	No	?	NA	NA	NA
5	Yes	Yes	Yes	Yes	No	No	?	NA	NA	NA
6	Yes	Yes	Yes	NA	NA	NA	NA	NA	NA	NA
7	No	No	Yes	NA	NA	NA	NA	NA	NA	NA
8	Yes	Yes	Yes	No	No	No	No	NA	NA	NA
9	Yes	Yes	Yes	No	No	No	No	NA	NA	NA
10	No	No	Yes	NA	NA	NA	NA	NA	NA	NA
11	Yes	Yes	Yes	No	No	NA	Yes	NA	NA	NA
12	No	No	Yes	NA	NA	NA	NA	NA	NA	NA
13	Yes	Yes	Yes	Yes	No	NA	Yes	NA	No	No
14	Yes	Yes	Yes	Yes	No	NA	Yes	NA	No	No
Criterion Measure	NA	NA	NA	NA	NA	NA	NA	Yes	NA	NA

* NA—Not applicable

Program Title: DRAWING TRIANGLES (Visual Perceptual Training)
Objective: The student will draw triangles of different sizes in different positions.

Instructional Sequence
The teacher says:

  1. "This is a triangle. It has three sides."

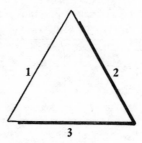

  2. "How many sides does a triangle have?"
  3. "Finish drawing the triangle."

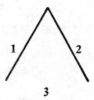

  4. "Finish drawing the triangle."

  5. "Draw a triangle."

1   2

3

6. "Picture A is bigger than picture B."

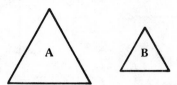

7. "Picture B is smaller than picture A."
8. "Picture A and picture B are the same because they are both triangles and they have 3 sides. A _____ has 3 sides."
9. "Triangles have to have 3 sides but they can be _____ or _____."
10. "All triangles do not look like this."

11. "This is a triangle too because it has _____ sides."

12. "Some other triangles look like this."

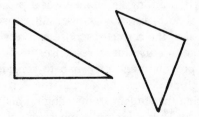  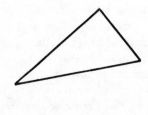

13. 'Cross out the pictures that are triangles."

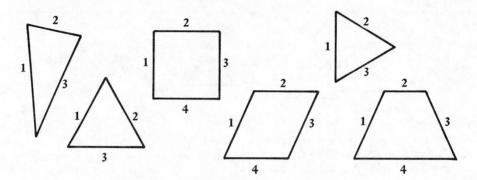

14. "Cross out the pictures that are triangles."

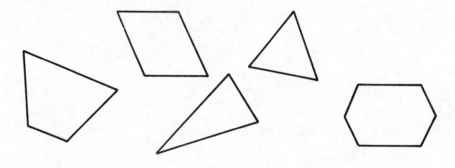

Criterion Measure

The teacher says, "Draw 5 different triangles on this sheet of paper." (If differences in size and position aren't apparent, have them draw several more until they demonstrate the objective or until you are certain they cannot do it.)

Knowledge-of-Results, Feedback, or Reinforcement

A major component of programmed instruction during its infancy was a procedure called *knowledge-of-results*. In its simplest form knowledge-of-results was a technique in which the student was informed of the correct response to a teaching frame shortly after completing the frame or making a response. In their attempts to provide knowledge-of-results, programmers often had to consider such mundane matters as preventing the student from looking at the correct answer without first responding, or preventing the student from changing his or her answer after viewing the correct response. This led to an emphasis on gimmickry or "hardware." Teaching machines locked the frame in place so that students were forced to respond before looking at the knowledge-of-results. Books were designed so that only one "teaching frame" in a sequence appeared on a page, and the correct response appeared on the next page. Needless to say, principles of learning or the "software" part of programming often were forgotten in order to establish an effective knowledge-of-results technique.

The notion behind knowledge-of-results was that the student could compare his or her response to the correct response and be reinforced (by the match) if they were the same. This simplistic view of human behavior overlooked a number of critical issues, such as the actual definition of reinforcement; the latency between response and reinforcing stimuli; the topography of the response; and, last but not least, the effect of knowledge-of-results that indicated a discrepancy—a mismatch. The current state of professional opinion indicates ambivalence regarding whether or not knowledge-of-results is an integral and necessary condition (Bivens, 1964; Moore and Smith, 1964). Some research supports its inclusion, some does not, some shows positive influence in favor of no knowledge-of-results (Lublin, 1965). What path should a novice programmer follow?

If programs are evaluated and revised by the programmer until the objectives are adequately met, then knowledge-of-results is not an absolutely critical component. Note that when objectives are met, criterion measures are completed correctly. This implies that the responses to instructional sequences must also be correct. The programmer who designs, builds, tests, revises, and retests an instructional sequence until it does, in fact, teach the desired behavior does not need knowledge-of-results in his or her program for *instructional purposes*. Too often knowledge-of-results has become a crutch which the programmer uses to hold up those students who do not learn from poorly designed instructional sequences. A programmer who develops an instructional sequence from which the learning disabled child can learn without depending upon knowledge-of-results is in an excellent position to add such information for other than instruction purposes.

A Final Note on Instructional Sequences

The emphasis in this material has been on paper-and-pencil types of instructional materials, but programmed instruction for learning disabilities need not rely solely on this media. Many creative instructors have utilized various audio-visual equipment and other easily adapted materials (Allouche, 1971–1972). Any one of the principles or corollaries in this section could be applied with equal effectiveness to audio tape recorders and presentations, motion pictures, or videotapes, and certainly to the type of materials prepared on site as noted in chapter 14.

A notable example of a situation where paper and pencil exercises are inappropriate is gross motor training. Motor skills involving large muscle groups call for extensive movements not possible with paper and pencil tasks. Therefore, it would probably be necessary to schedule or program an instructional sequence in an all-purpose room or gymnasium. The fact that no books or papers are used does not mean that the instructional sequence isn't programmed. Most of the instructional principles can be utilized; that is, the student can be called upon to make regularly scheduled, active responses—he could identify a correct movement before being called upon to produce the movement, and so on.

Again, the point of this final note is to encourage the programmer to take advantage of the many different forms of media available.

19

Implementation
and Revision

The final stage of the procedure for developing remedial-instructional programs for specific learning disabilities is the one in which student responses are gathered and changes are made on the basis of objective evaluation. Implementation, or "testing" as it is sometimes called, means that the instructor is going to try out the instructional program with one or more students either from the target population or from a normal population (Brethower et al., 1964; Thiagarajan, 1971). For the instructional designer who is preparing a program for non-learning-disabled students the implementation and revision phase can be somewhat easier than it is for the teacher of learning disabled children. The number of students who can complete the program is a major difference in the two situations. Even a special learning disabilities class will not usually provide fifteen to twenty children with similar characteristics such as would be found in a usual classroom. Therefore, the teacher preparing a program for a learning disabilities problem will often have to make revisions based on limited data, data drawn from a normal population, or reasonably adequate data collected over an extended period of time from children with deficits (Morasky, 1971).

Revision of the material will follow the implementation however it is carried out and every change that is made will come about as the result of problems encountered or errors made *by the student* (Lumsdaine, 1963, 1965; Morasky, 1967). The implementation and revision phase of the systems approach to instructional programs is undoubtedly the most important in terms of student feedback and the application of empirical techniques to learning and instruction. **353**

Empiricism and the methods of science call for maximum objectivity and decision making based on that objectivity. The major purpose for testing a program is to determine as objectively as possible its functionality as an instructional instrument.

Why Test and Revise?

Consider a situation in which a remedial reading teacher presents X information in a multimedia format to a class of fifteen students during three sessions. The teacher's presentations are outwardly polished and well-organized with substantial content and highly imaginative use of audiovisual equipment. At the end of the sessions the teacher polls a student, an observer, and a supervisor to determine what *they* thought of the instruction. (Unfortunately, this was the only source of feedback the teacher had because no criterion measures were administered.) The individuals polled all say, "It was a nice presentation—polished—well-organized and really creative. . . ." Suppose, however, that the fifteen students already had 50 per cent of the information given and missed 25 per cent of what was new to them because the teacher used terms that were too abstract and presented no models or examples. How would the teacher know that the polished, well-organized, creative presentation was *not* effective and that it should be changed before being presented to another group? If the teacher had developed criterion measures and used them with the fifteen students, then the data from those measures could be used for revision instead of using the subjective, misleading, "polling" procedure. Evaluation of instruction can permit revision and reevaluation so that the teacher can gain from ten years of experience instead of having the proverbial "one year of experience . . . ten times over."

By implementing a program of instruction with a group of learning disabled students and evaluating the outcome, the teacher is moving away from the dangers of "selective perception," "subjectivity," and "experimenter bias." The results of the student's performance on criterion measures will indicate if revised instruction is necessary. Such information is based on student performance, not on highly questionable teacher introspection or equally questionable peer judgment. It is for these reasons that the instructor puts his or her product on the line, and attempts to determine if it really does teach.

Individual Testing

After spending many hours completing the task analysis, criterion measures, and instructional sequences, the instructor will often overlook simple details that can interfere with the effectiveness of a program. In order to identify and remedy these minor problems instructors should administer the program to an individual rather than a group. This, of course, presupposes that the program is suitable for one-to-one presentation, and that the programmer can arrange such a situation. Many classroom teachers, of course, would find it difficult to arrange time to try a program on one student from the target population.

If individual testing is possible from a practical standpoint, the programmer will discover several advantages for this means of limited evaluation prior to group testing (Horn, 1966). An individual can talk rather freely while advancing through the material, and from his or her descriptions of uncertainties and problems the programmer can locate directions that are unclear, materials that are cumbersome to maneuver, instructions that were omitted, examples that are misleading, and a host of other small yet bothersome problems.

The initial individual testing procedures for a learning disabilities program are fairly simple. Just arrange to have someone (preferably from the student target population) go through the program while being observed. If it is impossible for the individual testing to be done with a student who actually displays the disability in question because there is a limited number of students available, then the instructor should use a child from a normal population who has not yet acquired the behaviors taught in the program. The student is instructed to talk aloud about what he or she is doing and the problems he or she is encountering. From these comments the instructor should identify the source of difficulty and make necessary changes. For example, in the situation below a student in a special learning disabilities class is going through a program and making comments:

Individual testing procedures

> "Let's see . . . (*She skips the formal looking introduction and goes to the page that has considerable "white-space"*) I guess I start here . . . (*She reads the information presented which is in the form of a complex rule or generalization.*) Hmm . . . (*and she reads it again.*) Yeah . . . OK . . . now what do I do with these two things, A and B, down here? (*The instructor didn't give instructions in the material as to how to respond. Interaction with the instructor is not encouraged during individual testing so the instructor remains silent.*) Guess I pick one that is like this up here . . . (*and she looks back and forth, up and down, from paired choices to generalizations.*) Well, I suppose it's B. (*No mark is placed by B.*) OK . . . now for the next pair . . . this B is like that B, so I guess this one is B too. (*Did the student use her first choice as a model or example in the second choice? Maybe the instructor should add a model or example to the generalization.*) OK . . . on to the next page . . . Oh, another one of those difficult statements . . . let's see . . . (*and she reads the generalization and while reading an example that follows the generalization, she says*) Oh . . . I see . . . yeah, it means *that*. Well, I know that . . . (*and she skips the choices presented below.*)

From this short commentary it is possible to discern the student's need for an example to clarify the generalization, and the lack of directions that resulted in no responses at all on the second page. It would not matter in this case whether or not the student was from the intended student population since the problems encountered are of a procedural nature, which would influence the learning, but are not integral to the disability being remediated. After a few sample revisions the program will be ready for group testing.

Group Testing

The primary reason for group testing is to gather data regarding the correctness of student responses to instructional material and criterion measures. It is assumed that by this point in the development of the program most of the procedural problems have been recognized and corrected. The program is usually duplicated in sufficient numbers for large-group administration and students return the programs to the programmer after completion. The term *group* should not be interpreted here as "many people together in one place" but, rather, as an accumulation of data from many people. This accumulated testing data can be secured from several individual students or small groups of two or three persons and the accumulation time can be as much as several months. The idea is to collect as much evidence as possible that can be used to validate or revise the program of instruction. The programmer will check each program as the student completes it and prepare a table like the one in Figure 19-1.

After the table is filled out for the group having completed a program, then the programmer can identify problem areas. For example, if a program was given to thirty students and twenty-eight had Xs in column 9, that would indicate that response #9 and its associated information needed revision. The type of revision needed will vary from one response to another, and a strategy for determining what revisions to make will be discussed later in this chapter.

Another programming error can be indicated from the table. Suppose fifteen of the thirty students in the group-testing session missed item 11 and twenty-two missed items 16 and 17, but the fifteen who missed #11 all missed 16 and 17. In such a case the programmer should consider the relationship between 11, 16, and 17. Is the information or concept in #11 critical to or prerequisite to #16 and #17? Would incorrect learning in #11 lead logically to incorrect responses in #16 and #17? If the programmer decided that the answer to either of these questions was "yes," then revision of #11 might clear up the problem with #16 and #17; therefore, no revision of the latter two would be necessary.

Another piece of information that can be secured from the table involves the relationship between criterion measures and associated instructional sequences. If an instructor consults a table of group-testing results and discovers that a substantial number of students responded incorrectly to four out of eight criterion or subcriterion measures, then the instructional sequence responses associated with the four incorrect criterion measures ought to be examined. Instructional sequences associated with a criterion measure are those in which the student learns the behavior tested in the criterion measure. Suppose that in Program X, instructional sequence responses #9, #10, #11, and #12 are associated with criterion measures #21 and #22. Furthermore, suppose that the results of group testing indicate that 50 percent of the students responded incorrectly to criterion measures #21 and #22, and those same students missed instructional sequence items #9 and #11. Such data should be a signal for the programmer to look at the responses made to #9 and #11, to determine if they were similar to the incorrect responses in #21 and #22. Consistently incorrect responses by students will often make clear the reasons for incorrect learning, and appropriate revisions become obvious.

What happens when students do not respond incorrectly to any of the instructional sequence material, but have many wrong answers on criterion measures? This situation indicates that the students were not having difficulty with the instructional sequences; that is, they were learning to make new responses as the programmer had planned, but those new responses were not being used in the criterion measures. Revision of the instructional sequence is obviously necessary, and the programmer should immediately consider the relationship of the instructional sequence responses to the criterion measure responses. Once the program-

Student																		
												X = incorrect response						
						Responses												
	1	2	3	4	5	6	7	8	9	10	11	12	13	14	15	16	17
1									X							X	X
2			X								X						X
3									X							X	X
4									X		X						X
5					X	X			X							X	X
6									X		X		X				X
7									X								
8											X					X	X
9					X				X							X	X
10																X	
11									X		X					X	X
12									X		X					X	

FIGURE 19-1
Student Checklist

mer has established that the two sets of responses are relevant to each other, then he or she can begin to revise the instructional sequences according to a specific revision strategy.

A Strategy and Checklist for Revision

In any instructional sequence where the error rate exceeds 10 percent, the instructor should consider possible revisions in order to reduce subsequent error rates. We will say more later in this chapter about the arbitrary error rate level of 10 percent, but for the present it is a benchmark from which to work. How does the programmer revise? How does he or she know what is needed? Where does he or she begin? Table 19-1 provides a revision checklist as a guide for programmers to follow when revisions seem necessary.

As an example of how the revision checklist can be used, consider the following item from a learning disabilities program entitled "Rhyming Words and Phrases." This program was tape recorded and the student used a response sheet.

> Making up words or groups of words that rhyme can be lots of fun, and you don't even need any special stuff. All you need to do is think of words. Not any words, just words that sound alike such as back

TABLE 19-1
Revision Checklist

Apply the checklist questions to individual response items. In each question it is assumed that the error rate on the items was sufficiently high to warrant revision (10 percent +).

1. Does the sequence rate "yes" responses to all questions from the instruction sequences checklist (chapter 17)?
2. Was the student sufficiently directed in regard to how he or she should respond?
3. Is there information in the sequence that leads the student to respond incorrectly? Is he or she guessing?
4. Is the information too verbally presented? Are there too many words? Are the words too difficult? too abstract?
5. Would a graphic presentation help? picture? graph? photograph?
6. Would an example or two help explain the rule or generalized statement?
7. Should the response be multiple-choice instead of production? or vice-versa?
8. Are the multi-choice items appropriate?
9. Should this response item be combined with another to form one larger step?
10. Should this response item be divided into two or more smaller steps?
11. Has the programmer made some incorrect assumptions about the entering behavior of the students?

and rack. There are hundreds of words in your language that rhyme. Poets use rhyming words often. Poems (which poets write) are groups of words that rhyme.

Two words that rhyme are—

1. boat—beach
2. make—lake

The instructor found it difficult to have one student go through the program before group testing so a special class of fifteen children completed the instruction. After group testing the programmer was dismayed to discover that twelve students out of a total sample of fifteen got this particular response item incorrect. No individual testing was possible, and his subjects were not available for consultation so the instructor made a quick survey of the completed student program. He was able to dig out the following additional information:

- 9 students made no response
- 2 students circled the wrong response
- 1 student placed a check by the wrong response
- 3 students either circled or placed checks by the correct response

With this additional information the instructor was ready to begin applying the revision checklist questions to this particular instructional sequence item.

Previous to the group-testing session, the programmer had applied the instructional sequence checklist questions to the entire program, and it was his opinion that an affirmative response was more or less appropriate to each question, so he progressed to question 2 on the revision checklist: "Was the student sufficiently directed in regard to how he or she should respond?" A look at the item in question confirms that the answer to this question is an obvious "no." The student is not even informed that he or she should respond at all, let alone directed to the nature of the response. The following rewritten question resulted from question 2 on the revision checklist:

(Place a check on your response sheet by the two words that rhyme.)

_____A. boat—beach
_____B. make—lake

Question 3, "Is there information in the sequence that leads the student to respond incorrectly? Is he or she guessing?" seemed to deserve a "yes" in the opinion of the instructor. Upon looking at the paragraph about rhyming words the instructor decided that the relationship between rhyming and the ends of words sounding alike was not explicit; therefore, a student would probably have to guess at the existence of this connection. The following revision was made:

Not any words . . . just words that sound alike at the end such as back and rack.

With this revision the students should have sufficient information to respond without guessing.

The information might be sufficient given a revision, but is there too much information as suggested in question 4 of the revision checklist? Our fictional instructor applied question 4 to the instructional sequence and decided to eliminate the following phrases and sentences:

~~Making up words or groups of~~ words that rhyme ~~can be lots of fun, and you don't even need any special stuff. All you need to do is think~~

are

~~of words. Not any words . . . just~~ words that sound alike at the end such as "back" and "rack." ~~There are hundreds of words in your language which rhyme. Poets use rhyming words often. Poems (which poets write) are groups of words which rhyme.~~

After applying questions 1 through 4 on the revision checklist, the revised instructional item was shorter and more direct than the original version, and it seemed as if the problem of students not responding would no longer appear so markedly as in the first testing session. Furthermore, the additional information in the revised copy might increase learning and, hence, the percentage of correct responses. What about questions 5 through 11 on the revision checklist? Might they also suggest revision? The instructor responsible for the rhyming program did not believe changes were necessary when he applied questions 5, 6, and 7, but question 8 had implications for change in light of the deletions made in an earlier revision. Specifically, question 8 asks, "Are the multiple-choice items appropriate?" and the incorrect alternative in the original version would contain information to which the student had not yet been exposed; that is, *only* words that have similar final sounds rhyme—words that have similar initial sounds do not. In short, the programmer would be presenting two choices; one which was correct, and one which was incorrect though not so obviously, if one were attempting to generalize a phenomenon from limited exposure. As a result, the incorrect alternatives, "boat"—"beach," were changed to "boat"—"run."

Having rewritten some of the content, eliminated some of the content, and given directions for appropriate responding, the instructor believed that the revised instructional sequence was substantially improved over the original and the specific desired learning was much more likely to be achieved. He did not discern any revisions associated with questions 9 through 11, so the newly prepared instructional sequence item sounded like this:

Words that rhyme are words that sound alike at the end such as "back" and "rack." Place a check on your response sheet by the two words that rhyme.

_____**A.** boat—run

_____**B.** make—lake

This rather lengthy example illustrates how to approach the problem of revision and how to use available data to guide the revisions you make. The revision checklist is more useful if data are available in the form of student responses, and data become available only when the program is actually implemented with the target population. Of course, the procedural errors in the example given might have been picked up and revised in an individual testing session. Other sequencing errors might become evident when working with a learning disabled population. The important point of this entire chapter, however, is that *giving* instruction is not the end of the teaching process with learning disabled children. You must evaluate the results in order to determine effectiveness and to develop a sequence or program of instruction that you can honestly label "valid." The teacher who has implemented and revised a variety of programs dealing with a range of high-frequency learning disability problems will have at hand an inventory of proven professionally prepared materials.

A word of caution: Do not be misled by a program's superficial appearance into believing that it *must work* and that data collection would be a waste of time. Rest assured that the "sirens of superficiality" will be there to lure you from the implementation and revision path, and the costs of such divergence will be paid by some student who continues to have a disability even after your instruction.

Revise the Instruction or the Criterion Measure?

If error rates on a particular criterion measure or even a set of measures are unusually high, why not suspect the criterion measure of some fault and consider revising it? There are specific reasons "why not." Remember, criterion measures are the result of a careful, systematic analysis of a task that was selected and defined equally as carefully and systematically as the analysis. The criterion measure was developed as the tool for determining whether or not the student could perform the desired behavior. At one point in criterion measurement development, the programmer must agree that a correct response on the criterion measure is adequate evidence that the student has learned what the instructor wanted him or her to learn. If the instructor could not agree to that condition, then the criterion measure was reworked until it did meet that standard. After meeting such a significant benchmark, one cannot readily change the standard simply because large numbers of students cannot meet it correctly. The materials used to *teach* those students need to be changed, not the materials used to *test* them.

On the other hand, there are two occasions when modifications of criterion measures are justified: (1) when an error in the task analysis is detected and/or (2) when the measure is structured such that knowledgeable students are led to make inappropriate responses. In the first instance, the instructor is really retreating to the initial stage of the programming procedure and then progressing forward with new information. That is, when he or she recognizes an error in the

Justification for modifying criterion measures

task analysis and completes a new analysis correctly, then the next logical step is to develop criterion measures to evaluate the newly identified skills associated with the task.

The best example we have ever seen of an error in task analysis leading to an incorrect criterion measure is reflected in the measure shown below. It is not from a learning disabilities program, but, nevertheless, it illustrates the problem quite well. It was taken from a college level program on "Basic Measurement Techniques."

> Each of the items on the left below exemplifies a type of scale. Write "Nominal," "Ordinal," or "Interval" in the space to the right of each item according to the type of scale it exemplifies.
>
> **A.** ton-pound-ounce   _____
> **B.** 66:23 = 200:100   _____
> **C.** College 1, College 2   _____
> **D.** Greater—Lesser   _____

We would guess from the criterion measure shown above that there are three types of scales and that each of the items in the measure can be identified as exemplifying one of the scales. A student of statistics will recognize quickly, however, that a fourth type of scale, "ratio," is exemplified by item B, yet is not even named in the measure. A survey of the remainder of the program would reveal that ratio scales were never mentioned. The programmer simply made an error in analyzing the task of "identifying scales used in social research." There are four, not three, different types of scales and item B can be either of two types, so the criterion measure should be revised to include clear-cut examples of each. Once the error has been detected it is appropriate for the programmer to revise the criterion measure accordingly.

The second reason for revising a criterion measure after the program testing stage is much more obvious than the first. If the direction and/or structure of the measure are such that students who know the correct response are led to respond incorrectly, then the measure should be revised. A common example of this problem is the measure that asks students to sequentially manipulate items in several different ways. On such a measure the students will sometimes omit intermediate or final responses simply because they don't comprehend entirely what they are supposed to do. This problem can be readily cleared up by dividing the measure into parts and giving individual directions for each part.

A Final Note about Program Implementation and Revision

A problem mentioned earlier in this chapter was that of determining a cutoff level for the percent of correct and incorrect responses. Any figure that an instructor selects will be arbitrary, and logical support can be found for a variety of different levels. It seems highly impractical for a teacher to insist on a 100 percent response rate to the instructional sequence and criterion measure responses in a program. Yet, is 90 percent or 78.5 percent any more appropriate? The solution to the dilemma is, of course, that each individual instructor must decide upon the level he or she will accept, keeping in mind the learning disabilities problem, the subject matter, the task, the program development budget, the critical necessity for mastery performance, and the specific disability of the student target population. For example, it is reasonable for the programmer in industry to say, "I'll be content with 85 percent correctness because the students scoring lower than that can be transferred to a new job."

It is not as reasonable for a classroom teacher or a learning disabilities specialist in a public school situation to assume the same position as the industrial programmer in spite of preconceived notions about motivation and intelligence. On the other hand, the classroom teacher might find that 93 percent correct performance is within the bounds of the normal school budget and expected on-the-job hours, and an increase beyond that level is impractical. Not only might it be impractical to reduce the incorrect response rate to less than 7 percent, but it also might prove to be a much more difficult task than achieving the 93 percent correct level was. The inability to perform in the case of that remaining 7 percent might be due to factors that are not readily identifiable; therefore, the research necessary for adequate evaluation and revision could be beyond the limits of practicality. With such concern in mind, the best answer the author can give to the question of performance cutoff levels is this: It depends on a number of variables that the individual programmer can best assess; therefore, it is a level that must be named by the individual programmer.

20

An Illustration
of the
Systems Approach

We selected the following case study to demonstrate a systems approach to remediation. Diagnostic steps might vary according to screening and testing procedures established in different situations; however, the general range of information available at the initial stages of the case is quite typical. Although specific approaches and activities have been selected for example here, this type approach can be involved with almost any theoretical orientation. The selection of specific activities and materials is based more upon the assumptions adopted by the user than upon the systems approach requirements.

The Case of Deborah L.

Deborah, a normal appearing and healthy young 6½ year old, was referred to the University Clinic for Learning Disabilities jointly by her parents and the first grade teacher at the school Debbie had attended for the past year and one half. The letter of referral said in part:

> Although Debbie had essentially a normal kindergarten experience, she has had a rough time of it in first grade. Her reading skills simply have not been developing adequately and she is falling farther and farther behind. She seems to generally enjoy school but lately even this general enthusiasm has begun to wane as her inability to meet

demands placed upon her in the schoolroom seems to have gotten to her.

Subsequent phone and face-to-face conversations with the teacher and the child's mother yielded the following information.

1. The child was perhaps the poorest reader in the classroom.
2. She tended to do generally well in other activities, excelling particularly in drawing.
3. Her vocabulary was somewhat limited, stilted, and tended toward repetitious use of the same phrases, appropriately used but not as flexible and ranging as her classmates.
4. Debbie misused a number of simple words in an almost aphasic sense sometimes using "hit" for "sit" and similar substitution errors.
5. She seemed to have little trouble with the understanding and use of generally flowing speech and followed complex oral directions at least adequately.

A check of school and medical records and interviews with the child's kindergarten teacher, the school nurse, and the family pediatrician provided these data:

1. No outstanding medical problem appears to be present.
2. A history of normal growth and development is present.
3. Visual and aural acuity are within normal limits.
4. Her school attendance record is normal with only a slight increase in absences during the last few months.
5. Kindergarten file notes indicated some concern over her general attention span and responsiveness but reading readiness behaviors are rated as "ok."

Background information

Deborah was seen by a learning disability specialist in the clinic following a half-day's observation of her at school. Informal evaluation procedures indicated that she was capable of following instructions, could hear and identify environmental noises, and showed average comprehension of a story read to her. She was cooperative and friendly.

Her performance on the *Wepman Auditory Discrimination Test* indicated a below-level capability in the area of auditory discrimination. This was further checked by administration of the *Goldman-Fristoe-Woodcock Test of Auditory Discrimination* and Debbie was found to be at the 33 percentile rank on the quiet test and the 22 percentile rank on the noise test.

On the *Illinois Test of Psycholinguistic Abilities* she was found to be significantly below average on *auditory reception, grammatic closure,* and *auditory sequential memory.* The test administrator's notes indicated that Deborah did well once her attention was assured and in those cases where she was directed into a face-to-face attention situation. A phone call to her classroom teacher cross-validated this anecdotal information as the teacher reported better performance when Deborah was close to the teacher in the classroom or when she was receiving instructions in a one-to-one mode.

As a final formalized test of her behaviors Deborah was administered the *Durrell Analysis of Reading Difficulty.* She was found to be deficient in both oral and silent reading, listening skills, and in word analysis. Other areas are within the normal range.

The diagnostic team of the clinic presented the following guidelines to those ready to work on remediation.

Remediation
guidelines

Debbie has apparently normal intellectual, perceptual and sensory capabilities. Her deficit behavior is most obvious in activities related to classroom reading. It is our opinion that her problem is one of failing to be at criterion level in auditory discrimination for a child her age, primarily a failure to discriminate initial sounds in words. Under explicit demands for careful attention and at a sufficiently slow pace to allow her time to attend to her own receptive processes and subsequent responses she performs all right as far as quality of discrimination is concerned. The most basic aspect of the problem seems to be that of never having adequately learned the strategy of attending to the cues offered by auditory stimuli. By not attending at critical times she has failed to learn many of the simple but crucial habitual discrimination patterns most children her age have. This is reflected in her reading difficulty and in her misuse of words (based primarily on initial letter confusion) and in some failure to be attentive.

We would recommend that remediation be directed toward building attention strategies and the acquisition of now deficit auditory discrimination behaviors. Given these two objectives we feel that her prognosis is good.

The person with primary responsibility for Deborah's remedial work was her classroom teacher, Ms. Watson. Also available for help was Ms. Telson, the learning disabilities specialist from the clinic. Ms. Telson was part of the diagnostic team, and had responsibility for coordination between that team and the classroom teacher.

Although the prognosis for the remediation of Deborah's problem was favorable, the task appeared to be quite formidable. The cost of program preparation in terms of time and effort would be high. Commercially produced materials were available but the school principal was not inclined to utilize the school's meager budget in this way. It was Ms. Watson's opinion, however, that she could produce the program with Ms. Telson's help and use it with several other students who exhibited disabilities identical to Deborah's. Over the years Ms. Watson had seen Deborah's problem occur with many children and she was certain that effective efficient materials could be used extensively. The cost-effectiveness of whatever she created would be quite acceptable over time.

Given the guidelines from the diagnostic team, Ms. Watson could identify the general problem area, that is, auditory discrimination, and with the advice of Ms. Telson she came to the conclusion that the assumptions associated with the systems approach were valid in Deborah's and the other cases that she had seen. She was ready, then, to begin the task analysis. The first step was to develop the final task description. Ms. Watson's first draft of the final task description looked like this:

Students will know the different initial sounds.

She knew that such a statement was not specific enough so she made another attempt which would more accurately describe Deborah's behavior after instruction:

**Students will identify different initial sounds from sets
of alternatives.**

Ms. Watson began to think about the actual operation of presenting sets of alternatives to Deborah and realized that more elaboration was needed in the final task description. Deborah's problem would probably be alleviated when Deborah could listen to a word with a specific initial sound and then identify the same word from among alternatives which were like that word. So the final task description was revised one more time:

**Given sets of words with minimally different initial sounds,
students will identify the one that is like a given model.**

Final task
description

From Ms. Watson's perspective the last statement was an adequate description of the type of task Deborah could *not* do now, but that she should be able to do after instruction. Ms. Watson believed that once Deborah could discriminate initial sounds as she would have to in the final task description her performance in class would substantially improve.

It was now time to consider the assumptions Ms. Watson would have to make about students like Deborah who would go through the instruction she was about to prepare.

Assumptions:

Entering
assumptions

1. The child can recognize what is meant in the instructions "Point to the one that is the same (or *like* this one)."
2. The child has no major auditory memory problems.

Note that Ms. Watson did not assume that students could attend to a complete sequence of model-alternatives-choice because that was a part of the problem and she meant to deal with that as a part of the program.

With the final task description and the assumptions completed Ms. Watson was ready to tackle the analysis of the task. She began by wondering if there was some type of sequence that is followed when discriminating initial sounds. Such a sequence, if it existed, could possibly be identified in flowchart form and, hence, taught to Deborah. "What do you do first when you listen to someone pronounce words?" she asked herself. "For that matter, what do you do last?" To Ms. Watson there did not seem to be a first or last or middle set of decisions or actions taken when one listened to normal conversations or word pronunciations. "I just hear the sounds in what appears to be one step," she thought. Whether she was correct or not in her analysis, Ms. Watson felt that the *Flowchart Type of Analysis* was not going to be very productive for her, so she began to examine the rules or generalizations used to make initial sound discriminations. (She realized, of course, that the very word "discrimination," which she was using to describe the task, indicated the type of analysis she ought to use. But to be thorough and afford herself the chance to work with all possible clues, she chose to consider each analysis technique in turn.)

The *Generalization Analysis Technique* seemed to be as fruitless for Ms. Watson as the flowchart had been. There were some rules or generalizations she could identify that related to the production of initial sounds, but the linguistic terminology she was familiar with was structural in nature and far too complex for Deborah's problem. If generalizations were to be formulated for producing initial sounds it would not have helped anyway inasmuch as the problem dealt with recognizing initial sounds, not producing them.

When Ms. Watson began to think of the discriminations that need to be made in order to recognize the different initial sounds in the English language, she immediately thought of the twenty-six letters of the alphabet.

"What we really need to do is make certain that Deborah and students like her can hear each letter (or the sound it makes) as being different from each other letter (or the sound it makes)," she reasoned. "But . . . some letters have multiple sounds . . . these sounds being called 'phonemes.' Does Deborah need to discriminate each phoneme from each other phoneme? Yes, she surely does. But do I need to teach that?"

Task analysis

Ms. Watson came to the conclusion that she would not have to teach discriminations that Deborah had already made—only those she had not made. With the help of Ms. Telson and other members of the diagnostic team it was determined that Deborah had consistent problems with the following letters and sounds:

> "f" as in fire, fat, fee
> "s" as in sail, sight, sold
> "t" as in tire, tight, told
> "h" as in hire, he, hold
> "g" as in git, gap, gold
> "j" as in jet, jot, jug

The six sounds listed above would be the basis for the auditory discrimination program to be developed by Ms. Watson. There would surely be other sounds that were difficult for students to discriminate, but those could be added to the program if and when they were identified by Ms. Watson.

The task analysis reveals for Ms. Watson that each of the six initial sounds would have to be discriminated one at a time from each of the other five sounds. There were in essence, then, six subtasks leading up to the final task. It was now time for Ms. Watson to begin developing criterion measures that would evaluate Deborah's ability to perform on those six subtasks and the final task.

The final criterion measure that Ms. Watson had to develop should correspond to the final task description. Here is what it looked like:

Script for Final Criterion Measure

(Instructions to the teacher) Slowly read the following directions to the child; make certain that the sample is done correctly before proceeding to the test items. "I am going to read a word and I want you to listen carefully to that word. After I have read the first word I will read other words . . . but *one* will sound like the first word. Listen for it. Let's try it.

Final criterion
measure

BOAT/ SHEEP CAR RUN CAN BOAT DOG

That's good . . . you heard 'boat.' Now, if you don't hear it the first time I will read all the words again and you just tell me when you hear the word by raising your hand. Let's try it again."

GARBAGE/ ROOF GARBAGE TOWEL SOMETHING

(If the child did not do the sample correctly, repeat the instructions and give the following samples. Raise the child's hand yourself at the proper time if necessary to illustrate the procedure. If the child has done the sample correctly begin at number 1 below.)

CAST/ LEG CAST
MOVE/ UP HOP MOVE
ZEBRA/ DUMP ZEBRA THROW CHEAT

(Circle the word identified by the student as being the same.)

1. FIRE/ HIRE FIRE TIRE SIRE
2. SAIL/ HAIL FAIL TAIL SAIL
3. HIT/ SIT FIT GIT HIT
4. SOLD/ FOLD SOLD TOLD HOLD GOLD
5. FEE/ SEE TEE HE FEE GEE
6. HUT/ GUT JUT TUT HUT
7. TUG/ JUG TUG HUG
8. FIRE/ HIRE SIRE TIRE FIRE
9. HOT/ GOT TOT JOT HOT
10. FAT/ FAT TAT HAT GAT SAT

11. SIGHT/ TIGHT FIGHT SIGHT
12. HAP/ SAP GAP TAP HAP JAP
13. TOG/ TOG FOG SOG JOG HOG
14. GIT/ HIT FIT GIT SIT
15. JUG/ HUG TUG JUG
16. GOT/ TOT JOT GOT HOT
17. FAIL/ SAIL FAIL TAIL HAIL
18. SIT/ FIT GIT HIT SIT
19. GOLD/ HOLD TOLD SOLD FOLD GOLD
20. JOT/ GOT TOT HOT JOT
21. TOLD/ TOLD SOLD GOLD HOLD
22. JOG/ TOG JOG FOG HOG
23. GAIL/ SAIL FAIL TAIL HAIL GAIL
24. JAIL/ SAIL GAIL TAIL HAIL JAIL

Ms. Watson had some initial concerns about the complexity of the instructions for the final criterion measure, but she was confident that once the child understood the directions the items would measure the behavior with which she was concerned. She had to admit that the measure was not a direct evaluation of Deborah's ability to discriminate initial sounds in everyday speech, but the possibility that this behavior would generalize to classroom situations was great enough that she was willing to accept this as an adequate measure. If Deborah displayed problems producing these sounds, a program could be developed to remediate that difficulty. Given that she had what she felt was an adequate final criterion measure, Ms. Watson was ready to decide whether or not to develop subcriterion measures for each of the six sounds. On the one hand she reasoned that such measures would allow her to monitor Deborah's progress in the instructional program, but, conversely, the first ones would be composed of words on which she had not been given instruction, so the question of valid measurement would arise. Ms. Watson decided to begin the program with the "f" sound but not give a criterion measure until the "s" and the "t" had also been covered. The first subcriterion measure followed this format:

Subcriterion measures

Script for the First Subcriterion Measure

(Instructions for the teacher)   Slowly read the following directions to the child; make certain that the sample is done correctly before proceeding to the actual test items. "I am going to say some words . . . when you hear me say a word the second time . . . raise your hand . . . like this (take the child's hand) . . .

CAR   HAVE   DOG   CAR   (Raise the child's hand)

Let's do it again . . .

LEAF   CREAM   LEAF   (Raise the child's hand)

Let's do this one without my help . . .

TOAD   FLOAT   TOAD

(If the child is doing the task correctly go on to number one below, if not repeat the instructions and the samples.)

1. FAIL TOAD SAIL FAIL TAIL
2. SEE FEE BOAT SEE TEE
3. FUN FUN SUN
4. TIGHT SIGHT FIGHT SIGHT
5. SAIL TAIL SAIL FAIL
6. SOLD TOLD FOLD SOLD
7. TELL FELL SELL TELL
8. FIRE HIRE SIRE TIRE FIRE
9. TAIL TAIL FAIL SAIL

The second criterion measure would be:
(Directions to the child are the same as in first criterion measure.)

1. HAIL SAIL TAIL HAIL
2. HUT TUT CUT HUT
3. HE TEE SHE HE
4. HIM SIM HIM TIM
5. HOG TOG HOG FOG

The third criterion measure would be:

1. JOG HOG JOG FOG
2. JIM TIM HIM JIM
3. JOT JOT TOT HOT
4. JAIL HAIL SAIL JAIL
5. JUG HUG JUG TUG

The fourth criterion measure would be:

1. GET JET GET SET
2. GAIL JAIL HAIL TAIL GAIL
3. GIN TIN SIN GIN
4. GUT HUT GUT TUT
5. GOT HOT TOT GOT

With the completion of the fourth criterion measure Ms. Watson had the structure for the instructional program. It would go as follows:

1. Instruction on the "f," "s," and "t" sounds
2. Criterion measure #1
3. Instruction on the "h" sound
4. Criterion measure #2

5. Instruction on the "j" sound
6. Criterion measure #3
7. Instruction on the "g" sound
8. Criterion measure #4
9. Final criterion measure

Now came the time for Ms. Watson to decide whether or not to develop statements of objectives. To whom did she need to communicate? Deborah's parents would like to be informed of the general purpose of the program and the final task description would be sufficient for them. How about Deborah? Ms. Watson believed that Deborah would do well if she knew in a very general way what was supposed to happen, but formal statements would be of little use. Would objectives be helpful for future users of the materials? Quite probably; but with her limited time schedule, Ms. Watson felt that the final task description would have to suffice for objectives. So the decision was made that no further objectives (beyond the final task description) would be necessary. As is usually the case with instructional programmers, Ms. Watson was anxious to get on with the development of instructional sequences.

Since the final behavior desired from the program involved auditory input, Ms. Watson decided to make the entire instructional portion of the program on audio cassette tapes so that students could use them independently. The script was also available for one-to-one instruction for children who had difficulty with the tape recorder.

Instructional sequence

Hi. This is tape number one of "Listening to Word Sounds." On this tape you will be listening to words I say and making marks on Worksheet Number 1. Do you have Worksheet Number 1 in front of you? If you don't, turn off the tape, go get your sheet and a pencil, then come back and turn the tape on again. (pause) Now that you have Worksheet Number 1 and a pencil let's begin to work. Listen to this word . . . BOAT. Now listen to these two words . . . TAR . . . WALK. Did they *both* sound just like the first word? No, they did not sound like the first word. The first word was BOAT. The other words were TAR and WALK and neither of those words sound like BOAT. Let's try another one. Listen to this word . . . MAPLE. Now listen to these two words . . . MAPLE . . . MAPLE. Did they sound the same as the first word? Yes, they did. They were all "MAPLE." Here is the next one. Listen to this word . . . DISH. Now listen to these two words . . . DISH . . . COAT. Were they *both* like the first word? No they were not, were they? "COAT" does not sound like DISH. Listen to this word . . . BOOK. Listen to these two words . . . BOOK . . . BOOK. Were they the same? Yes, they were. Take your pencil and finish the X in the space by the number 1 on your worksheet. (pause) Did you find and finish the X by the number one? If you did not, turn off the

tape recorder and tell your teacher that you did not finish the X. If
you did finish the X let's go on. Listen to this word . . . PAPER. Listen
to these two words . . . PAPER . . . LIGHT. Were they the same? No,
they were not, so you should not put an X in the space by number
two on your worksheet. Only put an X there if the words are all the
same. Let's do number three. Listen to this word . . . FIGHT. Listen to
these two words . . . FIGHT . . . FIGHT. Were they the same? Yes, so
you should place an X by the number three. Listen to number four.
FIGHT . . . listen . . . FIGHT . . . RUN. Were they the same? No, so
you should not have an X by number four. Listen to number five . . .
FEE . . . listen . . . LEE . . . ME. Place a mark on your worksheet only
if they were the same. Listen to number six . . . FIT . . . listen . . . FIT
. . . FIT. Mark an X if they were the same. Listen to seven . . . FOG . . .
listen . . . DOG . . . FOG. Mark an X if they were the same. Listen to
eight . . . FARM . . . listen . . . FARM . . . FARM. Listen to nine . . .
FOX . . . listen . . . FOX . . . BOX.

    Number ten . . . listen . . . FOG . . . listen . . . FOG . . . FOG
    Number eleven . . . listen . . . FAKE . . . listen . . . CAKE . . . FAKE
    Twelve . . . listen . . . FOOT . . . listen . . . FOOT . . . FOOT
    Thirteen . . . listen . . . FOX . . . listen . . . LOX . . . FOX
    Fourteen . . . listen . . . FOOT . . . listen . . . ROOT . . . ROOT
    Fifteen . . . listen . . . FIVE . . . listen . . . FIVE . . . FIVE
    Sixteen . . . listen . . . FEET . . . listen . . . FEET . . . FEET
    Seventeen . . . listen . . . FACE . . . listen . . . RACE . . . FACE
    Eighteen . . . listen . . . FIVE . . . listen . . . JIVE . . . FIVE
    Nineteen . . . listen . . . FIT . . . listen . . . FIT . . . BIT
    Twenty . . . listen . . . FELT . . . listen . . . FELT . . . BELT
    Twenty-one . . . listen . . . FARM . . . listen . . . MARM . . . FARM
    Twenty-two . . . listen . . . FOLD . . . listen . . . FOLD . . . FOLD
    Twenty-three . . . listen . . . FAT . . . listen . . . FAT . . . CAT
    Twenty-four . . . listen . . . FIGHT . . . listen . . . FIGHT . . . FIGHT
    Twenty-five . . . listen . . . FELL . . . listen . . . FELL . . . FELL
    You have come to the end of your worksheet and lesson number 1.
Turn off the tape recorder and take your worksheet to your teacher.

    Four other tape scripts like the one above were developed for the "f" sound.
In addition five tapes with twenty-five exercises on each were developed for each
of the other five sounds, so Ms. Watson had a total of thirty tapes and worksheets. In an attempt to sustain interest, resist fatigue, and attain maximum
generalization and transfer, Ms. Watson arranged the program schedule so that
only one worksheet could be completed per day. An individual student's progress could be monitored through the worksheets for five days and after the
sheets and tapes for a particular sound had been completed the subcriterion
measures could be administered. In this way the entire instructional portion of

the program would require thirty days to complete with the final criterion measure given on the thirty-first day.

Instructional
sequence
checklist

Ms. Watson applied the instructional sequences checklist to the materials she prepared and came to the conclusion that only item 10, corollary 4 deserved a negative response. Corollary 4 asks, "Do the choices in an identification task become more difficult, that is, move from those things most unlike the model to those things most like the model?" She had made an attempt to sequence the choices this way, but at the time she was not certain which discriminations would be more difficult than others. In light of this problem, however, she had always made the first few exercises consist of sounds that Deborah already knew although this, of course, would not help another child who had a different repertoire from Deborah's. The program was sequenced so that the target sounds were not used as a sound different from the model until they had been previously taught. When adequate data were available Ms. Watson could analyze the student responses with corollary 4 in mind.

Implementation
of the program

Implementation of the program with Deborah was the next step to be accomplished. A work space was set up in a somewhat isolated corner of the classroom so that Deborah could use the tape recorder there at scheduled times. A major question still remained, however. Would Deborah attend to the exercises on the tape? Ms. Telson and Ms. Watson were of the opinion that a trial and error procedure could be detrimental to program function if they were to discover that Deborah was not attending. With this rationale in mind they designed a positive reinforcement procedure in which Deborah would receive points or credits (she would know them as "points") which could be used to "buy" extra time in the play area, the gymnasium, the home economics area, etc. Inasmuch as a baseline of her performance prior to the implementation of this contingency had not been established, the teacher would not be able to show that it was positive reinforcement in the formal sense; but if performance levels were acceptable throughout the program, then their objective would have been achieved regardless of the procedure used.

Two daily records were maintained: one which Deborah kept in her desk which showed points earned, and one which Ms. Watson kept which showed the number of correct exercises (same as points earned), number of points spent, and balance of points remaining.

Before actually introducing Deborah to the reinforcement procedure and program, Ms. Watson had a child from another classroom listen to the tapes and attempt the exercises. This individual testing session was not intended as an evaluation of the efficiency of the exercise as much as a check on the clarity and sequencing of the directions. She found that the word "listen" did not need to be repeated in all twenty-five exercises with this child, but she kept in mind that Deborah might find such a stimulus to be a signal for attending. The worksheets seemed to be a confusing aspect so she put them in a packet with the child's name on the cover, and when a child asked for a tape a worksheet was also given out.

For the purposes of this case study, it is probably not useful or necessary to illustrate the complete records of Deborah's performance in the program. It suffices to say that Ms. Watson determined by the third day that Deborah was operating at an appropriate response rate. By the end of the second week (ten worksheets) and throughout the rest of the program Deborah's performance on worksheets and criterion measures averaged 87 percent correct responses, which was considered acceptable to Ms. Watson.

Over the next year Ms. Watson used the program that had been developed for Deborah with eight other children while at the same time making new tapes for other initial sounds. A check of the responses made by all nine children who had gone through the programs revealed a 9.6 percent average error rate, which was randomly distributed throughout the items, with the first two tapes of each new sound having a somewhat higher error rate and the last half of each remaining tape having a higher error rate than the first half. The possibility of fatigue influencing the children's performance was considered, but since all subcriterion and criterion measure scores were above 90 percent, Ms. Watson decided to leave the programs as they were.

The important aspects of the systems approach to learning disability problems that we can see from the foregoing example are the identification and breakdown of the task to be learned by the child (task analysis), the development of criterion measures, the decision about whether or not objectives should be stated, the development of instructional sequences, and the testing and revision of the entire package. A viable, effective instructional program was established and validated by a classroom teacher using a systematic and professional approach.

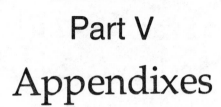

Part V

Appendixes

The five appendixes contained in this final section are designed to help the practitioner in further perfecting skills and in obtaining additional information and materials.

Appendix A contains additional examples of task analyses to help the practitioner develop this basic important skill. Specific examples are given along with suggestions for sharpening the process.

Appendix B is an introductory glossary to help the new practitioner more easily understand professional terminology frequently encountered in learning disability work.

Appendix C contains an annotated listing of some published works that might constitute a good personal library for the practicing learning disability worker.

Appendix D lists a number of professional periodicals to help the L.D. specialist find the most up-to-date information about the field.

Appendix E provides names and addresses of suppliers of publications, information, equipment, and supplies frequently needed by those working with learning disabled children.

Examples of
Task Analysis

The following task analyses are provided as examples of how various tasks can be broken down. In some cases the analyses are partial because smaller breakdowns might be necessary for effective teaching. Nevertheless, the authors are indebted to the programmers who provided these analyses.

From a Program Titled "Decoding Words"

Task Description

The student will decode unknown words using phonetic rules for short and long vowels.

Assumptions

This program is designed for first-grade students who have learned the sounds of the consonants and can identify them in initial, medial, and final position. The students will have been introduced to the short sounds of the vowels and given some practice in distinguishing them. The students will have a limited sight vocabulary.

Task Analysis

In order to do this task you must employ the following rules:

1. Every word must have a vowel. A consonant can't make a sound without the vowel beside it.

    m says mm with mouth closed—add a and say ma—add t and say mat.

2. When decoding a new word, look first for the vowel sound, then the beginning sound, then the ending sound.

    Set—First determine the sound of e, then add s and t.

    pat—pAt   fin—fIn

3. One vowel in the middle of a word (syllable) usually has its short sound.

    ran—bag—pet—zip

4. A single vowel that does not conclude a word usually has its short sound.

    band—glad—in—up—on

5. Vowels have two sounds, a short, weak sound and a long, strong sound. The long, strong sound is exactly like its name:

    ape, ate, east, ear, ice, idea, oats, old, use, uniform

6. A short vowel is marked with this sign ˘, a long vowel with ¯.

    hăt—pĕg   āte—mē

7. When a consonant follows the vowel, the vowel is protected and uses the short sound.

    pot—task—bag—sip

8. When a single vowel ends a one-syllable word, it has a long vowel sound.

    Me—no protection follows the e.

    I—we—go—he

9. When e is at the end of a word that has another vowel, the e is silent and the other vowel says its long sound.

    like—tame—bone

10. When there are two consecutive vowels, the first uses the long sound and the second is silent.

    road—heap—meat—bee

From a Program Titled "Beginning Multiplication Concepts"

Task Description

The general task is to multiply numbers by viewing them as sets.

Assumptions

In order to begin in this program the student must be able to do the following:

1. Count from 1 to 100

2. Recognize the numerals 1 to 100
3. Identify the set value of the numbers 1 to 100
4. Identify sets

Task Analysis

Rule: To multiply we join equivalent sets.
E.g.: * * * * * *

      * * * * * *

$2 + 2 + 2 + 2 + 2 + 2 = 12$
6 twos $= 12$
6 sets of 2 $= 12$

Rule: In horizontal multiplication sentences the sign $\times$ means "sets of" and we call it "times."
E.g.: $2 + 2 + 2 = 6$
3 sets of 2 $= 6$
we read "3 times 2 $= 6$"
we write "$3 \times 2 = 6$"

Rule: In multiplication we multiply two factors to get a product.
E.g.: factor $\times$ factor $=$ product
$3 \times 2 = 6$

Rule: factor $\times$ factor $=$ product. One factor tells how many sets there are. The other factor tells how many things are in each set. The total number of things is the product.
E.g.: * * * *

      * * * *

      * * * *

$4 \times 3 = 12$
4 sets
3 in each set
12 in all

Rule: An array can help us to write and understand multiplication sentences. An array is an arrangement of dots or objects into rows with the same number of things in each row. The number of rows one way is the number of sets. The number of rows the other way tells how many in each set. The total number is the product.
E.g.: * * * * *

      * * * * *

      * * * * *

5 rows going down	OR	3 rows going across
3 stars in each row		5 stars in each row
15 stars in all		15 stars in all
$5 \times 3 = 15$		$3 \times 5 = 15$

Rule: When you multiply the same factors, in any order, you get the same product.

E.g.: 3 × 6 = 18   * * * * * *
       6 × 3 = 18   * * * * * *
       3 × 6 = 6 × 3   * * * * * *

From a Program Titled "Place Values"

Task Description

The general task is to say the value of any numeral in its place value language.

Assumptions—Place Value Program

1. All words in this program have been previously taught and are in the reading and speaking vocabulary of the children.
2. All students taking this program already know how to say all numerals used in this program the conventional way.
3. All students know left and right directions.
4. All students can conceive the idea that larger numerals are made up of one or more digits and these students know the face value of each digit.
5. All students know the concept of ordinality and can use it in problem-solving situations.
6. All students are familiar with the mathematical terminology and meanings used in this program, with the exception of place value labeling and language.
7. Perception is normal in all students taking this program and should pose no problems in the program.
8. All numerals worked with in this program refer to whole numbers. The term "any given numeral" refers only to whole numbers.

Task Analysis—Generalization Approach— Place Value Program

1. Look at the numerals given and find the digit that is at the end when going in the *right* direction.
   examples   987   36   9
2. Look at the numerals given. Find the digit that is at the end when going in the *right* direction and label this digit "ones."
                       7 ones   6 ones   9 ones
   examples   987   36   9
3. Look at the numerals given and find the digit, if there is one, that is just to the *left* of the digit which was determined to be the "ones" digit.
   examples   987   36

4. Look at the numerals given. Find the digit, if there is one, that is just to the *left* of the "ones" digit and label this digit "tens."

$$8 \text{ tens} \quad 3 \text{ tens}$$

examples   987   36

5. Look at the numerals given and find the digit, if there is one, that is just to the *left* of the digit that was determined to be the "tens" digit.

examples   987

6. Look at the numerals given. Find the digit, if there is one, that is just to the *left* of the "tens" digit and label this digit "hundreds."

$$9 \quad \text{hundreds}$$

examples   987

7. Look at the numerals given and label from *right* to *left* each digit with the labels "ones," "tens" and "hundreds" respectively, as needed.

hundreds

examples   987 tens   36 tens   9 ones

                     ones   ones

8. When saying any given numeral aloud, say the numeral from *left* to *right*.

examples   987   36   9

9. When saying any given numeral aloud in place value language, read it from *left* to *right* saying the digit name first and the label second for each digit place.

examples   987 read aloud: nine hundreds, eight tens, and seven ones

              36 read aloud: three tens and six ones

               9 read aloud: nine ones

From a Program Titled "Map Studies"

Task Description

The general task is to recognize the different types of maps.

Discrimination Analysis

Unit	*Discriminative Attribute*
1. Globe map	1. Round, land and water sizes correct, most accurate map of earth.
2. Mercator map	2. Flat, usually square or rectangular, land and water size and shape distorted.
3. Polar map	3. North Pole centered, land masses distorted.

Unit	*Discriminative Attribute*
4. Lambert Projection	4. Land and water size and shape accurate only in east-west direction.
5. Mollweide map	5. Oval shape, land size accurate, land shape distorted.
6. Broken Projection map	6. Map split, land shape correct, water areas distorted.

From a Program Titled "Base Six Numeration"

Task Description

The task to be taught is an understanding of one-, two-, and three-digit numbers written in base six numeration.

Task Analysis

In order to do this task students will need to know the following:

1. To show that a numeral is written in base six numeration, the word six is written after the numeral (34 six).
2. There are only six digits used in base six numeration. These six digits are 0, 1, 2, 3, 4, and 5.
3. Base six is based on grouping sets of six instead of grouping sets of ten like our base ten numeration system.
4. The first place to the far right of the numeral is called the ones place.
5. Since base six is based on grouping sets of six, the largest digit that will ever be placed in the ones place is 5.
6. The second place is called the sixes or base place.
7. A quantity of six will be represented by placing the digit 1 in the sixes place (10 six).
8. Each succeeding set of six, up to 5 sets, will be represented by increasing the digit in the sixes place.
9. The largest quantity that can be represented by a two-digit numeral in base six is 35 which is written 55 six.
10. The third place is called the thirty-sixes place.
11. Each digit in the thirty-sixes place represents one set of thirty-six of six sets of six. Therefore, the quantity 36 will be written 100 six.
12. The largest quantity that can be represented by a three-digit base six numeral is 215 which is written 555 six.
13. To find the value of a three-digit base six numeral in base ten, find the value of each digit and add these amounts together.

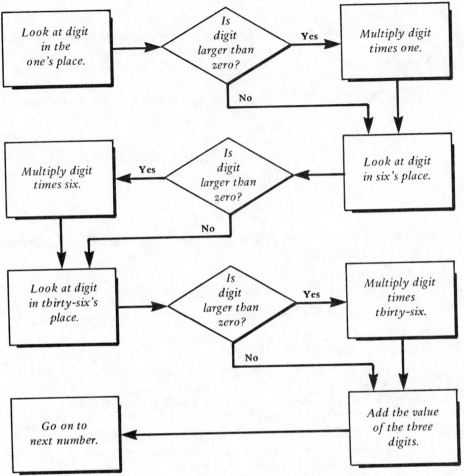

Flowchart Analysis: Changing Base Six Numeral to Base Ten Numeral.

From a Program Titled "Working with Sets"

Task Description

The general task is to identify and work with sets.

Task Analysis

1. Rule: A *numeral* tells us the *number* of *elements* in a *set*.

E.g.: The *numeral* for this set is 4.
E.g.: The *numeral* for this set is 6.

2. Rule: *Elements* are *objects* or *members* in a *set*.

E.g.: There are two (2) *elements* in this *set*.
E.g.: There are six (6) *elements* in this *set*.

3. Rule: Sometimes *sets* have *equal elements* in them.
   E.g.:   Set A and Set B both have 4 *elements* in them.
           Set A and Set B are *equal*.

   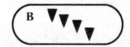

E.g.: Set X and Set Y are *equal*. They have *2 elements* each.

4. Rule: Sometimes *sets do not* have *equal elements* in them.
   E.g.:   Set A has 4 *elements*. Set B has 5 *elements*.
           Set A and Set B are *not equal*.
   E.g.:   Set X has 2 elements. Set Y has 4 elements.
           Set X and Set Y are *not equal*.
5. Rule: An *empty set does not* have *any elements* in it.

E.g.:   This is an *empty set.*
E.g.:   This is an *empty set.*

6. Rule: *One set* may be *greater than* another *set.* This sign shows that one set is greater.

E.g.:   Set A is *greater than* set B.
E.g.:   Set X is *greater than* Set Y.

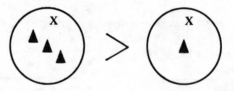

7. Rule: The *elements* of one set may be a *subset* or a part of the *elements* of another set.

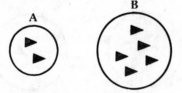

E.g.:   Set A is a *subset* of Set B.
E.g.:   Set X is a *subset* of Set Y.

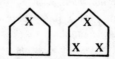

8. Rule: The *elements* of *one set* may be *added* to the *elements* of *another set.*

    E.g.: Set A can be *added* to the *elements* of Set B to *equal* the *elements* of Set C.

    E.g.: The *elements* of Set X can be added to the *elements* of Set Y to *equal* the *elements* of Set Z.

9. Rule: The *order* in which *sets* are *added does not affect* the sum.

E.g.:

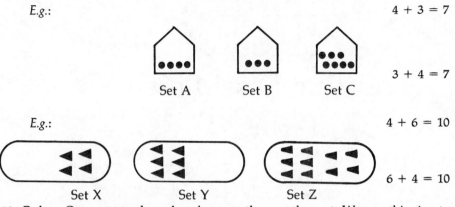

$$4 + 3 = 7$$

Set A   Set B   Set C

$$3 + 4 = 7$$

E.g.:

$$4 + 6 = 10$$

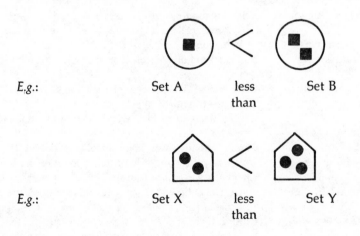

$$6 + 4 = 10$$

Set X   Set Y   Set Z

10. Rule: One set may have *less* elements *than* another set. We use this sign to show *less than.*

E.g.:

Set A   less than   Set B

E.g.:

Set X   less than   Set Y

B

A Glossary of
Learning Disability
Terms

Acuity: Level of functioning capability of a sensory mode (e.g., visual acuity).

Agnosia: Inability to recognize objects or events even though the sense organs are functioning adequately.

Agraphia (dysgraphia): Inability to produce written material. Ability to copy may be intact.

Anoxia: Oxygen deficiency.

Aphasia: Inability to use language symbols as in speech.

Apraxia: Inability to produce meaningful movement.

Articulation: The production of speech sounds.

Association: Cognitive development of relationships by integrating experiences.

Asymbolia: Inability to understand and use symbols.

Auditory blending: The ability to put separate sounds together to form a meaningful whole; e.g., PAY + PER = PAPER.

Auditory discrimination: The ability to distinguish between sounds of varying intensity, frequency, or composition.

Auditory memory: The ability to recall what has been heard.

Behavior modification: A technique for systematically changing or developing targeted behaviors.

Binocular vision: Vision that involves joint focusing of both eyes.

Body image: The concept of how one's own body relates to and/or affects other objects.

Central nervous system (CNS): The brain and spinal cord.

Cerebral dominance: The control of some set of behaviors by one side or hemisphere of the brain.

Channels of communication: Sensory-motor pathways by which language or communication is effected (e.g., visual-motor).

Clinical teaching: An approach to instruction that emphasizes recognition of and response to the individualized needs of a pupil.

Closure: The process of obtaining or achieving a complete idea, often from the presentation of only partial information.

Congenital: Present at birth.

Cross-modal: Involving more than one sensory channel.

Decoding: The receptive process wherein undifferentiated signals are provided with meaning (e.g., random sounds become perceived as speech).

Developmental reading: Reading growth that is normal or average in pattern, rate, and sequence.

Directionality: Awareness of up-down, right-left, front-back.

Discrimination: Distinguishing differences among stimuli.

Dyscalcolia: Inability to calculate; an arithmetic disability.

Dysgraphia: *See* agraphia.

Dyslexia: Inability or impairment in reading.

Echolalia: Meaningless or senseless repetition or mimicry of words or sounds.

Emotional lability: Unstable shifts or swings in moods or emotions.

Encoding: The expression of meaning in language through speech or motion.

Endogenous: Due to hereditary or genetic factors.

Etiology: The cause of a condition.

Exogenous: Due to something other than hereditary or genetic factors.

Expressive language: The production of language for communication.

Feedback: Information received from monitoring a response or activity usually by the individual actually producing the response or activity.

Figure-ground perception: The ability to focus on one or more parts of a stimulus field while the remaining parts become background.

Grapheme: A written language symbol that stands for an oral language unit.

Handedness: Right or left hand preference in an individual.

Haptic: Touch or tactual.

Hyperactive: Excessive motor activity exhibited.

Hypoactive: Deficient motor activity exhibited.

Hyperkinesis: *See* hyperactive.

Hypokinesis: *See* hypoactive.

Ideation: Reflective thought.

Impulsivity: Sudden behavior without forethought or concern for subsequent results.

Inner language: Formation of simple concepts without use of receptive or expressive language, as in young children's play.

Itinerant teacher: A teacher who travels among several schools usually providing individual help for children with special problems.

Kinesthesia: The sense whereby muscular movement and position are perceived.

Laterality: Sidedness (*see* directionality).

Linguistics: Science of language development, structure, and use.

Memory span: The length of time one is capable of remembering.

Modality: Usually refers to a sensory track such as visual or auditory.

Morpheme: The smallest meaningful unit in a language; e.g., an individual letter.

Multisensory: Involving more than one sense.

Ocular pursuit: The process of the visual tracking of movement.

Ontogeny: The development of an organism.

Perceptual-motor: The interaction of any perceptual mode with motor behavior (e.g., visual-motor).

Perseveration: Continuation of a piece of behavior after it is no longer appropriate.

Phoneme: The smallest unit of sound in a language system.

Phonetics: Speech sounds.

Phylogeny: Evolutionary development of a species.

Psycholinguistics: The study of the language process from the shared viewpoint of the disciplines of psychology and linguistics.

Psychomotor: Interaction of motor or movement behaviors with psychological processes.

Receptive language: The process of understanding language produced by others (e.g., reading, listening).

Resource teacher: A specialist who is capable of providing regular classroom teachers with suggestions and ideas useful in remediation activities.

Reversals: Production, usually in writing, of mirror images of stimuli (e.g., *p* for *q*).

Sensory-motor: Combined behaviors involving both sensory modes and motor behavior.

Spatial orientation: Awareness of one's own position in relationship to such factors as distance and direction.

Stereopsis: Three-dimensional perception.

Strauss syndrome: The pattern of symptoms considered to be characteristic of the brain-injured individual.

Strephosymbolia: A synonym for dyslexia.

Syndrome: A pattern or cluster of symptoms.

Tactile: Touch.

Task analysis: The examination of a certain task for the purpose of noting its component parts or subtasks.

Visual memory: The ability to recall what has been seen.

Word blindness: An early term for dyslexia.

A Suggested Library

Selections for a practitioner's personal professional library are of course a matter of individual preference. Theoretical and programmatic biases would necessarily influence choices. However, people relatively new to the field or attempting to build their own professional library frequently ask for suggestions. The publications listed here represent, first of all, a range of problems and approaches. Second, they are all readable, easily used works, and are readily available. In obtaining copies, the purchaser should request the latest edition since one or two of the older items may be in the process of revision now or at a later date.

Books

The books listed here represent a sampling of the literature available. In many cases, equally useful alternative selections might be suggested. No attempt is made to rate comparatively the value or worth of those noted here.

Learning Disability Books

Bush, W. and Giles, M. *Aids to Psycholinguistic Teaching*. Columbus: Charles E. Merrill, 1977. *Contains a listing of diagnostic teaching procedures for specific psycholinguistic disabilities. The format parallels the ITPA and activities are divided according to 1–8 grade levels.*

Dunn, L. (ed.) *Exceptional Children in the Schools*. New York: Holt, Rinehart & Winston, 1973. *A compilation of chapters dealing with a number of different areas of exceptionality including specific learning disabilities. The material in other chapters is often useful and applicable to the learning disability field.*

Gardner, W. *Children With Learning and Behavior Problems.* Boston: Allyn and Bacon, 1974.
A very useful outline of how to apply the behavior management approach to children in learning situations. The text is readable, practical, and offers many specific directions.

Goodman, L. and Mann, L. *Learning Disabilities in the Secondary School.* New York: Grune and Stratton, 1976.
A textbook outlining issues of identification along with programming and instructional concerns as they relate to the older child and young adult. This work contains a number of useful tables and lists.

Hammill, D. and Bartel, N. *Teaching Children With Learning and Behavior Problems.* Boston: Allyn and Bacon, 1978.
A very useful handbook for those looking for specific ideas and activities. A number of different academic areas are covered including reading, arithmetic, spelling, writing, and some general problem areas.

Heilman, A. *Principles and Practices of Teaching Reading.* Columbus: Charles E. Merrill, 1972.
A general textbook dealing with overall problems and practices involved in teaching reading. This work is of particular value to the practitioner who has not received any formal training in teaching reading.

Johnson, S. *Arithmetic and Learning Disabilities.* Boston: Allyn and Bacon, 1979.
A new book that is one of the very few efforts to focus on the interrelationship of learning disabilities and classroom arithmetic activity. The practitioner is offered a handbook of practical diagnostic and remedial help with many practical suggestions ready for immediate application.

Kephart, N. *Slow Learner In the Classroom.* Columbus: Charles E. Merrill, 1971.
The classic outline of the perceptual-motor orientation to learning problems. The text outlines both the theoretical and applied aspects of this orientation and serves as a basic introduction to other supplementary publications similarly oriented.

Kirk, S. and Kirk, W. *Psycholinguistic Learning Disabilities: Diagnosis and Remediation.* Urbana: University of Illinois Press, 1971.
Essentially a handbook for using the descriptive diagnostic data provided by the ITPA in planning remedial activities. This relatively brief work helps the reader develop competency

in reading and using ITPA profiles as guidelines for remedial decisions.

Mann, P. and Suiter, P. *Handbook in Diagnostic Teaching: A Learning Disabilities Approach.* Boston: Allyn and Bacon, 1974.
A useful compilation of do-it-yourself diagnostic techniques for the classroom teacher. Spelling and reading are specifically covered along with developmental screening activities for a large number of academically relevant behaviors (e.g., auditory discrimination).

Meyers, E., Ball, H., and Crutchfield, M. *The Kindergarten Teachers' Handbook.* Los Angeles: Gramercy Press, 1973.
A brief paperback offering a number of useful suggestions for the practitioner. Ideas relating to assessment, prescriptive teaching, behavior management, and similar topics are included.

Myers, P. and Hammill, D. *Methods for Learning Disorders.* New York: John Wiley, 1976.
A college-level textbook in learning disabilities. The practitioner who wishes a relatively brief overview of the approach of a number of prominent contributors to learning disabilities (e.g. Gillingham, Fernald, Orton) will find this book useful as an orientation for further reading.

Ross, A. *Psychological Disorders of Children.* New York: McGraw-Hill, 1974.
Deals with the psychological problems of children who are displaying such problem behaviors as aggression and withdrawal. Written from a behavioral viewpoint, this book should assist the reader in achieving additional insight into the emotional aspects that frequently accompany learning disabilities as well as providing some hints on how to deal with them.

Smith, R. (Ed.) *Teacher Diagnosis of Educational Difficulties.* Columbus: Charles E. Merrill, 1969.
Deals with material similar to Mann and Suiter (mentioned above) but on a more complex and technical level.
Particularly useful because of the wide range of areas covered (e.g., written expression, arithmetic, personal-emotional-social skills).

Vallett, R. *The Remediation of Learning Disabilities.* Belmont, Calif.: Fearon, 1967.
As subtitled, a handbook of psychoeducational resource programs. This publication, available in loose-leaf form, offers modular programs for use in such areas as sensory-

motor integration, language development, and conceptual skills.

Wiederholt, L., Hammill, D., and Brown, V. *The Resource Teacher: A Guide to Effective Practices.* Boston: Allyn and Bacon, 1978.
This very practical book is a useful compilation of material related to a number of curriculum areas and can save the practitioner many hours of searching in libraries and files.

Programming Books

Anderson, R. C. and Faust, G. W. *Educational Psychology.* New York: Dodd, Mead, 1973.
In spite of the title this book offers more coverage of instructional programming techniques and concepts than traditional educational psychology information. Task analysis, objectives, evaluation, entering behaviors, and various associated topics are discussed from both research and applied standpoints. This is an excellent book to have in your library for basic reference use. Although the emphasis is on normal classroom application, extrapolation to special educational circumstances should be facilitated by the many clear examples.

Brethower, D. M., Markle, D. G., Rummler, G. A., Schrader, A. W., and Smith, D. E. P. *Programmed Learning: A Practicum.* Ann Arbor, Mich.: Ann Arbor Pub., 1964.
This is probably one of the best books available for applied or "practicum" experience with instructional programming. It

is not a "facts and theory" book. It is packed with examples and exercises from which the reader (participant) can learn to prepare instructional programs. Subject matter/task analysis and revision of materials are covered particularly well. Many of the examples were taken from industrial settings, which might cause some difficulty for the practitioner who cannot project the transfer to learning disabilities program development.

Merrill, M. D. (Ed.) *Instructional Design: Readings.* Englewood Cliffs, N.J.: Prentice-Hall, 1971.
This book provides an excellent anthology of writers and researchers in the area of instructional design-programming. Most of the articles are at a moderately high level of abstraction; therefore, the book cannot be recommended as a skill development source. However, the practitioner who seeks the theory and research behind task analysis, objectives, instructional processes, and evaluation will find this book to be a very fine addition to a professional library.

Popham, W. J. and Baker, E. L. *Planning Instructional Sequences, Establishing Instructional Goals and Systematic Instruction.* Englewood Cliffs, N.J.: Prentice-Hall, 1970.
Active responding, basic concepts, concreteness, and emphasis on systematic procedure characterize these three, short, educationally oriented books. Aimed at the typical classroom teacher, these books provide fine practice in the technique of identifying goals or objectives and relating those ends to the activities which occur in the classroom. Given the humor and frequency of the examples, the reader should have little difficulty perceiving the applicability of the technique to special educational situations.

Sources of
Current Information

In addition to having a standard resource library to which one may refer when necessary, the effective L.D. worker, whether practitioner, theorist, or researcher, needs to be kept abreast of current events, contemporary research, new and pending legislation, and to have access to reviews of publications and materials. Periodicals are the most productive source of such information.

A number of different professional periodicals carry articles relevant to Learning Disabilities. Those listed here deal with this area. In some cases they will also carry articles dealing with other areas sometimes only peripherally related to learning disabilities. In other instances, the focus is not directly upon Learning Disabilities but upon another area. However, in the journals listed here, L.D. topics and related information are frequently included.

If the individual worker cannot afford to subscribe to each, effort should be made, at least, to have local public, school, and college/university libraries subscribe.

Academic Therapy
1539 Fourth Street
San Rafael, California 94901
Similar in many respects to the *Journal of Learning Disabilities*, this periodical covers a slightly wider range of behaviors through an interdisciplinary approach. It is directed toward the practitioner who is working with the "inefficient" learner.

Contributions range from sample programs to theoretical research. Published quarterly.

Exceptional Children
1920 Association Drive
Reston, Virginia 22091
This publication is the oldest regular periodical publication in the field. Published by the Council for

Exceptional Children, it deals with a broad spectrum of exceptionality including learning disabilities. Its content covers research as well as applied matters but it is definitely oriented toward the practitioner. It contains several useful subsections such as media reviews, reader's forum, and a professional convention and meeting calender. Published eight times a year.

The Learning Disability Quarterly
Department of Special Education
University of Kansas Medical Center
435 H.C. Miller Bldg.
39th and Rainbow
Kansas City, Kansas 66103
The newest of the L.D. periodicals, this journal offers research reports with applied focus, interpretative reviews of the literature, articles regarding practices in personnel preparation, and articles oriented toward the practical needs of the learning disability practitioner. The journal is published by the Division for Children with Learning Disabilites of the Council for Exceptional Children four times a year.

Journal of Learning Disabilities
101 East Ontario Street
Chicago, Illinois 60611
This journal features programs, materials, and techniques for the practitioner along with some reporting of research and commentary on issues. It has not been as rigorous in reporting research as some other journals but is getting stronger in this area. Published ten times a year.

The Journal of Special Education
3515 Woodhaven Rd.
Philadelphia, Pennsylvania 19154
Articles in this periodical range from biographical sketches of important figures in special education, to discussion of debatable topics, to reporting of research. The technical level of the articles is generally higher than in the *Journal of Learning Disabilities* or *Academic Therapy*. Entire issues will sometimes be primarily devoted to a single topic such as the role of cultural deprivation in handicapped children or perceptual-motor and modality issues. Published quarterly.

The Reading Teacher
International Reading Association
Six Tyre Ave.
Newark, Delaware, 19711
Published by the International Reading Association, this journal seeks to provide a forum of exchange for information and opinion relevant to instruction in reading in the elementary classroom. Though some research is reported, the emphasis is primarily upon applied information. Published eight times a year.

Teaching Exceptional Children
1920 Association Drive
Reston, Virginia 22091
Also published by the Council for Exceptional Children, this journal is primarily a handbook of applied ideas for the active practitioner. Containing no research reports, it deals with practical tips, new ideas, and accounts of use of different types of techniques and methods. Published quarterly.

E

Major Sources of Learning Disability Materials*

Academic Therapy Publications
1539 Fourth St.
San Rafael, CA 94901

Adapt Press, Inc.
808 West Avenue North
Sioux Falls, SD 57104

Addison-Wesley Publishing Co.
2725 Sand Hill Rd.
Menlo Park, CA 94025

Allied Education Council
P.O. Box 78
Galien, MI 49113

Allyn and Bacon, Inc.
470 Atlantic Ave.
Boston, MA 02210

Alpern Communications
220 Gulph Mills Rd.
Radnor, PA 19404

American Book Co.
450 W. 33 St.
New York, NY 10001

American Education Publications
245 Long Hill Rd.
Middletown, CT 06457

American Guidance Associates
1526 Gilpin Ave.
Wilmington, DE

American Guidance Service, Inc. (AGS)
Publishers' Building
Circle Pines, MN 55014

* This is a list of some major sources but it should not be considered exhaustive. It includes publishers and producers of texts and reference books, general materials (games, equipment, supplies, remedial programs), films, and also assessment and evaluation instruments and materials. Most will furnish brochures and catalogues upon request, though it may be necessary to be somewhat specific in making requests since some produce separate lists and catalogues for different purposes and use.

American Speech and Hearing Association
9030 Old Georgetown Rd.
Washington, DC 20014

Ann Arbor Publishers
P.O. Box 338
Worthington, OH 43085

Appleton-Century-Crofts
440 Park Avenue South
New York, NY 10016

Arrow Book Club (Scholastic Book
   Services)
50 West 44 St.
New York, NY 10036

Association for Childhood International
3615 Wisconsin Ave., N.W.
Washington, DC 20036

Association for Learning Disabilities
   (ALD)
220 Brownsville Rd.
Pittsburgh, PA 15210

Baldridge Reading Instructional Materials
14 Grigg St.
Greenwich, CT 16830

Baker and Taylor Co.
Audio-Visual Services Division
P.O. Box 230
Monence, IL 60954

Bantam Books, Inc.
666 Fifth Ave.
New York, NY 10019

Barnell-Loft
958 Church St
Baldwin, NY 11510

Basic Books, Inc.
10 E. 53 St.
New York, NY 10022

Bausch & Lomb Optical Co.
Rochester, NY 14602

Beckley-Cardy
1900 N. Narrangansett
Chicago, IL 60639

Behavioral Research Laboratories
P.O. Box 577
Palo Alto, CA 94302

Bell and Howell
7100 McCormick Rd.
Chicago, IL 60645

Benefic Press
10300 W. Roosevelt Rd.
Westchester, IL 60153

Bobbs-Merrill Co.
4300 W. 62 St.
Indianapolis, IN 46206

Book-Lab, Inc.
1449 37 St.
Brooklyn, NY 11218

Borg-Warner Educational Systems
7450 N. Natchez Ave.
Niles, IL 60648

Bowmar
Box 3623
Glendale, CA 91201

William C. Brown Co.
2460 Kerper Blvd.
Dubuque, IA 52001

Bradley Wright Films
309 N. Duane Ave.
San Gabriel, CA 91775

Burgess Publishing
7108 Olms Lane
Minneapolis, MN 55435

California Test Bureau, A Division of
   McGraw-Hill
Del Monte Research Park
Monterey, CA 93940

CANHC Film Distribution
P.O. Box 1526
Vista, CA 92083

Catalog of Standardized Tests
Bureau of Educational Research and
   Service
University of Iowa
Iowa City, IA 52240

Center for Applied Linguistics
1717 Massachusetts Ave., N.W.
Washington, DC 20036.

Children's Press
1224 West Van Buren St.
Chicago, IL 60607

Churchill Films
662 N. Robertson Blvd.
Los Angeles, CA 90069

Communication Research Associates
P.O. Box 110012
Salt Lake City, UT

Consulting Psychologists Press
577 College Ave.
Palo Alto, CA 94306

Continental Press, Inc.
Elizabethtown, PA 17022

Council for Exceptional Children
1920 Association Dr.
Reston, VA 22091

Craig Corp.
921 W. Artesia Blvd.
Compton, CA 90220

Creative Playthings, Inc.
Edinburg Rd.
Cranbury, NY 08540

Creative Publications
P.O. Box 10328
Palo Alto, CA 94303

Crippled Children and Adults of Rhode
    Island
The Meeting Street School
33 Grotto Ave.
Providence, RI

Cuisenaire Company of America, Inc.
12 Church St.
New Rochelle, NY 10885

Curriculum Information Center, Inc.
Brooks Towers
1020 15th St.
Denver, CO 80202

Developmental Learning Materials
7440 N. Natchez Ave.
Niles, IL 60648

Devereaux Foundation
Devon, PA

Dexter & Westbrook, Ltd.
958 Church St.
Rockville Centre, NY 11510

DIAL, Inc.
Box 911
Highland Park, IL 60035

Doubleday & Co.
Garden City, NY 11530

Durrell Publication, Inc.
P.O. Box 743
Kennebunkport, ME 04046

Economy Company
1901 N. Walnut Ave.
Oklahoma City, OK 74103

Educational Aids
845 Wisteria Drive
Fremont, CA 94538

Edmark Associates
655 S. Orcas St.
Seattle, WA 98108

Educational Activities, Inc.
1937 Grand Ave.
Baldwin, NY 11520

Educational Development Laboratories, A
    Division of McGraw-Hill
1121 Avenue of the Americas
New York, NY 10020

Educational Performance Associates
563 Westview Ave.
Ridgefield, NJ 07657

Educational Service, Inc.
P.O. Box 219
Stevensville, MI 49127

Educational Teaching Aids Division
A. Daigger & Co.
159 W. Kinzie St.
Chicago, IL 60610

Educational Testing Service
Princeton, NJ 08540

Educator's Publishing Service
75 Moulton St.
Cambridge, MA 02138

Edukaid of Ridgewood
1250 E. Ridgewood Ave.
Ridgewood, NJ 07450

Electronic Future, Inc.
57 Dodge Ave.
North Haven, CT 06473

Encyclopaedia Britannica Educational
  Corp.
425 N. Michigan Ave.
Chicago, IL 60611

Essay Press
Box 5
Planetarium Station
New York, NY 10024

Fearon Publishers
6 Davis Dr.
Belmont, CA 94002

Field Educational Publications, Inc.
2400 Hanover St.
Palo Alto, CA 94002

Flaghouse Inc.
18 West 18th St.
New York, NY 10011

Follett Educational Corp.
1010 W. Washington Blvd.
Chicago, IL 60607

Alvyn M. Freed
391 Munroe St.
Sacramento, CA 95825

Garrard Publishing Co.
1607 N. Market St.
Champaign, IL 61820

General Learning Corp.
250 James St.
Morristown, NJ 07960

Ginn & Co.
191 Spring St.
Lexington, MA 02173

Globe Book Co.
175 Fifth Ave.
New York, NY 10010

Gramercy Press
P.O. Box 77632
Los Angeles, CA 90007

Grolier Educational Corporation
845 Third Ave.
New York, NY 10022

Grune & Stratton
11 Fifth Ave.
New York, NY 10003

Gryphon Press
220 Montgomery St.
Highland Park, NJ 08904

Guidance Associates
1526 Gilpin Ave.
Wilmington, DE 19800

E.M. Hale & Co.
1201 S. Hastings Way
Eau Claire, WI 54701

J.L. Hammett Co.
165 Water St.
Lyons, NY 14489

C.S. Hammon & Co.
515 Valley St.
Maplewood, NJ 07040

Harcourt Brace Jovanovich, Inc.
757 Third Ave.
New York, NY 10017

Harper & Row Publishers, Inc.
10 East 53 St.
New York, NY 10022

D.C. Heath & Co.
125 Spring St.
Lexington, MA 02173

Marshall S. Hiskey
5640 Baldwin
Lincoln, NB 68507

Hoffman Information Systems, Inc.
5632 Peck Rd.
Arcadia, CA 91006

Holt, Rinehart and Winston, Inc.
383 Madison Ave.
New York, NY 10017

Houghton Mifflin Co.
One Beacon St.
Boston, MA 02107

Houston Press
University of Houston
Houston, TX 77000

Ideal School Supply Co.
11000 South Lavergne
Oak Lawn, IL 60453

Imperial Film Company, Inc.
Instructional Material Distributor
8 Surry Road
Norwood, MA 02062

Initial Teaching Alphabet Publications,
Inc.
6 E. 43 St.
New York, NY 10017

Psychological Test Specialists
Box 1441
Missoula, MT 59801

Instructional Industries, Inc.
Executive Park
Ballston Lake, NY 12019

Instructo Corp.
200 Cedar Hollow Rd.
Paoli, PA 19301

The Instructor Publications
7 Bank St.
Dansville, NY 14437

International Reading Association
800 Barksdaie Rd.
Newark, DE 19711

Jones-Kenilworth Co.
8301 Ambassador Row
Dallas, TX 75247

Journal of Learning Disabilities
101 East Ontario St.
Chicago, IL 60611

Journal of Special Education
433 S. Gulph Rd.
King of Prussia, PA 19406

The Judy Co.
310 N. Second St.
Minneapolis, MN 55401

Kenworthy Educational Service
P.O. Box 3031
138 Allen St.
Buffalo, NY 14201

Keystone View Co.
2212 E. 12 St.
Davenport, IA 52803

Kimbo Educational Co.
Box 246
Deal, NJ 07723

Laidlaw Bros.
Thatcher & Madison Sts.
River Forest, IL 60305

Language Research Associates
Box 95
950 E. 59 St.
Chicago, IL 60637

Lansford Publishing Co.
P.O. Box 8711
San Jose, CA 95155

Lawren Productions Inc.
P.O. Box 1542
Burlingame, CA 94010

Learning Concepts
2501 N. Lamar
Austin, TX. 78705

Learning Corporation of America
1350 Avenue of the Americas
New York, NY 10019

Learning Disability Quarterly
University of Kansas Medical Center
39th & Rainbow
Kansas City, KS

Learning Research Associates
1501 Broadway
New York, NY 10036

Learning Resource Center, Inc.
10655 S.W. Greenburg Rd.
Portland, OR 97223

Learning Resource Division, EDL
202 Miriam Dr.
Lakland, FL 33803

Learning Through Seeing
LTS Bldg.
Box 368
Sunland, CA 91040

J.P. Lippincott Co.
E. Washington Square
Philadelphia, PA 19105

Litton Educational Publishing Inc.
450 W. 33 St.
New York, NY 10001

Love Publishing Co.
6635 E. Villanova Pl.
Denver, CO 80222

Lyons and Carnahan Educational
    Publishers
407 E. 25 St.
Chicago, IL 60616

The Macmillan Co.
866 Third Ave.
New York, NY 10022

Macmillan, Inc.
866 Third Ave.
New York, NY 10022

Mafex Associates, Inc.
11 Barron Ave.
Johnstown, PA 16906

McCormick-Mathers Publishing Co.
450 W. 33 St.
New York, NY 10001

McGraw-Hill Book Co.
1221 Avenue of the Americas
New York, NY 10020

McGraw Hill/Early Learning
Paoli, PA 19301

David McKay Co.
750 Third Ave.
New York, NY 10017

Merrill Publishing Company
444 N. Lake Shore Dr.
Chicago, IL 60611

Charles E. Merrill
1300 Alum Creek Dr.
Columbus, OH 43216

Miller-Brody Productions
Room 2020
342 Madison Ave.
New York, NY 10017

Milton Bradley Co.
74 Park St.
Springfield, MA 01101

Modern Curriculum Press
13900 Prospect Rd.
Cleveland, OH 44136

William C. Morrow
105 Madison Ave.
New York, NY 10016

The C.V. Mosby Co.
11830 Westline Industrial Dr.
St. Louis, MO 63141

Motivational Research Inc.
P.O. Box 140
McLean, VA 22101

National Council of Teachers of English
1111 Kenyon Rd.
Urbana, IL 61801

National Education Association
    Publications
1201 16 St., N.W.
Washington, DC 20036

National Medical Audiovisual Center
    Annex
Station K
Atlanta, GA 30324

National Reading Conference, Inc.
Reading Center
Marquette University
Milwaukee, WI 53233

New Readers Press
Box 131
Syracuse, NY 13210

New York Association for Brain Injured
Children
305 Broadway
New York, NY 10007

New York State Education Dept.
Division for Handicapped Children
Special Education Instructional Materials
Center
800 N. Pear
Albany, NY 12204

Noble & Noble, Publishers
1 Dag Hammarskjold Plaza
New York, NY 10017

Northwestern University Press
1735 Benson Ave.
Evanston, IL 60201

Open Court Publishing Co.
Box Eighth St.
LaSalle, IL 61301

Orton Society
8415 Bellona Lane
Towson, MD 21204

F.A. Owen Publishing Co.
7 Bank St.
Dansville, NY 14437

Peek Publications
P.O. Box 11065
Palo Alto, CA 94303

Perceptual Development Laboratories
6737 Southwest Ave.
St. Louis, MO 63143

Phonovisual Products
12216 Parklawn Dr.
Rockville, MD 20852

Pro-Ed
7701 Cameron Rd.
Office Park
Austin, TX 78751

Prentice-Hall, Inc.
Englewood Cliffs, NJ 07632

J.A. Preston Corp.
71 Fifth Ave.
New York, NY 10003

Priority Innovations
P.O. Box 792
Skokie, IL 60076

The Psychological Corp.
304 E. 45 St.
New York, NY 10017

Psychological Test Specialists
Box 1441
Missoula, MT 59801

Psychotechnics
1900 Pickwick Ave.
Glenview, IL 60025

G.P. Putnam Sons
200 Madison Ave.
New York, NY 10016

Rand McNally & Co.
P.O. Box 7600
Chicago, IL 60680

Random House
201 E. 50 St.
New York, NY 10022

Reader's Digest Services
Educational Division
Pleasantville, NY 10570

The Reading Laboratory, Inc.
55 Day Street
South Northwalk, CT 06854

The Reed Clarke Company, Inc.
6444 Fly Rd.
East Syracuse, NY 13057

Rheem Califone
5922 Bancroft St.
Los Angeles, CA 90016

Scholastic Magazine and Book Services
50 W. 44 St.
New York, NY 10036

Science Research Associates
259 E. Erie St.
Chicago, IL 60611

Scott, Foresman and Co.
1900 East Lake Ave.
Glenview, IL 60025

Silver Burdett Co., A Division of General
  Learning Corp.
250 James St.
Morristown, NJ 07960

Simon & Schuster, Inc.
630 Fifth Ave.
New York, NY 10020

The L.W. Singer Co.
201 E. 50 St.
New York, NY 10022

Skill Development Equipment Co.
1340 North Jefferson Ave.
Anaheim, CA 92807

Slosson Educational Publications
140 Pines St.
East Aurora, NY 14052

Society for Visual Education
1356 Diversey Parkway
Chicago, IL 60614

Special Child Publications
4635 Union Bay Place, N.E.
Seattle, WA 98105

Special Education Materials Inc.
484 South Brodway
Yonkers, NY 10705

Stanley Bowman Co.
4 Broadway
Valhalla, NY 10595

Steck-Vaughn Co.
Box 2028
Austin, TX 78767

C.H. Stoelting Co.
424 N. Homan Ave.
Chicago, IL 60624

Swank Motion Pictures Inc.
201 S. Jefferson
St. Louis, MO 63166

Teachers College Press
Teachers College
Columbia University
1234 Amsterdam Ave.
New York, NY 10027

Teachers Publishing Corp.
22 W. Putnam Ave.
Greenwich, CT 06830

Teaching Aids
159 W. Kinzie St.
Chicago, IL 60610

Teaching Resources Corp.
100 Boylston St.
Boston, MA 02116

Teaching Technology Corp.
7471 Greenbush Ave.
North Hollywood, CA 91609

Charles C. Thomas Publisher
301-27 E. Lawrence Ave.
Springfield, IL 62717

3M Visual Products
3M Center
St. Paul, MN 55101

Trend Enterprises
P.O. Box 3073
St. Paul, MN 55165

Tweedy Transparencies
207 Hollywood Ave.
East Orange, NJ 07018

United States Department of Health,
  Education and Welfare
Washington, DC 20025

United States Government Printing Office
Superintendent of Documents
Washington, DC 20025

University of Chicago Press
5801 Ellis Ave.
Chicago, IL 60637

University of Illinois Press
Urbana, IL 61801

University of Iowa Press
Bureau of Research
Iowa City, IA 52242

The University of Iowa
Audio-Visual Center
Iowa City, IA 52240

The Viking Press, Inc.
625 Madison Ave.
New York, NY 10022

George Wahr Publishing Co.
316 State St.
Ann Arbor, MI 41808

Webster Division
McGraw-Hill
Manchester Rd.
Manchester, MO 63011

Weekly Reader Paperback Book Club
American Education Publications
A Xerox Company
55 High St.
Middletown, CT 06457

Wenkart Publishing Co.
4 Shady Hill Square
Cambridge, MA 02138

Western Psychological Services
12031 Wilshire Blvd.
Los Angeles, CA 90025

Western Publishing Education Services
1220 Mound Ave.
Racine, WI 53404

Westinghouse Learning Corp.
P.O. Box 30
Iowa City, IA 52240

Wheeler Publishing Co.
10 E. 53 St.
New York, NY 10022

John Wiley & Sons
605 Third Ave.
New York, NY 10016

Winston Press, Inc.
25 Groveland Terrace
Minneapolis, MN 55403

Winter Haven Lions Research Foundation
Box 1112
Winter Haven, FL 33880

World Publishing Company
110 E. 59 Street
New York, NY 10022

Xerox Education Publications
Education Center
Columbus, OH 43216

Zaner-Bloser Co.
612 North Park St.
Columbus, OH 43215

Richard Zweig Associates
20800 Beach Blvd.
Huntington Beach, CA 92648

References

Adamson, G., & Van Etten, C. Prescribing via analysis and retrieval of instructional materials in the educational modulation center. *Exceptional Children*, 1970, *36*, 531-533.

Adkins, P., & Walker, C. A call for early learning centers. *Academic Therapy*, 1972, *7*, 447-451.

Affleck, J., Lehning, T., & Brow, K. Expanding the resource concept: The resource school. *Exceptional Children*, 1973, *39*, 446-453.

Allen, K., Turner, K., & Everett, P. A behavior modification classroom for head start children with problem behaviors. *Exceptional Children*, 1970, *37*, 119-127.

Alexander, J. F., Barton, C., Schiavo, R. S., & Parsons, B. V. Systems—Behavioral intervention with families of delinquents: Therapist characteristics, family behavior, and outcome. *Journal of Consulting and Clinical Psychology*, 1976, *48*, 656-664.

Allouche, B. An example of a multimedia teaching system: The teaching program with audiovisual support. *Bulletin de Psychologie*, 1971-1972, *25*, 830-843.

Ames, L. Learning disabilities: The developmental point of view. In H. Myklebust (Ed.), *Progress in learning disabilities* (Vol. 1). New York: Grune and Stratton, 1968.

Ammerman, H., & Melching, W. *The derivation, analysis, and classification of instructional objectives*. (Tech. Rep. 66-74). Alexandria, Va., Resources Research Office, 1966.

Anderson, R., & Faust, G. The effects of strong formal prompts in programmed instruction. *American Educational Research Journal*, 1967, *4*, 345-352.

Arena, J. (Ed.). *Building spelling skills in dyslexic children*. San Rafael, Calif.: Academic Therapy Publications, 1968.

Ashlock, P., & Grant, M. *Educational therapy materials from the Ashlock Learning Center*. Springfield, Ill.: Charles C. Thomas, 1972.

Ashlock, P., & Stephen, A. *Educational therapy in the elementary school: An educational approach to the learning problems of children*. Springfield, Ill.: Charles C. Thomas, 1966.

Atkinson, B., & Seunath, O. The effect of stimulus change on attending behavior in normal children and children with learning disabilities. *Journal of Learning Disabilities*, 1973, *6*, 569–573.

Ayllon, T., & Azrin, N. *The token economy: A motivational system for therapy and rehabilitation.* New York: Appleton-Century-Crofts, 1968.

Ayllon, T., Layman, D., & Kandel, H. J. A behavior-educational alternative to drug control of hyperactive children. *Journal of Applied Behavior Analysis*, 1975, *8*, 137–146.

Ayres, A. *Sensory integration and learning disorders.* Los Angeles, Calif.: Western Psychological Services, 1972.

Ayres, J. Tactile functions, their relationship to hyperactive and perceptual motor behavior. *American Journal of Occupational Therapy*, 1964, *6*, 6–11.

Bailey, E. *Academic activities for adolescents.* Evergreen, Colo.: Learning Pathways, 1975.

Baker, H. Psychological services: From the school staff's point of view. *Journal of School Psychology*, 1965, *3* (4), 36–42.

Baker, H., & Leland, B. *Detroit tests of learning aptitude.* Indianapolis: Test Division of Bobbs-Merrill Co., Inc., 1935.

Baldwin, A., & Baldwin, C. *Cognitive control of mother-child interactions.* Washington, D.C.: U.S. Office of Education, 1970.

Baldwin, C., & Baldwin, A. Personality and social development of handicapped children. In C. Sherrick, J. Swets & L. Elliott (Eds.), *Psychology and the handicapped child.* Washington, D.C.: United States Department of Health, Education and Welfare, 1974.

Baldwin, R., & Kenny, T. Medical treatment of behavior disorders. In J. Hellmuth (Ed.), *Learning disorders* (Vol. 2). Seattle: Special Child Publications, 1966.

Baller, W., & Charles, D. *The psychology of human growth and development.* New York: Holt, Rinehart & Winston, 1968.

Baller, W., Charles, D., & Miller, E. Midlife attainment of the mentally retarded: A longitudinal study. *Genetic Psychology Monographs*, 1967, *75*, 235–329.

Bannatyne, A. *Language, reading and learning disabilities: Psychology, neuropsychology, diagnosis and remediation.* Springfield, Ill.: Charles C. Thomas, 1971.

Barsch, R. Evaluating the organic child: The functional organizational scale. *Journal of Genetic Psychology*, 1962, *100*, 345–354.

Barsch, R. The concept of language as a visuo-spatial phenomenon. *Academic Therapy Quarterly*, 1965a, *1*, 2–11.

Barsch, R. *A movigenic curriculum.* Wisconsin State Department of Public Instruction, Wisconsin Bureau of Handicapped Children, 1965b. (Bulletin No. 25)

Barsch, R. *Achieving perceptual-motor efficiency: A space-oriented approach to learning.* Seattle: Special Child Publications, 1967.

Bassler, J. Interdisciplinary need in reading. *Illinois Journal of Education*, 1967, *58*, 3–4.

Bateman, B. Learning disabilities—Yesterday, today, and tomorrow. *Exceptional Children*, 1964, *31*, 167–177.

Bateman, B. An educator's view of a diagnostic approach to learning disorders. In J. Hellmuth (Ed.) *Learning disorders* (Vol. 1). Seattle: Special Child Publications, 1965.

Bateman, B., & Frankel, H. Special education and the pediatrician. *Journal of Learning Disabilities*, 1972, *5*, 178–186.

Becker, J., & Sabatino, D. Frostig revisited. *Journal of Learning Disabilities*, 1973, *6*, 180–184.

Beery, K., & Buktenica, N. *Developmental test of visual-motor integration.* Chicago: Follett Educational Corporation, 1967.

Behavior patterns of children in school. In *Vital Health Statistics.* United States Department of Health Education and Welfare, Public Health Services, 1972, *11*, 1–78.

Bellamy, G., Greiner, C., & Buttars, K. Arithmetic computation for trainable retarded students: Continuing a sequential instructional program. *Training School Bulletin*, 1974, *70*, 230–240.

Belmont, I., & Birch, H. The effect of supplemental intervention on children with low reading-readiness scores. *Journal of Special Education*, 1974, *8*, 81–89.

Belmont, L., & Birch, H. Lateral dominance and right-left awareness in normal children. *Child Development*, 1963, *34*, 257-270.

Bender, L. A visual motor gestalt test and its clinical use. *Research Monographs*, American Orthopsychiatric Association, 1938, No. 3.

Berkowitz, P., & Rothman, E. *The disturbed child.* New York: New York University Press, 1960.

Berry, K. *Models for mainstreaming.* San Rafael, Calif.: Dimensions Publ. Co., 1973.

Bialer, I. Conceptualization of success and failure in mentally retarded and normal children. *Journal of Personality*, 1961, *29*, 303-320.

Bijou, S. Systematic instruction in the attainment of right-left form concepts in young and retarded children. In J. Holland & B. Skinner (Eds.), *An analysis of the behavioral processes involved in self-instruction.* Final Report, 1965, USOE, NDEA, No. 191, Title VII Project.

Birch, H., & Gussow, J. *Disadvantaged children: Health, nutrition, and school failure.* New York: Harcourt, Brace and World, 1970.

Birch, J. *Mainstreaming; Educable mentally retarded children in regular classes.* Reston, Va.: Council for Exceptional Children, 1974.

Bivens, L. Feedback complexity and self-direction in programmed instruction. *Psychological Reports*, 1964, *14*, 155-160.

Black, F. A word explosion in learning disabilities: A notation of literature trends 1962-1972. *Journal of Learning Disabilities*, 1974, *7*, 323-324.

Blackham, G. *The deviant child in the classroom.* Belmont, Calif.: Wadsworth, 1967.

Blair, J. A comparison of mother and teacher ratings on the Preschool Attainment Record of four year old children. *Exceptional Children*, 1970, *37*, 299-300.

Blanco, R. *Prescriptions for children with learning and adjustment problems.* Springfield, Ill.: Charles C. Thomas, 1972.

Bliesmer, E. Informal teacher testing in reading. *The Reading Teacher*, 1972, *26*, 268-272.

Bloom, B. (Ed.). *Taxonomy of educational objectives, the classification of educational goals, handbook I: Cognitive domain.* New York: David McKay, Inc., 1956.

Bloom, B., Krathwohl, D., & Masia, B. *Taxonomy of educational objectives, the classification of educational goals, handbook II: Affective domain.* New York: David McKay, Inc., 1964.

Boder, E. A neuropediatric approach to the diagnosis and management of school behavioral and learning disorders. In J. Hellmuth (Ed.), *Learning Disorders* (Vol. 2) Seattle: Special Child Publications, 1966.

Boehm, A. *Boehm test of basic concepts.* New York: Psychological Corporation, 1967.

Bonham, S. *Suggested procedures for designing instructional systems for secondary students with learning disabilities.* An interim report of activities. Worthington, Ohio: Ohio Division of Special Education, 1975.

Borschbaum, M. Coursey R., & Murphy, D. The biochemical high-risk paradigm: Behavioral and familial correlates of low-platelet Monoamine Oxidose activity. *Science*, 1976, *194*, 339-341.

Boshes, B., & Myklebust, H. Neurological behavioral study of children with learning disorders. *Neurology*, 1964, *14*, 7-12.

Braud, L., Lupin, M., & Braud, W. The use of electromyographic biofeedback in the control of hyperactivity. *Journal of Learning Disabilities*, 1975, *8*, 420-425.

Brenner, A. *The Anton Brenner developmental gestalt test of school readiness.* Beverly, Hills, Calif.: Western Psychological Services, 1964.

Brethower, D. Markle, D., Rummler, G., Schrader, A., Smith, D. *Programmed learning: A practicum.* Ann Arbor: Ann Arbor Publishing, 1964.

Brien, R., & Laguna, S. Flowcharting: A procedure for development of learning hierarchies. *Program Learning Educational Techniques*, 1977, *14*, 305-314.

Brown, V. Learning about mathematics instruction. *Journal of Learning Disabilities*, 1975, *8*, 476-485.

Brown, V., Hammill, D., & Wiederholt, L. *The test of reading comprehension.* Austin, Texas: Pro-Ed, 1978.

Browne, D. *A demonstration center for secondary learning disabled students.* Cushing, Oklahoma: Wilson School Child Service Demonstration Center, 1974.

Bruininks, R., & Rynders, J. Alternatives to special class placement for educably mentally retarded children. In E. Meyen, G. Vergason, & R. Whelan (Eds.), *Alternatives for teaching exceptional children.* Denver: Love, 1975.

Bryan, T. Learning disabilities: A new stereotype. *Journal of Learning Disabilities,* 1974, 7, 304–309.

Bryan, T. An observational analysis of classroom behaviors of children with learning disabilities. *Journal of Learning Disabilities,* 1974b, 7, 26–34.

Bryan, T. & Eash, M. Chicago institute for learning disabilities: Project child. *Learning Disability Quarterly,* 1978, 1, 71–72.

Bryan, T., & McGrady, H. Use of a teacher rating scale. *Journal of Learning Disabilities,* 1972, 5, 199–206.

Bryan, T., & Wheeler, R. Perception of learning disabled children: The eye of the observer. *Journal of Learning Disabilities,* 1972, 5, 484–488.

Bryant, N. D. Research institute for the study of learning disabilities (Columbia University). *Learning Disability Quarterly,* 1978, 1, 68–70.

Bryen, D. Teacher strategies in managing classroom behavior. In D. Hammill & N. Bartel (Eds.), *Teaching children with learning and behavior problems.* Boston: Allyn and Bacon, 1975.

Buros, O. (Ed.). *The third mental measurements yearbook.* New Brunswick: Rutgers University Press, 1949.

Buros, O. (Ed.). *The fourth mental measurements yearbook.* Highland Park, N.J.: Gryphon Press, 1953.

Buros, O. (Ed.). *The fifth mental measurements yearbook.* Highland Park, N.J.: Gryphon Press, 1959.

Buros, O. (Ed.). *The sixth mental measurements yearbook.* Highland Park, N.J.: Gryphon Press, 1965.

Buros, O. (Ed.). *The seventh mental measurements yearbook.* Highland Park, N.J.: Gryphon Press, 1972.

Bush, W., & Giles, M. *Aids to psycholinguistic teaching.* Columbus, Ohio: Charles E. Merrill, 1977.

Caldwell, B. *Pre-school inventory.* Princeton, N.J.: Cooperative Tests and Services, 1970.

Calvert, D., Olshin, G., Dewcerd, M., & Berson, M. Office of Education describes model projects for young handicapped children. *Exceptional Children,* 1969, 36, 229–248.

Carpenter, R., & Sells, C. Measuring effects of psychoactive medication in a child with a learning disability. *Journal of Learning Disabilities,* 1974, 7, 545–550.

Carrow, M. Some general principles of language theory. In *A theoretical approach to the diagnosis and treatment of language disorders in children.* San Antonio, Texas: Harry Jersig Speech & Hearing Center, 1968.

Case, R. Gearing the demands of instruction to the developmental capacities of the learner. *Review of Educational Research,* 1975, 45, 59–87.

Case, P. S. A systems approach to modifying behavior in a children's residential center. *Child Care Quarterly,* 1976, 5, 35–41.

Chalfant, J., & Scheffelin, M. Central processing dysfunction in children: A review of research. *National Institute of Neurological Diseases & Stroke Monographs,* 1969, No. 9.

Chappell, G. Language disabilities and the language clinician. *Journal of Learning Disabilities,* 1972, 5, 610–619.

Churchill, M. Study links learning disabilities with delinquency. *ETS Developments,* 1978, 25, 6–7.

Clemmens, R., & Davis, J. Complimentary roles of the pediatrician and educator in school planning for handicapped children. *Journal of Learning Disabilities,* 1969, 2, 524–532.

Clements, S. *Minimal brain dysfunction in children: Terminology and identification. Phase one of a three-phase project.* Washington, D.C.: United States Department of Health, Education and Welfare, 1966.

Clements, S. *Minimal brain dysfunction in children.* (Public Health Service Publication No. 2015) Washington, D.C.: United States Department of Health, Education and Welfare, 1969.

Cohen, H., Birch H., & Taft, L. Some considerations for evaluating the Doman-Delacato "Patterning" method. *Pediatrics*, 1970, 45, 302-314.

Cohen, N., Douglas, V. Characteristics of the orienting response in hyperactive and normal children. *Psychophysiology*, 1972, 9, 238-245.

Cohn, R. The neurological study of children with learning disabilities. *Exceptional Children*, 1964, 31, 179-185.

Comly, H. Cerebral stumulants for children with learning disorders. *Journal of Learning Disabilities*, 1971, 4, 484-490.

Conners, C. Recent drug studies with hyperkinetic children. *Journal of Learning Disabilities*, 1971, 4, 476-483.

Connolly, A., Nachtman, W., & Pritchett, E. *Keymath diagnostic arithmetic test.* Circle Pines, Minn.: American Guidance Service, Inc., 1971.

Corey, S. The nature of instruction. In P.C. Lange (Ed.), *Programmed instruction: NSSE 66th yearbook.* Chicago: University of Chicago Press, 1967.

Cott, A. Megavitamins: The orthomolecular approach to behavioral disorders and learning disabilities. *Academic Therapy*, 1972, 7, 245-259.

Cowgill, M., Friedland, S., & Shapiro, R. Predicting learning disabilities from kindergarten reports. *Journal of Learning Disabilities*, 1973, 6, 577-582.

Coy, M. The Bender visual-motor gestalt test as a predictor of academic achievement. *Journal of Learning Disabilities*, 1974, 7, 317-319.

Cratty, B. *Active learning: Games to enhance academic abilities.* Englewood Cliffs, N.J.: Prentice-Hall, 1971.

Cratty, B. Motor activities and learning disabilities, a look ahead. In M. Krasnoff (Ed.), *Learning disabilities: A decade ahead.* Ann Arbor, Mich.: Institute for the Study of Mental Retardation and Related Disabilities, 1974.

Cravioto, J. Nutrition and learning in children. In N. Springer (Ed.), *Nutrition and Mental Retardation.* Ann Arbor, Mich.: Institute of the Study of Mental Retardation and Related Disabilities, 1972.

Cruickshank, W. A teaching method for brain injured and hyperactive children. *Special Education and Rehabilitation Monograph*, Series, No. 6. Syracuse, N.Y.: Syracuse University Press, 1961.

Cruickshank, W. To the editor. *Exceptional Children*, 1968, 35, 93-94.

Cruickshank, W. Some issues facing the field of learning disability. *Journal of Learning Disabilities*, 1972, 5, 380-388.

Cruickshank, W. Introduction and overview of the problem of the conference. In M. Krasnoff (Ed.), *Learning disabilities: A decade ahead.* Ann Arbor, Mich.: Institute for the Study of Mental Retardation and Related Disabilities 1974.

Cruickshank, W., Bice, H., Wallen, N., & Lynch, K. *Perception and cerebral palsy.* Syracuse, N.Y.: Syracuse University Press, 1965.

Cruickshank, W. *Learning disabilities in home, school and community.* Syracuse, N.Y.: Syracuse University Press, 1977.

Cushenbery, D. The Joplin Plan: The teachers' viewpoints. *Academic Therapy*, 1966, 1, 230-234.

Cutler, C., Hirshoren, A., & Cecirelli V. Comparison of discrimination and reproduction tests of children's perception. *Perceptual and Motor Skills*, 1973, 37(1), 163-166.

Cutts, N. (Ed.). *School psychologists at midcentury: A report of the Thayer conference on the functions, qualifications, and training of school psychologists.* Washington, D.C.: American Psychological Association, 1955.

Czerniejewski, C., & Tillotson, K. Community program for the learning disabled child. *Academic Therapy*, 1973, 9, 57-60.

Davids, A. An objective instrument for assessing hyperkinesis in children. *Journal of Learning Disabilities*, 1971, 4, 499-501.

Delacato, C. *The treatment and prevention of reading problems: The neuro-psychological approach.* Springfield, Ill.: Charles C. Thomas, 1959.

Delacato, C. *The diagnosis and treatment of speech and reading problems.* Springfield, Ill.: Charles C. Thomas, 1963

Delacato, C. *Neurological organization and reading.* Springfield, Ill.: Charles C. Thomas, 1966.

De La Cruz, F., & La Veck, G. The pediatrician's view of learning disorders In J. Hellmuth (Ed.), *Learning disorders* (Vol. 1) Seattle: Special Child Publications, 1965.

Denckla, M. Clinical syndromes in learning disabilities: The case for "splitting" vs. "lumping." *Journal of Learning Disabilities,* 1972, *5,* 401–406.

Denckla, M. Research needs in learning disabilities: A neurologist's point of view. *Journal of Learning Disabilities,* 1973, *6,* 441–450.

Deutsch, C. Environment and perception. In M. Deutsch, I. Katz & A. Jensen (Eds.), *Social class, race, and psychological development.* New York: Holt, Rinehart & Winston, 1968.

Deutsch, C. Environmentally determined learning disabilities. In M. Krasnoff (Ed.), *Learning disabilities: A decade ahead.* Ann Arbor, Mich.: Institute for the Study of Mental Retardation and Related Disabilities, 1974.

Developmental indicators for the assessment of learning. Chicago: Office of the Superintendent of Public Instruction, 1972.

Dillard, H., & Landsman, M. The Evanston early identification scale: Prediction of school problems from the human figure drawings of kindergarten children. *Journal of Clinical Psychology,* 1968, *24,* 227–228.

Doll, E. Neurophrenia. *American Journal of Psychiatry,* 1951, *108,* 50–53.

Doll, E. *The Vineland social maturity scale.* Circle Pines, Minn.: American Guidance Service, 1953.

Doll, E. Preschool Attainment Record, Research Edition. Circle Pines, Minn.: American Guidance Service, 1967.

Doman, R., Spitz, E., Zucman, E., Delacato, C., & Doman, G. Children with severe brain injuries: Neurological organization in terms of mobility. *Journal of the American Medical Association,* 1960, *174,* 119–124.

Doman, G., Delacato, C., & Doman, R. *The Doman-Delacato developmental profile.* Philadelphia: Institutes for the Achievement of Human Potential, 1964.

Douglas, V. Sustained attention and impulse control: Implications for the handicapped child. In C. Sherrick, J. Swerts, & L. Elliott (Eds.), *Psychology and the handicapped child.* Washington, D.C.: United State Department of Health, Education and Welfare, 1974.

Dunn, L. *Peabody picture vocabulary test.* Circle Pines, Minn.: American Guidance Service, 1965.

Dunn, L. (Ed.). *Exceptional children in the schools.* New York: Holt, Rinehart, & Winston, 1973.

Dunsing, J. Learning disabilities: Art, science, or witchcraft. *Academic Therapy,* 1973, *8,* 451–460.

Dunsing, J., Kephart, N. Motor generalizations in space and time. In J. Hellmuth (Ed.), *Learning Disorders* (Vol. 1). Seattle: Special Child Publications, 1965.

Durkin, D. Some questions about questionable instructional materials. *The Reading Teacher,* 1974, *28,* 13–17.

Durrell, D. *Durrell analysis of reading difficulty.* New York: Harcourt Brace Jovanovich, 1955.

Dykman, R., Ackerman, P., Clements, S., Peters, J. Specific learning disabilities: An attentional deficit syndrome. In H. Myklebust (Ed.), *Progress in learning disabilities* (Vol. 2). New York: Grune and Stratton, 1971.

Eaves, R. C., & McLaughlin, P. A systems approach for the assessment of the child and his environment: Getting back to basics. *Journal of Special Education,* 1977, *11,* 99–111.

Edgington, R. Public school programming for children with learning disabilities. *Academic Therapy,* 1967, *2,* 166–169.

Evans, J. Multiple-choice discrimination programming. Paper presented at the meeting of the American Psychological Association, New York, 1961.

Fairfield Public Schools pre-kindergarten descriptive inventory. Fairfield, Conn.: Fairfield Public Schools, 1972.

Feder, B. Consultation with guidance personnel in crisis situations. *Journal of School Psychology,* 1967, *6* (1), 13–17.

Ferinden, W., & Jacobsen, S. Early identification of learning disabilities. *Journal of Learning Disabilities,* 1970, *3,* 589–593.

Fernald, G. *Remedial techniques in basic school subjects.* New York; McGraw-Hill, 1943.

Flanagan, J. *Tests of general ability, form A, grade K–2.* Chicago: Science Research Associates, Inc., 1960.

Flavell, J. Developmental studies in mediated memory. In L. P. Lipsitt & H. W. Reese (Eds.), *Advances in child development and behavior* (Vol. 5). New York: Academic Press, 1970.

Flavell, J., Beach, D., & Chinsky, J. Spontaneous verbal rehearsal in a memory task as a function of age. *Child Development,* 1966, *37,* 283–299.

Fleck, S. A general systems approach to severe family pathology. *American Journal of Psychiatry,* 1976, *133,* 669–673.

Ford, M. New directions in special education. *Journal of School Psychology,* 1971, *9,* 73–83.

Frankel, H. Portland public schools' prescriptive program. In P. Mann (Ed.), *Mainstream special education.* Reston, Va.: Council for Exceptional Children, 1974.

Freeman, R. Drug effects on learning in children: A selective review of the past thirty years. *Journal of Special Education,* 1966, *1,* 17–44.

Freeman, R. Controversy over "Patterning" as a treatment for brain damage in children. *Journal of the American Medical Association,* 1967, *202,* 385–388.

Freidus, E. Methodology for the classroom teacher. In J. Hellmuth (Ed.), *The special child in century 21.* Seattle: Special Child Publications of the Seguin School, 1964.

Frierson, E., & Barbe, W. (Eds.). *Educating children with learning disabilities.* New York: Appleton-Century-Crofts, 1967.

Frostig, M. Testing as a basis for educational therapy. *Journal of Special Education,* 1967, *2,* 15–34.

Frostig, M. Futures in perceptual training. In M. Krasnoff (Ed.), *Learning disabilities: A decade ahead.* Ann Arbor, Mich: Institute for the Study of Mental Retardation and Related Disabilities, 1974.

Frostig, M., & Horne, D. The Frostig program for the development of visual perception: Teacher's guide. Chicago: Follett, 1964.

Frostig, M., & Horne, D. *The developmental program in visual perception: Intermediate pictures and patterns.* Chicago: Follett, 1966(a).

Frostig, M., & Horne, D. *The developmental program in visual perception: Advanced pictures and patterns.* Chicago: Follett, 1966(b).

Frostig, M., & Horne, D. Marianne Frostig Center of Educational Therapy. In M. Jones (Ed.), *Special education program: Within the United States.* Springfield, Ill.: Charles C. Thomas, 1968.

Frostig, M., Horne, A., & Horne, D. The developmental program in visual perception: Beginning pictures and patterns. Chicago: Follett, 1966.

Frostig, M., Lefever, D., & Whittlesey, J. A developmental test of visual perception for evaluating normal and neurologically handicapped children. *Perception and Motor Skills,* 1961, *12,* 383–394.

Frostig, M., Lefever, D., & Whittlesey, J. *The Marianne Frostig developmental test of visual perception.* Palo Alto, Calif.: Consulting Psychology Press, Inc., 1964.

Frostig, M., & Maslow, P. Language training: A form of ability training. *Journal of Learning Disabilities,* 1968, *1,* 105–115.

Fry, E. Teaching machines: An investigation of constructed versus multiple-choice methods of response. *Automated Teaching Bulletin,* 1959, *1,* 11–12.

Gaddes, W. A neuropsychological approach to learning disorders. *Journal of Learning Disabilities,* 1968, *1,* 523–534.

Gagnè, R. The analysis of instructional objectives for the design of instruction. In R. Glaser (Ed.), *Teaching machines and programmed learning, II.* Washington, D.C.: NEA, 1965.

Gagnè, R. Instructional variables and learning outcomes. In M. Wittrock & D. Wiley (Eds.), *The evaluation of instruction: Issues and problems.* New York: Holt, Rinehart & Winston, 1970.

Gallagher, J. Children with developmental imbalances: A psychoeducational definition. In W. Cruickshank (Ed.), *The teacher of brain-injured children. A discussion of the bases for competency.* Syracuse, N.Y.: Syracuse University Press, 1966.

Gallagher, J. The special education contract for mildly handicapped children. *Exceptional Children,* 1972, *38,* 527-535.

Gallegos, R., & Phelan, J. Using behavioral objectives in industrial training. *Training and Development Journal,* 1974, *28* (4), 42-48.

Gardner, W. *Children with learning and behavior problems: A behavior management approach.* Boston: Allyn and Bacon, 1974.

Gearheart, B. *Learning disabilities: Educational strategies.* St. Louis, Mo.: C. V. Mosby, 1973.

Geschwind, N. Neurological foundations of language. In H. Myklebust (Ed.), *Progress in learning disabilities* (Vol. 1). New York: Grune and Stratton, 1968.

Gesell, A. *Gesell developmental schedules.* New York: Psychological Corp., 1949.

Gesell, A., & Amatruda, C. Developmental diagnosis: Normal and abnormal child development. In H. Knoblock & B. Pasamanick (Eds.) *Gesell and Amatruda's developmental diagnosis.* New York: Harper and Row, 1974.

Gesell, A., & Ilg, F. *Infant and child in the culture of today.* New York: Harper & Row, 1943.

Gesell, A. & Thompson, H. Twins T. and C. from infancy to adolescence: A biogenetic study of individual differences by the method of co-twin control. *Genetic Psychology Monographs,* 1941, *24,* 3-122.

Getman, G. The visuomotor complex in the acquisition of learning skills. In J. Hellmuth (Ed.), *Learning disorders* (Vol. 1). Seattle: Special Child Publications, 1965.

Getman, G., & Kane, E. *The physiology of readiness: An action program for the development of perception for children.* Minneapolis: Programs to Accelerate School Success, 1964.

Getman, G., Kane, E., Halgren, M., & McKee, G. *Developing learning readiness.* Manchester, Mo.: Webster Division, McGraw-Hill, 1968.

Gibson, E. A systematic application of the concepts of generalization and differentiation to verbal learning. *Psychological Review,* 1940, *47* (3), 196-229.

Gickling, E., & Theobald, J. Mainstreaming: Affect or effect. *The Journal of Special Education,* 1975, *9,* 317-328.

Giffin, M. The role of child psychiatry in learning disabilities. In H. Myklebust (Ed.), *Progress in learning disabilities* (Vol. 1). New York: Grune and Stratton, 1968.

Gilbert, T. Mathetics: The technology of education. *Journal of Mathetics,* 1962(a), *1* (1), 7-74.

Gilbert, T. Mathetics: II. The design of teaching exercises. *Journal of Mathetics,* 1962(b), *1* (2), 7-56.

Gillingham, A., & Stillman, B. *Remedial work for reading, spelling, and penmanship.* New York: Hackett & Wilhelms, 1936.

Gillingham, A., & Stillman, B. *Remedial work for reading, spelling, and penmanship* (6th ed.). New York: Hackett & Wilhelms, 1946.

Gillingham, A., & Stillman, B. *Remedial training for children with specific disability in reading, spelling, and penmanship* (7th ed). Cambridge, Mass.: Educators Publishing Service, 1965.

Glaser, R. *Investigations of the characteristics of programmed learning sequences.* Pittsburgh: University of Pittsburgh, 1961.

Glaser, R. Instructional technology and the measurement of learning outcomes: Some questions. *American Psychologist,* 1963, *18,* 519-521.

Glaser, R., & Klaus, D. Proficiency measurement: Assessing human performance. In R. Gagnè (Ed.), *Psychological principles in system development.* New York: Holt, Rinehart & Winston, 1962.

Glass, G., & Robbins, M. A critique of experiments on the role of neurological organization in reading performance. *Reading Research Quarterly,* 1967, *3,* 5-51.

Goldbeck, R., & Briggs, L. An analysis of response mode and feedback factors in automated instruction. In W. Smith & J. Moore (Eds.), *Programmed learning.* Princeton, N.J.: Van Nostrand, 1962.

Goldberg, H. The ophthalmologist looks at the reading problem. *American Journal of Ophthalomogy,* 1959, 47, 67-74.

Goldberg, H., Drash, P. The ophthalmologist and the disabled reader. In J. Hellmuth (Ed.), *Learning disorders* (Vol. 3). Seattle.: Special Child Publications, 1968.

Goldman, R., & Fristoe, M. *Test of articulation.* Circle Pines, Minn.: American Guidance Service, Inc., 1969.

Goldman, R., Fristoe, M., & Woodcock, R. *Test of auditory discrimination.* Circle Pines, Minn.: American Guidance Service, Inc., 1970

Goldstein, K. The modifications of behavior consequent to cerebral lesions. *Psychiatric Quarterly,* 1936, 10, 586-610.

Gollagher, J. Changes in verbal and non-verbal ability of brain-injured mentally retarded children following removal of special stimulation. *American Journal of Mental Deficiency,* 1962, 66, 774-781.

Goodman, L., & Mann, L. *Learning disabilities in the secondary school.* New York: Grune and Stratton, 1976.

Gotkin, L., & Goldstein, L. Learning from teaching machines. In P. Lange (Ed.), *Programmed instruction: 66th yearbook of NSSE.* Chicago: University of Chicago Press, 1967.

Graubard, P. Teaching strategies and techniques for the education of disruptive groups and individuals. In P. Graubard (Ed.). *Children against schools.* Chicago: Follett, 1969.

Graubard, P. Children with behavioral disabilities. In L. Dunn (Ed.), *Exceptional children in the schools.* New York: Holt, Rinehart & Winston, 1973.

Gray, B., & Fygetakis, L. Mediated language acquisition for dyphasic children. *Behavior Research and Therapy,* 1968, 6, 263-280.

Gray, B., & Ryan, B. *A language program for the nonlanguage child.* Champaign, Ill.: Research Press, 1973.

Greene, D. A study of learning problems and interprofessional relationships. In R. Wold (Ed.), *Visual and perceptual aspects for the acheiving and underachieving child.* Seattle: Special Child Publications, 1969.

Gronlund, N. *Stating behavioral ovjectives for classroom instruction.* London: Macmillan, 1970.

Grosenick, J. Integration of exceptional children into regular classes: Research and procedure. *Focus on Exceptional Children,* 1971, 3, 1-9.

Gross S., Carr, M. Dornseif, A., & Rouse, S. Behavioral objectives in a reading skills program, grades 4-8. *The Reading Teacher,* 1974, 27, 782-789.

Hafner, D. A shift in emphasis in programming for handicapped children. *Exceptional Children,* 1972, 39, 59-60.

Hainsworth, P., & Siqueland, M. *Early identification of children with learning disabilities: The Meeting Street School screening test.* Rhode Island: Crippled Children and Adults of Rhode Island Inc., 1969.

Hall, C., & Lindzey, G. *Theories of personality.* New York: John Wiley, 1970.

Hall, K., Cartwright, G., & Mitzel, H. CARE: Computer assisted renewal education. In P. Mann (Ed.), *Mainstream special education.* Reston, Va.: Council for Exceptional Children, 1974.

Hall, R., Fox, R., Willard, D., Goldsmith, L., Emerson, M., Owen, M., Davis, F., & Porcia, E. The teacher as observer and experimenter in the modification of disrupting and talking-out behaviors. *Journal of Applied Behavior Analysis,* 1971, 4, 141-149.

Hallahan, D. P. University of Virginia learning disabilities research institute. *Learning Disability Quarterly,* 1978, 1, 77-78.

Hallahan, D., & Cruickshank, W. *Psychoeducational foundations of learning disabilities.* Englewood Cliff, N.J.: Prentice-Hall, 1973.

Hallahan, D., Kauffman, J., & Ball, D. Selective attention and cognitive tempo of low achieving and high achieving sixth grade males. *Perceptual and Motor Skills,* 1973, 36, 579-583.

Hallahan, D., Tarver, S., Kauffman, J., & Graybeal, N. A comparison of the effects of reinforcement and response cost on the selective attention of learning disabled children. *Journal of Learning Disabilities.* 1978, *11*, 430-438.

Hammill, D. Learning disabilities: A problem in definition. *Prise Reporter,* October 1972, No. 4. Harrisburg, Pa.: Pennsylvania Resources and Information Center for Special Education.

Hammill, D. & Bartel, N. (Eds.). *Educational perspectives in learning disabilities* New York: John Wiley, 1971.

Hammill, D., & Bartel, N. *Teaching children with learning and behavior problems: A resource book for preschool, elementary, and special education teacher.* Boston: Allyn and Bacon, 1978.

Hammill, D., Goodman, L., & Wiederhol, J. Visual-motor processes: Can we train them? *The Reading Teacher,* 1974, *27,* 469-478.

Hammill, D., & Larsen, S. *Test of written language.* Austin, Texas: Pro-Ed, 1978.

Hammill, D., & Wiederholt, J. *The resource room: Rationale and implementation.* Philadelphia: Buttonwood Farms, 1972.

Hammill, D., & Wiederholt, J. Review of the Frostig Visual Perception Test and the related training program. In L. Mann and D. Sabatino (Eds.), *The first review of special education.* Phildelphia: Buttonwood Farms, 1973.

Hammock, J. Criterion measures: Instruction vs. selection research. Paper presented at the meeting of the American Psychological Association, Chicago, Ill., 1960.

Hardy, J. Perinatal factors and intelligence. In S. Osler and R. Cooke (Eds.), *The biosocial basis of mental retardation.* Baltimore: John Hopkins Press, 1965.

Haring, N., & Miller, D. Precision teaching in regular junior-high-school classrooms. In E. Deno (Ed.), *Instructional alternatives for exceptional children.* Reston, Va.: Council for Exceptional Children, 1973.

Haring, N., & Ridgway, R. Early identification of children with learning disabilities. *Exceptional Children,* 1967, *33,* 387-395.

Harris, A. *How to increase reading ability* (5th ed.). New York: David McKay, 1970.

Harris, A., & Jacobson, M. Basic vocabulary for beginning reading *The Reading Teacher,* 1973, *26,* 392-395.

Hartman, A. *Preschool diagnostic language program.* Harrisburg, Pa.: Department of Public Instruction, 1966.

Hasazi, J. E., & Hasazi, S. E. Effects of teacher attention on digit-reversal behavior in an elementary school child. *Journal of Applied Behavior Analysis,* 1972, *5,* 157-162.

Hawley, C., & Buckley, R. Food dyes and hyperkinetic children. *Academic Therapy,* 1974, *10,* 27-32. Head Start test collection—School readiness measures. Princeton, New Jersey: Educational Testing Services, 1971.

Hayes-Roth, F., Longabaugh, R., & Ryback, R. Mental health: Systems and nonsystems. *International Journal of Mental Health,* 1977, *5,* 5-31.

Heath, E, & Early, G. Intramodal and intermodal functioning of normal and L. D. children. *Academic therapy,* 1973, *9,* 133-149.

Herb, D. *The organization of behaviors.* New York: John Wiley, 1949.

Hegge, T., Kirk, S., & Kirk, W. *Remedial reading drills.* Ann Arbor, Mich.: George Wahr, 1970.

Heimstra, N., & Ellingstad, V. *Human behavior: A systems approach.* Monterey, Calif.: Brooks-Cole Publishers, 1972.

Hendershot, C. *Programmed learning: A bibliography of programs and presentation devices, I and II.* Bay City, Mich.: Author, 1967.

Herrick, M. Disabled or disadvantaged: What's the difference? *The Journal of Special Educational,* 1973, *7,* 381-386.

Hess, B. *Local project assistant, direct introvention project-special learning disabilities.* Unpublished manuscript, Milwaukee, Wisconsin Public Schools, 1974.

Hess, R. Educability and rehabilitation: The future of the welfare class. *Journal of Marriage and the Family,* 1964, *26,* 422-429.

Hewett, F. A hierarchy of educational tasks for children with learning disorders. *Exceptional Children,* 1964, *31,* 207–214.

Hewett, F. Educational engineering with emotionally disturbed children. *Exceptional Children, 1967, 33,* 459–467.

Hewett, F. *The emotionally disturbed child in the classroom.* Boston: Allyn and Bacon, 1968.

High, C. Pupil behavior rating scale. In B. Gearheart. *Learning disabilities: Educational strategies.* St. Louis, Mo.: C. V. Mosby, 1973.

Hinshelwood, J. Congenital word-blindness, with reports of two cases. *Ophthalmological Review,* 1902, *21,* 91–99.

Hively, W. Programming stimuli in matching to sample. *Journal of Experimental Analysis of Behavior,* 1962, *5,* 279–298.

Hobbs, N. Helping disturbed children: Psychological and ecological strategies. In H. Dupont (Ed.), *Educating emotionally disturbed children.* New York: Holt, Rinehart & Winston, 1969.

Hobbs, N. (Ed.). *Issues of classification of children.* San Francisco, Calif.: Jossey-Bass, 1974.

Hoepfnew, R., Stern, C., & Numedal, S. (Eds.). *Preschool/kindergarten test evaluations.* Los Angeles: Center for the Study of Evaluation and the Early Childhood Research Center, 1971.

Hopkins, B., Schutte, R., & Garton, K. The effects of access to a playroom on the rate and quality of printing and writing of first- and second-grade students. *Journal of Applied Behavior Analysis, 1971, 4,* 77–87.

Horn, R. *Developmental testing.* Ann Arbor, Mich.: Center for Programmed Learning for Business, 1966.

Hughes, J. Electroencephalogy and learning. In H. Myklebust (Ed.), *Progress in learning disabilities* (Vol. 1). New York: Grune and Stratton, 1968.

Ilg, F., Ames, L., & Apell, R. School readiness as evaluated by Gesell developmental, visual, and projective tests. *Genetic Psychology Monographs,* 1965, *71,* 61–91.

Illinois Office of the Superintendent of Public Instruction. *Developmental Indicators for the Assessment of Learning.* Chicago: OSPI, 1972.

Jenkins, J., & Mayholl, W. Describing resource teacher programs. *Exceptional Children,* 1973, *40,* 35–36.

Johnson, D. Educational principles for children with learning disabilities. *Rehabilitation Literature,* 1967, *28,* 317–322.

Johnson, D. Perception and educational planning. In M. Krasnoff (Ed.), *Learning disabilities: The decade ahead.* Ann Arbor, Mich.: Institute for the Study of Mental Retardation and Related Disabilities, 1974.

Johnson, D., & Myklebust, H. *Learning disabilities: Educational principles and practices.* New York: Grune and Stratton, 1967.

Johnson, M., & Kress, R. Individual reading inventories: Sociological and psychological factors in reading. 21st Annual Reading Institute, Temple University, 1964.

Johnson, R., & Grismer, R. The Harrison School center: A public school-university cooperative resource program. In E. Deno (Ed.), *Instructional alternatives for exceptional children.* Reston, Va.: Council for Exceptional Children, 1973.

Johnson, S. The marginal child: Workshop proceedings. Plattsburgh, New York: State University of New York at Plattsburgh, 1962.

Johnson, S. *Arithmetic and learning disabilities.* Boston: Allyn and Bacon, 1979.

Johnson, S., Morasky, R., & Plumeau, F. Symposium: Strategies for three teacher-parent workshops. Paper presented at the meeting of the Association for Children with Learning Disabilities, Houston, Texas, 1974.

Jones, J. Dyslexia: Identification and remediation in a public school setting. *Journal of Learning Disabilities,* 1969, *2,* 533–538.

Kaluger, G., & Kolson, C. *Reading and learning disabilities.* Columbus, Ohio: Charles E. Merrill, 1969.

Karlsen, B., Madden, R., & Gardner, E. *Stanford diagnostic reading test.* New York: Harcourt, Brace, Jovanovich, 1968.

Karnes, M. *Helping young children develop language skills: A book of activities.* Washington, D.C.: Council for Exceptional Children, 1968.

Kass, C. Introduction to learning disabilities. *Seminars in Psychiatry,* 1969, *1,* 240-244.

Kass, C., & Myklebust, H. Learning disability: An educational definition. *Journal of Learning Disabilities,* 1969, *2,* 377-379.

Keele, D., Keele, M., Huizinga, R., Bray, N., Estes, R., & Holland, L. Role of special pediatric evaluation in the evaluation of a child with learning disabilities. *Journal of Learning Disabilities,* 1975, *8,* 40-45.

Keogh, B. (Ed.). Early identification of children with learning disabilities. *Journal of Special Education Monograph,* 1970, No. 1.

Kephart, N. *The brain-injured child in the classroom.* Chicago: National Society for Crippled Children and Adults, 1963.

Kephart, N. Perceptual-motor aspects of learning disability. In E. Frierson & W. Barbe (Eds.), *Educating children with learning disabilities.* New York: Appleton-Century-Crofts, 1967.

Kephart, N. On the value of empirical data in learning disability. *Journal of Learning Disabilities,* 1971, *4,* 393-395.

Kephart, N. *The slow learner in the classroom* (2nd ed.). Columbus, Ohio: Charles E. Merrill, 1971a.

Kirk, S. Behavioral diagnosis and remediation of learning disabilities. *Proceedings of the Conference on Exploration into the Problems of the Perceptually Handicapped Child, First Annual Meeting,* April 6, 1963, *1.*

Kirk, S. *Educating exceptional children.* Boston: Houghton Mifflin, 1962.

Kirk, S. Learning disabilities: The view from here. On progress in parent information, professional growth, and public policy. *Selected papers, Association for Children with Learning Disabilities.* San Rafael, Calif.: Academic Therapy Publications, 1969.

Kirk, S. *Educating exceptional children* (2nd ed.). Boston: Houghton Mifflin, 1972.

Kirk, S., & Kirk, W. *Psycholinguistic learning disabilities: Diagnosis and remediation.* Urbana, Ill.: University of Illinois Press, 1971.

Kirk, S., McCarthy, J., & Kirk, W. *Illinois test of psycholinguistic abilities* (rev. ed.). Urbana, Ill.: University of Illinois Press, 1968.

Kirk, W. A tentative screening procedure for selecting bright and slow children in kindergarten. *Exceptional Children,* 1966, *33,* 235-241.

Kleffner, F. Aphasia and other language deficiencies in children: Research and teaching at Central Institute for the Deaf. In W. Daly (Ed.), *Speech and language therapy with the brain-damaged child.* Washington, D.C.: Catholic University of America Press, 1962.

Knight, S. Programming for the retarded reader. *Programmed Instruction,* 1964, *3,* 51-53.

Koppitz, E. *The Bender gestalt test for young children.* New York: Grune and Stratton, 1964.

Koppitz, E. Brain damage, reading disability and the Bender Gestalt Test. *Journal of Learning Disabilities,* 1970, *3,* 429-433.

Kornetsky, C. Medication and control of behavior. In M. Krasnoff (Ed.), *Learning disabilities: The decade ahead.* Ann Arbor, Mich.: Institute for the study of Mental Retardation and Related Disabilities, 1974.

Krasnoff, M. (Ed.). *Learning disabilities: The decade ahead.* Ann Arbor, Mich.: Institute for the study of Mental Retardation and Related Disabilities, 1974.

Kratoville, B. L. (Ed.). *Youth in Trouble.* San Rafael, Calif.: Academic Therapy Publications, 1974.

Kroth, R. *Communicating with the parents of exceptional children.* Denver, Colo.: Love, 1975.

Lahey, B. B. Behavior modification with learning disabilities and related problems. In M. Hersen, R. Eisler & P. Miller (Eds.), *Progress in behavior modification* (Vol. 3). New York: Academic Press, 1976.

Lahey, B. B., Busemeyer, M. K., O'Hara, C., & Beggs, V. E. Treatment of severe perceptual-motor disorders in children diagnosed as learning disabled. *Behavior Modification,* 1977, *1,* 123-140.

Landreth, G., Jacquot, W., & Allen, L. A team approach to learning disabilities. *Journal of Learning Disabilities,* 1969, *2,* 82–87.

Larsen, S. The learning disabilities specialist: Role and responsibilities. *Journal of Learning Disabilities,* 1976, *9,* 498–508.

Larsen, S. (Ed.). *Code of ethics and competencies for teachers of learning disabled children and youth.* Kansas City, Kan.: Division for Children With Learning Disabilities of the Council for Exceptional Children, 1978.

Larsen, S., & Hammill, D. The relationship of selected visual-perceptual abilities to school learning. *The Journal of Special Education,* 1975, *9,* 281–291.

Lawson, L., Jr. Ophthalmological factors in learning disabilities. In H. Myklebust (Ed.), *Progress in learning disabilities* (Vol. 1). New York: Grune and Stratton, 1968.

The learning resource center for exceptional children. *Exceptional Children,* 1970, *36,* 527–530.

Lee, J., & Clark, W. *Lee-Clark reading readiness test: Kindergarten and grade 1.* Monterey, Calif.: Test Bureau/McGraw-Hill, 1962.

Lerner, J. W. *Children with learning disabilities.* Boston: Houghton Mifflin, 1971.

Lerner, J. W. *Children with learning disabilities* (2nd ed.). Boston: Houghton Mifflin, 1976.

Lerner, J. Systems analysis and special education. *Journal of Special Education,* 1973, *7,* 15–26.

Lindsey, J. A multi-modular learning disability program. New Iberia, La.: Iberia Parish School Board, 1974.

Linn, S. Spelling problems: Diagnosis and remediation. In J. Arena (Ed.), *Building spelling skills in dyslexic children.* San Rafael, Calif.: Academic Therapy Publications, 1968.

Lipton, M., & Wender, E. Report to the nutrition foundation from the national advisory committee on hyperkinesis and food additives. Washington, D.C.: Office of Education and Public Affairs, 1977.

Llorens, L. Activity analysis for cognitive-perceptual-motor dysfunction. *American Journal of Occupational Therapy,* 1973, *27,* 453–456.

Long, N., & Newman, R. A differential approach to the management of surface behavior of children in school. *Teachers' Handling of Children in Conflict: Bulletin of the School of Education of the University of Indiana,* 1961, *37,* 47–61.

Long, N., & Newman, R. Managing surface behaviors of children in school. In N. Long, W. Morse, & R. Newman (Eds.), *Conflict in the classroom.* Belmont, Calif.: Wadsworth, 1965.

Lovitt, T. Self-management projects with children with behavioral disabilities. *Journal of Learning Disabilities,* 1973, *6,* 138–150.

Lowell, R. Reading readiness factors as predictors of success in first grade reading. *Journal of Learning Disabilities,* 1971, *4,* 563–567.

Lublin, S. Reinforcement schedules, scholastic aptitude, autonomy need, and achievement in a programmed course. *Journal of Educational Psychology,* 1965, *65,* 295–302.

Lumsdaine, A. Some problems in assessing instructional programs. In R. Filep (Ed.), *Prospectives in Programming.* New York: Macmillan, 1963.

Lumsdaine, A. Assessing the effectiveness of instructional programs. In R. Glaser (Ed.), *Teaching machines and programmed learning, II: Data and directions.* Washington, D.C.: NEA, 1965.

Mackie, R. *Special education in the United States: 1948–1966.* New York: Teachers College Press, 1969.

Mager, R. *Preparing instructional objectives.* Palo Alto, Calif.: Fearon, 1962.

Maietta, D. Current halloos confronting special learning disabilities. *Seminars in Psychiatry,* 1969, *1,* 245–252.

Mann, P. (Ed.). *Mainstream special education.* Reston, Va.: Council for Exceptional Children, 1974.

Mann, P., & McClung, R. Training regular teachers in learning disabilities. In P. Mann (Ed.), *Mainstream special education.* Reston, Va.: Council for Exceptional Children, 1974.

Mann, P., & Suiter, P. *Handbook in diagnostic teaching.* Boston: Allyn and Bacon, 1974.

Mann, P., Suiter, P., & McClung, R. *Handbook in diagnostic teaching* (2nd ed.). Boston: Allyn and Bacon, 1979.

Markle, S. Teaching machines versus programmers. *Audiovisual Communication Review*, 1962, *10*, 286-292.

Markle, S. Empirical testing of programs. In P. Lange (Ed.), *Programmed instruction: 66th yearbook of the NSSE*. Chicago: University of Chicago Press, 1967.

Markle, S. *Good frames and bad*. New York: John Wiley, 1969.

Markle, S. Some thoughts on task analysis and objectives in educational psychology. *Educational Psychologist*, 1973, *10*(1), 24-29.

Markle, S., & Tiemann, P. (Producers) *Programming is a process*. Chicago, Ill.: University of Chicago, 1967. (Programmed film)

McCarthy, J. Psychoeducational diagnosis: A derivative of classroom behavior. Paper presented at the meeting of the National Catholic Educational Association Annual Meeting, Palos, Ill., 1966.

McCarthy, J. Learning disabilities: Where have we been? Where are we going? In *Selected Convention Papers*, Council for Exceptional Children Convention, April, 1969.

McCarthy, J., & Paraskevopoulos, J. Behavior patterns of learning disabled, emotionally disturbed, and average children. *Exceptional Children*, 1969, *36*, 69-74.

McClain, W. The modification of aggressive classroom behaviors through reinforcement, inhibition, and relationship therapy. *Training School Bulletin*, 1969, *65*, 122-125.

McClurg, W. Dyslexia: Early identification and treatment in the schools. *Journal of Learning Disabilities*, 1970, *3*, 372-377.

McDonald, T., & Moorman, G. Criterion referenced testing for functional literacy. *Journal of Reading*, 1974, *17*, 363-366.

McGahen, F. E., & McGahen, C. *The early detection inventory*. Chicago: Follett, 1972.

McGrady, H., Jr. Language pathology and learning disabilities. In H. Myklebust (Ed.), *Progress in Learning disabilities* (Vol. 1). New York: Grune and Stratton, 1968.

McIntosh, D., & Dunn, L. Children with major specific learning disabilities. In L. Dunn (Ed.), *Exceptional children in the schools*. New York: Holt, Rinehart & Winston, 1973.

Mechner, F. Science education and behavioral technology. In R. Glaser (Ed.), *Teaching machines and programmed learning II*. Washington, D.C.: NEA, 1965.

Meichenbaum, D. *Cognitive-behavior modification*. New York: Plenum Press, 1977.

Meier, J. Prevalence and characteristics of learning disabilities found in second grade children. *Journal of Learning Disabilities*, 1971, *4*, 1-16.

Meisgeier, C. The Houston plan: A proactive integrated systems plan for education. In E. Deno (Ed.), *Instructional alternatives for exceptional children*. Reston, Va.: Council for Exceptional Children, 1973.

Meyan, E. L., & Deshler, D. D. The Kansas research institute in learning disabilities. *Learning Disability Quarterly*, 1978, *1*, 73-74.

Meyers, E., Ball, H., & Crutchfield, M. *The kindergarten teacher's hanndbook*. Los Angeles: Gramercy Press, 1973.

Model demonstration of specific learning disabilities child service. Conway, Arkansas: Educator's Consulting Services, 1974.

Moore, W., & Smith, W. Role of knowledge of results in programmed instruction. *Psychological Reports*, 1964, *14*, 407-423.

Morasky, R. A method for evaluating criterion measures. Paper presented at the meeting of the National Society for Programmed Instruction, Boston, 1967.

Morasky, R. *Discrimination programming as a behavioral control technique*. Unpublished doctoral dissertation, University of Michigan, 1968.

Morasky, R. Progress report: Phase I, program development in learning disabilities. Grant T 15 MH 12713-01CET. National Institute of Mental Health, 1971.

Morasky, R. *Learning experiences in educational psychology.* Dubuque, Iowa: William Brown, 1973.

Morgan, W. A case of congenital word-blindness. *British Medical Journal,* 1896, 2, 1378–1379.

Morse, W. Intervention techniques for the classroom teacher of the emotionally disturbed. In P. Knoblock (Ed.), *Educational programming for the emotionally disturbed children: The decade ahead.* Syracuse, N.Y.: Syracuse University Press, 1965.

Morse, W. The education of socially maladjusted and emotionally disturbed children. In W. Cruickshank & G. Johnson (Eds.), *Education of exceptional children and youth.* Englewood Cliffs, N.J.: Prentice-Hall, 1967.

Moss, J. Disabled or disadvantaged: There is a difference! *The Journal of Special Education,* 1973, 7 (Symposium No. 9), 387–391.

Murphy, H., & Durrell, D. Murphy-Durrell Reading Readiness Analysis. New York: Harcourt Brace Jovanovich, Inc., 1965.

Myers, P., & Hammill, D. *Methods for learning disorders.* New York: John Wiley, 1969.

Myers, P., & Hammill, D. *Methods for learning disorders* (2nd ed.). New York: John Wiley, 1976.

Myklebust, H. *The psychology of deafness: Sensory deprivation, learning and adjustment.* New York: Grune and Stratton, 1964.

Myklebust, H. *Development and disorders of written language.* New York: Grune and Stratton, 1965.

Myklebust, H. Learning disabilities in psychoneurologically disturbed children: Behavioral correlates of brain dysfunctions. In J. Zubin & G. Jervis, (Eds.), *Psychopathology of mental development.* New York: Grune and Stratton, 1967.

Myklebust, H. (Ed.). *Progress in learning disabilities* (Vol. 1). New York: Grune and Stratton, 1968.

Myklebust, H. *The Pupil Rating Scale: Screening for learning disabilities.* New York: Grune and Stratton, 1971.

Myklebust, H., & Boshes, B. *Minimal brain damage in children* (Final report, United States Public Health Service Contract 108-65-142, United States Department of Health, Education and Welfare). Evanston, Ill.: Northwestern University Publications, 1969.

Myklebust, H., & Johnson, D. Dyslexia in children. *Exceptional Children,* 1962, 29, 14–25.

National Advisory Committee on Handicapped Children. *Special Education for Handicapped Children. First Annual Report.* Washington, D.C.: United States Department of Health, Education and Welfare, 1968.

Nacman, M. A systems approach to the provision of social work services in health settings. *Social Work in Health Care,* 1975, 1, 133–143.

Neef, N. A., Iwata, B. A., & Page, T. Public transportation training: *In vivo versus* classroom instruction. *Journal of Applied Behavior Analysis,* 1978, 11, 331–344.

Neff, H. *The Cherokee project.* Albuquerque, N.M.: Bureau of Indian Affairs Field Support Services Office, 1974.

Newcomer, P., & Hammill, D. *Psycholinguistics in the schools.* Columbus, Ohio: Charles E. Merrill, 1976.

Newcomer, P., & Hammill, D. *The test of language development.* Austin, Texas: Pro-Ed, 1977.

Nichol, H. Children with learning disabilities referred to psychiatrists: A follow-up study. *Journal of Learning Disabilities,* 1974, 7, 118–122.

Nieves, R. Model demonstration program for learning disabled children in Puerto Rico. Hato Rey, Puerto Rico: Department of Education, Commonwealth of Puerto Rico, 1974.

Norfleet, M. The Bender Gestalt as a group screening instrument for first grade reading potential. *Journal of Learning Disabilities,* 1973, 6, 383–388.

Ogburn, K. Interaction with appropriate consequences. *Journal of Learning Disabilities,* 1974, 7, 204–206.

O'Grady, D. Psycholinguistic abilities in learning-disabled, emotionally disturbed, and normal children. *Journal of Special Education,* 1974, 8, 157–165.

Ogurzsoff, S., Pennock, M., Sykes, S., & Vogel-Sprott, M. Problem drinkers and treatment agencies in an urban community: A systems approach. *Canadian Journal of Public Health,* 1976, 67, 232–236.

Ong, B. The pediatrician's role in learning disabilities. In H. Myklebust (Ed.), *Progress in learning disabilities* (Vol. 1). New York: Grune and Stratton, 1968.

O'Neal, P., & Robins, L. Childhood patterns predictive of adult schizophrenia. *American Journal of Psychiatry*, 1958(a), *115*, 385-391.

O'Neal, P., & Robins, L. The relation of childhood behavior problems to adult psychiatric status. *American Journal of Psychiatry*, 1958(b), *114*, 961-969.

Orton, S. Specific reading disability, strephosymbolia. *Journal of the American Medical Association*, 1928, *90*, 1095-1099.

Orton, S. *Reading, writing, and speech problems in children.* New York: Norton, 1937.

Orton, S. A neurological explanation of the reading disability. *Education Record*, 1939, *20*, (Supplement 12), 58-68.

Osgood, C. *Method and theory in experimental psychology.* New York: Oxford University Press, 1953.

Osgood, C. Motivational dynamics of language behavior. In M. Jones (Ed.), *Nebraska symposium on motivation.* Lincoln, Nebraska: University of Nebraska Press, 1957.

Osgood, C., & Miron, M. (Eds.). *Approaches to the study of aphasia.* Urbana, Ill.: University of Illinois Press, 1963.

Page, T., Iwata, B. A., & Neef, N. A. Training pedestrian skills to retarded persons: Generalization from the classroom to the natural environment. *Journal of Applied Behavior Analysis*, 1976, *9*, 433-445.

Paine, R. Minimal brain dysfunction. *National project on learning disabilities.* (Public Health Publication No. 2015). Washington, D.C.: Government Printing Office, 1969.

Pannbacker, M. A speech pathologist looks at learning disabilities. *Journal of Learning Disabilities*, 1968, *1*, 403-409.

Pate, J., & Webb, W. *First grade screening test.* Circle Pines, Minn.: American Guidance Service, 1966.

Pearlman, E., & Pearlman, R. The effect of remedial-reading training in a private clinic. *Academic Therapy*, 1970, *5*, 298-304.

Piaget, J. *[The origins of intelligence in children]* (M. Cook, trans.). New York: International Universities Press, 1952.

Pitcher-Baker, G. Does perceptual training improve reading? *Academic Therapy*, 1973, *9*, 41-45.

Popham, W., & Baker, E. *Establishing instructional goals.* Englewood Cliffs, N.J.: Prentice-Hall, 1970.

Powers, H. Dietary measures to improve behavior and achievement. *Academic therapy*, 1973, *3*, 203-214.

Project Re-Ed. *A demonstration project for teachers of emotionally handicapped children.* Nashville, Tenn.: Department of Mental Health, 1963.

Quay, H. Dimensions of problem behavior and educational programming. In P. Graubard (Ed.), *Children against schools.* Chicago: Follett, 1969.

Rabinovitch, R. Reading and learning disabilities. In S. Arieti (Ed.), *American Handbook of Psychiatry.* New York: Basic Books, 1959.

Rappoport, S. Personality factors teachers need for relationship structure. In W. Cruickshank (Ed.), *The teacher of brain-injured children: A discussion of the bases for competency.* Syracuse, N.Y.: Syracuse University Press, 1966.

Raskin, L., & Taylor, W. Problem identification through observation. *Academic Therapy*, 1973, *9*, 85-89.

Redelheim, P. Learning-disabled or culturally disadvantaged: A separate piece? *The Journal of Special Education*, 1973, *7* (Symposium No. 9) 399-407.

Redl, F., & Wineman, D. *The aggressive child.* Chicago: Free Press, 1957.

Resnick, L. Programmed instruction and the teaching of complex intellectual skills: Problems and prospects. *Harvard Educational Review*, 1963, *33*(4), 72-104.

Resnick, L., Wang, M., & Kaplan, J. Task analysis in curriculum design: A hierarchically sequenced introductory mathematics curriculum. *Journal of Applied Behavior Analysis*, 1973, *6*(4), 679-710.

Reynolds, M., & Balow, B. Categories and variables in special education. *Exceptional Children*, 1972, *38*, 357–366.

Reynolds, M., & Birch, J. *Teaching exceptional children in all America's schools*. Reston, Va.: Council for Exceptional Children, 1977.

Rhodes, W. The disturbing child: A problem of ecological management. *Exceptional Children*, 1967, *33*, 449–455.

Rhodes, W. A community participation analysis of emotional disturbance. *Exceptional Children*, 1970, *36*, 309–316.

Richardson, S., Hastorf, A., & Dornbusch, S. Effects of physical disability on a child's description of himself. *Child Development*, 1964, *35*, 893–907.

Riegel, R., Taylor, A., & Danner, F. Teaching potentially educationally handicapped children to classify and remember. *Exceptional Children*, 1973, *40*(3), 208–209.

Roach, E., & Kephart, N. *The Purdue perceptual-motor survey*. Columbus, Ohio: Charles E. Merrill, 1966.

Robbins, M. A study of the validity of Delacato's theory of neurological organization. *Exceptional Children*, 1966, *32*, 517–523.

Roberts, H. A clinical and metabolic reevaluation of reading disability. In *Selected Papers on Learning Disabilities, Fifth Annual Convention, Association for Children With Learning Disabilities*. San Rafael, Calif.: Academic Therapy Publications, 1969.

Rood, M. The use of sensory receptors to activate, facilitate, and inhibit motor response, autonomic and somatic, in developmental sequence. In C. Sattley (Ed.), *Approaches to the treatment of patients with neuro-muscular dysfunction*. Dubuque, Iowa: Brown, 1962.

Rose, C., & Helper, J. *Child services demonstration center evaluation: Summary report*. Denver, Colo.: Colorado Department of Education, 1974.

Rosenberg, S. (Ed.). *Directions in psycholinguistics*. New York: Macmillan, 1965.

Rosner, S. Ophthalmology, optometry, and learning difficulties. *Journal of Learning Disabilities*, 1968, *1*, 451–455.

Ross, A. *Psychological disorders of children*. New York: McGraw-Hill, 1974.

Ross, A. *Learning disabilities: The unrealized potential*. New York: McGraw-Hill, 1976.

Roth, J. An intervention strategy for children with developmental problems. *Journal of School Psychology*, 1970, *8*, 311–314.

Royal, M. Performance objectives and C-R tests— We wrote our own. *The Reading Teacher*, 1974, *27*, 701–703.

Rude, R. Readiness tests: Implications for early childhood education. *The Reading Teacher*, 1973, *26*, 572–580.

Sabatino, D. Resource rooms: The renaissance in special education. *Journal of Special Education*, 1971, *6* (Symposium No. 8) 335–347.

Sartain, H. Instruction of disabled learners: A reading perspective. *Journal of Learning Disabilities*, 1976, *9*, 489–497.

Schramm, W. Programmed instruction today and tomorrow. In W. Schramm (Ed.), *Four case studies of programmed instruction*. New York: Fund for the Advancement of Education, 1964.

Schulman, J., Kaspar, J., & Throne, F. *Brain damage and behavior: A clincial experimental study*. Springfield, Ill.: Charles C. Thomas, 1965.

Schwartz, L., & Oseroff, A. Clinical teacher model for interrelated areas of special education. In P. Mann (Ed.), *Mainstream special education*. Reston, Va.: Council for Exceptional Children, 1974.

Shafto, F., & Sulzbacher, S. Comparing treatment tactics with a hyperactive pre-school child: Stimulant medication and programmed teacher intervention. *Journal of Applied Behavior Analysis*, 1977, *10*, 13–20.

Shedd, C. Some characteristics of a specific perceptual-motor disability-dyslexia. *Journal of the Medical Association of Alabama*, 1967, *37*, 150–162.

Shepherd, M., Oppenheim, A., & Mitchell, S. Childhood behavior disorders and the child guidance clinic. *Journal of Psychology and Psychiatry*, 1966, *7*, 39–52.

Sherrick, C., Swets, J., & Elliott, L. (Eds.). *Psychology and the handicapped child.* Washington, D.C.: United States Department of Health, Education and Welfare, 1974.

Sherrington, C. *The integrative action of the nervous system.* New Haven: Yale University Press, 1948.

Siegel, E. Learning disabilities: Substance or shadow. *Exceptional Children,* 1968, *34,* 433–437.

Skinner, B. *Science and human behavior.* New York: Macmillan, 1953.

Skinner, B. The science of learning and the art of teaching. *Science,* 1958, *128,* 969–977.

Skinner, B. Teaching machines. *Scientific American,* 1961, *205*(36), 90–102.

Skinner, B. *The technology of teaching.* New York: Appleton-Century-Crofts, 1968.

Slingerland, B. *Screening tests for identifying children with specific language disabilities.* Cambridge, Mass.: Educators Publishing Service, 1964.

Sloan, W. *Lincoln-Oseretsky motor development scale.* Los Angeles: Western Psychological Services, 1954.

Smith, J., & Smith, D. *Child management: A program for parents.* Ann Arbor, Mich.: Ann Arbor Publishers, 1966.

Smith, P., & Marx, R. Some cautions on the use of the Frostig test: A factor analytic study. *Journal of Learning Disabilities,* 1972, *5,* 357–362.

Smith, R. (Ed.). *Teacher diagnosis of educational difficulties.* Columbus, Ohio: Charles E. Merrill, 1969.

Smith, R., & Neisworth, J. Fundamentals of informal educational assessment. In R. Smith (Ed.), *Teacher diagnosis of educational difficulties.* Columbus, Ohio: Charles E. Merrill, 1969.

Solomons, G. Guidelines on the use and medical effects of psychostimulant drugs in therapy. *Journal of Learning Disabilities,* 1971, *4,* 471–475.

Spache, G. *Diagnostic reading scales.* Montery, Calif.: California Test Bureau, 1972.

Spalding, R., & Spalding, W. *The writing road to reading.* New York: Morrow, 1957.

Spinks, S. A resource approach to learning disabilities. Hattiesburg, Miss.: Hattiesburg Public Schools, 1974.

Stevens, G., & Birch, J. A proposal for clarification of the terminology used to describe brain-injured children. *Exceptional Children,* 1957, *23,* 346–349.

Stewart, M. Use of drugs to help children with learning problems. In J. Hartstein (Ed.), *Current concepts in dyslexia.* St. Louis: C. V. Mosby, 1971.

Stick, S. The speech pathologist and handicapped learners. *Journal of Learning Disabilities,* 1976, *9,* 520–526.

Stolurow, L. A systems approach to instruction. In D. Merrill (Ed.), *Instructional design.* Englewood Cliffs, N.J.: Prentice-Hall, 1971.

Strang, R. *Reading, diagnosis and remediation.* Newark, Del.: International Reading Association, 1968.

Strauss, A., & Kephart, N. *Psychopathology and education of the brain-injured child* (Vol. 2). New York: Grune and Stratton, 1955.

Strauss, A., & Lehtinen, L. *Psychopathology and education of the brain-injured child.* New York: Grune and Stratton, 1947.

Strauss, A., & Werner, H. Disorders of conceptual thinking in the brain-injured child. *Journal of Nervous and Mental Disease,* 1942, *96,* 153–172.

Swift, M., & Spivack, G. Therapeutic teaching: A review of teaching methods for behaviorally troubled children. *Journal of Special Education,* 1974, *8,* 259–289.

Szasz, T. The myth of mental illness. *American Psychologist,* 1960, *15,* 113–118.

Tarnopol, L. *Learning disorders in children.* Boston: Little, Brown, 1971.

Tarver, S., Hallahan, D., Cohen, S., & Kauffman, J. The development of visual selective attention and verbal rehearsal in learning disabled boys. *Journal of Learning Disabilities,* 1977, *10,* 491–500.

Tarver, S., Hallahan, D., Kauffman, J., & Ball, D. Verbal rehearsal and selective attention in children with learning disabilities: A developmental lag. *Journal of Experimental Child Psychology,* 1976, *22,* 375–385.

Taylor, F., Artuso, A., Soloway, M., Hewett, F., Quay, H., & Stillwell, R. A learning center plan for special education. *Focus on Exceptional Children,* 1972, *4,* 1-7.

Telford, C., & Sawrey, J. *The exceptional individual: Psychological and educational aspects.* Englewood Cliffs, N.J.: Prentice-Hall, 1972.

Terrance, H. Discrimination learning with and without errors. Unpublished doctoral dissertation, Harvard University, 1960.

Thiagarajan, S. *The programming process.* Worthington, Ohio: Charles Jones Publishing Co., 1971.

Throne, J. Learning disabilities: A radical behaviorist point of view. *Journal of Learning Disabilities,* 1973, *6,* 543-546.

Thurstone, L. A factorial study of perception. *Psychometric Monographs,* 1944, No. 4.

Topaz, P. Publisher's message. *Journal of Learning Disabilities,* 1973, *6,* 128-129.

Torgeson, J. K. The role of nonspecific factors in the task performance of learning disabled children: A theoretical assessment. *Journal of Learning Disabilities,* 1977, *10,* 27-34.

Touzel, S. Secondary L.D. curricula—A propsed framework. *Learning Disability Quarterly,* 1978, *1,* 53-61.

Trembley, P. The changing concept of intelligence and its effect on special class organization. *Journal of Learning Disabilities,* 1969, *2,* 520-523.

Ullman, C. Measures of learning disability for different purposes. *Journal of Learning Disabilities,* 1971, *4,* 186-192.

Underwood, B. Studies of disturbed practice: VIII. Learning and retention of paired nonsense syllables as a function of intra-list similarity. *Journal of Experimental Psychology,* 1953, *45,* 133-142.

U.S. Department of Health, Education and Welfare, Public Health Services. Behavior patterns of children in school. In *Vital Health Statistics,* 1972, *11,* 1-78.

Valett, R. *A psychoeducational profile of basic learning abilities.* Palo Alto, Calif.: Consulting Psychologists Press, 1966(a).

Valett, R. *The Valett developmental survey of basic learning abilities.* Palo Alto, Calif.: Consulting Psychologists Press, 1966(b).

Valett, R. *The remediation of learning disabilities.* Belmont, Calif.: Fearon, 1967.

Vallett, R. *A psychoeducational inventory of basic learning abilities.* Belmont, Calif.: Fearon, 1968.

Valett, R. *Modifying children's behavior.* Belmont, Calif.: Fearon, 1969(a).

Valett, R. *Programming learning disabilities.* Belmont, Calif.: Fearon, 1969(b).

Valk, J. Neuroradiology and learning disabilities. In M. Krasnoff (Ed.), *Learning disabilities: The decade ahead.* Ann Arbor, Mich.: Institute for the Study of Mental Retardation and Related Disabilities, 1974.

Vane, J. *Vane kindergarten test.* Brandon, Vt.: Clinical Psychology Publishing Co., Inc., 1968.

Van Etten, G., & Adamson, G. The Fail-Save Program: A special education service continuum. In E. Deno (Ed.), *Instructional alternatives for exceptional children.* Reston, Va.: Council for Exceptional Children, 1973.

Vargas, J. *Writing worthwhile behavioral objectives.* New York: Harper and Row, 1972.

Vaughn, J., & Duncan, R. Individually guided education: A temporary systems approach to change. *Viewpoints,* 1974, *50,* 39-59.

Vuckovich, M. Pediatric neurology and learning disabilities. In H. Mykelbust (Ed.), *Progress in learning disabilities* (Vol 1). New York: Grune and Stratton, 1968.

Walker, S. Drugging the American child: We're too cavalier about hyperactivity. *Psychology Today,* 1974, 43-48.

Waugh, K., & Bush, W. *Diagnosing learning disorders.* Columbus, Ohio: Charles E. Merrill, 1971.

Waugh, R. On reporting the findings of a diagnostic center. *Journal of Learning Disabilities,* 1970, *3,* 629-634.

Wedell, K. Variations in perceptual ability among types of cerebral palsy. *Cerebral Palsy Bulletin,* 1960, *2,* 149-157.

Wedell, K. Diagnosing learning difficulties: A sequential strategy. *Journal of Learning Disabilities,* 1970, *3,* 311-317.

Wedell, K. Perceptuo-motor disabilities and research. In M. Krasnoff (Ed.), *Learning disabilities: The decade ahead.* Ann Arbor, Mich.: Institute for the Study of Mental Retardation and Related Disabilities, 1974.

Weinstein, L. Project re-ed schools for emotionally disturbed children: Effectiveness as viewed by referring agencies, parents, and teachers. *Exceptional Children,* 1969, *35,* 703-711.

Weintraub, F., Abeson, A., & Braddock, A. State law and education of handicapped children: Issues and recommendations. Reston, Va.: Council for Exceptional Children, 1975.

Weiss, H., & Weiss, M. *A survival manual: Case studies and suggestions for the learning disabled teenager.* Yorktown Heights, N.Y.: Center for Educational Services, 1974.

Wepman, J. *Auditory discrimination test.* Chicago: Language Research Associates, Inc., 1958.

Wepman, J. Auditory discrimination, speech, and reading. *Elementary School Journal,* 1960, *60,* 325-333.

Wepman, J., Jones, L., Bock, R., & Van Pelt, D. Studies in aphasia: Background and theoretical formulations. *Journal of Speech and Hearing Disorders,* 1960, *25,* 323-332.

Whitcraft, C. Approaching cooperative research in learning disabilities through psycholinguistics. *Journal of Learning Disabilities,* 1971, *4,* 568-571.

Whitcraft, C., & Allen, J. *A research and training program in selected aspects of lexical and syntactical development in the mentally retarded* (Final report, Project No. 532163, Grant No. DEG-0-9-532163[032]). Washington, D.C.: U.S. Office of Education, Bureau of Research, 1972.

Wiederholt, J. ACLD professional advisory board recommendations: A report and analysis. *Journal of Learning Disabilities,* 1974(a), *7,* 450-452.

Wiederholt, J. Historical perpectives on the education of the learning disabled. In L. Mann & D. Sabatino (Eds.), *The second review of special education.*

Philadelphia: Journal of Special Education Press, 1974(b).

Wiederholt, J. L. Educating the learning disabled adolescent: Some assumptions. *Learning Disability Quarterly,* 1978, *1,* 11-23.

Wiederholt, J. L., Hammill, D. D., & Brown, H. *The resource teacher: A guide to effective practices.* Boston: Allyn and Bacon, 1978.

Willower, D. Special education: Organization and administration. *Exceptional Children,* 1970, *36,* 591-594.

Wilson, J., & Robeck, M. *Kindergarten evaluation of learning potential.* New York: McGraw-Hill, 1963.

Wilson, M. Prevention of learning disabilities. *The school psychologist—Newsletter, Division 16, American Psychological Association,* 1968, *22,* 89-92.

Winett, R., & Winkler, R. Current behavior modification in the classroom: Be still, be quiet, be docile. *Journal of Applied Behavior Analysis,* 1972, *5,* 499-504.

Wiseman, D. A classroom procedure for identifying and remediating language problems. *Mental Retardation,* 1965, *3,* 20-24.

Wiseman, D. Remedial education: Global or learning-disability approach. *Academic Therapy,* 1970, *5,* 165-175.

Witkin, H. *Psychological differentiation.* New York: John Wiley, 1962.

Wold, R. (Ed.). *Visual and perceptual aspects for the achieving and underachieving child.* Seattle: Special Child Publications, 1969.

Wolfensberger, W. *Normalization.* Toronto: National Institute on Mental Retardation, 1972.

Wright, L. Conduct problems or learning disability? *Journal of Special Education,* 1974, *8,* 331-336.

Yates, J. Model for preparing regular classroom teachers for mainstreaming. *Exceptional Children,* 1973, *39,* 471-472.

Ysseldyke, J., Shinn, M., & Thurlow, M. The University of Minnesota Institute for research in learning disabilities. *Learning Disability Quarterly,* 1978, *1,* 75-76.

Author Index

A

Abeson, A., 49
Ackerman, P., 264
Alexander, J., 143
Allen, J., 65
Allen, K., 257
Allen, L., 185
Allouche, B., 351
Amatruda, C., 10
Ames, L., 76
Ammerman, H., 327
Anderson, R., 340
Apell, R., 76
Arena, J., 63
Ashlock, P., 119, 214
Atkinson, B., 345
Ayllon, T., 253, 255, 257
Ayres, A., 89, 135, 136
Ayres, J., 136
Azrin, J., 253, 255

B

Bailey, E., 46
Baker, E., 326
Baker, H., 179
Baldwin, A., 245, 247
Baldwin, C., 245, 247
Ball, H., 21, 179
Baller, W., 85
Balow, B., 221
Bannatyne, A., 62
Barsch, R., 89, 110, 142
Bartel, N., 16, 63, 83, 137
Barton, C., 143
Bassler, J., 56
Bateman, B., 4, 5, 17, 21,
    26–27, 37, 60, 65
Beach, D., 21
Becker, J., 179
Beery, K., 226
Bice, H., 117

Bijou, S., 151
Birch, H., 11, 77, 106
Birch, J., 10, 227–228, 281
Bivens, L., 351
Black, F., 34
Blanco, R., 119, 214
Bliesmer, E., 174
Bloom, B., 122, 326
Bock, R., 95, 111
Boehm, A., 179
Bonham, S., 237
Borschbaum, M., 48
Boshes, B., 18, 129
Braddock, D., 49
Braud, L., 52
Braud, W., 52
Bray, N., 68
Brenner, A., 177
Brethower, D., 145, 321, 322,
    337, 353
Brien, R., 296

Briggs, L., 340
Brown, V., 48, 137, 181
Browne, D., 238
Bruininks, R., 223, 228
Bryan, T., 45, 172, 180, 260
Bryant, N., 45
Bryen, D., 253, 256
Buckley, R., 35
Buktenica, N., 179
Buros, O., 177
Bush, W., 63, 128, 190, 214
Buttars, K., 291

C

Caldwell, B., 180
Carpenter, R., 70, 72
Carr, M., 335
Cartwright, G., 51
Case, P., 143
Case, R., 87
Cecirelli, V., 321, 342
Chalfant, J., 11, 56
Charles, D., 85
Chinsky, J., 21
Clements, S., 4, 11, 56, 264
Clemmens, R., 67
Cohen, H., 106
Cohen, N., 263
Cohen, S., 21
Cohn, R., 69
Comly, H., 71, 72
Connolly, A., 199
Corey, S., 145, 295
Cott, A., 71
Coursey, R., 48
Coy, M., 179
Cratty, B., 34, 41, 110
Cravioto, J., 35
Cruickshank, W., 33, 77, 107,
       117, 121, 281; (1961)
       99, 119; (1972) 36, 42;
       (1973) 11, 13, 35, 40,

Cruickshank, W. (*Continued*)
       65, 71, 77, 185; (1974)
       37, 42, 53
Crutchfield, M., 179
Cutler, C., 321, 342
Cutts, N., 189
Czerniejewski, C., 235

D

Davids, A., 72
Davis, F., 257
Davis, J., 67
Delacato, C., 89, 104–106
De La Cruz, F., 66
Denckla, M., 42, 57, 69, 70
Deshler, D., 45
Deutsch, C., 35, 37, 52
Doll, E., 11, 170, 181
Doman, G., 104–106
Doman, R., 104–106
Dornbusch, S., 249
Dornseif, A., 335
Douglas, V., 263, 264
Duncan, R., 146
Dunn, L., 180, 221–224, 228
Dunsing, J., 41, 108
Durkin, D., 205
Durrell, D., 199
Dykman, R., 264

E

Eash, M., 45
Eaves, R., 143
Edgington, R., 223
Ellingstad, V., 146
Emerson, M., 257
Estes, R., 68
Evans, J., 302
Everett, R., 257

F

Faust, G., 340
Feder, B., 185
Fernald, G., 9, 135–137
Flavell, J., 21
Fleck, S., 143
Ford, M., 37
Fox, R., 257
Frankel, H., 60, 65
Freeman, R., 70, 106
Freidus, E., 119, 120
Fristoe, M., 181, 199
Frostig, M., 33, 34, 40, 89, 95,
       116–119, 139, 179
Fry, E., 342
Fygetakis, L., 127

G

Gaddes, W., 69
Gagne, R., 321, 343, 344
Gallagher, J., 21, 223
Gallegos, R., 148, 291, 315
Gardner, E., 181
Gardner, W., 77, 243, 248,
       253
Garton, K., 257
Gearheart, B., 5, 21, 22, 32,
       82, 107, 122
Gesell, A., 10, 68, 86, 262
Getman, G., 74, 89, 110,
       139–142
Gibson, E., 344
Gickling, E., 227
Giffin, M., 76
Gilbert, T., 145, 302
Giles, M., 63, 128, 214
Gillingham, A., 134–135
Glaser, R., 195, 310, 314, 317,
       321, 322
Goldbeck, R., 340

Goldman, R., 181, 199
Goldsmith, L., 257
Goldstein, K., 9
Goldstein, L., 144
Goodman, L., 46, 180
Gotkin, L., 144
Grant, M., 119, 214
Graubard, P. 251, 257
Gray, B., 125, 127
Graybeal, N., 21
Greiner, C., 291
Gronlund, N., 326
Grosenick, J., 224
Gross, S., 335
Guilford, 82
Gussow, J., 77

H

Hafner, D., 224
Hainsworth, P., 180
Halgren, M., 74, 139, 142
Hall, C., 83
Hall, K., 51
Hall, R., 257
Hallahan, D., 21, 45; (1973)
    11, 13, 35, 40, 65, 71,
    77, 185
Hammill, D., 16, 34-36, 48,
    51, 180, 181, 226;
    (1969) 4, 27, 103, 116,
    169; (1976) 5, 27, 35,
    82; (1978) 48, 63, 83,
    137
Hammock, J., 314
Haring, N., 4, 237
Harris, A., 136, 174
Hartman, A., 127, 128
Hasazi, J., 257
Hasazi, S., 257
Hastorf, A., 249
Hawley, C., 35

Hebb, D., 108, 116
Hegge, T., 134
Heimstra, N., 146
Hendershot, C., 145
Hess, R., 77
Hewett, F., 99, 262, 263
High, C., 174
Hinshelwood, J., 74
Hirshoren, A., 321, 342
Hively, W., 343, 345
Hobbs, N., 37, 259
Holland, L., 68
Hopkins, B., 257
Horn, R., 355
Horne, D., 116-119
Hughes, J., 69
Huizinga, R., 68

I

Ilg, F., 68, 76, 262
Iwata, B., 296

J

Jacobson, M., 174
Jacquot, W., 185
Jenkins, J., 233
Johnson, D., 33, 42; (1967) 4,
    5, 22, 26, 31, 86,
    129-134, 174
Johnson, S., 11, 31, 48, 137,
    289
Jones, L., 95, 111

K

Kaluger, G., 62
Kandel, H., 257

Kane, E., 74, 89, 110, 139, 142
Kaplan, J., 291
Karlsen, B., 181
Karnes, M., 63
Kaspar, J., 260
Kass, C., 6, 14, 21
Kauffman, J., 21
Keele, D., 68
Keele, M., 68
Keogh, B., 35, 46
Kephart, N., 29, 34, 89, 95,
    107-111, 139, 180
Kirk, S., 11-12, 15-16, 21, 56,
    134, 229; (1968) 21, 24,
    30, 31, 64, 95, 111-116,
    179; (1971) 111, 114,
    130; (1972) 5, 15, 35,
    83, 90, 251, 253
Kirk, W., 128, 130, 134;
    (1968) 21, 24, 30, 31,
    64, 95, 111-116, 179
Klaus, D., 314, 317, 321, 322
Knight, S., 151
Kolson, C., 62
Koppitz, E., 178, 179
Kornetsky, C., 41
Krasnoff, M., 33
Krathwohl, D., 122
Kratoville, B., 48
Kroth, R., 283

L

Laguna, S., 296
Lahey, B., 257
Landreth, G., 185
Larsen, S., 35, 39, 40, 45, 51,
    181
LaVeck, G., 66
Layman, D., 257
Lefever, D., 95, 116, 179
Lehtinen, L., 10, 117

Leland, B., 179
Lerner, J., 18, 35, 55, 83, 146, 229
Lindzey, G., 83
Linn, S., 174
Lipton, M., 48
Llorens, L., 293
Long, N., 252
Lovitt, T., 263
Lowell, R., 174
Lublin, S., 351
Lumsdaine, A., 353
Lupin, M., 52
Lynch, K., 117

M

Mackie, R., 18
Madden, R., 181
Mager, R., 326
Mann, L., 46
Mann, P., 43, 53, 63, 119, 137, 174, 214
Markle, D., 145, 321
Markle, S., 149, 291, 337, 340, 342
Marx, R., 179
Masia, B., 122
Maslow, P., 89, 116
Mayholl, W., 233
McCarthy, J., 242; (1968) 21, 24, 30, 31, 64, 95, 111, 179
McClung, R., 43, 53, 137
McGrady, H., 57, 63, 64, 180
McIntosh, D., 221
McKee, G., 74, 139, 142
McLaughlin, P., 143
Mechner, F., 296
Meichenbaum, D., 21
Meier, J., 20, 170
Melching, W., 327

Meyan, E., 45
Meyers, E., 179
Miller, D., 237
Miller, E., 85
Miron, M., 111
Mitchell, S., 242, 245, 247
Mitzel, H., 51
Montessori, M., 116
Moore, W., 351
Morasky, R., 289, 317, 343, 353; (1971) 147, 289, 314, 353; (1973) 99, 119, 120, 147
Morgan, W., 9
Morse, W., 251, 252
Moss, J., 35
Murphy, D., 48
Myers, P., 4, 5, 27, 35, 82, 103, 116, 169
Myklebust, H., 4-6, 18, 22-23, 26, 31, 64, 76, 86; (1967) 129-134, 174, 180

N

Nachtman, W., 199
Nacman, M., 143
Neef, N., 296
Neff, H., 238
Neisworth, J., 32, 169
Newcomer, P., 34, 48, 181
Newman, R., 252
Nieves, R., 238
Norfleet, M., 179

O

Ogburn, K., 255-256
Ogurzsoff, S., 143

O'Neal, P., 250
Ong, B., 57, 66
Oppenheim, A., 242, 245, 247
Orton, S., 9, 11, 74, 134, 135
Oseroff, A., 51
Osgood, C., 82, 111, 113
Owen, M., 257

P

Page, T., 296
Paine, R., 56
Pannbacker, M., 63
Paraskevopoulos, J., 242
Parsons, B., 143
Pate, J., 179
Pearlman, E., 235
Pearlman, R., 235
Pennock, M., 143
Peters, J., 264
Phelan, J., 148, 291, 315
Piaget, J., 86, 108, 116
Pitcher-Baker, G., 35
Plumeau, F., 289
Popham, W., 326
Porcia, E., 257
Powers, H., 35
Pritchett, E., 199

Q

Quay, H., 242

R

Rabinovitch, R., 56
Raskin, L., 172

Redelheim, P., 35
Redl, F., 264
Resnick, L., 291, 344, 345
Reynolds, M., 221, 281
Rhodes, W., 258
Richardson, S., 249
Roach, E., 95, 110, 180
Roberts, H., 71
Robins, L., 250
Rood, M., 136
Rosenberg, S., 65
Rosner, S., 74, 189
Ross, A., 21, 77, 87, 260
Roth, J., 263
Rouse, S., 335
Royal, M., 174
Rude, R., 174
Rummler, G., 145, 321
Ryan, B., 125
Rynders, J., 223, 228

S

Sabatino, D., 179, 226
Sartain, H., 39
Scheffelin, M., 11, 59
Schiavo, R., 143
Schrader, A., 145, 321
Schramm, W., 144
Schulman, J., 260
Schutte, R., 257
Schwartz, L., 51
Sells, C., 70, 72
Seunath, O., 345
Shafto, F., 257
Shedd, C., 172
Shepherd, M., 242, 245, 247
Sherrington, C., 108
Shinn, M., 45
Siegel, E., 36
Siqueland, M., 180

Skinner, B., 82, 116, 144, 253, 337
Slingerland, B., 180
Sloan, W., 180
Smith, D., 77, 321, 344
Smith, J., 344
Smith, P., 179
Smith, R., 32, 165, 169, 174
Smith, W., 351
Solomons, G., 72
Spache, G., 180
Spitz, E., 106
Spivack, G., 260, 261
Stevens, G., 10
Stewart, M., 71
Stick, S., 39
Stillman, B., 134-135
Stolurow, L., 146
Strang, R., 82
Strauss, A., 9, 10, 108, 117
Suiter, P., 63, 119, 137, 174, 214
Sulzbacher, S., 257
Swift, M., 260, 261
Sykes, S., 143
Szasz, T., 253

T

Taft, L., 106
Tarver, S., 21
Taylor, F., 226, 231, 235
Taylor, W., 172
Terrance, H., 345
Theobald, J., 227
Thiagarajan, S., 145, 353
Thompson, H., 68
Throne, F., 260
Thurlow, M., 45
Thurstone, L., 117
Tiemann, P., 145

Tillotson, K., 235
Topaz, P., 34
Torgeson, J., 21, 87
Touzel, S., 274
Trembley, P., 174
Turner, K., 257

U

Ullman, C., 185, 196
Underwood, B., 344

V

Valett, R., 5, 19-20, 121-122, 178, 181, 257; (1969) 19-21, 28, 119, 121-122, 230, 250, 257
Vane, J., 181
Van Pelt, D., 95, 111
Vargas, J., 326
Vaughn, J., 146
Vogel-Sprott, M., 143
Vuckovich, M., 67, 76

W

Walker, C., 41
Wallen, N., 117
Wang, M., 291
Watson, J., 253
Waugh, K., 190
Waugh, R., 186
Webb, W., 179
Wedell, K., 41, 42, 117

Weinstein, L., 257
Weintraub, F., 49
Wender, E., 48
Wepman, J., 24, 64, 82, 95,
  111, 181
Werner, H., 9, 10, 117
Wheeler, R., 172
Whitcraft, C., 57, 64, 65
Whittlesey, J., 95, 116, 179
Wiederholt, J., 35, 48, 180,

Wiederholt, J. (*Continued*)
  181, 226, 274; (1974)
  35, 36, 43, 52, 102
Willard, D., 257
Willower, D., 220
Wineman, D., 264
Wiseman, D., 128, 226
Witkin, H., 41
Woodcock, R., 181, 199
Wright, L., 242, 250

Y

Yates, J., 227
Ysseldyke, J., 45

Z

Zucman, E., 106

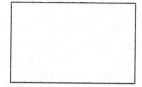

Subject Index

A

Aphasia, 27
Arithmetic problems, behavioral approach to, 137-139
Association for Children with Learning Disabilities, 12, 36, 47, 62, 177, 282
Aversion behavior, 166-168

B

Batteries, test, 176-181
  in reading, 174-176
Behavior:
  analysis, 208
  aversion, 166-168
  bits, 198-199, 209
  checklists, 169-176

Behavior (*Continued*)
  criterion performance, 208
  modification, 253-257
  necessary entering, 295-296
  problems (*see* Problem behaviors)
  repertoire, 208
  sequences, analysis of (*see* Flowchart task analysis)
  swings, 167
Behavioral approach (*see* Systems approach)
Behavioral deficit approach (*see* Educational-strategy approach)
Behavioral engineering, 98-100
Behavioral objectives (*see* Objectives, behavioral)
Brain (*see also* Central nervous system; Neurology):

Brain (*Continued*)
  dysfunction, 130
  injury, 10, 130
    minimal, 26, 68, 69, 76
  lateral dominance of, 9, 11
Bureau of Education of the Handicapped, 57, 61

C

Central nervous system (*see also* Brain; Neurology):
  levels of function of, 93
  role of, in learning disabilities, 5, 8, 26, 48, 89
Children with Specific Learning Disabilities Act of 1969, 37
Classroom:
  model layout of, 230-231
  typical, description of, 32

Clinics, private, 235
Communication (*see also* In-
    formation gathering):
    behavior, channels of,
        114-116 (*see also* Lan-
        guage-communication
        behavior)
    interdisciplinary, 185-191
    problems in, 188-199
Community programs, in
    learning disabilities,
    235
Computer programs, in learn-
    ing disabilities, 51-52
Council for Exceptional chil-
    dren, 49-50, 62, 282
Counseling, 268-274
    the family, 274-283
    the learning disabled,
        268-274
    the teacher, 283-287
Counselors, roles of, 280-281
Crisis intervention approach,
    263-266, 279-280
Criterion measures, 314-325,
    334, 361 (*see also* Sub-
    criterion measures)
    and behavioral objectives,
        327-335
    in illustrative case study,
        369-370
    multiple choice, 320-321
    preparation of, 148-149
    production-type, 320-321
    real-life, 317-320
    revision of, 361-362
    rule statement, 318-319
    simulated, 317-318
    written, 318
Cross-validation, 187
Culture, effect of, on problem
    behaviors, 258-259
Curriculum and facility plan-
    ning, 52-53

D

Decision-making plan, 98-99
Development stages orienta-
    tion, 84-87, 102-111,
    129-134, 261-263
DIAL, 177
Discrimination task analysis,
    302-313
Disparity principle, 5, 19,
    21-24
"Drawing triangles" program,
    347-350
DTVP, 116-119, 179
*Durrell Analysis of Reading Dif-
    ficulty*, 199, 209, 212
Dyslexia, 27, 62

E

Education field, 60
Educational-strategy ap-
    proach, 250-253
Environment, effect of on
    problem behaviors,
    258-259
Evaluation:
    judgments, 195-197
    neurological, 68-69
Expectancy age (EA), 23

F

Flowchart task analysis,
    296-302, 312-313
Frostig Center for Educational
    Therapy, 117
Frostig-Horne training pro-
    gram, 118-119

G

Generalization task analysis,
    310-313

H

Hyperkinesis, assessment of,
    73-74

I

Identification grid, 159, 160
Indices, behavioral, 170-171
Information gathering,
    185-188 (*see also* Com-
    munication)
    evaluative, 195-197
    frame of reference in,
        193-195
    relevancy and usefulness
        of, 191-199
    subdivisions of, 198-199
    syntax-cleaning in, 191-193
Instructional design, behav-
    ioral engineering ap-
    proach to, 98-100
Instructional programs:
    implementation of (*see*
        Testing)
    revision of, 353-354,
        358-361
Instructional sequences,
    336-337, 351-352
    checklist for, 346-347, 374
    in illustrative case study,
        372-374
    preparation of, 150

Instructional sequences
(*Continued*)
  principles for, 337–346
  responses to (*see* Responses
      to instructional se-
      quences)
Instruments, testing, 161–162,
      166–168, 176–181
Integration behaviors,
      130–131
Interpersonal relationships,
      189–190
Intervention strategy, 263–266
ITPA, 95, 96, 111–116,
      128–130, 179, 209, 210

J

Junior high programs, in
      learning disabilities,
      236–237

K

Key-Math, 199, 209, 211
Knowledge-of-results,
      350–351

L

Language, 63–65
  behavior, levels of organi-
      zation of, 113–114
  disability (*see* Learning dis-
      abilities, psycholinguis-
      tic)
  problems, 125–134
    developmental approach
        to, 129–134
  training programs, 127–134

Language-communication be-
      havior, model for,
      111–116
Learning, 336 (*see also* Instruc-
      tional sequences)
  levels of, 131
Learning centers:
  community and private,
      235–236
  cooperative, 234–235
  early, 236
  resource, 233–235
Learning disabilities (*see also*
      Problem behaviors):
  age range in, 46–47
  assessment approach to,
      and model, 94–97,
      116–119
  aversion behavior in,
      166–168
  basic process approach to,
      and model, 87–90,
      102–103, 107–111,
      139–142
  behavioral classifications of,
      16–17, 26–32, 131
  categories, objections to,
      16, 47 (*see also* Problem
      behaviors, categories
      of)
  characteristics of, 5,
      19–20
  clinical teaching approach
      to, 132–133
  deficit-behavior (task) ap-
      proach to, and model,
      90–93, 111–116,
      134–135, 137–139
  definitions of, 5–7, 12
  developmental approach to,
      and model, 84–87,
      102–111, 129–134
  diagnosis and prescription,
      187–188

Learning disabilities
(*Continued*)
  illustrative case study of,
      364–375
  incidence of, 17–19
  literature on, 281–282
  management approaches to,
      and models, 97–100,
      119–122, 137, 143–144
  measurement of, 23–24
  models and approaches,
      103–104
  multidimensional definition
      of, 132
  neurological involvement in
      (*see* Brain; Central ner-
      vous system; Neurol-
      ogy)
  perceptual ability in, 168
  perceptual-motor approach
      to, 107–111
  perceptual-motor problems
      in, 139–142
  psycholinguistic, model of,
      95, 96, 111–116
  psychoneurological,
      129–130
  structural levels of, 26
  types of, 25–32
  visual-perceptual, 117–119
Learning Disabilities Act, 56, 61
Learning disability approach
      (*see* Educational-strat-
      egy approach)
Learning disability field,
      33–35
  code of ethics in, 39
  communication problems
      in, 188–199
  consumer protection in,
      39–40
  curriculum and facilities,
      52–53
  definition of, 35–38

Learning disability field
(*Continued*)
  delivery of services in,
    51-53
  federal funding for, 61
  historical development of,
    9-13, 102
  instruments and techniques
    in, 50-51
  interdisciplinary approach
    to, 55-57, 185-191 (*see
    also names of disciplines*)
  organizational consolidation
    in, 49
  organizations of, 282
  research in, 34-35, 40-45,
    48-49
  role definitions in, 189-190
  special interests in, 282-283
  specialists in, 39, 42, 56,
    186, 188-191, 229-230
  state legislation in, 49-50
  training in, 42-46
  transitional period in,
    102-103
Learning disabled children:
  concerns of, 269-274
  counseling of, 268-274
Learning quotient (LQ), 18,
    24, 129
Life-skill preparation, 47
Linguistic development pro-
    gram, 125-127 (*see also*
    Language)
Literature sources, 281-283

M

Madison plan, 232
Mainstreaming, 47, 220,
    226-228

Mainstreaming Act (*see* Public
    Law 94-142)
Maturity stages, 68
Measurement, direct, 317-321
Measures:
  criterion (*see* Criterion mea-
    sures)
  real-life, 317-320
Medicine, 65
Model-approach match,
    103-104
Motor coordination, 167
Motor patterns, 108-109
Motor problems (*see* Percep-
    tual-motor match; Per-
    ceptual-motor prob-
    lems)
Movement behavior, research
    in, 41
Movigenic program, 142

N

National Advisory Committee
    on Handicapped Chil-
    dren, 18, 37
Neurology, 67-70 (*see also*
    Brain; Central nervous
    system)

O

Objectives, behavioral,
    326-335
  criterion measures and,
    327-335
  preparation of, 149-150
  from task analysis, 331-332
Ophthalmology, 74-75

Optometry, 74-75
Organizations, learning dis-
    ability, 49, 282

P

Parents:
  counseling of, 274-283
  responses of, 247-248
  roles of, 280-281
Patterning theory, 104-107
PCL system, 125-127
PDL program, 127-129
Pediatrics, general, 66-67
Perceptual-motor approach,
    107-111
Perceptual-motor match,
    109-110
Perceptual-motor problems,
    139-142
Perceptual-Motor Survey, 110,
    180, 199, 209, 213
Performance levels, 167-168
Personnel, specially trained,
    229-230
Pharmacology, 70-74
Phonics training, 134-135
Placement, 156 (*see also*
    Screening programs)
*Pre-Kindergarten Descriptive In-
    ventory*, 177
Problem behaviors, 240-242
    (*see also* Learning dis-
    abilities)
  in arithmetic, 137-139
  behavior modification ap-
    proach to, 253-257
  categories of, 26-32,
    242-245
  crisis intervention approach
    to, 263-266

Problem behaviors
(*Continued*)
  developmental teaching approach to, 261–263
  disparity in (*see* Disparity principle)
  educational-strategy approach to, 250–253
  environmental-ecological approach to, 258–259
  general, 19–21
  in language, 125–134
  learning-related areas of, 243
  nonattending, 260
  observable, 242–245
  overgeneralization in, 245
  perceptual-motor, 139–142
  in reading, 134–137
  responses to, and effects of, 247–250
  situations, 245–247
  therapeutic teaching approach to, 259–261
  "too little, too much, inappropriate," 244–245
Program, validation of, 150–151
Programmed instruction, 144–145
  systems approach to, 146–151
Psychiatry, 75–76
Psychoeducational strategy (*see* Educational-strategy approach)
Psycholinguistics, 64, 113 (*see also* Learning disabilities, psycholinguistic)
Psychologists, school, 189
Psychology, 76–77
Public Law 91-230, 44
Public Law 93-380, 37

Public Law 94-142, 37–38, 45
Purdue Perceptual-Motor Survey, 110, 180, 199, 209, 213

R

Reading:
  performance objectives in, 172–174
  problems, 134–137
Reading readiness batteries, 174–176
Reference areas, 193–195
Remedial areas, identification of, 208–214
Remedial materials:
  criteria for, 200–205
  goodness of fit of, 201–203
  guidelines for choosing, 205–208
  preparation of, 214–219
  selection of, 208–214
Remedial system, principles for, 285–286
Remedial teaching, 62–63 (*see also* Learning disabilities; Problem behaviors)
Resource centers, 233–235
Responses to instructional sequences:
  active, 337–340
  alternative, 344–346
  correct, cut-off level of, 362–363
  model of, 343–344
  production and identification of, 342
  relevant, 340–342
Revision checklist, 358–361
Role definition, 189–190

Ruleg analysis, 310
Rule statement, 318–319

S

School, restructure of, 230–232
Screening programs, 155–162
  evaluation of, 184
  grids, 159, 160, 163
  implementation of, 182–184
  informal techniques of, 168–176
  instrumentation of, 161–162, 166, 176–181
  purposes and objectives of, 158, 162–164
  scope and format of, 164–165
  timing of, 165–166
Secondary school programs, 237–238
Service delivery, 51–53
  contract, 223
  external support of, 235–236
  individualization of, 220–223
  internal support of, 232–235
  models of, 220–221, 228–239
  normalization principle in, 223 (*see also* Mainstreaming)
  personnel roles in, 223, 225
Sociology, 77–78
Special education, 57, 60–62, 220
  contract, 223

Specialists (*see* Learning disabilities, specialists in)
Speech development program, 125-127
Speech pathology, 63
State statutes, special education, 49-50
Strauss syndrome, 10-11
Subcriterion measures, 315-316
    in illustrative case study, 370-372
Symbolic behavior, 113 (see also Language-communication behavior)
Symbolization, 131
Syntax-cleaning, 191-193
Systems approach, 143-144, 146-151, 289
    illustrative case study of, 364-375
Systems-management programs, 120-122, 143-144 (*see also* Learning disabilities, management approaches to, and models)

T

Task analysis, 148, 208, 291-294 (*see also* Criterion measures; Objectives, behavioral)
    assumptions, entering behavior, 295-296, 367
    discrimination, 302-310, 312-313
    examples of, 378-387
    final description in, 294-295, 308, 315, 367
    flowchart, 296-302, 312-313
    generalization in, 310-313
    in illustrative case study, 368-369
Teacher, counseling of, 283-287
Teaching (*see also* Remedial teaching):
    developmental, 261-263
    therapeutic, 259-261
Teaching frames, 337-338, 350-351
Testing, 353-358
    group, 356-358

Testing (*Continued*)
    in illustrative case study, 374-375
    individual, 354-356
Tests:
    formal, 161-162, 166-168, 176-181
    informal, 168-176

V

VAKT method, 136-137
Vineland Social Maturity Scale, 170, 181
Vision education, 74-75
Visual perception, remediation of, 117-119, 139-142
Visuomotor system, 139-142
Vocational preparation, 47

W

Weights, statistical, 23-24